# URBAN POVERTY
## AND THE
# LABOUR MARKET

## ACCESS TO JOBS AND INCOMES
## IN ASIAN AND LATIN AMERICAN CITIES

Edited by Gerry Rodgers

INTERNATIONAL LABOUR OFFICE    GENEVA

ISBN 92-2-106499-9 (hard cover)
ISBN 92-2-106500-6 (limp cover)

*First published 1989*

# *Preface*

"Poverty, like beauty, lies in the eye of the beholder" wrote Orshansky,[1] and that summarises one of the difficulties faced by those who would compare poverty in different settings. The justification for such comparisons must lie in there being enough common threads, across areas with differing economic, social and cultural characteristics, to merit trying to draw some of them together. That, at least, is one rationale for this book, which brings together studies of urban poverty and labour markets from Latin America and from South and South-East Asia. The objective here is not only to document poverty — although that does no harm when the poor are so often forgotten in the design of macro-economic policy — but also to try to assess some of the mechanisms which underlie poverty. In particular, questions of labour market structure and access deserve close attention. Linking such issues to poverty is not as straightforward as one might think; the most widely available data sources are often scanty on this relationship, and concepts and disaggregations devised for regular labour market circumstances are often deficient for vulnerable, low-income groups.

The objectives of the studies included in this book, then, are to document trends in different dimensions of urban poverty; to assess how they affect particular groups of the population; to analyse concurrent trends in labour market outcomes; and to examine the relative importance of labour market and other factors in the evolution of poverty. The longer-term objective is to contribute to the design of labour market policies, in the context of overall strategies for the reduction of urban poverty which take advantage of complementarities between labour market and other anti-poverty policies. The studies take diverse approaches, reflecting the different situations they cover, as well as the differing perspectives of their authors and differences in the availability and use of data and results from past research. But underlying this diversity is a common concern to find out more about patterns of urban poverty and their origins in labour processes. In furthering this aim, the book is a co-operative effort of all its contributors, most of whom have reworked their chapters more than once in order to encompass common themes.

This book was started in the ILO's Employment and Development Department, and completed in the International Institute for Labour Studies. It was jointly prepared by these two entities within the International Labour Organisation. A third entity of the ILO which also contributed a great deal was the Programa Regional de Empleo para América Latina y el Caribe (PREALC) in Santiago de Chile and Panama; four of the studies in the volume were either prepared or supervised by PREALC staff. I am very grateful to those concerned, and in particular to Victor Tokman, Director of PREALC at the time, for his support. I am also grateful to Jack Martin, former Director of the Employment and Development Department, for supporting this work, and especially to the former Director of the International Institute for Labour Studies, Elimane Kane, who, sadly, is no longer with us. Several readers of an earlier version gave very helpful comments: Jacques Charmes, Wouter van Ginneken, Bill House, Jean-Pierre Lachaud, Adriana Marshall, Janine Rodgers, S. Sethuraman and Guy Standing. The cover of the book was designed by Ximena Subercaseaux. I would also like to thank Françoise Weeks and Christine Sutton, who typed and organised most of the text, for the work they put into this volume.

Gerry Rodgers
Labour Market Programme
International Institute for Labour Studies

*Note*

[1] Mollie Orshansky: "Counting the poor: Another look at the poverty profile", in *Social Security Bulletin* (Washington, DC), Jan. 1965.

In memory of Elimane Kane

وَقُلِ اعْمَلُوا فَسَيَرَى اللهُ عَمَلَكُمْ وَرَسُولُهُ
وَالْمُؤْمِنُونَ وَسَتُرَدُّونَ إِلَى عَلِمِ الْغَيْبِ وَالشَّهَادَةِ
فَيُنَبِّئُكُمْ بِمَا كُنْتُوْ تَعْمَلُونَ

# Contents

# List of tables

# Chapter 1

## Introduction: Trends in urban poverty and labour market access

*GERRY RODGERS*

### I. The urban poor and the labour market

The aim of this book is to document ways in which labour market structures and mechanisms result in or aggravate urban poverty in developing countries. It is perhaps not very fashionable to be concerned with poverty in the 1980s. The United Nations Third Development Decade began with reaffirmation of social objectives, but in practice international attention during the decade has been focused on financial crisis and economic adjustment. As for labour markets, the main objective has been to improve efficiency, in the expectation that this will improve resource allocation and help to achieve production and monetary objectives; there has been a tendency to tolerate persistent high unemployment as an unavoidable evil.

A view of labour markets which stresses their contribution to efficient factor allocation leads naturally to an interpretation of labour market structures and barriers as impediments to efficiency, whether they be trade unions, inflexible wage levels, or restrictions on market entry. The policy implications are straightforward: such impediments should be removed, or their effects compensated by appropriate price changes. But the logic of this is questionable; the labour market cannot be analysed as if it were just another commodity market. Our starting-point is, rather, that the disparities and differentials found in the labour market, the various institutions and mechanisms governing job access and security, and the legal and social frameworks, all form part of a broader social process governing the use and remuneration of labour. We frequently use the term "labour processes" to indicate that the issues are not limited to the market, and that there is a multiplicity of mechanisms rather than a single social relationship. The thesis of this book is that poverty arises from these labour processes, as much as from more obvious factors such as overall levels of production and productivity; and that inequalities in access to labour markets need to be understood as part of a process of social and economic stratification of which poverty is one result.

Poverty, then, derives in large part from the structure of the labour market and of the associated labour processes. We can identify at least five inter-related sets of issues: *(a)* the overall levels of labour productivity and remuneration; *(b)* differentiation in jobs and rewards; *(c)* unequal access to work of any sort; *(d)* the possibilities for labour supply; and *(e)* the dynamics of poverty, for individuals and society as a whole, in response to changing labour market situations. We shall study each of these in more detail later. They in turn lead to two distinct outcomes, which are easier to separate in theory than in practice: the overall incidence of poverty; and the determination of who is poor. One can observe differences in the incidence of poverty among labour market groups, without it being clear to what extent labour market structure is responsible for the overall level of poverty. Nor can this issue be readily resolved, for the interpretation of observed patterns depends on the underlying models. But many clues will be found in this book, suggesting that labour market differentiation and inequality are themselves important determinants of the overall level of poverty − in relative, but also in absolute terms.

Nine case studies or regional reviews follow, which examine the interactions between urban poverty and labour markets − five from Latin America, and four from South and South-East Asia. These studies concentrate mainly on individual cities, but it has not been possible to limit the analysis systematically in this way, because available data are not always disaggregated in such a way as to permit the identification of particular cities. In fact, the analysis of interactions between poverty and the labour market is bound to be plagued by data problems, because the data required depart somewhat from conventional disaggregations of the labour market. The studies aim to answer several questions: who are the urban poor, and what are their main labour market characteristics; what role do different labour processes or labour market relationships play in the generation of poverty, and what labour market options are open to the poor; how has poverty evolved in recent years of world recession, and what labour market mechanisms and outcomes have been important in this process? Most of the studies investigate both dynamic and static relationships, identifying trends in labour market patterns and poverty, and exploring their interdependence. In the rest of this Introduction, the main empirical findings are compared and contrasted in the light of the relevant theoretical and conceptual issues. But first a digression on the relationship between urban and rural poverty is called for.

## *II. Urban poverty and rural poverty*

Urban poverty is, to a greater or lesser degree, a reflection of rural poverty in most developing countries. Cities offer rural migrants a possible escape from joblessness, underemployment, oppressive agrarian structures or low productivity subsistence work. But the number of potential migrants among the rural poor is too great for urban economies to readily absorb them all. The existence of a rural labour reserve then intensifies competition in the urban labour market, and permits urban producers to maintain an insecure, unorganised and low-paid workforce. Thus the persistence of rural poverty puts pressure on urban labour processes, and contributes to the growth of low-income strata in the cities. Attempts to tackle urban poverty directly — through job-creation schemes, the provision of public services or forms of social security unavailable in rural areas — tend to widen the urban-rural gap, and so increase the incentives to migrate. Eventually, increased in-migration might well undermine any gains from policies to reduce urban poverty directly.

So the idea that "development" is primarily an urban issue, a question of industrialisation and the creation of an urban wage labour force, which was widespread in the 1950s and 1960s, has lost influence. Although a prominent development economist could still in the late 1970s publish a book on "urban bias" (Lipton, 1977), arguing that development planning and research was biased towards urban areas, he was by then largely preaching to the converted. This is not to say that rural areas now receive a disproportionate share of resources or policy interest, or even that rural poverty is adequately documented and understood. The lags are long, and policy institutions and research results take time to build up. But there is now a receptive audience for the view that the eradication of poverty, whether rural or urban, requires substantial intervention in rural areas.

However, the studies in this book focus on urban poverty, for even if rural poverty is quantitatively more important, there is disquieting evidence that urban poverty is persistent and in many countries growing; and there are grounds for suspecting that this has more to do with the specific ways in which urban labour markets operate than with changes in the countryside. In particular, global recession has adversely affected urban poverty through labour market mechanisms. At the same time, views of migration are also changing — the image of the rural poor flooding into towns captures only part of reality, for migrants are by no means all poor, whether before or after migration. Many if not most urban jobs are found prior to migration, so one can start to ask, in many countries, whether the distinction between urban and rural labour markets is really clear cut: the basic issue is a more general one of access to jobs. Networks of contacts and influence may make access to good urban jobs easier for some strata of the rural population than it is for many of the urban poor.

This must of course be adapted to regional realities, and notably to the absolute level of urbanisation. In a country where a tenth of the population is urban, the options and alternatives are essentially rural, so that urban labour market analysis depends heavily on the analysis of rural economic structures. Where the population is more evenly divided — and this means that the bulk of production is urban, since labour productivity is invariably higher in urban areas — urban labour market analysis does not depend on rural analysis. Even in countries where the rural economy predominates, its structure and operation may depend on urban patterns of processing and trade; or long-established cities may exist where economic forces and institutions have little to do with rural production processes.

The figures for urbanisation in table 1.1 should be regarded as a very rough guide, because definitions of urban areas vary greatly. In particular, many smaller or outlying urban areas in Africa are heavily agriculture-based, and would elsewhere be regarded as essentially rural, whereas the Indian census

*Table 1.1.   Urbanisation in low and middle-income countries, estimates for 1984*

|  | Percentage of population in urban areas |
|---|---|
| Low income: | |
| China and India | 23 |
| Other low income | 22 |
| Lower-middle income | 37 |
| Upper-middle income | 65 |
| By region (unweighted averages [1]): | |
| Sub-Saharan Africa (34 countries) | 25 |
| North Africa (5 countries) | 46 |
| South Asia (7 countries) | 19 |
| South-East Asia (6 countries) | 25 |
| East Asia (4 countries) | 51 |
| West Asia (11 countries) | 56 |
| Latin America, Caribbean (22 countries) | 57 |

[1] Excludes city States and countries with a population less than 1 million.
Source. World Bank, 1986.

reports "villages" with 20,000 people or more. But urbanisation shows a clear pattern: low-income countries average around 20-25 per cent of their population living in urban areas, with three regions in particular at about this level — sub-Saharan Africa, South Asia and South-East Asia; the other major developing regions — North Africa, West Asia and Latin America — all have urbanisation levels close to or above 50 per cent, and this is also true of East Asia if China is excluded. In so far as urban poverty persists in these latter regions in particular, it seems unlikely that its solution lies primarily in rural interventions. Moreover, urban populations continue to grow faster than rural; even in India, where the proportion of the population dependent on agriculture obstinately refused to decline for many years despite industrial growth, the most recent data suggest a significant shift away from primary activities.[1]

The importance of urban labour markets should therefore not be understated. But there are differences between regions not only in the extent of urbanisation, but also in its nature, and these differences have substantial implications for labour market structure. Many small towns do not have autonomous labour markets, in that economic activity is heavily focused on trade and on servicing agricultural activities, and labour moves relatively freely between such "urban" activities and agriculture. Such towns, in an economic sense, are mere appendages of the rural economy. At the other extreme, the labour market of large cities depends on rural activities only indirectly, in that production is largely independent of the agricultural sector, and there is a well-defined urban labour force, subject at most to secondary modification through seasonal inflows and outflows of rural migrant labour. In the case studies the stress is on large cities, to permit a focus on urban processes *per se*. We have thus been able to avoid extensive analysis of rural relationships in a book concerned with urban labour processes. So without arguing that urban-rural linkages are unimportant, we have paid relatively little attention to them.

## III. The identity of the urban poor

The "poor" do not constitute an analytical category with respect to the labour market. One can see ways in which poverty generates particular labour market strategies and types of vulnerability; but the poor are heterogeneous, and their strategies, options and responses are correspondingly diverse. Equally, while particular labour processes contribute to poverty, the relationships vary and their importance depends on social, economic and cultural context. Some groups of workers will almost always be poor — garbage sifters, marginal hawkers, those forced by poverty itself to take advantage of any opportunity of earning an income. Many more will be vulnerable to poverty by virtue of an insecure or irregular labour force status: for instance, many types of casual workers, or the erratically self-employed. But the congruence between labour market status and poverty is less than complete, and will depend on overall levels of productivity and patterns of social organisation and social security. Moreover, many forms of poverty — such as those associated with poor health or old age — are not primarily associated with labour market mechanisms, and they are more likely to respond to formal or informal social support systems than to labour market intervention.

Because of this looseness in the relationship between poverty and labour markets, we must start by considering the nature of urban poverty and the characteristics of the urban poor. At least four different criteria for identifying poverty are used in this book: absolute consumption; relative consumption or income; access to a range of public or semi-public goods and services; and subjective criteria, based on perceptions and behavioural responses among the poor. Of these, the first is both easiest to use and most widespread; and while it can readily be criticised, simplicity and data availability are virtues not to be despised. In Latin America an Economic Commission for Latin America and the Caribbean study (Altimir, 1979) has considerably influenced poverty analysis by standardising on two poverty lines: a food basket, defined in relation to nutritional criteria but subject to a good deal of variation in composition — those with incomes insufficient to purchase the food basket are considered "destitute"; and an extended basket, covering non-food consumption, arbitrarily specified as double the value of the food basket, which defines the "poor". The destitute thus constitute a subgroup among the poor. Since the minimum food basket reflects in some degree changing societal standards, a degree of relativity is introduced into the poverty measure; and the poverty lines appear to identify important population groups across a diversity of economic settings. In this book, the ECLAC standard is used in the studies in Panama City [2] (22 per cent classified poor in 1983, no figures for destitution), urban Costa Rica (25 per cent poor in 1982, of which 4 per cent were destitute), Guatemala City (64 per cent poor in 1983, of which 22 per cent destitute) and Santiago de Chile (45 per cent poor in 1985, of which 19 per cent destitute). Similar but not identical approaches are reported in the reviews of alternative poverty measures for Jakarta and Manila, the calorie-based or rice-based poverty measures for India have a similar rationale to that measuring destitution in Latin America, and the estimates for Brazil, which are indirect calculations based on minimum wages, derive from a similar logic in so far as minimum wages are themselves based on some concept of minimum consumption levels.

Despite the similarities, one should beware of making direct international comparisons of the incidence of poverty, even in these simplified terms. The discussion of poverty estimates and their problems in several chapters (especially Evers's discussion of Indonesian data) should serve as a warning. It is not obvious that poverty in India, in relation to a calorie intake standard alone, is even conceptually comparable with "destitution" in Panama, measured in relation to a more balanced and varied diet. Thus it would not be very meaningful to compare estimated proportions of the population below the various poverty lines across the countries studied here. Poverty entails deprivation, and deprivation involves some concept of what is socially acceptable, as well as of relative position — i.e. poverty is necessarily relative, in part at least. Several of the case studies have attempted to examine relative poverty more directly, but data limitations restrict them to examination of inequality in the overall household distribution of income or consumption (Panama, where the bottom 10 per cent of households is used as a proxy for destitution, Brazil, Guatemala, Santiago de Chile, Jakarta, Manila).

Access to public services as an aspect of poverty is discussed only in passing in this book, but the two South-East Asian studies discuss subjective measures of poverty in more detail. Evers (Jakarta) argues that self-defined poverty levels are not only conceptually superior, but also help in understanding the behaviour patterns and labour market responses of the poor. In this he is following a long tradition, and the argument that perceived needs are important determinants of labour supply is well taken. But the data required for such an approach are highly specialised, and are not replicated in any of the other studies.

The social and demographic characteristics of the poor are perhaps as important as the overall magnitude of poverty for investigating interactions with the labour market. Most chapters have something to say about the characteristics of the poor, and on the whole similar characteristics can be identified in very different economic and social situations. Low levels of education are a widespread characteristic of urban poverty, and this is hardly surprising, but there are aspects of the distribution of education which are worth noting. In studies which separate destitution from poverty (Costa Rica, Chile, Guatemala), for instance, the large difference in access to education above the primary level is between poor and non-poor, that between poverty and destitution being much smaller. There are also other signs (e.g. in the Panamanian and Philippine studies) that lack of access to secondary education is a key correlate of poverty; in Panama 35 per cent of workers with primary education fell below the poverty line, compared with only 11 per cent of those with some secondary education, and the figures were similar in the Philippines. In the urban West Bengal study all measures of above-primary education were powerful predictors of expenditure levels. These results are somewhat contrary to the conventional wisdom that the major target is to extend primary education to all sections of the population; and the reason may lie in the way urban labour markets respond to secondary-level qualifications.

In terms of demographic characteristics, there is a general tendency to find poor households to have high proportions of dependent children and older non-workers,[3] and to be large. The latter point is perhaps less obvious than the former, but it should be noted that most of the studies use per capita measures of income or expenditure. Since larger households tend to have more children, and children normally consume less than adults, per capita measures of welfare are biased downward for large households. The one study which corrects household size for the weighting of children (Costa Rica) finds that this distinctly reduces the differences between poverty groups in household size, although it does not eliminate them altogether.

Those studies which investigate the sex ratio of households find this to be strongly related to poverty, in that women are more vulnerable to poverty than men. The Brazilian study finds poverty to be notably higher in households with a high proportion of women among active household members, especially where the household head was female. This pattern, however, was true mainly in the Southeast; in the Northeast, structural labour market characteristics were much more important than demographic ones. Female headship was important in Costa Rica (the destitution rate was 3.5 times higher in households with a female head), the absence of a male worker was a powerful determinant of expenditure levels in West Bengal, and, although it was not examined in all studies, the sex balance of households seems likely often to be an important factor; this of course merely reflects unequal labour market access for men and women, on which more is said below.

Many other characteristics of households will be important in specific contexts. Caste is strongly related to poverty in India; recent migrants may sometimes be disproportionately represented among the poor, e.g., in Jakarta (but this may not be typical), and there may be discrimination on an ethnic or racial basis, which is suggested by some of the analysis in Guatemala. But probably the most important characteristics are those which condition labour market insertion.

## IV. Labour market structure and the insertion of the poor

For some authors, overall levels of productivity and pay should dominate the analysis of poverty. If some variation in rewards to labour is accepted, then the basic issue is one of raising productive capacity and concurrently raising employment levels. However, the studies in this book, which cover very diverse income and productivity levels, do not support this view. For instance, the proportion of the population estimated to be below the poverty line in the Chilean study is not greatly different from that in India, despite the large differences in labour productivity between the two countries. There are two obvious causes. First, as was already noted, poverty estimates are not comparable across such different circumstances, since the concept and measurement of poverty rises to reflect rising societal standards of living; but the corollary is that rising living standards are not a sufficient condition for a reduction in poverty. Second, the degrees of heterogeneity and inequality in the economy make a considerable difference. Development processes are not independent of heterogeneity and poverty, indeed disparities are created by the nature of the growth process and by the interests of the groups controlling different aspects of the process. Understanding poverty thus implies understanding the nature and causes of differentiation. The broader issue of aggregate growth and output levels remains important — but there are writings enough on that, and this book focuses on structure and differentiation.

## 1. Labour market categories

Labour markets are characterised by heterogeneity in many dimensions. The key research issue is how to represent this heterogeneity in models in which it derives logically from labour market functioning. Perhaps the most influential theoretical approach lies in the concept of labour market segmentation, which developed in the North American literature but is now widely applied in industrialised countries (Doeringer and Piore, 1971; Reich et al., 1973; Wilkinson, 1981). Several models have been developed of why labour markets should be structured into segments made up of jobs of different kinds with different levels of reward, and separated by barriers which limit mobility and other forms of interaction. In developing countries these models have merged with earlier streams of thought on economic dualism, and their most common expression is in the distinction between "formal" and "informal" sectors. There seem to be two main ways in which segmentation models of the division of labour can be developed: horizontally and vertically.

Horizontal segmentation denotes the separation of complete production systems, in which all labour has some common characteristic. This may involve a separation by type of enterprise or product, associating the labour process within each segment with a particular production process. The distinction between formal and informal sectors is a case in point, if they really are independent of each other. Vertical segmentation, by contrast, involves the use of labour from different segments in a single production process. Thus a large enterprise with both regular and casual labour, or using subcontracted or home workers, or operating in different sectors of the labour market and distinguishing groups of workers on the basis of race or gender, is operating in a vertically segmented labour market. The distinction may break down at the economy-wide level, in that apparently horizontally segmented markets may in fact form part of an aggregative interdependent system; but for examining the detail of labour market functioning it remains useful.

While the distinction between formal and informal sectors is widely used, it does provide a good example of the dangers and difficulties involved in segmentation models. Definitions of the informal sector vary greatly, but the usual characteristics include a lack of official registration, a dominance of self-employment, a low capital-labour ratio, often the production of low-quality goods or services, high levels of competition, easy entry, restricted access to credit and limited capacity for accumulation. These characteristics are by no means coincident or universal, and as a result there are many "informal" sectors with different levels of productivity, organisation, labour use and remuneration. At the same time, vertical segmentation within the "formal" sector may create dependent subcontractors, or forms of casual labour which are hardly distinguishable from casual wage labour in the informal sector — and indeed alongside informal labour arrangements in large enterprises will probably exist formal labour arrangements among small enterprises.

To avoid these problems it would be desirable to adapt the disaggregation of the labour market to the problem at hand. One way to tackle the issue of poverty is to pose the problem as one of labour market vulnerability in terms of lack of the credentials, skills or assets required for job access; lack of protection through legal restraints or collective organisation; irregularity and insecurity in work; vulnerability through need. A number of labour market disaggregations which have been proposed (notably by Bromley and Gerry, 1979; and Harriss, 1982) use ideas such as these, combined with the underlying idea that the co-existence of different forms of labour allows an intensification of exploitation. A possible classification for the analysis of urban poverty which builds on their work would separate:

*(a)* protected wage work (contracts and legal constraints operate; jobs are protected from market forces by restrictions on entry);

*(b)* competitive, regular wage work (entry is relatively open and market forces operate, but employment is nevertheless continuous and perhaps subject to contract — i.e. one can identify continuing jobs);

*(c)* unprotected wage labour (heterogeneous; includes much casual labour, domestic service, wage workers in petty trade; characterised by insecurity and/or irregularity). Various forms of disguised wage labour (e.g. outwork) might also be included here;

*(d)* self-employment and family labour in "productive" small-scale production;

*(e)* "marginal" activities, which range from peripheral low-productivity work such as shoe-shining and hawking to semi-legal and illegal activities.

This classification can encompass both vertical and horizontal segmentation; and it identifies two groups *(c)* and *(e)* which are particularly vulnerable to poverty. Nevertheless, poverty is also likely to be present in other categories, and the border between *(d)* and *(e)* is difficult to define, so more detailed subdivisions will be desirable in specific cases. Each production structure distributes the workforce across these categories, and in so doing generates characteristic patterns of poverty. In many economies larger enterprises operate with labour from *(a)* and *(c)*; the availability of credit, market access and the monopoly power of large firms will all affect the relative importance of *(d)* and *(e)*, and *(e)* in particular will also reflect the extent of unemployment and of urgent needs for income.

This classification, however, represents an objective which it is difficult to achieve with existing data sources. In this book, all the studies are forced by data availability to use more limited breakdowns. Most adopt informal-formal sector classifications for some purposes; in Latin America the studies on Chile, Guatemala, Panama and Costa Rica all work with somewhat analogous definitions of the informal sector, built up from widely available conventional work status, occupation and industry data, following a methodology developed by PREALC. This identifies the informal sector mainly with non-professional self-employment and domestic service, and sometimes wage employment in small enterprises (PREALC, 1982). Such disaggregations do not meet the objectives of a labour classification such as that proposed in the preceding paragraph; but they are nevertheless often a step in the right direction, and helpful in the absence of more detailed disaggregation. As Harriss comments, after critically examining the informal sector concept, "in spite of the limitations of the dualistic approach, we are often in the position of having to work with it". Nevertheless, several studies succeed in distinguishing various forms of casual or subsistence work, or consider concepts of "protection" or "regularity" in work, or glean some clues from conventional industry or work status disaggregations, all of which can add elements to the analysis not available from a formal-informal sector model.

The key issue is the extent to which these labour market categories coincide with marked differences in the incidence of poverty. In Brazil Jatobá proposes a labour market breakdown which combines criteria based on the presence of enforceable labour contracts with income criteria for the self-employed, and the two sectors thus identified are denoted "organised" and "unorganised". A wage criterion is then used to separate low-income workers. The study also separates "protected" (by labour legislation) and "unprotected" workers. These breakdowns are quite effective both in analysing regional inequality (the differences between regions arise more from the regional *incidence* of protection and organisation in the labour market than from regional differences in the *effects* on poverty of protection or organisation) and in identifying the poor: 16 per cent of protected workers were "poor" (below the minimum wage) in 1983, compared with 52 per cent of unprotected workers, 11 per cent of organised sector workers, and 66 per cent of unorganised sector workers. But the strength of these results derives in part from the inclusion of an income criterion in the definition of "organised" and "unorganised", while "protected" workers were covered by minimum-wage legislation among other factors. Household-level poverty data, rather than individual earnings, would have avoided this bias, but these were not available in the data source used.

The use of the informal sector concept in the other Latin American studies gives mixed results. The tendency for the poor to be clustered in the informal sector was strongest in Costa Rica, where 75 per cent of destitute household heads were working in the informal sector, and 54 per cent of other poor household heads, compared with 32 per cent for the non-poor groups. Poverty in the informal sector was evenly divided between the self-employed and wage workers in small firms (included in the informal sector here), but there was still extensive poverty among employees of large firms. The general pattern was similar for household secondary workers except that, for this group, poverty was even more extensive among formal sector wage workers than for household heads. In Panama the difference in poverty between the formal and informal sectors was smaller (35 per cent of the poor were in the informal sector, including domestic service, as compared with 28 per cent of the non-poor), while in Santiago there was no difference at all for household heads, and a fairly small difference for secondary workers (larger for spouses than for offspring). The Jakarta study also reports a formal-informal sector breakdown of poverty, using a registration criterion to identify informal enterprises. The study allows for the simultaneous participation of households in three classes of economic activity — formal, informal and subsistence; if we exclude households engaged in both formal and informal, but not subsistence, activities (only 3 per cent of cases) then the incidence of poverty among households not engaged in informal sector activities was between 13 to 24 per cent, while for those in informal sector activities it averaged 60 per cent. Nevertheless, more than half the poor were reported as working in the formal sector.

The Indian studies avoid the use of an informal sector concept as such. Harriss argues that protection of workers can to some extent be equated with registration of enterprises, if short-term and casual workers can be separated. This distinction proves to be important: in Bombay 40 per cent of casual workers fell below the poverty line, as compared with 10 per cent of regular workers in small firms and 12 per cent of regular workers in large firms. Similar results from the city of Coimbatore reinforce the importance of the nature of the labour contract, rather than the size of the enterprise. Bardhan's study of West Bengal supports this conclusion, with casual labour distinctly more frequent among the bottom third of the expenditure distribution (12.4 per cent of workers) than among the remainder (6.1 per cent), while the proportion of casual labour in the household is a significant negative factor in a multivariate analysis of expenditure levels. This result is also found in other parts of the world; e.g. a study in Tunis (van Durme, 1987) shows casual workers to be highly concentrated among the poor (17 per cent of the poor, 9 per cent of other low-income groups, only 1 per cent of middle-income groups). The Latin American studies do not provide figures on this, but fairly high levels of poverty among private sector wage labour may be due to similar factors.

Do these disaggregations identify the poor more effectively than if one used traditional occupation, industry or work status breakdowns? On the whole, despite data imperfections, the answer is yes. Distributions of the poor by occupation and industry in the Manila, Costa Rica and Santiago studies point to certain types of activity which are vulnerable to poverty — construction and domestic service in Manila, for instance — and this clearly helps to locate the poor. But apart from well-defined activities such as domestic service, these patterns tend to be fairly weak, precisely because they aggregate dissimilar types of labour use and remuneration. Another case in point is the category of "self-employed", usually classed in the informal sector, and where the incidence of poverty is often assumed to be high. In this respect, the data in the West Bengal study are instructive. The multivariate regression on expenditure suggests that the influence of self-employment on income is negative. But if we look at the detailed distribution of self-employed households by expenditure class, there is considerable heterogeneity; for instance, in the largest class of self-employed (service and production work, including street vendors) the distribution is bi-modal, with these households being clustered in the second lowest and second highest expenditure classes (Chapter 9, table 9.4). This work-status category therefore tells us little about poverty if it is not combined with additional information, such as the scale of operation, the command over resources and markets, and the return to labour. In the other studies there is equally little sign of self-employment as such effectively identifying the poor. In Manila the earnings of the self-employed are distinctly higher than those of wage workers, on average; Harriss's review of several Calcutta case studies does show a clearer pattern than Bardhan, and employees in small firms appear to do worse than the self-employed. In Madras 70 per cent of the self-employed fell below the poverty line, but the same is true of unorganised sector employees. In Guatemala City 31.6 per cent of the self-employed were below the poverty line in 1980, but so were 30.9 per cent of private sector wage workers.

To sum up, data constraints made it difficult to apply disaggregations of the labour market which fully reflect patterns of segmentation, and differences in vulnerability and security. "Standard" disaggregations of the workforce, however, are deficient in the identification and analysis of urban poverty. Some improvement was usually obtained with formal-informal breakdowns, despite both theoretical and empirical imprecision, but distinctly better results can be expected from disaggregations which more accurately identify different forms of labour vulnerability, protection and control over work. When it was possible to move in this direction, through separating out casual or unprotected forms of work, for instance, the identification of poverty became clearer, facilitating an understanding of its origins.

## 2. Job access

The segmentation patterns described above can only persist if there are forces controlling and differentiating access to jobs of different types, in different labour market segments. In a smoothly functioning market economy, of course, access to jobs and rewards would depend on individuals' leisure preferences and productivities, so the problem of access would not need to be studied; it would be sufficient to analyse the characteristics of labour supply and demand, and the processes by which they are brought into equilibrium. But one can argue that the interaction between poverty and labour markets can indeed be posed as essentially one of access, for labour markets are in general highly stratified, with mobility impeded by institutional barriers, and dependent on characteristics, credentials and resources to which access is unequally distributed. If this view is accepted, then a better starting-point will be an enumeration of the access routes into different parts of the labour market. These will vary greatly from situation to situation. Some will be purely particularistic — the "principle of particularism" as Harriss calls it — in that access to particular categories of work is obtained through inter-personal networks, which themselves reflect social structures in terms of kin, caste, community or ethnic origin. Other restrictions on access depend on generalist criteria:

— qualifications acquired through the educational system;

— skills and experience acquired through apprenticeship or on-the-job training;

— personal characteristics likely to appeal to employers, which — depending on the job — may include docility, initiative, autonomy, etc.; sex, age and migrant status may also be important here;

— access to capital (important mainly for self-employment, but also relevant where migration, job purchase or some other initial investment is called for) through own resources, through ability to provide collateral for loans, and through ability to call on family, community or state institutions for support;

— access to a market for output from self-employment (viable locations for trade, ability to sell goods produced, etc).

There are also characteristics which may well have a negative effect, such as experience of unemployment, irregular employment history, personal appearance or accent, or inadequate health or nutritional status.

Differentiation in the labour market is grounded in differential access to these credentials. To some extent, there is an underlying issue of information — knowledge about access routes, and how to obtain the credentials concerned, is clearly also unequally distributed. This is related to the supply side, covered in more detail below. On the demand side, human capital models would explain differentiation in terms of relative productivities; and such explanations obviously have some validity. But the educational qualifications required for access to any particular job usually rise with the average education level of the population. Evidently education plays a rationing, rather than a purely productivity-measuring role — and one which systematically discriminates against the poor. As noted above, urban poverty appears to be particularly closely associated with lack of schooling above the primary level, and it is mainly secondary-level qualifications which provide desirable labour market entry points. Access to capital is likewise distributed in ways which bear little relation to productivity, and even less to welfare. In so far as the point of initial access can condition subsequent prospects, the net outcome is surely to intensify stratification.

For those who fail to gain access to the more desirable strata of the labour market, it is not obvious that easy-entry low-income jobs are available. Much of the informal sector is also highly protected. Labour market ports of entry may exist, such as portering, casual construction labour or domestic service; and the marginal jobs, right down to begging, prostitution and theft or other illegal activities, may provide a minimum income for those without alternatives. Migrants will sometimes have the option of return. But many face a lifetime of occasional, casual work, of eking out a living through taking on whatever menial tasks they can find.

Evidence on these issues in the case studies is not abundant. The difficulty of labour market access shows up to some extent in the level of open unemployment, and also in the observed levels of labour supply, and these issues are discussed separately below. But the more specific questions of access routes to different parts of the labour market, and patterns of discrimination among groups of workers, can only be inferred indirectly from the conventional survey data used in the studies; detailed analysis requires case study material, discussed in detail mainly by Harriss and Evers, though clues about access patterns can be gleaned from several other studies.

The importance of lack of education as a condition which distinguishes the poor is apparent in most of the studies, but is not necessarily dominant, and if educational credentials are insufficient for access to the upper reaches of the labour market they may be of little help. For instance, Bardhan finds that wages vary much less by level of education in casual jobs than they do in regular jobs. Perhaps the most important way in which education interacts with poverty is at the inter-generational level: poverty and low levels of education of parents are associated with early drop-out from school and labour market entry of children (Rodgers and Standing, 1981), limiting the possibilities for acquiring educational credentials or training, and perpetuating the existence of an unskilled lower stratum of the labour force.

The effect on poverty of discrimination by sex, age, and ethnic origin is also widely documented in the studies. In India both Bardhan and Harriss report evidence of sex discrimination in the form of large wage differentials, even for virtually identical occupations. In Bombay this was particularly true of casual workers, but in urban West Bengal Bardhan reports that discrimination was greater in regular than in casual jobs. In Panama, while comparable proportions of male and female workers were earning below the minimum wage in formal sectors, a much larger proportion of females fell below the minimum-earnings line in informal sectors. There is also a good deal of indirect evidence of discrimination against women, in that poor households tend to have a high proportion of female members.

Ethnic discrimination is also often a major influence. In India caste is a ubiquitous factor affecting entry to particular labour market segments, often controlled by particular caste groups, while scheduled castes or tribes are heavily over-represented among casual labour and contract labour. In Guatemala City a majority of the poor are reported to be of indigenous origin, and similar phenomena are observed elsewhere. The evidence on age discrimination is much less regular — among the poor in Costa Rica one finds disproportionate numbers of older household heads, while in Guatemala it is younger household heads who are disadvantaged. Clearly a mixture of factors intervene, including the extent of wage progression in internal labour markets in regular jobs, and life-cycle patterns of dependency.

Migration is more complex. It has long been presumed in the development literature that rural to urban migrants form a relatively low-wage, easily exploited urban stratum. In the study on Guatemala City it is suggested that migrants are clustered in marginal areas of the city with poor housing, and tend to be concentrated in the informal sector. But while some empirical work supports this, and there is widespread evidence of low-income ports of entry for migrants such as domestic service or construction work, on balance the evidence that migrants systematically do badly in urban labour markets is unconvincing. For instance, recent migrants often suffer distinctly less unemployment than longer-term residents, and their occupational and work status structure is not significantly worse.[4] This could be in part due to the omission from most analysis of short-term, circulating migrants — Evers notes that this is important in Jakarta — or of those who return to rural areas or smaller towns after having failed to obtain labour market access. But it could also be due to the mechanisms which Harriss reports from Bombay and other Indian cities: that migration *reflects* job access rather than being the initial step in job search. He argues that access to urban jobs for migrants does not involve entry at the bottom of the market, but rather a horizontal shift in which the level of urban labour market entry reflects the position in the rural hierarchy, so that migrants are distributed throughout the urban structure. Thus Harriss reports that, in Coimbatore, migrants made up 30 per cent of permanent wage workers, 35 per cent of short-term workers, 32 per cent of casual workers and 47 per cent of the self-employed. The rigidity of hierarchical position is then reflected in very low levels of mobility within urban labour markets, such mobility as occurs mainly being between jobs of a similar status. This position is not altogether supported in the Jakarta study, where some upward mobility seems to occur, and Indian labour markets may be particularly segmented in this respect. But even in Jakarta it seems that the links between job access and urban poverty are not primarily conditioned by flows of migrants, or at least that migration, job access and urban poverty are closely intertwined only in certain limited sectors of the labour market.

Much migration seems to occur after a job has been located, usually through a network of contacts built on kin, community, caste or similar lines, which often appear to dominate the process of job access for the poor. Harriss cites several examples, and the closed nature of these networks is strikingly illustrated by his finding from Coimbatore that only 21 per cent of casual workers could name someone in permanent wage work among their extended kin. Even in regular jobs in large-scale industry in India, it is common for workers to have the right to determine who shall replace them if they leave. In the "modern" Panamanian economy Camazón et al. report that in poorer areas of Panama City 54 per cent of workers obtained their jobs through friends or relatives. In Jakarta such networks seem to be institutionalised in the *"pondok"* system, although they appear to be less effective in providing entry to the formal sector. It is not obvious whether such fragmented labour markets lead to increased poverty; they reduce competition, and so may make it harder for employers to push wages down; and they appear to generate a sense of community solidarity which provides support in times of particular hardship. But at the same time they inhibit access to work, and perhaps perpetuate underprivileged urban strata on the margins of the regular economy, swelling the ranks of casual workers in sectors where entry is unconstrained.

Do sectors with unconstrained entry exist? Most of the studies suggest that to some extent they do, albeit with reservations. The destitute are widely found clustered in construction, domestic service, and commerce, and the presumption is that the unorganised components of these sectors — casual unskilled construction work, hawking of goods on the streets, certain types of personal services, and subsistence activities of the type discussed by Evers — can be entered more or less freely. Harriss comments, however, that this is not true for market portering in Coimbatore, where one has to be a member of a gang, and accounts of individual experiences [5] remind us that when income opportunities are few and needs are great, the struggle to control those opportunities will be intense. Thus free entry is perhaps not entirely the appropriate term; and the evidence on open unemployment suggests that the concept of free entry needs to be handled with care.

### 3. The question of unemployment

There was, at least until the late 1970s, a widespread tendency (from which the present writer was not immune!) to dismiss open unemployment as relatively unimportant in developing countries. According to the conventional wisdom, labour underutilisation was much more important than open unemployment, and the latter was a major issue only in certain rather unusual economies (e.g. in the Caribbean) or among fairly well-off groups — "the educated unemployed" who could afford to engage in extended job search. For example, Sinclair (1978), in his review of literature on this subject, assumed that a substantial fraction of unemployment was in some sense voluntary, and while this has been contested on both conceptual and empirical grounds [6] the view persists,[7] and has coloured much labour market work.

The growth of open unemployment in developing countries since the mid-1970s must at least raise questions as to the validity of a development model which links poverty to labour underutilisation rather than open unemployment; this book can shed some light on the issue, and on the distribution of unemployment across the population. Table 1.2 summarises the main quantitative relationships between poverty and unemployment presented in the case studies. There are problems of comparability, both in the definition of poverty and income groups, and in the measurement of unemployment.[8] But even allowing a considerable margin of error because of these factors, there is a powerful and almost unanimous conclusion: unemployment tends to be

*Table 1.2. Unemployment and poverty (percentages)*

| | Poverty or income group [1] | | | |
| --- | --- | --- | --- | --- |
| | Very poor | Poor | Middle | High |
| *Urban Costa Rica, 1982* | | | | |
| Unemployment rate [2] | 11.0 | 6.0 | 2.0 | 2.0 |
| *Guatemala City, 1980* | | | | |
| Unemployment rate | 5.0 | 2.9 | 4.7 | 1.9 |
| Including "discouraged workers" | 10.6 | 10.8 | 10.0 | 7.7 |
| Including estimated underemployment | 20.6 | 19.6 | 10.0 | 7.7 |
| *Metropolitan Panama, 1983* | | | | |
| Unemployment rate | 14.8 | 11.1 | 3.8 | 3.8 |
| *Santiago de Chile, 1982* | | | | |
| Unemployment rate, heads | 50.0 | 18.3 | 5.3 | 5.3 |
| Unemployment rate, spouses | 25.5 | 19.4 | 6.8 | 6.8 |
| Unemployment rate, children | 63.6 | 45.4 | 23.7 | 23.7 |
| *Santiago de Chile, 1985* | | | | |
| Unemployment rate, heads | 23.7 | 9.1 | 3.1 | 3.1 |
| Unemployment rate, spouses | 23.4 | 14.6 | 4.5 | 4.5 |
| Unemployment rate, children | 30.1 | 16.5 | 12.7 | 12.7 |
| *Urban West Bengal, 1977-78* | | | | |
| Percentage of household members unemployed | 9.5 | 11.4 | 7.8 | 6.0 |
| Percentage of households with a member unemployed | 19.3 | 21.6 | 14.9 | 11.4 |
| Percentage of unemployed for more than 12 months | 74 | 78 | 83 | 84 |

[1] The subgroups are not strictly comparable between countries, because of varying definitions of poverty. They should therefore be interpreted as conveying the relative position. Unemployment rates are also not strictly comparable because of varying definitions and reference periods.　[2] 100 minus the employment rate. Similar data for 1971 give virtually no unemployment − 1 per cent in each of the three groups.
Sources. Given in full in the following chapters.

higher among the poor, not among the relatively well off. All the Latin American studies give the same result. The general pattern is the same in West Bengal, although unemployment is higher among the poor than among the very poor. The relationship is particularly strong in Santiago, where no less than half of very poor household heads were unemployed in 1982, but only 5.3 per cent in higher-income groups; a large part of the fall in unemployment in Chile from 1982 to 1985 was due to job-creation programmes in public works aimed precisely at unemployment among the poor, but this hardly weakened the relationship. Although we do not have such clear evidence for Brazil, there is indirect evidence pointing in the same general direction; Jatobá comments that a 1980 survey of São Paulo found that 42 per cent of the unemployed belonged to the 28 per cent of households which were either low-skill blue-collar, household servants or self-employed, which again suggests an association of unemployment with poverty.

This does not mean that unemployment is a problem only among the poor. Middle-income groups have fairly high unemployment rates in several countries studied. In West Bengal we can see a weak but monotonic tendency for the duration of unemployment to be longer among higher-income groups, which would be consistent with their having resources sufficient to engage in longer job search. But the dominant relationship clearly links unemployment with poverty. The "luxury" unemployment hypothesis, then, is decisively rejected. This result, incidentally, holds good in many other countries. In Sri Lanka, which provided the archetypal model of unemployment as in large degree a problem of upper-income groups (an argument developed in ILO, 1971), Richards and Gooneratne (1980) found, using a 1973 survey, that unemployment rates were systematically highest among the lowest-income groups. In Malaysia Visaria (1981) found unemployment falling from 12.3 per cent in the bottom urban income decile to 2.1 per cent in the top for males, from 13.9 per cent to 2.1 per cent for females (although the pattern was somewhat irregular in intervening income deciles). Urrutia (1985) found unemployment to be higher in lower-income deciles in Colombia in the 1970s. In Tunis van Durme (1987) found the unemployment rate of heads to be lowest among the highest-income groups in 1975, and to be relatively high (although not the highest) among the very poor. In Abidjan Lachaud (1988) found open unemployment to be strongly associated with poverty, especially for household heads and male secondary household workers, with unemployment falling from 41.1 per cent among the destitute to 11.7 per cent among the highest-income groups.

But what do the figures in table 1.2 mean? In some sense, the relationship between unemployment and poverty is definitional — households with all members unemployed will have no labour income, and will fall below the poverty line in the absence of other income sources. Urrutia argued that because of this the relationship between unemployment and income in Colombia should not be taken as reliable evidence of a relationship between unemployment and poverty. He preferred to use education level as a proxy for "permanent income", defining those with less than primary education as poor, and found that unemployment is spread fairly evenly across education levels. However, there seem to be several flaws in this logic. The "human capital" assumption that education can proxy for permanent income is particularly vulnerable in the presence of unemployment, for the relationship between education and permanent income is likely to be systematically affected by experience of unemployment. If one wants to work with a permanent income concept, expenditure levels (used to measure poverty in several case studies) are probably a better proxy, although not all aspects of poverty concern permanent income. Also, given difficulties in initial job access because of labour market segmentation, unemployment will tend to be higher among those entering the labour market for the first time, i.e. the relatively young; but these will tend to have higher than average educational levels simply on account of the expansion of the educational system, introducing a positive bias into the relationship between unemployment and education. Urrutia's argument therefore does not disturb the conclusion that unemployment is concentrated among the poor.

Given the importance of income shortfalls because of unemployment, the crucial issue is other income sources. In part, this will come from other household members who remain in work. The figures for West Bengal show that the percentage of households with a member unemployed is roughly double that of individuals unemployed, which indicates the extent to which other family members remain employed. But the unemployment of a household head will under these circumstances have particularly severe consequences for poverty. This is clear in the Santiago data, where the unemployment rate of heads is much higher, in relation to other household members, among the poorest groups.

There are of course other sources of income support. None of the countries concerned has an adequate state unemployment insurance scheme, but community or family solidarity is likely to be of assistance. Many families will draw on savings, if they have any; others, perhaps many, will fall into debt, and although there is little information on this, where it is important it may severely constrain future labour market options.[9] But probably the most obvious response to unemployment among the poor is an intense search for low-productivity subsistence activities. The Jakarta study, in particular, argues that measurements of open unemployment are maladapted for analysing poverty; that loss of job or inadequate job access shows up in intensified subsistence activity, which may or may not be consistent with a classification of individuals by regular survey techniques as "employed" or "unemployed". The point is well taken, but table 1.2 does clearly show measured open unemployment to be valid and important as well. How important obviously varies a great deal. In Santiago it was clearly *the* major problem. In Guatemala City it seems to be of secondary importance, although the extended estimates of underemployment, including discouraged workers, show how quickly a 5 per cent unemployment rate can turn into 20 per cent labour underutilisation. The West Bengal figures show how a 10 per cent unemployment rate affects 20 per cent of households, which is also an important mechanism by which the impact of open unemployment spreads, and the multivariate analysis in West Bengal shows unemployment to be a highly significant determinant of poverty. Overall, it seems that while poverty makes unemployment difficult to stand — and forces changes in labour supply strategy, intensive job search and subsistence activities — the simple inability to obtain work remains an important determinant of urban poverty.

The case studies do not provide much information on under-employment, in its various forms, with the exception of the Costa Rica and Santiago studies, both of which examine the relationship between hours of work and poverty. In both cases, only destitute households among the poor had working hours which differed greatly from the population average. In both cases, short working hours were a significant feature of destitution. In Santiago 27 per cent of destitute household heads worked less than 30 hours per week in 1985 (against an average 12 per cent of the total population) and this was true of 51 per cent of spouses (population average 23 per cent). In urban Costa Rica there was a similar relationship, even stronger for household heads (44 per cent, against a population average of 10 per cent). These results probably reflect the incidence of irregular casual work. But for secondary household workers there was an interesting supplementary pattern: in destitute households secondary workers were disproportionately found in both the less-than-30-hours and the more-than-50-hours groups. In other words, not only underemployment but also what might arguably be regarded as overemployment were both present. Evers also notes that long working hours are commonplace in Jakarta, especially among women, one-third of whom worked over 60 hours per week without counting housework and subsistence activities. Presumably this is a widespread phenomenon. For different groups and at different times, then, poverty will be associated with unemployment, and inadequate or irregular access to employment reflected in short weekly working hours; but also with long working hours, reflecting low productivity and urgent income needs.

### 4. The supply of labour

The supply of labour by poor households depends on demographic and life-cycle characteristics discussed above. But the response of households to poverty also involves changes in labour supply strategies, particularly involving secondary workers — predominantly women, but also male children and older workers. The success of these strategies obviously depends on issues of labour market access discussed above, and secondary workers are subject to particularly intense discrimination. Moreover, the term "strategy" may itself be misleading, implying a well-worked out plan for the allocation of family labour resources. While this may sometimes be accurate, it is probable that the strategy will more often consist of attempts to obtain additional income by any means available, perhaps through the forced withdrawal of children from school, or through a search for additional work by household members who are already in full-time employment. In many households there will be crises, arising from the dismissal or incapacity of the main income earner, from household division, or from some other source of increased dependency, and these will force undesirable levels of labour supply. In fact, arguably the most general influence of poverty on the labour market is the influence of extreme need on patterns of labour supply and production. The nature of these patterns varies, for so does the degree of exploitation and the accessibility of work. In some situations, the result will be a mixture of subsistence activity and low-productivity self-employment. More frequently, wage employment of some type will be involved, the urgent need for income of the poor facilitating the payment of below-subsistence wages or the imposition of intolerable working conditions, while self-employment and wage employment alike are subject to predation from a host of intermediaries, money-lenders and functionaries.

Many of the studies provide information on these patterns, but it is difficult to separate the influence of poverty from other household determinants of labour supply, and from the broader issue of access to the labour market. Moreover, the variation in female labour supply, which is always much larger than that for men, depends considerably on cultural and status factors which vary regionally and internationally. In India female labour force participation is highest among the poor, both in urban West Bengal and in Bombay — in Bombay the adult female labour force participation rate for casual labour households was 35 per cent, while for factory or small-sector households it was only 9 or 10 per cent. A similar pattern seems possible in Jakarta, although the data do not permit a direct comparison. On the other hand, in the Latin American studies economic activity rates are relatively low among the poor. In Guatemala the estimated labour force participation rate is 44 per cent among the destitute, compared with 48 per cent overall; in Costa Rica 61 to 67 per cent among the poor, compared with 72 per cent among other population groups; in Panama 52 to 53 per cent among the poor compared with 57 per cent among other groups. In Santiago a breakdown of labour force participation by relationship within the household shows the participation of heads to be only weakly related to poverty, but the rates for spouses and children were significantly lower among the poor.

Lower levels of labour supply among the poor may in the first instance reflect household characteristics — an excess of individuals who are in some way handicapped, ill, underfed, or otherwise disadvantaged.[10] In such cases poverty is in part the result of low ability to supply labour. To some extent the data from urban West Bengal show this; in the poorest group, only 77 per cent of usually economically active males were actually in the labour force in the reference week (compared with at least 95 per cent in all other groups). But one can also suppose, as in several of the Latin American studies, that lower measured labour supply among the poor also reflects "discouraged worker" effects. Since unemployment levels are highest for the poorest groups, the abandonment of job search by secondary household members seems a plausible explanation of at least part of the difference in measured labour supply.

How can this be reconciled with the income needs of the poor? Evers suggests one possibility — that among the poorest groups, subsistence production provides a substantial fraction of household income; that it substitutes for inadequate income opportunities elsewhere; and that it is very poorly measured by conventional surveys. This relates to well-known difficulties with the concept of "unpaid family worker", the measurement of which is a perennial source of understatement of labour supply, as well as with the appreciation of domestic labour. If Evers's results for Jakarta are true elsewhere — we have little evidence, but some of the qualitative discussion about Guatemala City points in the same direction — then what occurs is not labour force withdrawal, but a shift away from the labour market towards other, more marginal ways of meeting income needs.

But the variation in these patterns highlights the interdependence between labour supply and labour market structure. In several countries an industry or labour market segment has grown up to take advantage of or perhaps create a low-skill, low-wage and unorganised female labour force. In urban West Bengal, for instance, female wages appear to be about half those of men. Under such circumstances, intense poverty seems linked to entry to these low-status, low-income labour market segments — for women, and probably school-age children as well. Elsewhere these labour market segments do not exist or are less important, perhaps because of alternative subsistence options, or because other forms of production organisation result in different patterns of labour market segmentation. In either case labour supply response among the poor is conditioned by the structure of labour demand.

# V. Recession, labour markets and poverty

The erratic behaviour of the world economy since 1970 has affected the countries studied in greatly differing degrees. Apart from Chile, driven into recession by monetarist policies in the mid-1970s, the Latin American countries covered here maintained reasonably high rates of GDP growth throughout the 1970s; but all went into severe recession in the early 1980s, although the onset was somewhat delayed in Panama. In Asia the effects were less dramatic; GDP growth in the Philippines was already much lower in the late 1970s than before 1973, but really severe recession only arrived in 1983. India was sufficiently insulated from the world market, and sufficiently aided by remittances from migrants to the Gulf, to mitigate the effects of world recession; indeed, growth appeared to be accelerating in India in the early 1980s when it was declining elsewhere. Indonesia's growth was uneven but high, on average, reflecting its favoured position as an oil exporter at a time of rapidly rising oil prices.

In parallel with these changes in growth rates, many changes in labour market patterns can be seen. Some clearly result from short-term changes in economic growth; others appear to be the outcome of longer-term secular processes. Many of them have influenced trends in poverty, directly and indirectly. We will now try to isolate some of the ways in which this has occurred, and assess their importance. Most of the better quantified material on this comes from the Latin American studies,[11] several of which examine the recession in detail; comparable time series were much harder to establish elsewhere, although some clues can be picked up here and there.

The studies focus mainly on the late 1970s and early 1980s. By the time of writing — 1988 — several of the countries considered had recovered somewhat from the worst of the recession, although economic growth remains precarious and indebtedness a continuing constraint. The relationships between labour market outcomes and poverty observed in the 1970s and early 1980s can provide some clues as to how the poor have been faring since, and suggest possible trends for the 1990s.

## 1. Trends in urban poverty

Although levels of poverty are not directly comparable across countries, it is nevertheless interesting to compare such trends in the incidence of poverty as can be discerned for the 1970s and early 1980s. Variations in poverty, even if only very approximately measured, give a first idea of how much the effects of the fluctuations in the world and national economies during this

*Table 1.3.  Trends in the extent of urban poverty, 1965-85*

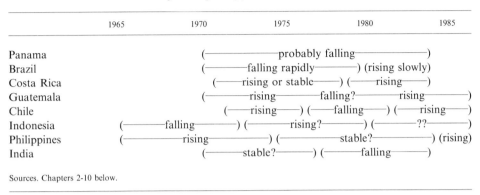

| | 1965 | 1970 | 1975 | 1980 | 1985 |
|---|---|---|---|---|---|
| Panama | | (————————probably falling————————) | | | |
| Brazil | | (————falling rapidly————) (rising slowly) | | | |
| Costa Rica | | (————rising or stable————) (————rising————) | | | |
| Guatemala | | (————rising————falling?————rising————) | | | |
| Chile | | (————rising————) (————falling————) (————rising————) | | | |
| Indonesia | (————falling————) (————rising?————) (————??————) | | | | |
| Philippines | (————rising————) (————stable?————) (rising) | | | | |
| India | | (————stable?————) (————falling————) | | | |

Sources. Chapters 2-10 below.

*Table 1.4.  Trends in relative urban poverty (inequality), 1965-85*

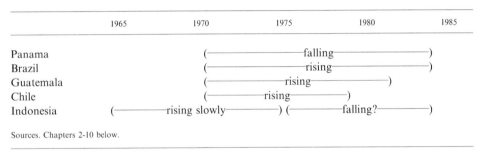

| | 1965 | 1970 | 1975 | 1980 | 1985 |
|---|---|---|---|---|---|
| Panama | | (————————falling————————) | | | |
| Brazil | | (————————rising————————) | | | |
| Guatemala | | (————rising————) | | | |
| Chile | | (————rising————) | | | |
| Indonesia | (————rising slowly————) (————falling?————) | | | | |

Sources. Chapters 2-10 below.

period were borne by low-income groups. Tables 1.3 and 1.4 are based on figures presented in the following chapters. Table 1.3 mostly uses direct poverty estimates, but account has also been taken of time series for wages. There are considerable data uncertainties, and it should be regarded as a very rough first approximation. There is much variation between countries, and all countries which have data for several points in time show fluctuations and trend reversals. Only Brazil shows an unambiguous decline in the extent of poverty in the 1970s (albeit coinciding with an increase in inequality, both between households and between regions), but most countries covered here had periods of improving or at least stable poverty during the 1970s, especially the late 1970s; where this does not emerge from rather erratic poverty estimates, it can been seen in wage series discussed below.[12] However, the pattern appears to depend much more on internal political and economic forces than on the world economy. In the 1980s, on the other hand, there was a widespread tendency for poverty to increase, with world recession clearly a major cause; Indonesia, as an oil exporter, probably does not fit this pattern (we do not have poverty estimates for the 1980s, but real wages appeared to be rising). Otherwise the only clear exception is India, much less dependent on external trade, where the incidence of urban poverty fell by about 5 percentage points from 1978 to 1983. But even in India there are hints in Harriss's chapter that the position of the destitute was not improving. Panama may also be an exception, probably because wage policy shifted the burden of adjustment onto higher-income groups.

## 2. Labour market mechanisms and poverty trends

### A. Labour market structure

The overall rate of urban employment creation is in one sense the fundamental variable for understanding the ways macro-economic trends affect urban poverty. But while aggregate employment is an important element, interpretation depends on understanding its structure. Changing rates of job creation generate changes in unemployment, in overall labour supply, in the sectoral distribution of work and its remuneration; and the aggregate level of employment is not necessarily a clear indicator of overall labour market evolution. In the Panama study, for instance, where aggregate employment elasticities are discussed, there is substantial variation in the relationship between output and employment with the economic cycle, suggesting the presence of underlying changes in labour market structure.

These changes in structure can, following the argument developed above, best be examined in terms of changing patterns of segmentation and of forms of labour. Several studies show adaptation of the labour market to recession through relative growth of the informal sector, however defined. The Brazilian study analyses this in most detail, finding first that the share of informal sector employment declined in the early 1970s, before starting to grow again; and then finding clear evidence of "informalisation" in the 1981-83 recession, as the organised sector's share of employment fell, particularly in the more modern and industrialised Southeast, which suffered more directly from the contraction of world markets. Jatobá argues that this contributed significantly to the increase in poverty from 1981 to 1983, given substantial earnings differences between organised and unorganised sectors. However, the overall shift in the employment structure was only of the order of 3 percentage points.

Several other studies point to a growth in informal sector employment or in self-employment. In Costa Rica there was a slight increase in the informal sector's share of employment in the peak of the recession; in Guatemala the informal sector grew faster than the formal in the 1970s; in Panama the share of the informal sector in employment grew from 25 per cent in 1978 to 30 per cent in 1983, with a shift away from wage labour towards self-employment in the informal sector. In Chile there was no such trend. In Manila the share of own-account work in total employment rose from 14 to 22 per cent from 1982 to 1985. The general interpretation is that these changes reflected labour market adaptation to the slow growth of labour demand in the modern sector, which seems plausible, but quantitatively these adjustments do not seem enormous (there were distinctly larger changes in wages and unemployment), nor are they necessarily closely related to poverty — there is no evidence of a close link in Panama, for instance.

In discussing labour market structure, above, it was argued that vulnerability in the labour market is a better basis for disaggregation than a formal-informal sector breakdown. The Brazilian and Indian studies give some information on this. In Brazil Jatobá finds the category of unprotected labour increasing in importance during the recession — in fact the shift into this category seemed to be somewhat greater than that into unorganised sector employment. In India Harriss finds that casual and vulnerable labour market groups grew in the 1970s. For instance, non-registered factory employment grew twice as fast as registered employment from 1971 to 1981. Recent National Sample Survey data back up his argument: the proportion of casual labour rose from 10 per cent in 1972/73 to 14.8 per cent in 1983 among urban male workers in India; for females the increase was from 23.7 per cent to 27.3 per cent (India, 1986). He also argues that India has seen a growth of informalisation in a different sense, through the growth of subcontracting, outwork, and the use of contract labour — phenomena which are of course allied to the growth of casual labour. In both cases there is a presumption that this has increased poverty.

Evidence on the importance of other changes in labour market structure is patchy. In Chile the State's role in the labour market shifted from 1974 to 1983, with public employment dropping by half. Elsewhere there has been growing government intervention, involving more white-collar workers and changing access routes to the labour market. But the implications for poverty are unclear.

### B. Unemployment

We concluded above that the importance of unemployment for poverty should not be underestimated; and the links between trends in unemployment and poverty in the studies underline this point. The extreme case is Chile, where poverty, and in particular destitution, was closely related to the unemployment rate over the past 15 years or so. The strength of this relationship is the result of the extraordinarily high levels of unemployment in Chile, especially from 1982 to 1985, and notably among household heads. But even where unemployment is lower, it has been rising and this, together with an increase in the proportion of household heads among the unemployed, has clearly been a widespread factor in increases in poverty in the early 1980s. In urban Southeast Brazil unemployment rose from 3.8 per cent in 1979 to 7.4 per cent in 1983 (the rise was less in the Northeast), and the proportion of household heads rose by several percentage points. In Manila rapidly rising unemployment was clearly a major factor in the growth of poverty from 1983 to 1985, and similar inferences can be made in other case studies. Given the widespread tendency for unemployment rates to rise in developing countries during the 1980s, especially but not exclusively in the Western Hemisphere, these results are worth stressing. Unorganised sectors do have some "sponge" capacity, as Jatobá argues, but it may be quite limited, and open unemployment is certainly the direct cause of much poverty.

### C. Wages and earnings

Most data on wages refer to regular jobs, and in so far as they refer to lower-income groups they often concern legislated minimum wages, not necessarily effectively covering all workers. Thus wage series tend to be biased towards protected segments of the labour market. This does not mean that they give no guide to trends in poverty. Wage trends in protected and unprotected segments are likely to be correlated and, because of variations in individual wages and in dependency between households, part of the population in the protected segment of the labour market will always be vulnerable to poverty. But such data have to be used with caution, and the complexity of wage structures often makes it difficult to isolate trends from incomplete information.

In some countries recession provoked very substantial changes in wage levels. In Costa Rica real wages fell by 30 per cent from 1979 to 1983; in the urban Philippines real wages dropped by 45 per cent from 1982 to 1985, earnings of own-account workers by 57 per cent. Such enormous changes are bound to increase poverty even if initially they only affect relatively protected labour market groups. In practice it is not only higher wage levels which are affected, and the Philippine data suggest that wage declines were just as large in low-income sectors as in high. In Brazil, where real wage changes were less dramatic (real wages in manufacturing fell 10 per cent from 1981 to 1983), there was a rapid growth in low-income employment, i.e. employment paying less than the minimum wage, in the 1981-83 recession; in fact, virtually all employment growth was of this kind, and it affected protected and unprotected workers, and (in the Southeast at least) organised and unorganised sectors alike. Thus the decline in real wages had a widespread impact. In Costa Rica the percentage of household heads earning less than the official minimum wage rose from 24 per cent to 31 per cent. However in Panama the pattern was different. Wage declines were concentrated on *higher* income groups in the 1970s and early 1980s, apparently because of the practice of awarding similar absolute wage increases to all groups. Thus from 1978 to 1983 the average real wage of weekly wage earners rose by 10 per cent, while for monthly salary earners there was a decline of 9 per cent. This was surely a major reason for Panama's relatively good performance in terms of poverty indicators.[13] In Chile the large changes in real wages were overshadowed by the even larger changes in unemployment, and changes in the incidence of destitution were most closely correlated with changes in unemployment; but changes in the incidence of poverty above the destitution level were more closely related to wage changes.

In countries less affected by the recession, changes were more difficult to pinpoint, but perhaps no less important. In India there is evidence of widening wage inequality, with some sign that real wages have been rising — albeit erratically — over the past decade or so in permanent, regular jobs, while they have been stagnating or even declining in casual work. Since the share of casual work in the total has been rising, this could be an important factor leading to increased poverty. There is a paradox, however, in that the aggregate evidence suggests that urban poverty has been declining in India, at least from

1977/78 to 1983. More research is required to clarify this. In Jakarta too there is some weak evidence that wage differentials have been increasing, as public sector real wages rose fairly rapidly in the 1970s while unskilled wages showed no real trend. When the latter started to rise in the early 1980s, there was some evidence that the increase was faster in large and medium-scale industry (Manning and Mazumdar, 1985). However, wage data for Jakarta are scarce, so that these patterns remain very uncertain.

How one interprets these changes depends to some extent on the forces responsible for wage determination. The State is clearly a major actor, through the fixing of public sector pay, its repression or promotion of worker organisation, or minimum-wage legislation. In much of Latin America the minimum wage, which can be a means for keeping wages down as well as keeping them up, acts as a reference standard even when the legislation is not enforced. As a result, in many countries, trends in minimum wages have clearly played a role in alleviating or worsening poverty. In Brazil the minimum wage rose by 15 per cent in the 1970s, dropping in the early 1980s. In Guatemala the minimum wage fluctuated around a downward trend in the 1970s before falling by 28 per cent from 1980 to 1985. One result was that the number of minimum-wage earners required for the average household to purchase only the basic food basket rose from 1.6 in 1972 to 2.5 in 1985.

But the State is only one actor, and the forces which tend to fragment the labour market also tend to generate differentials in levels and trends in earnings. Apart from the Indian case — indicative, but not conclusive — we have little evidence on this. Some groups are better able to defend their position than others, and it makes sense that in crises, casual labour is particularly exposed. In the Philippines sectoral breakdowns suggest that tertiary sector workers are especially vulnerable, and work status breakdowns that this is true of the self-employed. In Brazil there was a noticeable growth of low-income employment in the industrialised Southeast in the recession, and data from Costa Rica also indicated particular vulnerability in sectors producing tradeables. But to pursue this further requires appropriately disaggregated data, which can be matched with local labour market segmentation patterns.

### D. Labour supply

It was argued above that labour supply patterns are to a large extent conditioned by the structure and level of labour demand. We have also seen that household labour supply strategies change in the face of increasing poverty or unemployment. Trends in overall labour supply will reflect the balance of these — sometimes conflicting — forces, and their interaction with underlying social and cultural relationships. As a result we find a wide variety of labour supply trends. Sometimes, such trends and changes in poverty are fairly clearly related. In Colombia Urrutia (1985) found that during the 1970s there was a large increase in the labour supply of secondary workers, mainly but not exclusively women, among the urban lower-income groups, at a time when poverty was falling. He argues quite convincingly that increases in job opportunities rather than changing labour supply strategies were responsible; and that this was an important mechanism by which the benefits of economic growth reached the poor. In Brazil, too, as poverty declined in the 1970s labour force participation rates rose steadily; again, this can be interpreted as a response to increased opportunity. But during the 1981-83 recession, when wages were falling and essentially only low-income jobs were being created, female labour force participation rates continued to rise, while male rates stabilised. In contrast to the 1970s, then, the increase in female labour supply in 1981-83 might be explained as a supply response to increased need. But other interpretations are possible — the process might be seen as a more general, longer-term feminisation of the labour force, noted for some sectors of Indian industry by Harriss, and thus determined much more by the evolving structure of labour demand than by household response patterns.

Other evidence on changing labour supply patterns in response to trends in poverty is equally ambiguous. In Costa Rica there was a small rise in labour supply during the recession, concentrated on secondary workers, but there is no obvious sign of a pattern of this type in Guatemala, Panama or Chile. In Manila rising labour force participation in the early 1980s is interpreted by Alonzo as a response to declining real wages, but in Jakarta Evers argues that the labour supply responses come in forms of work which are very poorly measured in conventional surveys, so that available statistics are unreliable anyway. To this argument might be added another, that supply responses to poverty depend a great deal on household characteristics, and that different categories of households can be identified with quite distinct supply responses, which may or may not balance each other out in the aggregate figures. Again, more disaggregated analysis is required.

# VI. Concluding comments

The case studies are drawn from only two regions, and even within those regions, they were not picked to be representative. General conclusions therefore need to be drawn with prudence. Some broader inferences can nevertheless be derived from the evidence presented. The main one is that there are indeed specific ways in which urban poverty and labour markets interact. We have highlighted ways in which protection is extended to or withdrawn from parts of the labour force, especially in so far as there are trends towards "informalisation" or "casualisation"; the importance of particular wage and earnings structures; the specific role of unemployment; discrimination against particular groups, perhaps more against women and less against migrants than is commonly supposed. These structural aspects do not show up in aggregate employment and wage figures, and they underline the need to break down work and the labour force in ways which are analytically meaningful for the assessment of poverty and labour market vulnerability. It is especially important to be able to locate groups with insecure labour market access, particularly vulnerable to exploitation and deprivation. Conventional data sources permit us to go some way in this, through judicious disaggregation, but they need to be linked to more detailed, perhaps qualitative or anecdotal, material, if an adequate understanding of the labour market insertion of the poor is to be built up.

The studies show diverse patterns of change in poverty and labour market access in the 1970s and early 1980s. In the late 1970s, in a majority of the countries examined, urban poverty was probably declining. In the 1980s, however, this trend has been reversed, and urban poverty rose, in some cases sharply. Even where there is no evidence that poverty was rising overall, as in India, there were signs of increased labour market inequality as the extent of casual labour grew and their levels of living stagnated. But there is no uniformity in these patterns, nor should that be expected. Labour market institutions, structures and strategies vary greatly from one city or country to another, and it is these that mediate the relationships with poverty. The evolution of poverty depends on the position of different groups in relation to these structures, which determines how they fare when job opportunities, incomes and unemployment change. In short, it is broader labour processes which determine the evolution of urban poverty, occurring in specific social and historical contexts.

This conclusion also conditions the perception of policy. Some of the relationships and mechanisms discussed here suggest fairly immediate possibilities for policy intervention; and there are both successes and failures to ponder over in the experiences discussed below. Of course, in considering these experiences it is necessary to distinguish between political economy issues and policy analysis. The poor are on the whole not an effective lobby. Their interests are sometimes defended by those with political or bureaucratic power, but the rhetoric of policies to reduce poverty is often more prominent than effective action. A low-wage, unprotected labour force, or a labour reserve which can readily be drawn upon when the need arises, are seen in many developing countries as preconditions for rapid industrialisation; if adjustment to international recession or to monetary targets creates high levels of unemployment, then this is unfortunate, but it helps to damp down inflationary pressures. When these attitudes are carried to extremes, the effect on poverty can be disastrous — the most glaring example here is the case of Chile, but similar if less extreme patterns can be observed elsewhere. This suggests that the clearest policy issue is the need for effective mobilisation of the poor. The segmentation and fragmentation of the labour market takes on new meaning in this context, for it makes solidarity between different groups among the poor difficult to achieve, and indeed often creates competition rather than co-operation among low-income groups. The frequent assertion that trade unions in developing countries defend the interests of a relatively privileged group of regular workers is a case in point, and while too much is usually made of this point — it is more often used to undermine the protection of regular workers than to argue for the wider extension of such protection — it is clear that the interests of regular, secure workers diverge from the interests of those on the margins of the labour market.

However, the picture is not entirely bleak, and lessons may be learnt from the experiences discussed below. The relative success of Panama in limiting the effects of recession on poverty is worth noting; egalitarian wage policies, combined with effective action to prevent unemployment from rising, directed much of the burden of economic adjustment towards groups better able to bear it.[14] Broader issues of labour protection may also be important. The Brazilian study shows how the extent of protection (essentially through effective labour legislation) is closely related to the incidence of poverty, but also that protection was reduced during the recession, and that regional differentials in the incidence of protection remain important. There is thus a serious structural problem of implementation, related to the political economy issues noted above. A similar comment applies to minimum-wage policies, against which there is a substantial lobby, arguing that high minimum wages create unemployment or a privileged minority.[15]

The evidence on trends in poverty during the recession suggests that the design of macro-economic policy has an immediate effect on poverty, perhaps more direct than is commonly thought. The three most obvious mechanisms by which demand shortfalls are transmitted to the labour market are wage adjustments, increased open unemployment, and a shifting of workers towards absorptive informal sectors. In so far as the latter dominates, the apparent need for policy intervention is lessened — the informal sector acting as a buffer to absorb the worst of the impact on the labour market. But this did not seem to be the main mechanism in situations for which we have data: the share of the informal sector was found to grow to some extent in response to recession, but its absorptive capacity appeared limited, in the short term at least. This finding is related to the heterogeneous nature of the informal sector concept, within which the "free-entry" component is perhaps only a small fraction. Instead, open unemployment and real wage changes appeared to be important, and where there were serious failures of macro-economic policy, as in Chile and the Philippines, there has been an extraordinary growth in poverty as a result of a combination of these two factors. In general, these conclusions underline the need for direct promotion of employment through public works and other means, and for the social dimension to be much more effectively incorporated in macro-economic adjustment programmes, if growth in poverty is to be avoided.

Although we do not find the informal sector effective in absorbing the labour surplus provoked by economic recession, the promotion of employment in small-scale, informal sector and subsistence activities is one policy which might reach the urban poor. The Jakarta study suggests that just the elimination of administrative obstacles and excessive policing might contribute significantly. There is however a more general issue, that of access. Small-scale production is fragmented, and different forms of production and income generation are controlled either by larger-scale producers, or by particular ethnic or family groups. Those activities where entry is easy are marginal, produce little income and are not usually the target of policy. Thus policy has to face the problem of how to widen access; and this extends to many other forms of intervention to promote the interests of the poor in the labour market. For instance, making labour market information widely available is of little help when job access is controlled through particularistic networks. Many groups among the poor face discrimination in the labour market because of their personal characteristics; a policy of positive discrimination in their favour is required if significant progress is to be made. Education and training policy may help, but there is a prior question of access to education, and the interpretation of educational qualifications by the labour market — if educational levels rise among the whole population, including the poor, the poor may remain disadvantaged if their relative position in the educational hierarchy is unchanged. These structural problems will not respond readily to policy; it is necessary to face up to the structure of economic and social interests, many of which cannot be overcome without a major struggle.

It should be stressed that poverty in the urban labour market is heterogeneous, and requires more than a series of individual policy measures. A broadly based, multi-dimensional approach is needed, including not only actions aimed at the labour market but also a range of social policies covering housing, the pricing and distribution of essential goods, public services and various forms of social insurance. The aim here has not been to spell out the nature of such a package; attention is focused on mechanisms. Moreover, policy is specific to situations, and if sensible conclusions about the role of labour policy in reducing urban poverty are to be reached in particular contexts, they need to be grounded in an analysis of structures, mechanisms and differentiation in the labour markets concerned.

### Notes

[1] National Sample Survey data show the percentage of male workers engaged in agriculture and related activities to have dropped from 83 per cent in 1972-73 to 77 per cent in 1983 (India, NSS, 1986).

[2] In this chapter, unreferenced phrases such as "the study in Panama city" or the name of the author concerned refer to the appropriate chapter of this book, in the present case Chapter 5.

[3] Although there are notable exceptions, e.g. much higher dependency rates found among regular than among casual workers in Bombay, but not necessarily replicated in other Indian cities (see Harriss).

[4] See, for instance, Herrick and Hudson (1981) on Costa Rica, van Durme (1987) on Tunis, and Rodgers (1983) for a summary of several studies.

[5] See, for instance, Lapierre (1985), written in a semi-fictional fashion, but based on authentic accounts of life in the slums of Calcutta.

[6] For instance, by Standing (1981).

[7] In Berry and Sabot (1984), for example.

[8] It should be noted that the irregular unemployment of casual workers is not adequately represented in these figures, which mostly have a reference period of at least a week; the days of unemployment of irregular workers who obtained at least some days' work during the reference week will not be included in the unemployment estimates. See Chapter 8 for data showing how similar factors affect the comparison between unemployment estimates based on the "past week" and the "past quarter".

[9] This at least would be the expectation in the light of the consequences of indebtedness for rural labour.

[10] The effects of household age structure are in principle covered in most of the studies by calculating labour force participation rates in relation to the adult population aged 10 or 15 to 60 or 65, although households with a preponderance of members near these age limits are likely to be vulnerable to poverty. Sex structure will also have an effect; we have already noted that households without adult males are particularly vulnerable because of the greater difficulty of labour market access for women.

[11] A more thorough analysis of the effects of the recession on Latin American labour markets is to be found in Tokman and Wurgaft (1987).

[12] Urrutia's (1985) findings for Colombia are consistent with this pattern, in that he finds urban poverty increasing in the early 1970s and falling rapidly in the late 1970s. However, he does not present data for the 1980s.

[13] There was a somewhat similar pattern in Colombia; see Urrutia (1985).

[14] It seems, however, that such policies have been implemented much less effectively after the mid-1980s.

[15] The evidence for this position is weak, of course — one only has to compare unemployment rates in Chile, where there has been effectively no floor to wages, and in Panama or Brazil, where minimum-wage policy has been reasonably influential. See also PREALC (1983). However, as noted above, there are ambiguities about the ultimate objectives of minimum-wage policy.

## References

Altimir, Oscar, 1979: "La dimensión de la pobreza en América Latina", in *Cuadernos de la CEPAL*. Santiago, ECLAC.

Berry, Albert and Sabot, Richard H., 1984: "Unemployment and economic development", in *Économic Development and Cultural Change* (Chigaco), Vol. 33, No. 1.

Bromley, Ray and Gerry, Chris 1979: *Casual work and poverty in Third World cities*. New York, John Wiley.

Doeringer, Peter and Piore, Michael 1971: *Internal labour markets and manpower analysis*. Lexington, Massachusetts, Heath.

Harriss, John, 1982: "Character of an urban economy: 'Small-scale' production and labour markets in Coimbatore", in *Economic and Political Weekly* (Bombay), Vol. XVII, Nos. 23 and 24, 5 and 12 June.

Herrick, Bruce and Hudson, Barclay 1981: *Urban poverty and economic development: A case study of Costa Rica*. London, Macmillan.

India, Government of, National Sample Survey Organisation, 1986: *Sarvekshana* (New Delhi), Vol. IX, No. 4, Apr.

ILO, 1971: *Matching employment opportunities and expectations: A programme of action for Ceylon*. Geneva.

Lachaud, Jean-Pierre, 1988: "Pauvreté et marché du travail en Afrique: le cas d'Abidjan, Côte d'Ivoire", in *International Institute for Labour Studies Discussion Paper*. Geneva, IILS.

Lapierre, Dominique, 1985: *La cité de la joie*. Paris, Robert Laffont.

Lipton, Michael, 1977: *Why poor people stay poor*. London, Temple Smith.

Manning, Chris and Mazumdar, Dipak 1985: "Indonesian labour markets: An Overview", Paper prepared for Employment and Income Distribution Division, Development Research Department, World Bank. Washington, DC; mimeographed.

PREALC, 1982: *Mercado de trabajo en cifras, 1950-1980*. Santiago de Chile.

———, 1983: *Empleo y salarios*. Santiago de Chile.

Reich, Michael; Gordon, David and Edwards, Richard, 1973: "A theory of labour market segmentation", in *American Economic Review*, Papers and Proceedings, Vol. LXIII, No. 2, May.

Richards, Peter and Gooneratne, Wilbert, 1980: *Basic needs, poverty and government policies in Sri Lanka*. Geneva, ILO.

Rodgers, Gerry, 1983: "The impact of rural-urban migration on income distribution", in *Canadian Journal of Development Studies* (Ottawa), Vol. IV, No. 2.

Rodgers, Gerry and Standing, Guy (eds.), 1981: *Child work, poverty and underdevelopment*. Geneva, ILO.

Rowntree, B. S., 1901: *Poverty: A study of town life*. London, Macmillan.

Sinclair, Stuart W. 1978: *Urbanisation and labour markets in developing countries*. London, Croom Helm.

Standing, Guy, 1981: "The notion of voluntary unemployment", in *International Labour Review*, Vol. 120, No. 5.

Tokman, Victor and Wurgaft, José 1987: "The recession and the workers of Latin America", in ILO: *World recession and global interdependence*. Geneva.

Urrutia, Miguel, 1985: *Winners and losers in Colombia's economic growth of the 1970s*. New York, Oxford University Press for the World Bank.

van Durme, Patrick, 1987: "Trends in urban poverty and labour market access in Tunis". Geneva, ILO; mimeographed.

Visaria, Pravin, 1981: "Incidence of poverty and the characteristics of the poor in Peninsular Malaysia", in *World Bank Staff Working Paper*, No. 460. Washington, DC, World Bank.

Wilkinson, Frank (ed.), 1981: *The dynamics of labour market segmentation*. London, Academic Press.

World Bank, 1986: *World Development Report 1986*. New York, Oxford University Press for the World Bank.

# Chapter 2

## Urban poverty, labour markets and regional differentiation in Brazil

*JORGE JATOBÁ* [1]

## I. Introduction

This chapter compares Brazil's two most important regions, the Southeast and the Northeast, focusing on 1970-83, with particular emphasis on the labour market mechanisms set in motion in 1981-83, when Brazil was attempting to cope with a deep recession, rapid inflation, and a severe foreign debt crisis. The Southeast is more developed than the Northeast: not only does it account for the bulk of Brazil's output and labour force, but it has also achieved the most technical progress. Its economy is modern, and highly competitive nationally and internationally, and it has led Brazil's output growth and capital accumulation since the 1880s. The Northeast, in contrast, is now Brazil's poorest region. We will compare the labour market structures of the two regions, and examine how the response of these structures to economic growth and recession affects the extent and incidence of urban poverty. The data sources are the Demographic Censuses and the National Household Surveys (PNAD), published by the Brazilian Statistical Bureau (FIBGE). Data for 1981-83 came from a special tabulation of the National Household Survey provided by FIBGE at the request of a UNDP/ILO Technical Co-operation Project.

The origins of regional disparities in Brazil go back to the eighteenth century. Historically, the Southeast, led by São Paulo, clearly assumed the leading role in capital accumulation, while the Northeast was depressed and impoverished. By the 1950s there was already evidence in the Northeast of what has become a chronic phenomenon − a substantial underutilisation of labour in the urban centres where, despite emigration, a considerable number of people were either unemployed or, more frequently, underemployed. The latter were usually found in low-income and low-productivity occupations characterised by adverse working conditions, income instability, and a lack of protective labour and social security legislation.

From 1960 to 1980, despite considerable efforts to foster capital accumulation, high rates of output and employment growth, and changes in the output mix, the Northeast failed to reduce levels of labour force underutilisation. In contrast, the more homogeneous economy and labour markets of the Southeast provided, except during the 1962-66 recession, sufficient new jobs in the modern non-agricultural sectors to allow an overall increase in the relative importance of formal labour markets.[2]

There are several reasons why this did not happen in the Northeast (Neto, 1982). One is the relationship of its economy to that of the Southeast, for it is in the nature of regional integration for economic relationships to be more competitive than complementary. This confrontation between an economically mature region and one with a weak productive structure led to a loss of external markets by the latter and the capture of local markets by the former (see PIMES/UFPe, 1984, Chapter 1, section 1.2). In the Northeast this process not only led to the elimination of local jobs, but also inhibited the emergence of economic activities that would compete with those of the Southeast. Another factor was the nature of rural transformations, which tended to reduce labour absorption in rural activities (de Melo, 1976a). Moreover, regional industrialisation, while it created many jobs, also eliminated others as a result of competition that drove out goods produced in craft and semi-craft processes and small non-institutionalised urban manufacturing firms. Further, the labour absorption of new industries was limited to the extent that they used modern labour-saving techniques and high capital-labour ratios, and this was encouraged by fiscal and financial incentives that altered factor price ratios to lower the cost of capital relative to labour (Jatobá, 1974). Other factors that may have discouraged more rapid employment creation are: the weak backward and forward linkages in the region, which limited its capacity to internalise the income and employment effects of investment and output expansion; and a characteristic feature of late industrialisation, that the import substitution model was attempted without protectionist barriers.

By 1980, despite development efforts to reduce the differences in income levels and quality of life between the two regions, challenging problems remained. Whenever a social indicator was used to rank the level of development of the five Brazilian macro-regions (North, Northeast, Centre-West, Southeast and South), the Northeast would come out last or next-to-last, while the Southeast was always first. At the same time, the Brazilian economy was facing many difficulties, both internally and externally. The difficulties in the external sector, resulting from a process of capital accumulation financed during the 1970s by international private banks, tended to worsen as the ratio between debt service and exports reached critical levels. When oil prices and international interest rates rose in 1979, Brazilian economic policy-makers hesitated in taking timely adjustment measures and, as a consequence, the economy faced a serious foreign exchange predicament in 1980. Internally, inflation accelerated and reached the three-digit level for the first time.[3]

By the end of 1980 the Government had developed a stabilisation policy which led the economy, in 1981, to its most severe recession ever. Output and employment levels dropped dramatically. The economic crisis was felt first and most intensely in the Southeast, especially São Paulo, and later spilled over to the South and, eventually, to the Northeast (Osório et al., 1985). The level of economic activity and the labour markets of the more developed regions are more sensitive to stabilisation policies as they have a greater share of industrial output and modern jobs.

But the Northeast suffered as well. Brazil's GNP declined 1.6 per cent in 1981, while the Northeast managed only a 0.7 per cent increase in overall output.[4] However, 1981 was the third consecutive year of drought. The recession abated somewhat in 1982, allowing an overall output growth of 0.9 per cent for Brazil and a much better performance (10.9 per cent) for the Northeast. However, the foreign exchange crisis peaked in the second half of 1982, as export earnings dropped sharply because of international recession and protectionism, the terms of trade declined 50 per cent compared with 1977, and debt service reached unbearable levels. Foreign exchange reserves were exhausted in September 1982, leaving Brazil with no alternative but the IMF. As a result, by the end of 1982, stabilisation policies had been strengthened through tighter controls over credit, public expenditure and imports. The full effects of these measures were felt in 1983. As the recession advanced, the GNP fell 3.2 per cent and open unemployment rose by 24.6 per cent.[5] By then the recession had reached all sectors of economic activity and all regions, including the Northeast, where output growth was nil, and where the peak of the drought coincided with the peak of the recession.

During the downswing of the cycle, Brazilian society faced high social costs. Urban unemployment and underemployment rose sharply, real wages fell, and the cuts in public expenditure reduced transfers and benefits (education, health and social security expenses, etc.) to the lower-income groups of the population. Above all, the quality of life in urban areas deteriorated and, in the absence of welfare programmes such as unemployment insurance, the jobless suffered many economic and social hardships. Recession and drought altered the imbalances between Southeast and Northeast. The former, given its larger share of output and employment, was hit hard by the economic crisis, while the latter, although apparently suffering less from the recession, endured four years of drought.

## II. Growth and urban poverty: The regional dimension

### 1. The 1970s

From 1970 to 1974 Brazil was in the second stage of the economic boom that began in 1968. Overall output grew on average by 11 per cent per year (Fundação Getúlio Vargas, 1981), and the rate of investment reached 22.5 per cent of output. The Northeastern economy performed even better. Economic growth there reached 12.1 per cent per year while the rate of investment was close to 25 per cent (SUDENE, 1983). However, from 1975 onwards, output growth, but not capital accumulation, decelerated. GNP growth fell to 6.4 per cent per year for the country as a whole, while capital accumulation — measured by the rate of investment — remained around 22 per cent because foreign savings were financing public and state enterprise investments. Output growth in the Northeast moderated to 7.9 per cent per year while the investment rate climbed to 26 per cent.

Was poverty diminished as a result of rapid economic growth in the 1970s? Who was richer and who was poorer? Did the benefits of growth reach those who were poor in 1970? Were the results the same for both regions? Did the regional inequalities decrease as a result of growth?

These questions demand a clarification of the concept of poverty. We intend to be pragmatic and thus avoid the continuing debate about the definition and measurement of poverty (Sen, 1978, 1979). There is thus some arbitrariness, in terms of normative concepts, in our choices among alternative measures. In an effort to make the concept as explicit as possible, we have selected average monthly family income per capita equal to or less than one-quarter of Brazil's highest minimum wage as our measure of absolute poverty.[6] This takes account of the notion of destitution which is central to the concept of poverty. We have opted to complement this measure of absolute poverty with a relative measure, and so use some statistics drawn from income distribution data.

Pastore et al. show that poverty — measured by the number of families with an average monthly income per capita lower than a quarter of the highest minimum wage — decreased during the 1970s,[7] from 44 per cent in 1970 to 18 per cent in 1980. Among explanations for such a decrease, the most important seem to be a reduction in family size and an intensification of work by family members.[8] The reduced family size contributed to an increase in average family income per capita.[9] Work intensification by family members meant that more of them entered the labour market (including those previously unavailable for work because of age or physical condition), but also that all were working more hours per week. An important factor in the intensification of family work was the increase in female labour force participation rates — from 21 per cent in 1970 to 28 per cent in 1980.

We can distinguish three groups among the 18 per cent of families that remained poor in 1980. First, the totally unemployed, including families that were small, having no male household head, and dependent upon female workers with inadequate labour market qualifications.[10] As it was particularly difficult for members of such families to obtain jobs, their unemployment rate was high. Second, the partially unemployed, including large families, with both male and female heads present, often middle aged, but with a substantial proportion of women among those available for work. Third, those that remained poor despite having all available members working — small, young families, with both male and female heads, but where women did not predominate among members available for work. This group's poverty relates more to their low pay than to their ability to obtain work.

The study also shows that although both urban and rural poverty declined, the majority of the poor were still in rural areas — in both 1970 and 1980, for each poor urban family, there were two rural ones, which means that poverty in both areas decreased at about the same rate during the 1970s.

**Table 2.1. Urban poverty within and across regions, 1980 (percentages)**

|  | Urban poor families [1] | Regional distribution of urban poor families |
|---|---|---|
| Northeast | 26.59 | 50.61 |
| Southeast | 5.11 | 27.31 |
| (São Paulo) | (2.65) | (7.43) |
| Brazil | 10.4 | 100.00 |

[1] An urban poor family is defined as one with a monthly per capita income of one-quarter or less of the highest minimum wage.
Source. FIBGE/Demographic Census, 1980.

Nevertheless, urban and rural poverty have different weights. In 1980, while approximately 10 per cent of urban families were poor, the comparable figure in rural areas was 36 per cent. The rate of decline in poverty varied across regions.[11] In 1970, 41 per cent of poor families lived in the Northeast; by 1980 the Northeast's share was 50 per cent. The Southeast had 35 per cent of the country's poor families in 1970, but only 26 per cent in 1980. Thus, despite the overall decrease in poverty, regional differentials increased. According to 1980 census data, poor families in the Northeast tended to be large, 59.3 per cent had a self-employed head, and they supplied poor-quality labour. In the Southeast, however, 35 per cent of poor families were headed by women; 28 per cent had more women than men available for work and 32 per cent had only women available for work. However, these latter traits were also present in the Northeast.

We assume, for lack of appropriately disaggregated data, that the overall decline in poverty also occurred among poor *urban* families at the regional level. Families were becoming increasingly urbanised – in 1970, 58.8 per cent lived in urban areas; by 1980 the figure was 70.5 per cent. In the Northeast the proportion of urban families rose from 42.6 per cent in 1970 to 50.1 per cent in 1980, while in the Southeast the change was only slight – from 84.2 per cent to 84.8 per cent – over the decade. Thus it is likely that what was true for the urban plus rural trend was also true for the urban trend alone, i.e. at the same time that urban poverty was declining, it was also becoming increasingly unequal at the regional level. In 1980, 10.4 per cent of Brazilian urban families were poor – 26.6 per cent in the Northeast and 5.1 per cent in the Southeast (see table 2.1).

Poor urban families of the Northeast are characterised by: *(a)* a labour force participation rate (33 per cent among those aged 10 or more) lower than the regional average (44.2 per cent), reflecting both a large dependency ratio (42.4 per cent of family members under 18) and the difficulties facing family members in their efforts to find jobs; *(b)* a very low level of formal education (average only 1.7 years of schooling); *(c)* low educational standards of all family members (school enrolment of children aged 7-14 was only 60 per cent and the literacy rate of those of 15 and older was 52 per cent) (CNRH/IPEA,

*Table 2.2.  Family income distribution by National Household Survey region, 1980* [1]

|  | Gini coefficient | | Theil index | Percentage distribution by income deciles | | | | |
|---|---|---|---|---|---|---|---|---|
|  | Lower limit | Upper limit |  | 20 − | 50 − | 10 + | 5 + | 1 + |
| Rio de Janeiro (I) | .537 | .563 | .536 | 3.3 | 15.0 | 42.8 | 30.1 | 13.2 |
| São Paulo (II) | .482 | .507 | .427 | 3.9 | 18.0 | 37.6 | 25.5 | 10.4 |
| Minas Gerais and Espírito Santo (IV) | .556 | .570 | .603 | 3.4 | 14.3 | 44.7 | 31.3 | 13.0 |
| Northeast (V) | .584 | .593 | .727 | 3.5 | 14.0 | 49.7 | 36.4 | 15.8 |

[1] Regions I + II + IV make up the Southeast. Region V (Northeast) is formed by the states of Maranhão, Piauí, Ceará, Rio Grande do Norte, Paraíba, Pernambuco, Alagoas, Sergipe and Bahia. The data refer to both urban and rural family income, but given the high degree of urbanisation in 1980 (70 per cent), they can be considered an approximate guide to the income distribution of urban families.

Source. FIBGE/Demographic Census, 1980.

1985); *(d)* housing, water supply and sanitation levels much inferior to the Southeast, and increasingly so during the 1970s.[12]

Turning to measures of relative poverty, our most readily available indicator is the trend in income inequality,[13] and this shows that, despite the growth in real earnings for all income brackets during the 1970s, inequality increased in all regions (Hoffman, 1983), i.e. the average real income of the rich grew faster than that of the poor. Table 2.2 shows that the Northeast had the highest inequality indices and São Paulo the lowest; the Northeast had the smallest share (14 per cent) of income of the poorest 50 per cent of families, and São Paulo the greatest (18 per cent); and the Northeast had the largest share (15.8 per cent) of income of the richest 1 per cent of families and São Paulo the smallest (10.4 per cent). Inequality measures for other states of the Southeast fall between those for the Northeast and São Paulo.

The lower levels of inequality in São Paulo seem to have emerged during the 1970s. Census data on the distribution of labour incomes suggest that they result from a relatively stable income distribution pattern in São Paulo between 1970 and 1980, while inequality was increasing in other states.

### 2. The 1981-83 period

This study focuses on the 1981-83 recession, and its impact on relative and absolute urban poverty. Our data source is the National Household Survey for 1981 and 1983, which covers both urban and rural households in most regions.[14] The findings will then be compared with data on labour market outcomes in the same period, in the next section. From this we hope to understand better the relationship between labour market outcomes and urban poverty.

Data on family income show that the percentage of Brazilian families earning the nominal minimum wage or less rose from 18.4 per cent in 1981 to 19 per cent in 1983,[15] in the Northeast from 35.2 per cent to 35.4 per cent, and

*Table 2.3. Indicators of relative and absolute poverty, 1981-83*

| | Brazil | | Southeast | | Northeast | |
|---|---|---|---|---|---|---|
| | 1981 | 1983 | 1981 | 1983 | 1981 | 1983 |
| Gini coefficient | .579 | .597 | .567 | .581 | .572 | .601 |
| Percentage of income received by the 40 per cent poorest | 9.35 | 8.06 | 10.36 | 9.49 | 10.79 | 9.32 |
| Percentage of income received by the 10 per cent richest | 45.33 | 46.23 | 43.54 | 44.25 | 46.72 | 49.69 |
| Percentage of workers earning up to one minimum wage | 37.1 | 40.0 | 28.6 | 31.1 | 58.3 | 61.9 |
| Absolute poverty index | 0.196 | 0.220 | 0.142 | 0.162 | 0.328 | 0.366 |

Sources of basic data. FIBGE/PNAD. Table derived from Osório et al., 1985, table 2.15.

in the Southeast from 11.2 per cent to 12.1 per cent (between 1981 and 1983, real minimum wages dropped by 4.8 per cent). A study of personal income distribution trends at the regional level produced strong evidence of an increase in relative and absolute poverty during the recession period (Osório et al., 1985). Average real incomes dropped between 12 per cent and 14 per cent and manufacturing was the sector most affected by the period's stabilisation policies. As a result, manufacturing real wages fell by 10.2 per cent and, following a drop in aggregate demand, unemployment in the urban industrial areas rose to unprecedented levels.

Table 2.3 shows that there were increases both in relative poverty, measured by income distribution parameters, and in the absolute poverty index.[16] The Gini coefficients and the percentage of income going each year to the poorest 40 per cent and the richest 10 per cent demonstrate that there was rising income inequality, and the percentage of the working-age population earning one minimum wage or less increased as well. All these changes were larger in the Northeast than in the Southeast. This shows that the social costs of the recession were very high and affected all regions, but the Northeast did worse than the Southeast during periods of growth and of recession.

# III. Evolution and structure of urban employment and labour markets

## 1. The 1970s

The urban labour force grew at 6.0 per cent per year in the 1970s, while the working-age population (aged 10 and over) increased by 4.7 per cent; the result was a higher labour force participation rate each year.[17] The urban labour force was increasing at about the same pace (5.7 per cent) in the Northeast and the Southeast, although the participation rate grew faster in the Southeast alongside a slower growth of the working-age population (see table 2.4). There

*Table 2.4.    Urban labour force participation rates by sex, 1970-80 (percentages)*

|          | 1970      |           |        | 1980      |           |        |
|----------|-----------|-----------|--------|-----------|-----------|--------|
|          | Northeast | Southeast | Brazil | Northeast | Southeast | Brazil |
| Total    | 39.1      | 44.2      | 43.2   | 44.2      | 51.2      | 49.5   |
| Male     | 61.4      | 67.1      | 65.5   | 64.3      | 72.2      | 70.0   |
| Female   | 20.4      | 24.1      | 22.7   | 26.9      | 32.1      | 30.5   |

Source. FIBGE, Demographic Census, 1970 and 1980.

were increases in male and especially female participation rates (Paiva, 1984). In the 1970s more and more women of all age groups except the oldest were entering the labour market. The urban female participation rate rose from 22.7 per cent in 1970 to 30.5 per cent in 1980, and the proportion of women in the labour force grew from 27.4 per cent to 31.9 per cent. This could also be seen at the regional level.

The labour force also became increasingly urbanised in the 1970s, the urban share growing from 56 per cent to almost 70 per cent of the total labour force — from 39 per cent to 50 per cent in the Northeast and from 75 per cent to 85 per cent in the Southeast. Urban labour markets were thus under pressure, and in order to assess the economy's labour absorption record we need to examine employment trends. Overall, non-agricultural employment grew 6 per cent per year in the 1970s, i.e. almost 13.4 million people were absorbed. This was accompanied by an expansion of the informal sector — an outcome of a development process which appropriated different technologies over time. Sectors with widely different capital-output ratios and labour productivities existed side by side. This technological heterogeneity engendered a segmentation of the urban labour market, with different mechanisms of labour allocation and wage determination. Non-agricultural employment accounted for about 90 per cent of overall growth, and agriculture's share of total employment fell from 44 per cent to 29.3 per cent. Manufacturing, which accounted for about 29 per cent of GNP in 1980, was the outstanding growth sector, notably in the Southeast, especially São Paulo, where the bulk of manufacturing output is concentrated. By 1980 the Southeast accounted for more than two-thirds of manufacturing output and 69.2 per cent of manufacturing employment whereas the Northeast produced less than 10 per cent of manufacturing output and employed only 9.2 per cent of the manufacturing labour force. Nevertheless, manufacturing output growth in the Northeast was high, averaging around 10 per cent, and manufacturing employment grew by 8.8 per cent per year between 1970 and 1975. Although the expansion slowed from 1976 to 1980 the Northeast's performance was better than that of Brazil as a whole.

In short, Brazil's economy, pulled by the remarkable performance of manufacturing, was dynamic enough to create employment at a pace matching

*Table 2.5.*    *Informal sector and unemployment as a percentage of non-agricultural labour force, 1969-79*

| | 1969 [1] | | | 1976 | | | 1979 | | |
|---|---|---|---|---|---|---|---|---|---|
| | North-east | South-east | Brazil | North-east | South-east | Brazil | North-east | South-east | Brazil |
| Informal sector | 39.8 | 18.0 | 24.3 | 29.8 | 17.1 | 20.0 | 32.2 | 19.1 | 22.5 |
| Unemployment | 4.1 | 3.7 | 3.9 | 4.2 | 2.5 | 2.8 | 4.9 | 3.8 | 4.1 |

[1] In 1969 the age limit for labour force classification purposes was 14. In 1976 and in 1979 it was 10. This may have caused the decline in informal sector employment between 1969 and 1976 to be exaggerated.
Source. FIBGE/PNAD; 1969, 1976 and 1979.

the growth of the labour force. However, manufacturing employment as a proportion of total non-agricultural employment remained relatively low, especially in the Northeast, and the expansion of jobs in organised labour markets was not rapid enough to absorb all those entering the urban labour force. According to Paiva (1984), who organised the demographic census data to show the distribution of formal and informal sector non-agricultural employment, the proportion of the labour force engaged in informal labour markets remained stable in the 1970s. The estimates used data on labour force by sector of activity and work status: employee, employer, self-employed, and unpaid family workers. The formal sector in Paiva's study encompassed employees in manufacturing, commerce, transport, communication and storage, community services, construction and other activities; the informal sector consisted of all other workers in these industries as well as domestic workers (household servants). The overall finding was that, despite a rapid expansion in industrial employment, there was no decline in the share of the informal sector — remaining at about 38 per cent of non-agricultural employment in 1970 and 1980. The data also show that in 1980 the proportion of informal sector workers earning less than one minimum wage (38.5 per cent) was greater than in the formal sector (18.6 per cent), so the majority of poor workers were still in the informal sector.

The PNAD household surveys allow us to study the behaviour of the informal sector by region in the 1970s, and we will restrict the concept of the informal sector by deleting domestic workers and including only small business, self-employment and unpaid family workers. Between 1969 and 1976, the most rapid economic growth period, the informal sector in these terms declined from 24.3 per cent to 20 per cent of Brazil's total labour force. However, with slower economic growth in the late 1970s it rose again to 22.5 per cent (see table 2.5). The Northeast's informal sector was larger than average throughout, declining in the early 1970s and then increasing to 32.2 per cent of the labour force by 1979. In the Southeast between 1969 and 1976 the changes in the informal sector's relative importance were similar in direction, but smaller in amplitude. Slower economic growth in the late 1970s had different impacts on urban labour

*Table 2.6.    Urban labour force participation rates by sex, 1981-83 (percentages)*

|  | Brazil | | Southeast | | Northeast | |
|---|---|---|---|---|---|---|
|  | 1981 | 1983 | 1981 | 1983 | 1981 | 1983 |
| Total | 51.9 | 53.0 | 53.3 | 54.6 | 47.2 | 48.5 |
| Male | 71.5 | 71.6 | 72.6 | 73.0 | 67.0 | 66.7 |
| Female | 33.7 | 35.6 | 34.9 | 37.2 | 30.2 | 32.6 |

Source. FIBGE/PNAD. Participation rates for ages 10+.

markets across regions. Between 1976 and 1979 open unemployment rates increased faster in the Southeast (52 per cent) than in the Northeast (16.7 per cent) or Brazil (46 per cent). The Northeast's employment problems appeared more in informal sector underemployment than in unemployment.

## 2. The 1981-83 period

At the start of 1981 Brazil was in its most severe recession in modern history, at a time when labour participation rates were increasing rapidly and 1.5 million jobs had to be created each year just to absorb new entrants. Employment levels fell rapidly, mainly in metropolitan areas, where most modern economic activity was found. Labour markets adjusted in different ways. We will focus on urban labour market outcomes resulting from this, and their relation to the overall socio-economic status of the labour force.

### A. Labour force participation rates and growth

From 1981 to 1983 urban labour force participation rates continued to increase in Brazil and in the two regions studied (see table 2.6), due mainly to rising female participation rates. Male rates remained almost constant. This differs from the pattern of the 1970s when both male and female rates were increasing. The outcome of these changes, and of the growth in urban population, was an overall urban labour force growth of 3.8 per cent (the female labour force grew 5.6 per cent per year against 2.7 per cent for men),[18] faster in the Northeast (4.5 per cent) than the Southeast (3.5 per cent) both for males and females. This regional difference was not present in the 1970s.

One explanation for declining labour force growth is that some people, especially in middle- and upper-class families, may postpone labour market entry while awaiting better employment opportunities and better-paid jobs. Another explanation relies on the concept of hidden unemployment. During a severe recession, those who become discouraged simply stop looking for jobs, and are classified as no longer in the labour force. For Brazil there is evidence that there might have been about 800,000 hidden unemployed by 1983 (Infante, 1983). There must also have been a decline in urban population growth rates, either because of earlier fertility declines, or — more likely — because of lower rates of rural-urban migration in the recession. More rapid growth of the urban

*Table 2.7. Growth rates of urban non-agricultural labour force, employment and unemployment, 1981-83*

|  | Brazil | Southeast | Northeast |
|---|---|---|---|
| Labour force | 3.80 | 3.27 | 5.40 |
| Employment | 3.41 | 2.0 | 5.18 |
| Unemployment | 10.15 | 9.93 | 8.17 |
| Low-income employment | 11.09 | 12.2 | 11.22 |

Source. PNAD, special tabulations (MTb/SES — BRA/82/026).

labour force in the Northeast than the Southeast may also be associated with migration differences — the severe drought in the Northeast between 1979 and 1983 induced more rapid migration from rural areas. However, a statistical problem is that the FIBGE classified people engaged in the public works programmes, created to absorb rural workers displaced by the drought, as being in the urban construction sector, thus resulting in an overestimate of urban employment (Jatobá, 1985).

Deleting from the urban labour force those workers engaged in agricultural activities in urban areas produces a more refined concept of urban employment and unemployment. Unless otherwise stated, from now on we will use this concept, the urban non-agricultural labour force. Table 2.7 shows that its growth was similar to that of the urban labour force as a whole (3.8 per cent), although using this more restricted concept, the growth rate for the Northeast is even higher (5.4 per cent per year) than when urban agricultural activities were included (4.5 per cent). For the Southeast the reverse was true. Apparently, intra-regional rural-urban migration was stabilising in the Southeast in the 1970s, given the modernisation of its agriculture, when inter-regional migration to the Southeast was decreasing sharply, as employment opportunities became increasingly scarce in the modern sectors there. Conversely, for the Northeast, rural poverty, compounded by drought, was still an important impetus for migration to the cities, resulting in increased pressure on its urban labour markets.

### B. Employment growth

Table 2.7 shows that the growth of urban non-agricultural employment was less than that of the urban labour force, but was considerably faster in the Northeast than in the Southeast. What kind of employment opportunities were generated? Were these poorly paid jobs? In which sectors were workers absorbed? How was labour absorption distributed by work status, i.e. between employees protected or unprotected by contracts, the self-employed and unpaid family workers? How were employment opportunities distributed between formal and informal, or organised and unorganised labour markets? Did the number of poor workers increase in the recession? If so, how were they distributed between labour markets?

*Table 2.8.    Distribution of urban non-agricultural employment between poor and non-poor workers,*
*              1981-83 (thousands)*

|  | Brazil | | | Southeast | | | Northeast | | |
|---|---|---|---|---|---|---|---|---|---|
|  | 1981 | 1983 | Change | 1981 | 1983 | Change | 1981 | 1983 | Change |
| Urban non-agricultural workers | 28 998 | 31 044 | +2 046 | 16 520 | 17 194 | +674 | 5 330 | 5 912 | +582 |
| Poor workers | 7 507 | 9 371 | +1 864 | 3 466 | 4 424 | +958 | 2 288 | 2 864 | +576 |
| Non-poor workers | 21 491 | 21 673 | +182 | 13 054 | 12 770 | −284 | 3 032 | 3 048 | +16 |
| Poor workers as percentage of total urban workers | 25.9 | 30.2 | 91.1 | 21.0 | 25.7 | 142.0 | 42.9 | 48.4 | 99.0 |

Source. PNAD, special tabulations (MTb/SES — BRA/82/026).

*Table 2.9.    Composition   of   urban   non-agricultural   employment   by   work   status,   1981-83*
*              (percentages)*

|  | Brazil | | Southeast | | Northeast | |
|---|---|---|---|---|---|---|
|  | 1981 | 1983 | 1981 | 1983 | 1981 | 1983 |
| Employee | 75.9 | 74.9 | 78.2 | 76.7 | 70.0 | 70.2 |
|    Protected | 69.2 | 64.7 | 72.0 | 68.0 | 58.0 | 52.0 |
|    Unprotected | 30.8 | 35.3 | 28.0 | 32.0 | 42.0 | 48.0 |
| Employer | 3.2 | 3.4 | 3.7 | 3.9 | 1.8 | 1.7 |
| Self-employed | 19.2 | 19.8 | 16.6 | 17.9 | 26.0 | 25.3 |
| Unpaid family workers | 1.7 | 1.9 | 1.5 | 1.5 | 2.2 | 2.8 |

Source. PNAD, special tabulations (MTb/SES — BRA/82/026).

To answer these questions, we will use the concept of low-income employment, defined as the number of workers who earn one minimum wage or less per month.[19] Table 2.7 shows exceptionally high annual growth of low-income employment. Employment growth was concentrated in the lower-income group and this growth was more rapid in the Southeast than the Northeast, contrary to figures for overall urban employment. Indeed, low-income employment accounted for most of the absolute change in urban non-agricultural employment in Brazil from 1981 to 1983 (see table 2.8). For the Northeast 99 per cent of the growth was in low-income employment. More striking, however, is the Southeast, where the absolute growth of poorly paid employment exceeded that of total urban employment, so the number of non-poor workers fell. This means not only that the majority of new entrants into labour markets could be absorbed only at low-income levels, but also that

*Table 2.10.  Poor workers as a percentage of workers by work status, 1981-83*

|  | Brazil | | Southeast | | Northeast | |
|---|---|---|---|---|---|---|
|  | 1981 | 1983 | 1981 | 1983 | 1981 | 1983 |
| Employee | 23.5 | 29.0 | 18.8 | 23.7 | 41.5 | 48.8 |
| Protected | 11.0 | 16.3 | 8.5 | 13.9 | 22.2 | 28.4 |
| Unprotected | 51.4 | 52.2 | 45.0 | 44.7 | 68.2 | 70.8 |
| Employer | 0.6 | 1.4 | 0.5 | 1.7 | 0.6 | 1.0 |
| Self-employed | 31.9 | 31.8 | 28.7 | 30.1 | 43.5 | 43.9 |

Source. PNAD, special tabulations (MTb/SES — BRA/82/026).

many workers who managed to keep their jobs could do so only by accepting lower wages.

Table 2.8 also shows that poor workers as a proportion of total urban employment increased in all regions. It is remarkable that by 1983 almost half of the urban employed in the Northeast were poor workers. Thus, in 1981 and 1983, poverty was much more extensive among the urban employed in the Northeast than elsewhere. Clearly one result of the recession was a general impoverishment of the urban employed. Urban employment grew at the expense of more absolute and relative poverty, and the quality of life of workers deteriorated.[20]

For a more detailed analysis of trends in urban employment, we need to investigate both overall and low-income employment by work status. Table 2.9 shows that the Northeast's urban employment structure is different from that found elsewhere in Brazil. Employees and employers have smaller shares of total employment in the Northeast, while self-employed and unpaid family workers are more important. The percentage of workers lacking labour contracts ("unprotected" by labour legislation) is higher for the Northeast. This structure is typical of less-developed areas, and reflects the heterogeneity of labour markets having different mechanisms of labour allocation and income determination. The effect of the recession on the urban employment structure is also clear from table 2.9. For the Southeast the relative importance of employees declined while the share of the self-employed in overall employment increased. A decreasing percentage of employees fell in the protected category, and, for the Southeast and Brazil as a whole, the absolute number of protected workers decreased. For the Northeast the relative importance of employees did not change, but the share of unprotected wage workers increased substantially, a clear backward step in progress toward a developed labour market.

Table 2.10 shows that the majority of poor workers are in the unprotected wage and self-employed categories. Inter-regional differences are marked, and reflect the disparities in the level of development and modernisation of the labour markets. Not only were more poor workers concentrated in the *protected* wage sector in the Northeast than in the rest of

*Table 2.11.   Low-income employment as a percentage of total employment by main economic sectors,*
*1983*

|  | Brazil | Southeast | Northeast |
|---|---|---|---|
| Total | 30.2 | 27.7 | 48.4 |
| Industry | 18.9 | 13.8 | 44.8 |
| Construction | 28.8 | 18.2 | 57.5 |
| Commerce | 30.7 | 28.0 | 43.1 |
| Services | 34.7 | 31.0 | 48.9 |

Source. PNAD, special tabulations (MTb/SES — BRA/82/026).

Brazil, but, more importantly, the proportion of poor workers also rose among this group. However, impoverishment was not restricted to the relatively protected wage workers. Employers all over Brazil, mostly those engaged in small business, also became poorer. The total number of poor employers increased by 900,000 from 1981 to 1983. For the Southeast the absolute number of poor employers was four times greater in 1983 than 1981, which means that small low-income businesses were also hit hard by the recession.

Table 2.11 shows that poor workers in the Southeast are found more in services and commerce, but these figures are below the Brazilian average and much lower than the percentage for the Northeast, where poor workers are more evenly distributed across economic sectors. The greater concentration of poor workers in services and commerce is explained by relatively low skill requirements and by the easy entry and exit of small business employees, petty traders, street vendors, workers in low-skill occupations, etc., in labour markets which are more competitive than in industry. Construction is also a sector of easy entry for new low-skill entrants into the labour force, with a high percentage of low-paid jobs.

### C. Labour market segmentation

Brazil's labour markets are heterogeneous, with diverse types of labour allocation and labour market entry. In many sectors the modern and the antiquated lie side-by-side, and technologically advanced processes coexist with outdated ones, even in the same branch of production. This heterogeneity in the technological structure of the economy, together with absolute increases in the labour supply for which there is no match in terms of job growth, has generated underemployment and unemployment, and created a pattern of labour market segmentation. We need to understand the inner nature of this segmentation, what role it played during the recession and what kind of relationships have developed between segmentation and urban poverty. To evaluate which labour market mechanisms are operating through segmentation, that are either closely associated with or are major determinants of urban poverty, we need to examine how poor workers are distributed across the different labour markets.

*Table 2.12.   Segmentation of urban labour markets and unemployment rates, 1981-83 (percentages)*

| | Brazil | | | Southeast | | | Northeast | | |
|---|---|---|---|---|---|---|---|---|---|
| | 1981 | 1983 | Absolute growth, 1981-83 | 1981 | 1983 | Absolute growth, 1981-83 | 1981 | 1983 | Absolute growth, 1981-83 |
| Labour market shares: | | | | | | | | | |
| Organised | 67.9 | 65.5 | 1.60 | 72.3 | 69.1 | −0.23 | 52.8 | 49.9 | 2.32 |
| Non-organised | 32.1 | 34.5 | 7.03 | 27.7 | 30.9 | 7.39 | 47.2 | 50.1 | 8.20 |
| Urban unemployment rate | 6.1 | 6.9 | | 6.4 | 7.4 | | 6.5 | 6.9 | |

Source. FIBGE/PNAD, special tabulations (MTb/SES — BRA/82/026).

We used a dualistic model, identifying an "organised" or "formal" and a "non-organised" or "informal" segment. We shall use "organised" and "non-organised" to refer to these segments, to distinguish them from other labour market breakdowns. Criteria used to classify workers included work status, income and sectoral employment, following Infante (1985). The following categories are classified as organised:

1. All employees with labour contracts — protected wage workers, who are automatically covered by labour and social security legislation once the contract has been signed.
2. Employees without labour contracts who earn more than two minimum wages — the highest income segment among unprotected wage workers.[21]
3. Employees earning on average more than five minimum wages.
4. Self-employed individuals earning more than two minimum wages.
5. Civil service employees (public administration).[22]

The following are classified as non-organised:

1. Unprotected wage workers earning two minimum wages or less.
2. Employers earning five minimum wages or less.[23]
3. Self-employed individuals with two minimum wages or less, including own-account workers, and others in similar low-paid self-employed occupations.
4. Unpaid family workers, i.e. persons working 15 or more hours a week, helping household members in their productive activities, for which they receive no nominal income.
5. Domestic service workers, irrespective of income or whether or not they have labour contracts.

Table 2.12 shows that during the recession the relative size of organised employment was declining all over Brazil. Non-organised employment is relatively larger in the Northeast than in the Southeast or in Brazil as a whole, reflecting a less developed economic structure and more heterogeneous labour

*Table 2.13.    Sectoral employment by labour market segment, 1983 (percentages)*

| | Brazil | | Southeast | | Northeast | |
|---|---|---|---|---|---|---|
| | Organised | Non-organised | Organised | Non-organised | Organised | Non-organised |
| Industry | 84.0 | 16.0 | 89.6 | 10.4 | 61.1 | 38.9 |
| Construction | 54.0 | 46.0 | 62.2 | 37.8 | 31.4 | 68.6 |
| Commerce | 64.3 | 35.7 | 68.9 | 31.1 | 47.6 | 52.4 |
| Services | 60.5 | 39.5 | 61.9 | 38.1 | 52.2 | 47.8 |

Source. FIBGE/PNAD, special tabulations (MTb/SES — BRA/82/026).

markets. The shrinking organised labour markets and the expansion of non-organised employment are clearly seen in the differentials in employment growth rates. In the Southeast organised employment decreased slightly, whereas non-organised employment increased. For Brazil and the Northeast the pattern is similar. Hence, most of the growth in urban employment can be attributed to the expansion of non-organised employment.

Clearly the non-organised sector played a very important role in the adjustment of labour markets during the economic crisis; it acted like a "sponge", absorbing new entrants as well as workers displaced by the recession. It is easier to enter than the organised sector, where firms select workers according to their skills, experience, training and other traits; where formal education is required for the practice of most professions; or where one needs a large amount of capital to establish oneself as an employer. Although capital, skills, formal education and training are also useful in non-organised labour markets, they are less essential. Table 2.13 shows that non-organised employment is relatively larger in sectors where entry is not difficult, such as commerce or construction. The non-organised sector itself is very heterogeneous, offering prospective workers a variety of productive activities including small family-based business, petty trading, street vending, household service and a great number of self-employed occupations.

### D. Segmentation and poverty

In the literature on labour market segmentation in less-developed countries it is not unusual to find arguments associating urban poverty with informal or non-organised employment; in some conceptualisations poverty and informal employment are practically indistinguishable, as income is the sole criterion used in defining informal labour. We use a more refined definition of the non-organised labour market segments, and link this to poverty through an estimation of the labour market segmentation of low-income workers, defined as those workers earning one monthly minimum wage and less.[24]

Tables 2.14 and 2.15 show that the great majority of poor workers are in non-organised employment, and the majority of non-organised sector

*Table 2.14.   Percentage distribution of poor workers by labour market segment, 1981-83*

|  | Brazil | | Southeast | | Northeast | |
|---|---|---|---|---|---|---|
|  | 1981 | 1983 | 1981 | 1983 | 1981 | 1983 |
| Organised | 20.8 | 24.8 | 20.7 | 26.0 | 20.7 | 21.5 |
| Non-organised | 79.2 | 75.2 | 79.3 | 74.0 | 79.3 | 78.5 |

Source. FIBGE/PNAD, special tabulations (MTb/SES — BRA/82/026).

*Table 2.15.   Low-income employment as a percentage of overall employment by labour markets, 1981-83 (percentages)*

|  | Brazil | | | Southeast | | | Northeast | | |
|---|---|---|---|---|---|---|---|---|---|
|  | 1981 | 1983 | Growth, 1981-83 | 1981 | 1983 | Growth, 1981-83 | 1981 | 1983 | Growth, 1981-83 |
| Urban non-agricultural employment | 25.9 | 30.2 | 11.1 | 21.0 | 25.7 | 12.2 | 42.9 | 48.4 | 11.2 |
| Organised | 7.9 | 11.4 | 20.0 | 6.0 | 9.7 | 23.7 | 16.8 | 20.9 | 13.2 |
| Non-organised | 63.9 | 65.7 | 8.5 | 60.0 | 61.6 | 8.7 | 72.2 | 75.9 | 10.7 |

Source. FIBGE/PNAD, special tabulations (MTb/SES — BRA/82/026).

workers are poor. However, table 2.15 also shows that a significant number of workers in organised employment were poor, especially in the Northeast, so that poor workers are not confined to non-organised labour markets. What is most striking, however, is that the change in the percentage distribution of poor workers was towards the organised labour markets (table 2.14). For instance, while about a fifth of poor workers were engaged in organised employment in 1981, by 1983 the fraction, except for the Northeast, had increased to a quarter. Table 2.15 shows that the proportion of poor workers increased in both the organised and non-organised labour markets, although the increase was much more pronounced in the former, especially in the Southeast. For the Northeast the percentage distribution of poor workers between labour markets changed less (see table 2.14). The proportion of poor workers in non-organised sectors was of the same order in the Northeast as in the Southeast; the reason for the large difference between these regions is primarily due to the larger share of non-organised employment in the Northeast.

Table 2.16 shows that poor workers accounted for a substantial fraction of non-organised employment in all sectors, especially in services and commerce. The figures for the Southeast and for Brazil were not as large as those for the Northeast but were by no means negligible. However, although many poor workers can be found in non-organised employment, poverty is again not limited to that labour segment.

*Table 2.16.   Poor workers as a percentage of sectoral employment by labour market segments, 1983*

|  | Brazil | | | Southeast | | | Northeast | | |
| --- | --- | --- | --- | --- | --- | --- | --- | --- | --- |
|  | Employ-ment | Organ-ised | Non-organised | Employ-ment | Organ-ised | Non-organised | Employ-ment | Organ-ised | Non-organised |
| Total | 30.2 | 11.4 | 65.7 | 25.7 | 9.7 | 61.6 | 48.4 | 20.9 | 75.9 |
| Industry | 18.9 | 10.6 | 62.0 | 13.8 | 8.9 | 55.7 | 44.8 | 23.8 | 77.7 |
| Construction | 28.8 | 10.9 | 50.0 | 18.2 | 9.6 | 32.7 | 57.5 | 19.1 | 75.1 |
| Commerce | 30.7 | 14.2 | 60.6 | 28.0 | 14.3 | 55.4 | 43.1 | 18.4 | 65.6 |
| Services | 34.7 | 11.1 | 71.2 | 31.0 | 8.4 | 67.8 | 48.9 | 20.9 | 79.6 |

Source. FIBGE/PNAD, special tabulations (MTb/SES — BRA/82/026).

*Table 2.17.   Urban unemployment rates and proportion of unemployed heads of family, 1981-83 (percentages)*

|  | Brazil | | Southeast | | Northeast | |
| --- | --- | --- | --- | --- | --- | --- |
|  | 1981 | 1983 | 1981 | 1983 | 1981 | 1983 |
| Urban unemployment rates: | | | | | | |
|   Total | 5.6 | 6.4 | 6.1 | 6.9 | 5.7 | 6.2 |
|   Male | 5.7 | 6.6 | 6.2 | 7.2 | 5.9 | 6.3 |
|   Female | 5.4 | 5.9 | 6.0 | 6.4 | 5.4 | 5.9 |
| Urban unemployment rates of heads of family: | | | | | | |
|   Total | 0.84 | 1.10 | 1.15 | 1.44 | 0.54 | 0.69 |
|   Male | 1.07 | 1.45 | 1.49 | 1.90 | 0.65 | 0.89 |
|   Female | 0.34 | 0.39 | 0.44 | 0.51 | 0.29 | 0.26 |
| Unemployed heads of family as percentage of all unemployed: | | | | | | |
|   Total | 21.3 | 24.2 | 22.3 | 24.4 | 18.5 | 21.6 |
|   Male | 27.6 | 31.6 | 29.2 | 31.8 | 23.0 | 28.7 |
|   Female | 8.3 | 8.7 | 8.3 | 8.9 | 9.2 | 8.0 |

Source. FIBGE/PNAD, special tabulations (MTb/SES — BRA/82/026).

### E. Unemployment and poverty

Open unemployment, although rising slowly in the 1970s due to the deceleration of economic growth, was not considered a problem of great concern at that time. It seemed more serious for the Southeast than for the Northeast, where underemployment together with the low income levels of the labour force were the relevant labour market indicators. Such open unemployment as existed was seen as being mainly frictional, or identified with certain age or sex groups (the young, the elderly or women). The cyclical

*Table 2.18.   Urban unemployment rates by sex and age, 1981-83 (percentages)*

| | Unemployment rate | | | | | |
| --- | --- | --- | --- | --- | --- | --- |
| | Brazil | | Northeast | | Southeast | |
| | 1981 | 1983 | 1981 | 1983 | 1981 | 1983 |
| Total: | 5.6 | 6.4 | 5.7 | 6.2 | 6.1 | 6.9 |
| 10-17 | 11.4 | 11.4 | 9.3 | 7.7 | 12.8 | 13.6 |
| 18-24 | 9.7 | 11.0 | 11.1 | 12.5 | 10.4 | 11.6 |
| 25-49 | 3.5 | 4.5 | 3.6 | 4.2 | 3.8 | 4.9 |
| 50 and over | 1.8 | 1.9 | 1.4 | 1.3 | 2.0 | 2.1 |
| Male: | 5.7 | 6.6 | 5.9 | 6.3 | 6.2 | 7.2 |
| 10-17 | 12.6 | 12.4 | 11.1 | 7.8 | 13.8 | 14.9 |
| 18-24 | 10.1 | 11.6 | 11.4 | 13.0 | 10.8 | 12.4 |
| 25-49 | 3.5 | 4.7 | 3.5 | 4.4 | 3.9 | 5.2 |
| 50 and over | 2.0 | 2.3 | 1.5 | 1.5 | 2.3 | 2.5 |
| Female: | 5.4 | 5.9 | 5.4 | 5.9 | 6.0 | 6.4 |
| 10-17 | 9.4 | 9.9 | 5.7 | 7.5 | 11.3 | 11.6 |
| 18-24 | 9.1 | 9.9 | 10.5 | 11.5 | 9.7 | 10.2 |
| 25-49 | 3.4 | 4.1 | 3.8 | 3.9 | 3.6 | 4.4 |
| 50 and over | 1.2 | 1.1 | 0.9 | 0.7 | 1.4 | 1.2 |

Source. FIBGE/PNAD.

component of open employment increased as economic growth slowed in the later 1970s, although it never reached critical levels.[25] In the absence of any significant social legislation protecting the unemployed, to be jobless was a hardship that people could not bear for long, forcing them to accept any kind of temporary or short-term employment. Thus, the role played by underemployment during the more modest growth of 1975-80 was reinforced as a structural trait, at a time when the increase in the number of modern urban jobs could not keep pace with the absolute increases in the supply of labour.

However, at the start of 1981, when the economic crisis struck Brazil and there were massive lay-offs, unemployment became a very important labour market adjustment variable. Indeed, with the recession, open unemployment rose rapidly, mainly in the most important metropolitan areas, such as São Paulo and Rio de Janeiro. The urban employment rate rose from 3.9 per cent in 1979 to 5.6 per cent in 1981 and 6.4 per cent in 1983 (table 2.17), when around 2.5 million workers were jobless in the urban areas.[26] The rate was higher for the Southeast than for Brazil as a whole, while in the Northeast it was slightly lower and grew less rapidly. This suggests that unemployment in the Northeast was less important in labour market adjustment, in either absolute or relative terms, than in the Southeast. Variation in unemployment rates is more typical of regions where industrialisation is more advanced and where urbanisation and labour markets are more mature; hence the greater impact in the Southeast, due to its more complex and industrialised economic structure.

Unemployment varies systematically according to age and sex. Thus it is important to examine the disaggregated levels shown in table 2.18. Unemployment rates increased for both sexes and all ages, with some exceptions for the over-50s, but were somewhat lower for females. Unemployment rates were higher (frequently 10 per cent or more) for the younger groups − 10 to 17 and 18 to 24 − irrespective of sex, particularly in the Southeast. Young people are frequently new labour force entrants and face enormous difficulties in finding jobs. Unemployment increased, without exception, for urban workers aged 25 to 49, the prime working years. Most of the unemployed in this age group were, in all likelihood, married and with children, and probably more experienced and better-trained.

Unemployment of family heads increased faster than total unemployment. As table 2.17 shows, the only exception was Northeastern women. By 1983 about 1 per cent of the labour force were unemployed family heads and around 25 per cent of unemployed workers were family heads. The effect on family living standards was probably substantial, especially if there was no compensation either through more family members entering the labour market or through employed family members having longer working hours. In any event, hardship and impoverishment were the most likely outcomes.

## IV. Urban poverty and labour markets: Observable relationships and trends

We will now examine data on poverty and the labour market situations of the poor and try to link these with the findings of the analysis of trends and labour market outcomes. We will look in particular for mechanisms linking labour market outcomes to the distribution of poor workers among different segments and for regional differences in these patterns. As before, we discuss the 1970s and the 1981-83 recession separately. The evidence for the 1970s indicates that absolute urban poverty declined, although relative poverty, measured by income distribution statistics, increased. Notwithstanding the decline in absolute poverty, the regional distribution of those who remained poor became increasingly unequal, so that by 1980 the Northeast had a greater percentage of Brazil's poor families than in 1970, even though there was less absolute poverty in the region. The decline in absolute urban poverty paralleled a remarkable growth in non-agricultural employment, led by the expansion of manufacturing output in both regions. Although growth decelerated in the late 1970s, there were sufficient new jobs to match the expanding labour supply. Yet the cleavage between the organised and non-organised labour markets was unaffected. The relative importance of each labour market remained approximately the same, an indication that the rapid increase in the number of jobs in organised labour markets was less than what was needed to absorb the absolute increase in the urban labour force. Further, the majority of poor workers were still found in non-organised labour markets, the proportion being higher in the Northeast than the Southeast. Thus many families were still poor in 1980,[27] often because of unemployment, or because the majority of family members were women with difficult labour market access. Nevertheless, some families remained poor despite having all members employed, because they were able to find work only in low-paid jobs or occupations. It was also found that unemployment mainly strikes urban workers and is an important determinant of urban poverty.[28]

Among urban poor families in the Northeast, who accounted for about half of Brazilian urban poverty in 1980, a significant proportion of household heads were self-employed; labour force participation rates were lower than the average for the region, families were larger with a greater number of dependent children and youth, and a low level of formal education among those in the labour force, a trait closely associated with the poor quality of labour supplied. Urban poverty in the Southeast appeared to be more related to the sex-balance of the family, especially where the head or a majority of workers were women, than to the quality of labour supplied, family size, or the nature of the employment of family heads. Such findings pose different questions as to the source of poverty and require social policies quite different from those needed in the Northeast.

The increase in income inequality in the 1970s, which is taken here to mean also an increase in relative poverty, contrasts with the decline in absolute urban poverty. The data show that the increase in relative poverty was greatest for the Northeast, possibly because the labour markets there are more heterogeneous than in the Southeast, allowing for larger differences in the structure and trend of labour income. With slower economic growth in the late 1970s, there were some minor labour market adjustments; the most important consequences were a slight increase in open unemployment in the Southeast and a rise in underemployment in the Northeast, leading to a sharper cleavage of the urban labour market. However, neither outcome was of serious public concern since they did not create major social problems or political unrest among workers. Underemployment and labour market segmentation were the major structural labour market traits, mainly in the Northeast, while unemployment had always been historically low, and there were no dramatic labour market shocks to cause general concern.

With the recession deepening from 1981 to 1983, absolute and relative poverty grew all over Brazil, especially in the Northeast. In this period, unlike the 1970s, urban non-agricultural employment grew less rapidly than the labour force. The labour supply, in turn, increased more slowly, although urban labour participation rates continued to rise. Open unemployment increased everywhere. Urban labour force growth was faster in the Northeast than in the rest of Brazil, due to: (1) rural poverty, as a structural phenomenon, which led to intra-regional rural-urban migration, and (2) the drought, which aggravated rural poverty. Despite the recession, urban employment continued to grow. However, the growth was primarily in low-paid jobs; indeed in the Southeast the absolute number of better-paid workers (those earning more than the minimum wage) declined. Thus both entry and re-entry into the labour market were at low-income employment levels — a perverse labour market outcome and a good illustration of how, given the excess labour supply generated by a recession, labour market adjustments affect poverty. We can label this "perverse labour market selectivity" due to the economic crisis. Thus, in this period, the percentage of poor workers among the employed increased everywhere. Almost half the Northeastern urban workers were poor by 1983, although they accounted for less than one-third of all poor urban workers — nearly half of Brazil's poor urban workers were in the Southeast, because of the larger absolute size of the Southeastern labour market.

The analysis by work status showed that the self-employed and unpaid family (or household) workers are of greater relative importance in the Northeast than the Southeast, where employees and employers account for a greater share of regional employment. This reflects differences in the maturity of capitalist development, for the relationship between capital and labour in the Southeast reflects a more advanced capitalism where the majority of the labour force consists of protected wage workers.[29] However, because of the recession, the composition of urban employment in the Southeast became increasingly similar to that of the Northeast, and its structure moved away from the protected wage sector and toward other work statuses such as the unprotected wage sector, self-employment and unpaid family workers. These are the three categories where the majority of poor workers are found. Further, from 1981 to 1983 the percentage of poor workers in the protected wage sector increased in both regions. Hence, poverty increased even in the most capitalist segment of urban labour markets.

In terms of labour market segmentation, by 1983 31 per cent of urban workers were working in non-organised labour markets in the Southeast, against 50 per cent in the Northeast. This structure changed during the recession, with a shift of employment from organised to non-organised labour markets in relative (and in the Southeast in absolute) terms. By 1983 almost half of the non-organised labour market was in the Southeast, although this market accounts for a little less than one-third of that region's urban employment.[30] In the Northeast non-organised labour markets, which were already large, grew even larger because of the recession. Thus, there was an "informalisation" of urban labour markets as a result of the economic crisis, with the impact being greater in the Southeast. As a result, the modernisation of Brazilian labour markets suffered a setback, especially in the Southeast.[31] Trends similar to (but smaller than) those for the Southeast were also observed in the Northeast. This suggests an association between non-organised employment and poverty or, in more general terms, between segmentation and urban poverty.

The percentage of poor workers among all urban workers is much higher for the non-organised than for the organised labour market (see table 2.14). But poverty is not confined to the non-organised labour market, as in 1983 we find one in four poor workers in the organised labour market, and the proportion had been rising.[32] In fact, the proportion of poor workers increased in both labour markets for all Brazil. In the Southeast the increase in poverty was much more pronounced in the organised labour market, whereas in the Northeast poverty increased in both labour markets at about the same pace. Thus, while there is sufficient evidence to support the general proposition that segmentation is closely associated with poverty and that the mechanisms at work behind labour force allocation tend to place the majority of poor workers in non-organised labour markets, factors other than segmentation are also important.

Unemployment is an obvious major cause of poverty, especially in a country which has neither unemployment insurance nor any significant social legislation to protect the unemployed. During the recession unemployment gathered momentum, particularly in the Southeast, which accounted for almost 60 per cent of the increase in the number of unemployed from 1981 to 1983. Unemployment rates rose for both sexes and almost all age groups, especially among youth, for whom competition for first-entry jobs is intense; but unemployment also struck hard those aged between 25 and 49, most of whom had already been employed and had families. The proportion of unemployed family heads increased, mostly for males, and was significantly higher in the Southeast than the Northeast. The impact on poverty of unemployment is obviously greatest when family heads become jobless, since this cuts off the major or sole source of family income.

In summary, four trends emerged from the recession years: (1) low-income employment was almost the only source of employment growth for urban workers; (2) the cleavage of labour markets persisted, with poor workers continuing to be concentrated in non-organised employment; (3) there was rapid deterioration of labour income in organised labour markets, where the share of poor workers in total employment increased; and (4) unemployment increased, especially among youth but also among middle-aged heads of families. These are the relevant labour market outcomes and are consistent with the increase in relative and absolute poverty observed in Brazil and in its principal regions during the recession.

## V. The scope for labour market policy interventions

Clearly, the best short-term way to foster employment is to resume and maintain economic growth. Labour market policies should be considered as complementary, albeit not unimportant, in this process. Among possible labour market policies, we stress the following: support to small-scale production and all types of non-organised employment; stronger enforcement of the minimum wage law; real wage subsidies for particular groups; interventions to block exploitation of specific groups of workers by their employers; better organisation of the labour movement in order to strengthen bargaining power; emergency public works programmes for specific areas and groups of workers; the improvement of labour and social welfare legislation concerning the right to strike, collective bargaining, protection of unemployed workers; better labour market information; and stronger enforcement of labour legislation to enable more workers to enter protected labour markets.

The growing "informalisation" observed from 1981 to 1983 reinforced a structural trait of Brazil's labour markets. Even when the economy was booming, as in the 1970s, non-organised employment accounted for a significant proportion of total employment. It must not be excluded from any labour market policy since it is large, and became even larger in the 1980s. Policies designed to improve working conditions, productivity and real incomes of workers in such markets are likely to help them rise above the poverty line.

The notable increase in the number of workers in formal labour markets earning less than one minimum wage seems to indicate that employers have been successful in avoiding the minimum wage law. The rise in the number of urban workers in the unprotected wage sector means that employers have been able to hire many labourers "off the record" — i.e. by not signing individual labour contracts with them. By such methods, employers are able to underpay workers and thus to lower labour costs, since they evade paying social security taxes and other benefits such as the 13th month's salary, paid vacation, paid advance notice, etc. Workers tend to accept this exploitation because having a job is a matter of survival and they know that, under conditions of excess supply, it is very difficult to find better jobs elsewhere. Further, once a worker has a job even under these conditions, he or she avoids bringing an employer to the labour courts because of fear of losing that job. This obviously occurs more frequently during a recession, but also at other times, given the structural surplus of generally low-skilled workers generated by the rapid increase in the urban labour force.[33] Trying to enforce minimum-wage legislation in a recession might interfere with a spontaneous labour market mechanism, as such intervention might lead to higher wages and to an enhanced protected wage sector at the expense of higher unemployment rates or deeper segmentation. Nevertheless, the enforcement of the legislation during "normal" years might help increase the wages of the unskilled and the size of the protected wage sector, thereby helping to push many incomes over the poverty line.

To prevent exploitation of unorganised workers, it is necessary, but obviously not sufficient, that inspection by the labour authorities be strengthened. To improve the chances that workers in the protected wage sector obtain real wage increases, they should be better organised. A labour movement free of authoritarian interventions, together with more modern and democratic labour legislation, should provide workers with more bargaining power to gain and maintain wage increases. These institutional changes should help some workers overcome poverty; as seen above, many, and an increasing number of, poor workers were found in the protected wage sector. Further, increasing impoverishment of protected labour during the recession was a distinctive feature in the Southeast, where the core of Brazil's modern economy is located and where labour disputes have been most intense. As for the Northeast, simulations reported elsewhere (Ministério do Trabalho, 1985) demonstrated that, given the small size of its protected wage sector (reflecting a small modern economic sector), a resumption of economic growth would not lower the unemployment rate substantially. The lower output/employment elasticity there can also be attributed to the relatively larger size of the non-organised sector in the Northeast (50 per cent) than in the Southeast (31 per cent). Thus, in urban areas of the Northeast, local job-creation programmes would help reduce unemployment, above all among unskilled poor workers who have migrated to the cities, driven from the countryside either by rural poverty or the drought.

In the Southeast renewed growth would lower the cyclical component of unemployment quite rapidly, but would not be sufficient to also absorb new entrants and workers in non-organised labour markets. Thus, it is essential to broaden employment opportunities and to discourage lay-offs. The aim would be to weaken the discretionary power of employers to fire workers, for management tends to place the heaviest burden of the firm's adjustment to recession on the workers. Even though legislative measures would not block altogether management's power of dismissal, they might minimise unemployment during periods of adjustment to economic crisis and technological change.

The "poor worker" concept used here was based on the nominal minimum wage. However, union leaders, politicians, economists and others have asserted that the minimum wage is insufficient to assure a reasonable level of support of the individual worker, much less of a family. The nominal minimum wage has been functioning, in the Southeast's labour markets, as a "lighthouse", a signal to wage bargaining and wage determination in the private sector. For the Northeast's state and city governments it has served as a "floor" for wages of public administration employees. Under the wage laws prevailing since 1979, wage brackets are set up as multiples of the nominal minimum wage. Thus, changes in the minimum affect the whole wage structure in both the private and public sectors. Therefore, the Government's authority to determine the minimum wage is a powerful tool for labour market intervention because it not only affects the poor but also the wage structure and the distribution of wage income.

It is easier to handle minimum-wage policy in the broader context of an incomes policy. An incomes policy should aim, on the one hand, to stabilise the growth of aggregate demand to reduce the effect of swings in the level of economic activity on labour markets and on the impoverishment of workers — in other words, to avoid what happened during the recession. On the other hand, the policy should engender a more equitable distribution of the costs stemming from anti-inflationary policies and of the benefits of economic growth. Through an incomes policy, built within the framework of a social contract, it would be possible to minimise the adverse effects of stabilisation policies on employment and to protect the real income of more vulnerable groups, especially those in the lower-income brackets. However, labour market interventions and an incomes policy should complement other policies designed to combat urban poverty. The causes of poverty are deeply rooted in society and were inherited from the development style chosen after the Second World War. Redirecting the path of development toward the resolution of old social problems such as urban poverty seems an urgent necessity. Labour market interventions and an incomes policy would be easier in a democratic society profoundly concerned with pressing social needs. Therefore, within this framework, what is most needed to overcome poverty are policies to increase public spending in sectors such as housing, education, health and food, as well as a massive programme aimed at supporting small-scale production and tackling the issue of land reform. For this task labour market interventions are merely auxiliary tools, although by no means inconsequential ones.


### Notes

[1] Senior researcher and Associate Professor of Economics at PIMES/Department of Economics, Federal University of Pernambuco at Recife, Brazil. The author is grateful to the Industrial Relations Research Institute of the University of Wisconsin-Madison which provided all the facilities necessary for this research. Many people were helpful, especially Ricardo Infante, Glen Cain and Gerry Rodgers. Barbara Dennis made the text much more readable, and the author would also like to acknowledge the typing by Linda Dolan. However, none of these bears responsibility for any misconceptions and errors.

[2] A formal (or organised) labour market comprises, on the demand side, established firms and, on the supply side, wage workers. In this market workers and employers sign a labour contract. This contract gives workers access to social security benefits and assures them of the protection guaranteed by the Labour Code.

[3] The current account deficit reached US$12.5 billion in 1980. Interest payments accounted for 50.6 per cent of the deficit (US$6.3 billion). Inflation in 1980 reached an annual rate of 121 per cent.

[4] The Northeast's output growth rate is from SUDENE. The GNP data for Brazil as a whole are from the Getúlio Vargas Foundation. There are no data for the Southeast, so the ratio and averages must be taken as proxies for the performance of the Southeast as it accounts for more than 50 per cent of GNP.

[5] The aggregate open unemployment rate is not a very useful concept for heterogeneous labour markets as found in Brazil because it does not take account of other types of labour underutilisation. The concept of unemployment applies only to those workers who are actively searching for a job in the reference week of the household survey. Workers who in the reference week had ceased their job search are not considered members of the labour force and, consequently, are inappropriately classified in the inactive population.

[6] Until May 1984 there were various regional minimum wages. We used the highest minimum wage for the São Paulo-Rio area. However, since May 1984 there has been only one minimum wage. The use of the minimum wage as a reference point requires an analysis of changes in its real value over time. Between 1970 and 1980 the real value of the highest minimum wage increased by 15.2 per cent. Conversely, between 1981 and 1983 the highest real minimum wage fell by 4.8 per cent. Thus, since the real minimum wage changed, our measure of poverty is less than absolute in concept; this affects the analysis which follows.

[7] Pastore et al., 1983, examines the evolution of poverty in the 1970s, using the family as the unit of analysis. It takes overall poverty into account but does not focus on either urban or regional poverty. It uses representative samples of the 1970 and 1980 censuses. The text that follows draws heavily on the conclusions of this study.

[8] Large families (more than seven members) made up 25 per cent of the total number of families in 1970, but only 16 per cent in 1980. In the Northeast they declined from 29.9 per cent in 1970 to 22.7 per cent in 1980; and in the Southeast from 20.8 per cent in 1970 to 12.2 per cent in 1980. Thus, Northeastern families remained larger than those in the Southeast. Ibid., Annex (table 2).

[9] In the 1970s the fertility rate fell by 25 per cent, so reduced family size reflects a fall in the number of children. Since the use of "family per capita" measures weights children the same as adults, this measure overestimates the increase in income. I am grateful to Gerry Rodgers for this observation.

[10] In this study family members are considered to be available for work if they are *(a)* over 14, having completed first grade, and no longer in school, and *(b)* over 18 and not in school even if they have not completed first grade. Families are considered to be *totally unemployed* if no

family member is working, *partially unemployed* if some available family members are working, and *employed* if all available family members are fully engaged in labour markets.

[11] In 1970, 62.7 per cent of Northeastern families earned less than a quarter of the minimum wage per capita. By 1980 they accounted for only 32.5 per cent. However, their number represented a higher proportion of poor Brazilian families in 1980 (50 per cent) than in 1970 (41 per cent). See Pastore et al., 1983, Annex (table 14).

[12] According to census data: FIBGE, Demographic Census, 1970 and 1980.

[13] Poverty and inequality are not the same, and should not be confused, but "relative poverty" is close to the idea of income inequality. In this sense, the poor are those at the bottom of the income distribution profile. Distribution statistics measure only relative position, and do not consider changes in absolute income levels. Morley, in this respect, points out the following: "That is acceptable in an economy with constant income and population, because someone's gain is always someone else's loss. But when there is growth, someone's gain may not be someone else's loss. The distribution statistics ignore the increase in welfare that comes from such absolute increases in income." (Morley, 1982, p. 74).

[14] These data are not disaggregated by urban or rural location, but cover the 70 per cent of households that are urban very well, so we assume that they depict the basic trends and outcomes occurring in the cities.

[15] Since family size does not change rapidly, we can assume that changes in the distribution of income were not affected by this factor. Therefore, we consider variations in monthly family income as good approximations of variations in family income per capita.

[16] This is a variant of an index suggested by Sen (1973) and developed by Bhatty (1974) and Romão (1982). It includes the number of poor, how much their incomes are below the subsistence level, and a measure of inequality among them. The closer it is to one, the greater is absolute poverty.

[17] The labour force participation rate used here is the ratio of the labour force to the working-age population (10 years and over) for each attribute (sex, age).

[18] The measure of the urban labour force used here includes workers employed in agricultural activities within the urban perimeter.

[19] Morley (1982) observes that "the best indicator of the ability of the economy to create above subsistence employment opportunities is the percentage of below subsistence jobs, including unpaid family workers" (p. 94). Obviously, the minimum-wage law forbids an employer to hire a worker for less. An employer who signs a labour contract with a worker cannot pay less than the minimum wage, and failure to abide by the law, whenever a contract has been signed, might summon the employer to the Labour Courts; but many employers evade this law.

[20] Information about real wage trends is scarce. Between 1981 and 1983 the average real wage of manufacturing workers in São Paulo state fell by 10 per cent. See *Conjuntura Econômica*, Vol. 39, No. 10, p. 61.

[21] They lack automatic protection from social security and Labour Codes. The income limits fixed for this and other categories are based on studies of the urban informal sector in Brazil developed by Souza (1981) and Mello e Souza et al. (1982).

[22] All federal, state and municipal employees are considered "organised" irrespective of their income or whether they have labour contracts with the government.

[23] This will take into account small business or micro-firms often found in the urban informal sector of Brazil and other Latin American countries.

[24] The criteria used to classify workers into organised or non-organised sectors were the same as those described in section C above — except for income. The only difference is that the cut-off point in income was reduced, for all categories, to one minimum wage and less. As a result, some categories, such as formal protected wage workers, were excluded by definition from the classification.

[25] Cyclical unemployment is conceptualised as the unemployment stemming from either a slowdown or decline in the level of economic activity, while "frictional" unemployment refers to fairly short-term unemployment engendered by the process of job change. They are of course interdependent.

[26] The rates, estimated by taking the unemployed as a percentage of the urban labour force, include agricultural workers within the urban perimeter. All agricultural workers, however, were considered to be employed. If the number of unemployed was to be taken with respect to the more restricted concept of the urban nonagricultural labour force, rates would be slightly higher.

[27] These findings were drawn from Pastore et al. (1983).

[28] A household survey carried out at the beginning of 1980 for the city of São Paulo found that 42 per cent of the unemployed belonged to the 28.3 per cent of families who worked as low-skilled blue-collar labourers, as household servants and as a special category of self-employed workers (having a fixed site and using family labour). See Cacciamali (1985), pp. 86-128.

[29] Garcia et al. (1983), in their study of family labour force participation rates for Recife and São Jose dos Campos, not only found higher rates among the families of São José, but also that the major difference in the level and intensity of labour market insertion between the two cities was found in the labour force participation rates of families headed by blue-collar wage workers. This can be attributed to differences in the level of industrialisation which places a greater demand for manufacturing workers in São José than in Recife. Thus, a labour market placed in the heart of a region already industrialised is quite distinct from one located in an area where industrialisation has not yet reached full development.

[30] However, some studies have shown that "informalisation" in a state such as São Paulo is highly concentrated in the personal services sector, whereas in the Northeast it is widespread in other sectors, e.g. Souza (1981), p. 299.

[31] These findings conflict with those of Cacciamali (1985), who attempts to show that "informalisation", measured by a ratio of self-employed workers to the urban labour force, does not change much with variations in GNP. It is further argued that during the recession of 1981-83 the rate of "informalisation" increased much more slowly than open unemployment even for a region like the Northeast. She argued that such a phenomenon results from "barriers to entry" that, in the short run, lessen the ability of the informal sector to absorb workers displaced by the formal labour market as a consequence of the recession. Yet other studies have come to the same conclusions as ours. Souza and Araújo (1984) provided evidence based on the evasion of social security tax data for 1982 that "informalisation" as a result of the recession was an important feature of urban labour markets in the Northeast and the Southeast alike.

[32] Cacciamali (1985) pointed out that, at the start of the recession, many individual workers and families at the bottom of the income distribution in São Paulo city were already in the formal labour market.

[33] Morley (1982), p. 256, asserts that "no government, even the most well intentioned, can control the average level of their (unskilled workers') wages. What really must be done is to eliminate the oversupply of the unskilled".

### References

Baer, Werner, 1965: *Industrialisation and economic development in Brazil* (Homewood, Illinois, Irwin).

Bhatty, I. Z., 1974: "Inequality and poverty in India", in T. N. Srinivasan and P. Bardhan (eds.): *Poverty and income distribution in India* (Calcutta, Statistical Publishing Society).

Cacciamali, Maria Cristina, 1985: "Emprego e geração de renda no Brasil (ensaios)" (São Paulo, FIPE/IPEA/BID; mimeographed).

CNRH/IPEA, 1985: *Desigualdades sociais no Nordeste* (Brasília).

Fishlow, Albert, 1972: "Brazilian size distribution of income", in *American Economic Review* (Nashville, Tennessee), Vol. 62, pp. 390-402.

Fundação Getúlio Vargas, 1981: *Conjuntura Econômica*, Vol. 36, No. 12.

Furtado, Celso, 1963: *The economic growth of Brazil: A survey from colonial to modern times* (Berkeley, University of California Press).

Garcia, Brígida; Muñoz, Humberto; Oliveira, Orlandina, 1983: *Familia y mercados de trabajo: Un estudio de dos ciudades brasileñas* (Mexico, El Colegio de Mexico/UNAM).

García, Norberto E, 1982: "Absorción creciente con subempleo persistente", in *Revista de la Cepal*, Dec.

Hoffman, R, 1985: "Distribuição de renda no Brasil por unidade da Federação", in *Revista de Economia Política*, Vol. III, No. 1, pp. 31-41.

Infante, Ricardo, 1983: "Brasil: Ajustes dos mercados de trabalho urbano e o desemprego aberto" (Brasília; mimeographed).

————, 1985: "Características estruturais dos mercados de trabalho urbanos" (Brasília; mimeographed).

Jatobá, Jorge, 1974: "Factor price policies, technological change and labour absorption: The case of the Brazilian Northeast" (Nashville, Vanderbilt University, unpublished Ph.D. Dissertation).

———— (ed.), 1983: *Emprego no Nordeste: Modernização e heterogeneidade* (Recife, Massangana).

————, 1985: "Desenvolvimento regional, crise e mercado de trabalho: O caso brasileiro com especial atenção para o Nordeste, 1981-1983", in *Revista Econômica do Nordeste*, Oct./Dec.

de Melo, Mário Lacerda, 1976a: *O açúcar e o homem no Nordeste: Problemas sociais e econômicos do nordeste canavieiro* (Recife, Instituto Joaquim Nabuco).

————, 1976b: "Proletarização e emigração nas regiões canavieiras de Pernambuco" (Recife, UFPe; mimeographed).

Mello e Souza, Alberto e al., 1982: "Setor informal: Origens, características e dimensões" (Rio de Janeiro, FGV/IEAE; mimeographed).

Ministério do Trabalho, 1985: *Brasil: Recommendações para a formulação de políticas de emprego e rendas* (Brasília, Technical Report prepared in co-operation with UNDP/ILO Project BRA/82/026).

Ministério do Trabalho/SES, 1985: *Metodologia e estimativa do emprego a partir de painéis fixos para pares consecutivos da RAIS, 1979-1983* (Brasília, mimeographed).

Morley, Samuel A, 1982: *Labour markets and inequitable growth: The case of authoritarian capitalism in Brazil* (Cambridge, Cambridge University Press).

Neto, Leonardo G, 1982: "Emprego no Nordeste: Sugestões de políticas", in *Revista Econômica do Nordeste*, Vol. 13, No. 3.

Osório, Carlos; Gomes, Gustavo M.; Irmão, José F, 1985: *Recessão e desemprego nas regiões brasileiras* (Recife, Massangana).

Paiva, Paulo, 1984: "*Fifty years of population growth and labour absorption in Brazil: From 1950 to 2000*", Paper prepared for the Conference on Population Growth and Labour Absorption in the Developing World, Bellagio, July.

Pastore, José, 1979: *Desigualdade e mobilidade social no Brasil* (São Paulo, T. A. Queiroz).

Pastore, José; Zylberstajn, Hélio; Pagotto, Carmen, 1983: *Mudança social e pobreza no Brasil, 1970-1980* (São Paulo, FIPE/Livraria Pioneira).

PIMES/UFPe, 1984: *Desigualdades regionais no desenvolvimento brasileiro* (Four volumes) (Recife, Massangana).

Robock, Stefan H, 1963: *Brazil's developing Northeast: A study of regional planning and foreign aid* (Washington, DC, Brookings Institution).

Romão, M. C., 1982: "Índices de pobreza: Alternativas, decomposição e uso com dados agregados", in *Estudos Econômicos*, Vol. 12, No. 3, pp. 51-65.

Sen, A. K, 1978: *Three notes on the concept of poverty*, World Employment Programme research working paper, WEP 2-23-WP 65 (Geneva, ILO).

————, 1979: "Issues in the measurement of poverty", in *Scandinavian Journal of Economics*, Vol. 81, No. 2.

————, 1973: "Poverty, inequality and unemployment: Some conceptual issues in measurement", in *Economical and Political Weekly*, Special Number, pp. 1457-1464.

Singer, Paul, 1969: *Desenvolvimento econômico e evolução urbana* (São Paulo, Editora Nacional).

Souza, Aldemir and Araújo, Tarcísio, 1984: *Setor informal no Nordeste: Significado e evolução recente* (Recife, PIMES; mimeographed).

Souza, Paulo Renato, 1981: "Emprego e renda na pequena produção urbana no Brasil", in *Estudos Econômicos*, Mar.

SUDENE, 1983: *Produto e formação bruta de capital: Nordeste do Brasil, 1965-1981* (Recife).

Tolipan, Ricardo and Tinelli, Arthur C. (eds.), 1975: *A controvérsia sobre distribuição de renda e desenvolvimento* (Rio de Janeiro, Zahar).

# Chapter 3

## Poverty and the labour market in Costa Rica

*MOLLY POLLACK* [1]

## I. Introduction

This chapter is an attempt to evaluate the dimensions of poverty and how they affect different groups in urban Costa Rica, assessing the relative importance of the labour market and other factors in the evolution of poverty. In particular, we examine to what extent vulnerability to poverty is related to vulnerability to employment problems, which in turn depend on the characteristics of households and household members. It is important to study trends, so poverty in 1971, 1979 and 1982 is compared, albeit not always with the same variables due to the absence of consistent data. In order to estimate the scale of poverty we first discuss some basic concepts: the choice of the household as the unit of study; the definition of "biological" poverty in absolute terms; the selection of total income per household member to measure welfare; and the definition of a basic food basket to determine the poverty line. Three household groups are defined in relation to the poverty line: destitute, poor and non-poor households. For each group, household characteristics and poverty profiles of household members are determined and analysed in order to examine the following questions:

— Are the characteristics of households different among the three poverty groups?

— How are the income differentials explained by different factors?

— How have income differentials among these groups evolved from 1971 to 1982?

By using a methodology from an earlier study (Piñera, 1979), income differentials are decomposed into a demographic factor (percentage of adults) and two factors related to the labour market (income per employed household member, and employment rate).

From 1979 to 1982 Costa Rica underwent an economic crisis, so it is important to determine its effects on the magnitude of poverty and how different groups were affected. Unfortunately, the available data are unsatisfactory for a complete analysis, but some general indices of the impoverishment of households and labour market outcomes as a response to the crisis are given. The economic situation of households deteriorated because of the dramatic reduction in real wages and the increase in unemployment in this period, but some sectors were more affected than others.

The poverty and labour market situation is analysed in detail, and an attempt is made to identify factors which discriminate among poverty groups and which are related to the labour market insertion of household members. The labour market is divided into "formal" and "informal" sectors, and the insertion of heads and non-heads of household in these segments is presented for each group. This is perhaps our most important contribution, since it allows us to analyse the relationship between the labour market insertion of household members and the incidence of poverty among them. One of our hypotheses is that there has been a growth in the informal sector as one of the labour market mechanisms of adjustment to the economic crisis. That is, besides an increase in unemployment and a fall in real wages, employed household members have increased their participation in informal jobs. A related hypothesis examined below is that the labour market insertion of household members is a factor which discriminates among poverty groups, and in particular that there are relatively more destitute and poor household members employed in the informal sector than non-poor household members.

## II. The macro-economic context

Up to 1976 there was a reasonable employment level and a balance of trade in equilibrium. The unemployment rate fluctuated around 5 per cent and total underemployment, estimated in terms of equivalent unemployment, was about twice as much. Inflation was moderate, annual rates being below 10 per cent, and the terms of trade were relatively favourable. From 1978 onwards this situation deteriorated (table 3.1). A growing disequilibrium in the balance of trade led to the implementation of restrictive economic policies, and these in turn led to a drastic reduction in the gross domestic product and high unemployment rates. The currency was devalued by over 400 per cent, and the inflation rate reached almost 100 per cent in 1982.

The main goal of economic policy was to increase domestic aggregate demand through a more active monetary and fiscal policy. This led to the acceleration of the inflationary process from 1981 onwards. With respect to wage policy, the economic authority tried to at least maintain the real minimum wage by adjusting it according to past inflation. But since inflation was accelerating from 1979 to 1983, real wages fell by 30 per cent.

Besides the fall in real wages and the higher unemployment rate, there were two other mechanisms by which the labour market adjusted to the crisis. First the labour force participation rate increased from 50.5 to 51.5 per cent. Second, the traditional rural and informal urban sectors increased their share of the employed population between 1979 and 1982 from 27.7 to 29.2 per cent and from 14.5 to 15.2 per cent respectively (Pollack, 1985). The labour market adjustment was thus based on income reduction, higher unemployment and

*Table 3.1. Costa Rica: Main economic indicators, 1976-83*

| Year | Unemployment rate (%) | Equivalent unemployment rate [1] (%) | GDP rate of change (%) | Change in terms of trade (%) | Change in net foreign reserves (million US$) | Consumer Price Index change (%) |
|------|------|------|------|------|------|------|
| 1976 | 6.3 | 13.2 | 5.5 | 11.2 | 61 | 4.4 |
| 1977 | 4.6 | 11.2 | 8.9 | 24.1 | 110 | 5.3 |
| 1978 | 4.6 | 10.9 | 6.3 | −6.8 | 18 | 8.1 |
| 1979 | 4.9 | 12.5 | 4.9 | −1.6 | −113 | 13.1 |
| 1980 | 5.3 | 13.5 | 0.8 | −2.8 | 33 | 17.8 |
| 1981 | 9.7 | 17.4 | −2.3 | −14.8 | −65 | 65.1 |
| 1982 | 9.4 | 23.8 | −7.3 | −7.0 | 125 | 81.7 |
| 1983 | 9.0 | 19.9 | 2.3 | −7.1 | 60 | 10.7 |

[1] "Equivalent unemployment" is an estimate of the number of persons who would be wholly unemployed if labour demand were distributed in such a way that all employed persons were fully employed.
Sources. National Institute of Statistics, Ministry of Labour, Costa Rica; ECLAC.

growth of the informal sector. This led to a relative impoverishment of households and to a concentration of workers in low-income strata.

# III. Methodology

## 1. Data sources

Most data used here are taken from household surveys on employment and underemployment, undertaken by the National Institute of Statistics of the Ministry of Labour of Costa Rica. All figures for 1971 were taken from an ECLA study (Piñera, 1979), based on data from the household survey for 1971. Data for 1979 were taken from a previous study on household behaviour and economic crisis in Costa Rica (Pollack, 1985). All the analysis for 1982 is based on primary data from the above-mentioned survey, for July. It covers the whole country in both urban and rural zones. These data allowed the computation of household variables, such as number of household members, income, and so on, required to define poverty lines or to study poverty profiles of household members. This information made it possible to apply the economic theory of the family (Killingsworth, 1974; Ashenfelter and Heckman, 1974; Rodgers et al., 1980; Becker, 1981; Standing and Sheehan, 1978), and to classify households according to income strata into destitute, poor and non-poor groups.

## 2. Concepts and definitions

### A. The concept of poverty

No overall theory of poverty exists, but the subject has been widely studied, many definitions have been suggested, and different ways of identifying poverty groups have been developed. One of the most notable researchers in this

*Table 3.2.   Monetary equivalence for payments in kind (percentage of total income)*

|                        | Destitute and poor | Non-poor |
|------------------------|--------------------|----------|
| House                  | 30                 | 20       |
| Food                   | 50                 | 5        |
| Other                  | 10                 | 5        |
| House and food         | 80                 | 25       |
| House and other        | 40                 | 25       |
| Food and other         | 60                 | 10       |
| Food, house and other  | 90                 | 30       |

area is Sen (1976, 1978, 1981), whose "biological approach" is used here to define a poverty line. According to this approach, poor households are those whose total per capita income is not enough to cover their basic food needs, i.e. those who cannot meet minimum nutritional requirements, as defined by a basic food list or basket. This approach has been criticised for the relative arbitrariness involved in the selection of the basic foods, and for the complexity of defining nutritional intake requirements. Nevertheless, it is widely used, and in most countries expenditure surveys have been used to estimate the value of a "basic basket". In Costa Rica the Dirección General de Estadística calculates the value of the basic basket per person; the minimum nutritional requirements for July 1982 implied an expenditure of 712 colones. We use this as our basic poverty line.

### B. The concept of per capita income

To identify poor households, we need to specify the concept of income to be applied in comparison with the cost of the basic food basket. The income measure used here corresponds to total income received by all members of the family or household, including wages and salaries and other secondary incomes – pensions, rents, payments in kind, etc. Payments in kind were translated into monetary figures according to weights presented in table 3.2. They were estimated using information from other studies (Fishlow, 1972) and also the corresponding weights from the Consumer Price Index of San José.

### C. The concept of the household

In order to identify poverty groups it was necessary to define the household unit. All members of a family living and cooking under the same roof were considered as belonging to the same household unit. To determine whether a household is poor, we calculate total income per household member and compare this with the cost of the basic food basket. Per capita income was defined as the ratio between total household income and the number of household members. However, some adjustments need to be made in household size if individual welfare is to be measured, since welfare is not only determined by income but also by individual characteristics such as age, kind of activity, sex, etc. (see Rodgers, 1984, pp. 23-32). The ideal method would be to estimate household size according to adult-equivalent units. This approach is very difficult to implement due to lack of information and of an accepted adult-equivalence table. In this research the number of children was divided by two in all households, so that it is implicitly supposed that a child, irrespective of age, consumes one-half as much as an adult. Both definitions of income per household member (adjusted and unadjusted) are used separately, and the differences in poverty levels, derived from these estimates, are presented in section IV.

Once all concepts explained above are defined, households are classified into three poverty groups: destitute, poor and non-poor. Destitute households are those whose per capita income is less than the cost of one basic food basket. Poor households are those whose per capita income is equal to a value between one and two times the basic food basket. The non-poor are all households whose per capita income exceeds two basic food baskets.

There are still some restrictions concerned with the income data used here which could affect the poverty lines. First, income from sources other than labour is usually understated. The same problem arises with income from self-employment. However, there is reason to suppose that this understatement of incomes is more important in non-poor groups, since income from sources other than labour is more frequently obtained by higher-income households. Therefore, incomes around the poverty lines should be affected less than income in the non-poor strata.

# IV. Poverty and the labour market: 1971-82

## 1. Problems of comparability

Some analysis in this section compares poverty in 1971 with 1982. However, it is difficult to study poverty trends in Costa Rica because of inconsistencies between different data sources. Figures for 1982 are estimated by the author from household surveys on employment and unemployment. Figures for 1971 are taken from the ECLA study (Piñera, 1979). However, the methodologies used to estimate income per family member in 1971 and 1982 differ slightly. The ECLA study makes some adjustments to income as reported in the surveys, in order to estimate available personal income. The main adjustments attempt to correct cash income by incorporating payments in kind, capital income and transfer payments. Also, income is adjusted so as to be compatible with national accounts. The corresponding methodology for 1982 also attempts to correct income but in a different way. Two kinds of correction are carried out: one, in order to incorporate payments in kind, and, the other, to correct household size by allowing for differing consumption needs of adults and children, as noted above. Even though the two methodologies are different, the objective pursued is the same. In 1982 transfer payments are not included, but one of the main components of these subsidies are family allowances. Therefore, by giving a lower weight to the number of children, the effect should

*Table 3.3.   Characteristics of urban households, 1971 and 1982*

|  | Total | | Destitute | | Poor | | Non-poor | |
|---|---|---|---|---|---|---|---|---|
|  | 1971 | 1982 | 1971 | 1982 | 1971 | 1982 | 1971 | 1982 |
| Percentage of households | 100.0 | 100.0 | 4.0 | 4.4 | 13.0 | 20.2 | 83.0 | 75.4 |
| Household size | 5.3 | 4.9 | 7.2 | 5.3 | 6.9 | 5.4 | 4.9 | 4.7 |
| Household size | — | (4.9) | — | (5.6) | — | (4.8) | — | (3.8) |
| Percentage of children | 30 | 36 | 42 | 36 | 42 | 31 | 27 | 37 |
| Percentage of children | — | (32) | — | (57) | — | (33) | — | (29) |
| Percentage of adults | 70 | 64 | 58 | 64 | 58 | 69 | 73 | 63 |
| Employed/adults (%) | 39 | 61 | 28 | 59 | 34 | 57 | 47 | 70 |
| Active/adults (%) | 39 | 67 | 29 | 67 | 34 | 61 | 47 | 72 |
| Employed/active (%) | 99 | 93 | 99 | 89 | 99 | 94 | 99 | 98 |

Note. Figures in parentheses correspond to distributions across poverty strata before income adjustments.

at least be in the same direction as the inclusion of family allowances. Payments in kind are included in both estimates, but the ECLA study does not explain how they are weighted.

## 2. The magnitude of poverty and household characteristics

Table 3.3 shows that poverty increased in Costa Rica. Total poverty ("destitute" and "poor") increased from 17 to 24.6 per cent. If income had not been adjusted by the number of children and payments in kind, destitute households would have represented 20.5 per cent and poor households 36.7 per cent of the total. This difference of poverty reflects the sensitivity of poverty estimates to income and household size adjustments.

The main factors which discriminate between households in different strata are: household size, which is inversely related to income level; the percentage of children within the household, which increases as income decreases; the number of employed as a percentage of adult household members, which is weakly positively related to income level; the labour force participation rate of adults, which does not show a clear relationship with income; and the employment rate of households, which is positively associated with income. The percentage of children shows an interesting pattern. Before income corrections, it is negatively related with income level (figures in parentheses). Once income is adjusted to consider adult equivalent house-hold members, however, this relationship disappears. When comparing characteristics of households in 1971 and 1982 some differences can be seen: in 1982 households are smaller in size and have a higher percentage of children, more adults are economically active and employed,[2] but the unemployment rate is higher. With respect to changes in discriminating factors, the main conclusion from table 3.3 is that unemployment became a problem between 1971 and 1982,

*Table 3.4. Contribution to the explanation of per capita income differentials between urban households in different poverty strata*

| | Total differential | Total income | No. employed | No. of adults |
|---|---|---|---|---|
| | | No. employed | No. of adults | Household size |
| *1971* | | | | |
| Poor and destitute | 100.0 | 77.5 | 21.7 | 0.6 |
| Non-poor and poor | 100.0 | 62.8 | 21.8 | 15.2 |
| Non-poor and destitute | 100.0 | 67.9 | 21.8 | 10.3 |
| *1982* [1] | | | | |
| Poor and destitute | 100.0 | 94.8 | −4.4 | 9.6 |
| Non-poor and poor | 100.0 | 90.3 | 17.5 | −7.7 |
| Non-poor and destitute | 100.0 | 92.1 | 8.7 | −0.8 |
| *1982* [2] | | | | |
| Poor and destitute | 100.0 | 81.5 | −31.9 | 50.5 |
| Non-poor and poor | 100.0 | 70.6 | 18.0 | 11.5 |
| Non-poor and destitute | 100.0 | 75.1 | −2.5 | 27.5 |

[1] Income corrected for income in kind and number of children.   [2] Income with no adjustment at all.

especially among the poor, and since labour force participation rates are not significantly different among the three poverty levels this represents a real difference in employment levels between the three groups. One may conclude from this analysis that unemployment and certain household characteristics are important factors determining income differentials in urban Costa Rica, and that they discriminated better in 1982 than in 1971.

## 3. Factors explaining income differentials

By using a methodology that decomposes the sources of income differentials between different poverty strata (Piñera, 1979), table 3.4 is obtained. Three factors are identified. The first corresponds to differences in income per employed household member, the second reflects differences in the number of employed members among adults, and the third reflects the differences in the number of adults per household in the three groups. In 1971 and especially in 1982 the most important factor is the difference in income per employed household member. The second factor in importance is the employment rate of adult members of the family, which is less significant in 1982 than 1971. The demographic factor, represented by the number of adults per household, is the least important in determining income differentials among households classified by poverty group. However, it is convenient, at this point, to recall that household size was corrected by dividing the number of children by two in order to adjust per capita income. The number of adults is a very important factor in determining poverty if income is not adjusted, as shown by the second set of figures for 1982.

*Table 3.5.    Costa Rica: Urban poverty profiles according to head of household's characteristics, 1971 and 1982*

|  | Total | | Destitute | | Poor | | Non-poor | |
|---|---|---|---|---|---|---|---|---|
|  | 1971 | 1982 | 1971 | 1982 | 1971 | 1982 | 1971 | 1982 |
| *Sex* | | | | | | | | |
| Male | 79.8 | 84.3 | 52.8 | 62.9 | 75.3 | 82.3 | 81.9 | 86.2 |
| Female | 20.2 | 15.7 | 47.2 | 37.1 | 24.7 | 17.7 | 18.1 | 13.8 |
| *Education* | | | | | | | | |
| None | 3.9 | 4.4 | 10.2 | 10.1 | 8.7 | 8.9 | 2.9 | 2.8 |
| Primary | 60.3 | 48.7 | 80.0 | 79.6 | 80.0 | 65.5 | 56.1 | 41.3 |
| Secondary | 23.9 | 34.1 | 8.9 | 8.8 | 10.4 | 22.8 | 26.5 | 37.8 |
| University | 11.9 | 12.8 | 0.9 | 0.0 | 0.9 | 2.2 | 13.9 | 16.2 |
| Unknown | – | – | – | 1.5 | – | 0.6 | – | 2.0 |
| *Age* | | | | | | | | |
| 12-19 [1] | 0.3 | 1.4 | 0.0 | 0.0 | 0.6 | 3.4 | 0.3 | 0.9 |
| 20-29 | 15.2 | 22.8 | 10.3 | 13.8 | 8.9 | 13.1 | 16.3 | 25.9 |
| 30-39 | 27.5 | 31.8 | 28.4 | 20.1 | 29.4 | 25.3 | 27.1 | 34.3 |
| 40-49 | 24.0 | 21.2 | 27.5 | 18.5 | 28.6 | 26.3 | 23.1 | 19.9 |
| 50-59 | 17.9 | 16.1 | 16.2 | 28.5 | 15.3 | 21.3 | 18.3 | 13.9 |
| 60+ | 15.1 | 6.8 | 17.6 | 19.1 | 17.2 | 10.6 | 14.9 | 5.0 |
| *Economic activity* | | | | | | | | |
| Agriculture | 4.9 | 6.1 | 9.5 | 9.9 | 10.6 | 8.3 | 4.0 | 5.3 |
| Industry | 22.1 | 18.4 | 18.9 | 16.8 | 21.8 | 19.6 | 22.2 | 18.2 |
| Construction | 9.7 | 7.8 | 9.7 | 9.5 | 14.4 | 11.5 | 9.0 | 6.7 |
| Commerce | 18.0 | 24.3 | 15.7 | 28.4 | 15.7 | 22.7 | 18.4 | 24.5 |
| Services and others | 45.3 | 43.3 | 46.2 | 35.2 | 37.6 | 37.8 | 46.4 | 45.4 |
| *Occupational category* | | | | | | | | |
| Professional and technical | 11.4 | 12.0 | 0.0 | 0.0 | 1.8 | 2.5 | 13.1 | 15.3 |
| Administrative, clerical and sales | 35.6 | 27.7 | 12.1 | 15.9 | 17.8 | 22.3 | 38.9 | 29.8 |
| Manual workers | 41.1 | 40.1 | 52.4 | 43.6 | 59.5 | 49.1 | 38.1 | 37.5 |
| Service workers | 11.2 | 20.0 | 30.9 | 40.5 | 20.0 | 25.3 | 9.3 | 17.4 |
| Unknown | 0.6 | 0.2 | 4.6 | 0.0 | 0.8 | 0.8 | 0.5 | 0.1 |
| *Number of hours worked* | | | | | | | | |
| 1-20 | 19.1 | 4.4 | 44.4 | 25.2 | 26.3 | 7.1 | 16.7 | 2.4 |
| 21-40 | 4.8 | 21.7 | 8.5 | 31.5 | 5.6 | 23.1 | 4.5 | 20.7 |
| 41-50 | 50.0 | 42.9 | 25.5 | 29.6 | 38.9 | 40.4 | 53.0 | 44.4 |
| 51 and more | 26.1 | 29.1 | 21.6 | 13.7 | 29.2 | 28.1 | 25.7 | 30.3 |
| Unknown | – | 1.9 | – | 0.0 | – | 1.4 | – | 2.2 |

[1] In 1971 includes only household heads aged 15 to 19 years.
Source. Prepared by the author with data from National Household Surveys on Employment and Unemployment, 1982.

In summary, the difference in income per employed household member is the main factor influencing income differentials among households of the three poverty strata, and has gained importance between 1971 and 1982.

Demographic factors such as the number of adults per household are very significant if children are given the same weight as adults in adjusting income for family size, because destitute and poor households have relatively more children. But if the income adjustment is in terms of adult-equivalent household members, the demographic factor loses its significance.

### 4. Urban poverty profiles according to the characteristics of the household head: 1971 and 1982

Table 3.5 shows that most households had male heads in 1971 and 1982, the proportion being higher in 1982, in all three poverty strata. However, the sex of the head seems to be a discriminating factor in the analysis of poverty, since among the destitute and poor more households are headed by females than in non-poor households. Education is also a discriminating factor. In comparing educational levels between 1971 and 1982 one observes an improvement in the educational level of heads among both the poor and non-poor, but not among the destitute. Another factor is the age of the head of the household. Destitute households tended to be headed by older people, especially in 1982.

With respect to the insertion of heads of households into economic sectors, table 3.5 shows a higher concentration in commerce and services in 1982 and in industry and services in 1971. The economic sector in which household heads work is a discriminating factor for poverty, since the incidence of destitution is higher for heads employed in the agricultural sector in 1971 and 1982 and also in commerce in 1982. Poverty above the level of destitution is greater among household heads employed in agriculture and construction. The occupational category of household heads also discriminates between poverty strata. The incidence of poverty ("destitute" and "poor") is higher among workers in personal services and manual workers.

Underemployment, as measured by number of hours worked by household heads, is also a discriminating factor in 1971 and 1982. Most destitute households heads worked less than 40 hours a week in both years. This trend, however, seems to be improving.

In summary: sex, education and age of the household head were discriminating factors in 1971 and 1982. The occupational category, the number of hours worked and the labour market insertion of household heads are all also discriminating factors.

## V. Poverty in 1979 and 1982

In the economic crisis of 1979-82 Costa Rica experienced a drastic reduction in real wages of around 30 per cent and the unemployment rate doubled. An earlier study (Pollack, 1985) analysed household labour supply strategies in the face of this loss of purchasing power, and concluded that a segmented labour supply existed, which appeared as a consequence of the drastic reduction in real wages obtained by the head of household. In this case,

*Table 3.6.    Indicators of impoverishment of households whose head is a wage earner, 1979 and 1982*

|                                                                      | 1979 | 1982 |
|----------------------------------------------------------------------|------|------|
| *Distribution of household heads by income level*                    |      |      |
| 0-1 minimum wage                                                     | 24.4 | 30.8 |
| 1-2 minimum wages                                                    | 35.4 | 35.6 |
| 2 and more minimum wages                                            | 40.2 | 33.6 |
| *Distribution of income recipients according to income level of head* |      |      |
| 0-1 minimum wage                                                     | 25.5 | 32.5 |
| 1-2 minimum wages                                                    | 36.8 | 33.8 |
| 2 and more minimum wages                                            | 37.7 | 33.7 |

Source. Pollack (1985).

*Table 3.7.    Profile of employed household members by wage level of head, 1979 and 1982*

|                          | Wage level (multiple of minimum wage) | | | | | | | |
|                          | 0-1 | | 1-2 | | 2 and more | | Total | |
|                          | 1979 | 1982 | 1979 | 1982 | 1979 | 1982 | 1979 | 1982 |
|--------------------------|------|------|------|------|------|------|-------|-------|
| *Institutional sector*   | *24.3* | *31.6* | *35.2* | *32.7* | *40.5* | *35.7* | *100.0* | *100.0* |
| Public                   | 15.9 | 13.9 | 54.5 | 62.0 | 29.6 | 24.1 | 100.0 | 100.0 |
| Private                  | 29.3 | 38.8 | 38.0 | 33.2 | 32.7 | 28.0 | 100.0 | 100.0 |
| *Occupational category*  | *24.3* | *31.6* | *35.2* | *32.7* | *40.5* | *35.7* | *100.0* | *100.0* |
| Professional             | 0.5  | 0.8  | 9.1  | 6.6  | 90.4 | 92.6 | 100.0 | 100.0 |
| Administration/ managerial | 10.2 | 6.6 | 26.6 | 22.7 | 63.2 | 70.7 | 100.0 | 100.0 |
| Clerical and sales       | 6.9  | 5.8  | 31.7 | 32.9 | 61.4 | 31.3 | 100.0 | 100.0 |
| Manual workers           | 31.3 | 38.4 | 40.9 | 37.2 | 27.8 | 24.4 | 100.0 | 100.0 |
| Service workers          | 29.1 | 31.1 | 39.7 | 42.1 | 31.2 | 26.8 | 100.0 | 100.0 |
| *Economic sector*        | *24.3* | *31.6* | *35.2* | *32.7* | *40.5* | *35.7* | *100.0* | *100.0* |
| Agriculture              | 48.1 | 60.2 | 36.9 | 25.5 | 15.0 | 14.3 | 100.0 | 100.0 |
| Industry                 | 13.6 | 21.8 | 42.9 | 40.3 | 43.5 | 37.9 | 100.0 | 100.0 |
| Building                 | 14.4 | 17.6 | 44.0 | 45.8 | 41.6 | 36.6 | 100.0 | 100.0 |
| Public utilities         | 16.4 | 11.3 | 31.9 | 42.9 | 51.7 | 46.8 | 100.0 | 100.0 |
| Commerce                 | 18.3 | 22.9 | 39.6 | 33.5 | 42.1 | 43.6 | 100.0 | 100.0 |
| Services                 | 19.1 | 22.4 | 27.0 | 29.7 | 53.9 | 47.9 | 100.0 | 100.0 |

Source. Pollack (1985).

labour force participation rates increased substantially, in particular for secondary household members. Following that study, the main indicators of household impoverishment in 1979 and 1982 are presented in table 3.6. The percentage of household heads receiving a salary less than one minimum wage increased from 1979 to 1982, as did that of income recipients belonging to households whose head received less than the minimum wage. Moreover, the value of the minimum wage also declined in that period, as noted above. Taking into account this fall in real wages, the pattern visible in table 3.6, and the higher unemployment rate in 1982, it is clear that poverty increased substantially between 1979 and 1982 in Costa Rica.

An important question is in which sectors were the employed household members working in 1979 and 1982, because it determines how the crisis affected the different labour market segments and, therefore, the poverty of households with differing economic characteristics. From table 3.7 we can see that those employed in the private sector were more affected by the crisis than those in the public sector, since there is a greater concentration of private sector workers in lower-income strata in 1982 than 1979. In addition, employees in agriculture and industry who were manual or service workers, i.e. low-paid occupations which require fewer qualifications, increased as a proportion of the lower-income strata between 1979 and 1982.

From the above, it can be concluded that the effect of the crisis was a deterioration of the situation of poor households, in particular of those headed by manual or service workers and working in the sectors producing tradables. It seems likely that in 1982 the informal sector increased in importance as a labour market mechanism to face the crisis. This is studied with more suitable data in section VI for 1982, as this is the only year with the required statistics.

# VI. Poverty and labour market insertion in 1982

## 1. Institutional and economic insertion of heads of households

The pattern of labour market insertion of heads of household in 1982 is shown in table 3.8. It can be seen that destitution is more frequent among households with heads working in the private sector and in commerce, construction and agriculture. This could be a consequence of part-time and/or seasonal jobs, and also of the existence in those sectors of informal occupations. The incidence of non-destitute poverty is higher in households whose head works in industry, construction or agriculture. The distribution of households by occupational category of the head indicates that destitute and poor households are mainly those whose head is a manual or service worker.

## 2. Heads of households' insertion in formal and informal sectors

Using the PREALC definition of formal and informal sectors (PREALC, 1978), household heads are classified according to the labour market segment in which they work (table 3.8). The formal sector includes: public sector workers, employers and employees of larger firms (five or more employees), and self-employed professionals. The informal sector includes: non-professional self-employed workers, employers and employees of small firms (fewer than five workers) and unpaid family workers. The latter were excluded due to data

*Table 3.8.   Costa Rica: Occupational insertion of household heads by poverty strata, 1982*

|  | Total | Destitute | Poor | Non-poor |
|---|---|---|---|---|
| *Institutional sector* | | | | |
| Public | 27.3 | 3.6 | 17.5 | 31.3 |
| Private | 72.7 | 96.4 | 82.5 | 68.7 |
| *Economic sector* | | | | |
| Agriculture | 6.1 | 9.9 | 8.3 | 5.3 |
| Industry | 18.4 | 16.8 | 19.6 | 18.2 |
| Construction | 7.8 | 9.5 | 11.5 | 6.7 |
| Services | 42.8 | 33.1 | 36.9 | 45.0 |
| Commerce | 24.3 | 28.4 | 22.7 | 24.5 |
| Unknown | 0.5 | 2.1 | 0.9 | 0.4 |
| *Occupational category* | | | | |
| Professional | 12.0 | 0.0 | 2.5 | 15.3 |
| Administrative, clerical and sales workers | 27.7 | 15.9 | 22.3 | 29.8 |
| Manual workers | 40.1 | 43.6 | 49.1 | 37.5 |
| Service workers | 20.0 | 40.5 | 25.3 | 17.4 |
| Unknown | 0.2 | 0.0 | 0.8 | 0.1 |
| *Formal and informal sector* | | | | |
| *Formal sector* | 61.9 | 24.3 | 45.9 | 68.3 |
| Public sector | 27.3 | 3.6 | 17.5 | 31.3 |
| Employer large firm | 2.2 | 0.0 | 0.3 | 2.9 |
| Employee large firm | 31.6 | 20.7 | 28.1 | 33.2 |
| Independent professional | 0.8 | 0.0 | 0.6 | 0.9 |
| *Informal sector* | 38.1 | 75.8 | 53.5 | 31.7 |
| Independent non-professional | 17.6 | 40.2 | 23.8 | 14.6 |
| Employer small firm | 5.0 | 3.0 | 5.9 | 4.9 |
| Employee small firm | 15.5 | 32.6 | 23.8 | 12.2 |
| *Number of hours worked* | | | | |
| 1-30 | 9.8 | 44.2 | 13.0 | 6.9 |
| 31-40 | 16.3 | 12.5 | 17.2 | 16.2 |
| 41-50 | 42.9 | 29.6 | 40.4 | 44.4 |
| 51 and more | 29.1 | 13.7 | 28.1 | 30.3 |
| Unknown | 1.9 | 0.0 | 1.4 | 2.2 |

Source. Prepared by the author with data from Household Survey on Employment and Unemployment, July 1982.

problems. The figures in table 3.8 show that the incidence of poverty ("destitute" and "poor") is much higher among households whose head works in the informal sector, in particular households whose head is a non-professional independent worker or the employee of a small firm. In addition, the incidence of non-destitute poverty is high in households whose head is an employee of a large firm. Thus the formal-informal labour market insertion of household heads is a factor which discriminates effectively among poverty groups in Costa Rica in 1982; 75.8 per cent of destitute household heads are employed in the informal sector, while this proportion decreases to 53.5 and

**Table 3.9.** *Costa Rica: Occupational insertion of secondary household workers by poverty strata, 1982*

|  | Total | Destitute | Poor | Non-poor |
|---|---|---|---|---|
| *Institutional sector* |  |  |  |  |
| Public | 26.4 | 0.0 | 9.4 | 31.9 |
| Private | 73.6 | 100.0 | 90.6 | 68.0 |
| *Economic sector* |  |  |  |  |
| Agriculture | 3.1 | 4.5 | 2.9 | 3.1 |
| Industry | 24.5 | 21.1 | 34.5 | 21.9 |
| Construction | 4.0 | 1.9 | 6.3 | 3.4 |
| Services | 44.3 | 45.9 | 32.5 | 47.5 |
| Commerce | 23.3 | 26.6 | 22.9 | 23.3 |
| Unknown | 0.8 | 0.0 | 1.0 | 0.8 |
| *Occupational category* |  |  |  |  |
| Professional | 15.4 | 0.0 | 3.6 | 19.1 |
| Administrative, clerical and sales workers | 28.1 | 17.8 | 21.0 | 30.3 |
| Manual worker | 35.1 | 34.4 | 51.1 | 30.7 |
| Service worker | 21.3 | 47.7 | 24.0 | 19.7 |
| Unknown | 0.2 | 0.0 | 0.2 | 0.1 |
| *Formal and informal sector* |  |  |  |  |
| Formal sector | 64.6 | 34.7 | 53.7 | 68.6 |
| Public sector | 26.4 | 0.0 | 9.4 | 31.9 |
| Employer large firm | 0.6 | 0.0 | 0.2 | 0.7 |
| Employee large firm | 37.3 | 34.5 | 43.9 | 35.9 |
| Independent professional | 0.1 | 0.0 | 0.0 | 0.1 |
| Informal sector | 35.4 | 65.3 | 46.4 | 31.4 |
| Independent non-professional | 10.5 | 19.3 | 11.5 | 9.9 |
| Employer small firm | 0.9 | 0.0 | 1.3 | 0.8 |
| Employee small firm | 24.0 | 46.0 | 33.6 | 20.7 |
| *Number of hours worked* |  |  |  |  |
| 1-30 | 20.6 | 34.8 | 17.7 | 20.8 |
| 31-40 | 19.7 | 6.4 | 18.2 | 20.6 |
| 41-50 | 43.6 | 32.1 | 45.7 | 43.5 |
| 51 and more | 15.1 | 26.7 | 18.2 | 13.8 |
| Unknown | 1.1 | 0.0 | 0.2 | 1.3 |

Source. Prepared by the author with data from Household Survey on Employment and Unemployment, July 1982.

to 31.7 per cent for non-destitute poor and non-poor households respectively. Another important conclusion is the high incidence of poverty among wage earners, which while more striking in small firms, is also noteworthy in large firms.

### 3. Labour market insertion of secondary workers

Table 3.9 shows the distribution of non-household heads in different labour market sectors; note that all households classified as destitute have their employed secondary members working in the private sector (and this is also true of most non-destitute poor households). With respect to the sector of economic activity, secondary members of destitute households are mostly employed in services and commerce. The incidence of destitution is higher in households active in commerce, services and agriculture, while non-destitute poverty is higher in households whose members work in industry or construction. The high incidence of non-destitute poverty in industry may be in part due to the presence of trade unions, which in defending employment conditions and salaries, succeed in raising incomes at least above the level of destitution for the households concerned.

The incidence of poverty by occupational category of secondary household workers is similar to that for household heads. The incidence of destitution is higher among households whose members are service workers. The incidence of non-destitute poverty is higher in those households whose members are manual and service sector workers. The formal-informal sector insertion of non-household heads is very similar to that of household heads. The main difference is that most secondary workers from destitute and poor households engaged in the informal sector are employees in small firms, while household heads employed in the informal sector are mainly independent workers. Another difference between heads and non-heads is the number of working hours: 20.6 per cent of secondary household members work less than 30 hours per week, compared with only 9.8 per cent of household heads. However, among the destitute almost 45 per cent of household heads and 35 per cent of secondary household members work less than 30 hours. Therefore, the length of the working week is a discriminating factor among households. Even though this factor affects both heads and non-heads, it discriminates better among heads than among secondary household workers. This presumably reflects the existence of obstacles restricting access to full-time jobs which would allow the households concerned to escape poverty.

## VII. Conclusions

The main conclusions of this research are as follows. First, poverty increased in Costa Rica in 1982 as compared with both 1971 and 1979. This can to a large extent be explained by declining real wages and increasing open unemployment. However, more detailed analysis of the characteristics of poor households helps us to improve our understanding of the growth in poverty and its impact on households of different types. In particular, it was found that factors which discriminate against the poor include demographic structure and labour market characteristics of household heads and of other household members.

Household size and its composition (percentage of children) discriminate against the poor in Costa Rica. Destitute and poor households have relatively more children than non-poor households. But if per capita household income is adjusted in order to evaluate household size in terms of adult-equivalent members, the importance of this factor diminishes sharply.

Income differentials between poverty strata are — as one would expect — primarily determined by the differences in income per employed household member. This factor is the most significant in both 1971 and 1982, but is relatively more important in 1982. These differentials are the consequences of household members' characteristics (sex, education, age) as they interact with the characteristics of the jobs to which they have access.

The evidence distinguishes two groups among the poor: households subject to discrimination (e.g. those headed by women, or older people), or otherwise disadvantaged; and households headed by people without these specific disadvantages but who have access only to low-productivity jobs. In 1982 the latter group increased its share in overall poverty as a consequence of the decrease in total productivity, due in turn to restrictive economic policies.

One of the more interesting conclusions relates to the labour market insertion of household members when households are classified according to poverty strata. A hypothesis raised was that the informal sector played an important role in labour market adjustment to the economic crisis in Costa Rica. That is, not only did real wages fall and unemployment increase, but also relatively more household members were employed in the informal sector. This hypothesis was supported by the results obtained above. The importance of this finding is reinforced by a second result: that the distribution of household members across formal and informal segments of the labour market is an important factor which discriminates among poverty strata. The economic crisis therefore led to increasing poverty not only through its direct effect on wages and employment, but also through a variety of indirect labour market mechanisms.

### Notes

[1] PREALC, Santiago de Chile. The author is grateful for comments by Gerry Rodgers, Emilio Klein, Luis Riveros and Pilar Romaguera, and in particular to Andras Uthoff, whose suggestions throughout were very helpful.

[2] Though some of the change clearly results from definitional differences.

### References

Altimir, O., 1978: *La dimensión de la pobreza en América Latina* (Santiago, CEPAL).
———— and Piñera, S., 1977: *Análisis de la descomposición de las desigualdades de los ingresos primarios en países de América Latina* (Santiago, CEPAL).
Anker, R.; Buvinic, M.; Youssef, N., 1982: *Women's roles and population trends in the Third World* (London, Croom Helm).
Ashenfelter, O.; Heckman, J., 1974: "The estimation of income and substitution effects in a model of family labor supply", in *Econometrica*, Jan.
Becker, G., 1981: *A treatise on the family* (Cambridge, Massachusetts, Harvard University Press).

ECLA: *Estudio económico de América Latina* (various issues) (Santiago).

———, 1985: *La pobreza en Américana Latina: Dimensiones y políticas*, (Santiago).

Fishlow, A., 1972: "Brazilian size distribution of income", in *American Economic Review*, No. 62.

Killingsworth, M. R., 1974: "Determinants of the supply of labor time", in *Econometrica*, Jan.

Musgrove, P., 1980: "Household size and composition, employment, and poverty in urban Latin America", in *Economic Development and Cultural Change*, Jan.

Pollack, M. and Uthoff, A., 1984: "Costa Rica: Evolución macroeconómica, 1976-1983", in *Monografiá sobre Empleo*, No. 50 (Santiago, PREALC/ECIEL).

Pollack, M., 1985: "Household behaviour and economic crisis. Costa Rica 1979-1982", in *Documento de Trabajo*, No. 270 (Santiago, PREALC).

Piñera, S., 1979: *Medición, análisis y descripción de la pobreza en Costa Rica* (Santiago, CEPAL).

PREALC, 1978: *Sector informal: Funcionamento y políticas* (Santiago).

———, 1982: *Planificación del empleo* (Santiago).

———, 1983: *Empleo y salarios* (Santiago).

Rodgers, G., 1984: *Poverty and population: Approaches and evidence* (Geneva, ILO).

———, 1985: *Some issues in labour market research*, World Employment Programme research working paper (Geneva, ILO).

Rodgers, G. et. al., 1980: *Comparative analysis of women's labour force participation with the world fertility survey: Some preliminary views* (Geneva, ILO; mimeographed).

Rodgers, G.; Standing, G. (eds.), 1981: *Child work, poverty and underdevelopment: Issues for research in low-income countries* (Geneva, ILO).

Rodríguez, J., 1981: "La pobreza en América Latina: Un examen de conceptos y datos", in *Revista de la CEPAL* (Santiago), Apr.

Rowntree, S., 1901: *Poverty: A study of town life* (London, Macmillan).

Sen, A., 1976: "Poverty: An optimal approach to measurement", in *Econometrica*, No. 44.

———, 1978: *Three notes on the concept of poverty*, World Employment Programme research working paper (Geneva, ILO).

———, 1981: *Poverty and famines. An essay on entitlement and deprivation* (Oxford, Clarendon Press).

Standing, G.; Sheehan, G., 1978: *Labour force participation in low income countries* (Geneva, ILO).

# Chapter 4

# Poverty and labour market access in Guatemala City

RENÉ ARTURO
ORELLANA G.
RICARDO AVILA AVILA [1]

## I. Introduction

The experience of many countries in the Third World, and especially in Central America, has shown that the efforts and resources devoted to increasing production — including in those sectors which specifically produce goods and services to meet the basic needs of the least-protected groups — have not led to the elimination of poverty. This remains one of the most important problems facing these countries, and all the more acute because of the deterioration in the international economic environment. For experience has shown that economic growth alone does not guarantee a higher level of employment nor a better distribution of income, and that the origins of poverty lie in the extensive underutilisation of the labour force. In many countries such underutilisation originates in rural areas, and the problem is then transferred to urban areas through internal migration.

Underemployment and poverty are closely related, for lack of satisfaction of basic needs primarily affects those groups which have only a precarious foothold in the productive system; this in turn is linked to problems of structural heterogeneity in the economy and of labour market segmentation. GDP growth has not been sufficient to generate the number of new jobs required, nor to raise the income levels of the neediest groups, because growth has been concentrated in modern sectors of the economy, and in the large urban centres, especially capital cities where labour markets are more dynamic. An unequal distribution of technical progress between modern and traditional sectors has led to highly differentiated productivity growth, leaving the traditional sector labour force in a permanent situation of underemployment, low productivity and poverty. This process shows up in the segmentation of the labour market, with on one side the modern sectors, responsible for a high proportion of total production but a low percentage of total employment; and on the other, activities of a traditional type, employing the majority of the labour force, but with only a limited contribution to total production. This leads to situations in which workers with equal abilities obtain different incomes, depending on the production stratum of the enterprises in which they work.

According to estimates of the Instituto Nacional de Estadística, the population of Guatemala will be between 8.8 and 9.7 million in 1990. It was estimated that 70.9 per cent of households fell below the poverty line in 1980.[2] Extrapolated to 1990, this would imply between 6.2 and 6.8 million poor people. We can also calculate that in Guatemala City, with 63.5 per cent of the population below the poverty line, there will be between 762,000 and 889,000 people living in poverty. Such figures demonstrate eloquently the scale of a phenomenon which contravenes one of the most basic human rights.

"Poverty" is a situational syndrome, within which are associated subconsumption, undernutrition, precarious living conditions, low levels of education, an unstable insertion in the productive system, low levels of participation in institutions for social integration, and perhaps a scale of values different from the rest of society. This chapter focuses on the labour market and employment aspect of poverty. The aim is to assess the labour market insertion and employment characteristics of the poor, and by contrasting this with the situation of non-poor groups to highlight ways in which labour market variables are involved in the generation of poverty. This in turn makes it possible to examine how different types of intervention in the labour market might contribute to the reduction of poverty.

## II. The social formation

Guatemalan society is predominantly capitalist, in that the bulk of production is based on the use of wage labour. The economy is characterised by a social division which associates, at one extreme, the owners of the means of production and distribution, and at the other, a population lacking machines, tools or land. Thus in most parts of the production process, direct producers do not live from what they can produce from their land or capital goods, but rather from the sale of their labour in exchange for a wage. Another important aspect is that it has a dependent, underdeveloped social formation, which requires foreign investment and imported technology in order to develop.

The process of impoverishment observed among the rural masses has not been compensated by a sustained growth of living standards among the urban working class, in spite of economic growth. Rural misery has been accompanied by growth in unemployment, in underemployment and in the number of people obliged to undertake marginal activities in order to survive. The latter group has been particularly affected by the inflationary process of recent years.

The economy is also characterised by duality. It has a modern capitalist sector, with labour-saving production techniques. But this modern industrial sector has methods of recruitment which make job access difficult, and its penetration in the economy as a whole is slow. As a result the economy remains backward, in that large-scale capitalist enterprises co-exist with low-income, small-scale, informal production, often based on self-employment and using simple production techniques. Approaching two-thirds of national income depends on a limited number of agricultural export products, rendering the economy fragile. Artisans and peasants still live to a considerable extent from subsistence production. Most resources which can be reinvested in order to contribute to economic growth come from the larger enterprises, agrarian as well as industrial.

In summary, the influence of foreign capital and technology has created a modern, export-oriented capitalist sector, with a concentration of highly skilled labour in labour-saving production processes, but at the same time it has created within the economy an urban informal sector based on labour with little or no formal qualification, using rudimentary technology.

## III. Economic trends

### 1. Growth and poverty, 1960-80

The economy underwent a period of sustained growth from 1960 to 1980, although subject to conjunctural fluctuations. According to an ECLA study (ECLA, 1983), GNP grew from Q.1,285 million in 1960 to Q.2,196 million in 1970, and to Q.3,775 million in 1980, all in constant Quetzales of 1970, with an average annual growth rate of 5.5 per cent. GDP per capita grew by 2.4 per cent per year in the same period, from Q.324 to Q.521. In this period the economy diversified, urbanisation grew significantly, and society became both more modern and more stratified and complex. This process was accompanied by a considerable development of Guatemala's infrastructure. The main sources of this dynamism were the traditional export sector, incipient industrialisation stimulated by the creation of the Central American Common Market, and the expansion of both public and private investment. However, two decades of sustained growth were insufficient to reduce the levels of labour underutilisation and poverty, and the surplus generated by economic growth was not distributed equitably, rather profiting a small group whose incomes rose significantly. Thus despite economic dynamism, development has been deficient in many respects, and the gains from economic growth have been distributed unequally across population strata and economic segments. From 1970 to 1980 this trend can be clearly seen in the income distribution figures in table 4.1. The real incomes of the poorest groups were declining steadily, while those of the richest rose appreciably. One consequence has been that absolute poverty levels in Guatemala have not declined as a result of growth, and may in fact have increased. According to ECLA estimates of poverty, which are similar in order of magnitude to those reported in section I, 63 per cent of the population fell below the poverty line, a figure which is exceeded in Central America only by El Salvador with 70 per cent and Honduras with 68 per cent (ECLA, 1983).

Poverty is a multi-dimensional phenomenon, particularly characterised by food deficiencies, which reduce the capacity to make physical or intellectual efforts, by the type of participation in economic activity and by high rates of mortality (especially of infants) and morbidity. More than half the population has an unsatisfactory nutritional intake, and a substantial fraction has critically

*Table 4.1.    Trends in the distribution of urban household income, 1970-80 (Quetzales of 1980)*

| Income stratum | 1970 | 1980 | Annual change (%) |
|---|---|---|---|
| Total | 3 752 | 4 426 | +1.7 |
| 20 per cent poorest | 1 088 | 996 | −0.9 |
| 30 per cent under the median | 2 014 | 1 962 | −0.3 |
| 30 per cent over the median | 3 702 | 3 865 | +0.4 |
| 20 per cent richest | 9 098 | 12 393 | +3.1 |
| 10 per cent richest | 12 081 | 17 970 [1] | +4.0 |

[1] 12,970 in the original source; authors' correction.
Source. ECLA, 1983, table 9, p. 19.

low food intake, which in turn affects morbidity and mortality. In general, health conditions are precarious, but they have improved to some degree. Life expectancy at birth rose from 48.2 years in 1960 to 57.8 in 1980, while infant mortality fell from 92 to 69 per thousand live births in the same period. Public expenditure on health remained at about 1 per cent of GDP, and while the number of doctors per inhabitant rose, the number of hospital beds fell. Illiteracy fell from 61.1 per cent in 1960 to 45.6 per cent in 1980, and public expenditure on education rose slightly. But according to SEGEPLAN, only 49 per cent of children of primary school age actually attend school. Overall, 76 per cent of children are born in poor households, and 43 per cent in destitute households (for the definition of "poor" and "destitute" see section V).

## 2. The current situation

Like other Central American countries, since the late 1970s Guatemala has been passing through a deep economic and social crisis. It has experienced its worst ever economic depression, and the severest political convulsions of the past 50 years. The result has been a climate of instability and confusion. From 1977-80 onwards there was a progressive deceleration of economic growth, finally reaching negative values. The level of GDP in 1983 was comparable with that of 1979, or − in per capita terms − 1975. This situation derived from a set of economic, social and political factors, both internal and external, which distorted economic patterns and led to a fall in economic activity. The effects of the crisis fell initially on wage labour, gradually spreading to middle layers of the population, who are also starting to show signs of impoverishment. There have been arbitrary increases in the prices of goods and basic services, affecting worst those with the least resources, and resulting in a deterioration in living standards. This suggests that the socio-economic model of the 1960s and 1970s is now spent, for it has failed to meet national social objectives and even less to promote development, resulting in rapid inflation, speculation, high levels of unemployment, undernutrition, illiteracy, foreign indebtedness and fiscal deficit.

*Table 4.2. Average minimum wage, urban areas in selected years (in Quetzales)*

| Year | Nominal wage | Index of nominal wage | Real wage | Index of real wage |
|------|------|------|------|------|
| 1972 | 1.57 | 100.0 | 1.57 | 100.0 |
| 1975 | 1.86 | 118.8 | 1.24 | 78.9 |
| 1980 | 3.51 | 223.5 | 1.43 | 91.0 |
| 1985 [1] | 3.51 | 223.5 | 1.03 | 65.6 |

[1] January to March.

Source. Author's calculations with information from the Ministerio de Trabajo y Previsión Social; price data from the Instituto de Investigaciones Económicas y Sociales, Universidad de San Carlos.

# IV. The economically active population, employment and wages

The non-satisfaction of basic needs and precarious insertion in the labour market are closely related. There are good reasons to believe that those whose consumption in insufficient are to a large extent those who face occupational problems such as open or disguised unemployment or underemployment. This in turn interacts with the heterogeneous nature of growth in Guatemala, concentrated in modern sectors with little capacity for labour absorption. The overall trend has been for the active population to decline as a proportion of those aged 10 and over, from 46.5 per cent in 1964 to 41.0 per cent in 1981. Nevertheless, the labour force grew by 2.9 per cent per year in this period, generating considerable pressure on the labour market. Male labour force participation, 71.1 per cent in 1981, is much higher than that of women, 11.8 per cent, though no doubt part of the difference reflects undercounting of women's work. According to the 1981 census, about 62 per cent of male workers were engaged in agricultural occupations in Guatemala as a whole, compared with 8 per cent of women. Women were concentrated in service occupations (29 per cent), reflecting the importance of domestic service.

According to the ECLA study cited above (ECLA, 1983), the open unemployment rate in 1980 overall was 3.7 per cent; but if various categories of "discouraged" workers are included, i.e. those who have withdrawn from the labour force because of adverse labour market conditions, the rate rises to almost 10 per cent. If underemployment in terms of hours worked is added, a total unemployment nearer to 20 per cent is obtained, which gives an idea of the intensity of the problem of inadequate labour absorption, and its probable consequences for poverty. We discuss this in more detail below (table 4.7).

A major link between the labour market and the incidence of poverty concerns the minimum wage (table 4.2 indicates its evolution). Although the nominal minimum wage more than doubled from 1972 to 1985, the purchasing power of the minimum wage declined by 34.4 per cent. Additional evidence on the disadvantaged situation of the economically active population can be provided by comparing the nominal minimum wage and the estimated cost of

*Table 4.3.   Changes in minimum wages and of the cost of basic consumption baskets, 1972-85 (per day, current Quetzales)*

| Year | Guatemala City | | | Other urban areas | | | Rural areas | | |
|------|----------------|--|--|-------------------|--|--|-------------|--|--|
|      | Minimum wage | Food basket | Goods and services basket | Minimum wage | Food basket | Goods and services basket | Minimum wage | Food basket | Goods and services basket |
| 1972 | 1.57 | 2.54 | 6.08 | 1.57 | 2.00 | 3.62 | 0.95 | 1.48 | 2.30 |
| 1975 | 1.86 | 3.81 | 9.12 | 1.86 | 3.00 | 5.43 | 1.08 | 2.22 | 3.46 |
| 1980 | 3.51 | 6.25 | 14.95 | 3.51 | 4.90 | 8.90 | 2.35 | 3.64 | 5.67 |
| 1985 [1] | 3.51 | 8.66 | 20.72 | 3.51 | 6.79 | 12.33 | 2.35 | 5.04 | 7.85 |

[1] January-March.

Source. Author's calculations with information from SEGEPLAN and the Ministerio de Trabajo y Prevision Social.

a "minimum food basket" and a "basket of basic goods and services" for Guatemala City, other urban areas and rural areas (table 4.3).[3] In 1985 in all areas of the country the average minimum wage was insufficient to purchase the food basket, in fact sufficient for only around half of it, let alone the full basket of goods and services (including clothing, housing, transport, medicine, education and other elements). A family with two workers obtaining the minimum wage could barely purchase the food basket. This situation has deteriorated over time. Whereas in 1972 the minimum wage in the capital was 38 per cent less than the cost of the food basket and 74 per cent less than the goods and services basket, by 1985 these gaps had widened to almost 60 per cent and to 83 per cent respectively. The trend was similar in other parts of Guatemala.

Regular statistics at the national level on occupations and wages are not available, but the Social Security Institute keeps information on the number of affiliated workers in private enterprises and their monthly wages, covering about 25 per cent of workers and 50 per cent of wage workers. In the period 1979-85 these data suggest that overall employment in the private sector fell by 23 per cent, from 376,000 to 286,000. Nominal wages rose by 51 per cent, but real wages remained practically constant. The result was a decline in the aggregate wage bill of 25 per cent.

# V. Poverty and incomes in Guatemala City

In table 4.4 destitution is identified with the incapacity to purchase even the basic food basket discussed above, and poverty with the inability to purchase the basket of basic goods and services. It can be seen that destitution is relatively less frequent in the capital, and a larger proportion of the population overall falls in the non-poor category, but poverty above the level

*Table 4.4. Incidence of poverty, by area and poverty stratum (number of persons in thousands)*

| Area | Total | | Below poverty line | | | | | | Non-poor | |
|------|-------|-----|--------|------|----------|------|------|------|---------|------|
| | No. | % | Total | | Destitute | | Poor | | No. | % |
| | | | No. | % | No. | % | No. | % | | |
| Total | 6 382 | 100 | 4 841 | 70.9 | 2 651 | 38.8 | 2 190 | 32.1 | 1 991 | 29.1 |
| Guatemala City | 961 | 100 | 610 | 63.5 | 213 | 22.2 | 397 | 41.3 | 350 | 36.5 |
| Other urban | 1 387 | 100 | 935 | 67.4 | 484 | 34.9 | 451 | 32.5 | 453 | 32.6 |
| Rural | 4 484 | 100 | 3 296 | 73.5 | 1 954 | 43.6 | 1 342 | 29.9 | 1 188 | 26.5 |

Source. SEGEPLAN, 1983.

*Table 4.5. Functional distribution of income in Guatemala City by socio-economic stratum, 1980 (percentages)*

| Source of income | Total | Socio-economic stratum | | | |
|------------------|-------|-------------------|---------------------|------------------|----------------|
| | | Extreme poverty | Non-extreme poverty | Medium income | High income |
| Total | 100 | 100 | 100 | 100 | 100 |
| Own labour | 75.4 | 83.3 | 80.0 | 75.8 | 74.4 |
| Rent, interest, profits | 16.8 | 8.0 | 12.1 | 14.8 | 18.7 |
| Pensions, etc. | 3.1 | 5.3 | 3.8 | 5.1 | 2.0 |
| Transfers and other | 4.7 | 3.4 | 4.1 | 4.3 | 4.9 |

Source. ECLA, 1982.

of destitution is more frequent in the capital than elsewhere. Family size is larger in the poorest families — 5.8 members among the destitute, 5.0 among the other poor, and 3.9 among the non-poor. As a result the number of poor persons exceeds that of poor households. Most of the difference is in the number of children — 3.9 in destitute families, 3 in other poor families and 1.9 among the non-poor. Among factors which differentiate households in the different poverty strata, one is the age of the head — on average 40 in destitute households in Guatemala City, 42 in poor households, but nearly 47 in non-poor households; among adults illiteracy affects 32 per cent of the destitute, 17 per cent of the poor, and 7 per cent of the non-poor.

Although mean incomes are higher in the capital than other urban areas — Q.7,230 in 1980 against Q.3,286 — the income distribution is much more unequal — a Gini coefficient of .51 against .37. There is some evidence that inequality is increasing, in that a 1969 survey (Encuesta del Instituto de Investigaciones Económicas y Sociales, Universidad de San Carlos) found the bottom 50 per cent of households received 20 per cent of income, compared with 16.5 per cent in 1980. Overall, the 56.3 per cent of poor families in Guatemala

City obtain 22.6 per cent of income, while the 17.4 per cent of destitute families obtain just 3.7 per cent.

Table 4.5 gives an idea of the functional distribution of income in different poverty strata. The poverty categories here come from an ECLA study, and do not correspond exactly to those used above. In particular, only about 30 per cent of the population is classified as poor in this study. It can be seen that while income from own labour dominates in all groups, there is a distinct declining trend as one moves from poor to rich. This suggests in particular that income opportunities from self-employment are relatively limited for the poor.

# VI. Poverty and employment in Guatemala City

Poverty and the lack of satisfaction of basic needs are linked to the structural heterogeneity of the productive system and to labour market segmentation. The problem is not limited to open unemployment, but affects a substantial fraction of the employed, as well as part of the inactive population. Underutilisation of labour tends to be greatest in rural areas, but is also important in informal types of urban activity, which often provide the point of entry for recent migrants to urban areas. To analyse these structures we need to look both at household characteristics — size, number of working members — and occupational characteristics of the head; the economic situation of the household depends to a great extent on the possibility for the head to gain entry to the modern sector.

Labour force participation rates are fairly low among the poor; 44.1 per cent for the destitute compared with 47.8 for other poor households, according to the 1980-81 household survey on income and expenditure. Among those in the labour force, 8.5 per cent were not at work, 6.8 per cent unemployed on the conventional definition (actively looking for work) and 1.7 per cent otherwise not working. Table 4.6 gives a more detailed breakdown for the same period

Table 4.6. *Distribution of the population aged 10 and more in Guatemala City by labour force situation and poverty stratum, 1980 (percentages)*

| Labour force group | Total | Extreme poverty | Non-extreme poverty | Medium income | High income |
|---|---|---|---|---|---|
| Total | 100 | 100 | 100 | 100 | 100 |
| Labour force | 47.5 | 44.4 | 47.9 | 48.3 | 46.8 |
| At work | 45.5 | 42.2 | 46.5 | 46.0 | 45.5 |
| Unemployed | 2.0 | 2.2 | 1.4 | 2.3 | 1.3 |
| Inactive | 52.5 | 55.6 | 52.1 | 51.7 | 53.2 |
| Unemployment rate | 3.7 | 5.0 | 2.9 | 4.7 | 1.9 |
| Total participation rate [1] | 34.5 | 25.8 | 30.1 | 40.1 | 31.3 |

[1] As a percentage of total population.
Source. ECLA, 1982.

from the ECLA study (i.e using the poverty categories of table 4.5, which are not directly comparable with the "destitute"-"other poor" breakdown we have been using).

The proportion of those without a job who are looking for work, and are thus classified as unemployed, depends on the perceptions they have of the possibility to find work. As a result, in so far as the lack of employment opportunities is widespread and persistent, a part of the population will abandon the search for work and will thus cease to be classified as economically active. This no doubt partly explains the pattern in table 4.6, where the inactivity rate of adults is highest for the destitute, and unemployment for this group, although relatively high, is not exceptionally so. The inverted U-shaped pattern for labour force participation may well reflect the importance of discouraged workers in the poorest groups, and labour force withdrawal as an income effect among the richest.

Table 4.7 breaks down the pattern in more detail, using the same poverty breakdown as table 4.6. The level of unemployment is around 10 per cent in the three poorer groups, after adjusting for discouraged workers,[4] and there is not much variation by poverty stratum. However, labour force participation rates are low among the poor. In addition, including an estimated adjustment for underemployment, the difference between the two poorest groups and the others is clearer, with around 40 per cent either unemployed or underemployed in these groups, implying about 20 per cent overall unemployment after adjusting for the shorter hours worked by the underemployed. This compares with 10 per cent in the middle-income and 7.7 per cent in the high-income groups. Since poor families tend to have low labour force participation rates, high real unemployment rates and probably also high rates of unpaid or low-paid work, the problem of poverty can be explained in part by the difficulty of access to paid work, suggesting that economic policy to reduce poverty should concentrate on the creation of remunerated employment.

Three further aspects of work in poor households are captured in table 4.8: the sector of activity, the work status and the level of education. The concentration of the destitute in the tertiary sector comes out clearly, although over a third of workers in this group are also found in secondary activities. As for distribution by work status, the largest single category for the poor is "never worked", demonstrating the difficulty of initial job access among the poor (47 per cent of people in this category came from the poor group, compared with 28 per cent poor among workers as a whole). Unpaid family work is also important for the poor, but less so for the poorest where significant family enterprises are less frequent, limiting the possibilities for this type of work. As for education, the observed pattern is unsurprising, in that 93 per cent of the poorest workers had received no formal schooling, compared with 83 per cent of the "other poor" and 47 per cent of the non-poor.

Despite the high incidence of poverty, the capital continues to attract large numbers of rural migrants. Both push and pull factors are involved. Among the former are the unequal distribution of land and consequent

*Table 4.7.    Unemployment and underemployment in Guatemala City by poverty stratum, 1980
(thousands of persons and percentages)*

| Variable | Total | Extreme poverty | Non-extreme poverty | Medium income | High income |
|---|---|---|---|---|---|
| Total population | 1 001 | 66 | 240 | 451 | 244 |
| *Labour force* | | | | | |
| Not adjusted | 346 | 17 | 72 | 181 | 76 |
| Adjusted [1] | 368 | 18 | 78 | 190 | 82 |
| *Participation rate [2]* | | | | | |
| Not adjusted (%) | 34.5 | 25.8 | 30.1 | 40.1 | 31.3 |
| Adjusted (%) | 36.7 | 27.4 | 32.7 | 42.0 | 34.0 |
| *Working population* | | | | | |
| At work [3] | 333 | 16 | 70 | 172 | 75 |
| Open unemployment [4] | 13 | 1 | 2 | 9 | 1 |
| Open unemployment, including discouraged workers | 35 | 2 | 8 | 18 | 7 |
| Visible underemployment [5] | 28 | 5 | 23 | 0 | 0 |
| *Unemployment rates (%)* | | | | | |
| Open | 3.7 | 5.0 | 2.9 | 4.7 | 1.9 |
| Open, including discouraged workers | 9.2 | 10.6 | 10.8 | 10.0 | 7.7 |
| Visibly underemployed total | 7.6 | 29.4 | 29.5 | 0 | 0 |
| Un- and under-employment | 16.8 | 39.9 | 40.3 | 10.0 | 7.7 |
| Equivalent visible underemployment [6] | 2.5 | 10.0 | 8.8 | 0 | 0 |
| Total equivalent unemployment [7] | 11.7 | 20.6 | 19.6 | 10.0 | 7.7 |

[1] Adjusted for discouraged workers.    [2] As a percentage of the total population.    [3] With work which is remunerated in cash or in kind.    [4] Actively looking for work.    [5] Persons working less than a normal working day.    [6] Number of equivalent full-time jobs required to compensate for short hours worked by those "visibly underemployed".    [7] Total unemployment plus underemployment adjusted for hours worked.
Source. See table 4.6.

incapacity to achieve above-subsistence incomes, and low rural wages. At the same time, the capital appears to rural families, and especially youths, as the principal centre of economic and social opportunity, and migration is facilitated by improved transport and communications between the city and the countryside. But the absorption of rural migrants has proved difficult because of social and cultural barriers, and as a result the majority of migrants are segregated from the "modern" inhabitants. Migration is then reflected in the growth of marginal *barrios*, usually situated on the periphery of the city. Economic pull factors have been much weaker; migration is not a response to genuine expansion in urban labour demand, created by industrial expansion, but more the result of unemployment and rural economic pressures.

Flows of migrants, ill-prepared both culturally and occupationally, have placed growing demands not only on the narrow labour market, but also on the physical and social infrastructure of the city. Existing deficiencies in

***Table 4.8.*** *Characteristics of the economically active population in Guatemala City, by poverty stratum*

| Variable | Total | All poor | Extreme poverty | Non-extreme poverty | Non-poor |
|---|---|---|---|---|---|
| *Economic sector* (Percentage distribution within poverty groups) | | | | | |
| Primary | 2.3 | 2.1 | 1.9 | 2.2 | 2.4 |
| Secondary | 44.7 | 44.8 | 37.6 | 46.7 | 44.5 |
| Tertiary | 53.0 | 53.1 | 60.5 | 51.1 | 53.1 |
| Total | 100.0 | 100.0 | 100.0 | 100.0 | 100.0 |
| *Work status* (Percentage distribution across poverty groups) | | | | | |
| Employers | 100.0 | 17.2 | 0.1 | 17.1 | 82.8 |
| Own-account workers | 100.0 | 31.6 | 7.6 | 24.0 | 68.4 |
| Public employees | 100.0 | 14.0 | 2.6 | 11.4 | 86.0 |
| Private employees | 100.0 | 30.9 | 6.0 | 24.9 | 69.1 |
| Unpaid family workers | 100.0 | 35.2 | 2.6 | 32.6 | 64.8 |
| Never worked | 100.0 | 47.2 | 8.0 | 39.2 | 52.8 |
| Unknown | 100.0 | 64.3 | 48.9 | 15.4 | 35.7 |
| *Education level* (Percentage distribution within poverty groups) | | | | | |
| Less than primary | 57.4 | 84.9 | 92.8 | 82.9 | 46.6 |
| Primary | 11.6 | 7.3 | 3.8 | 8.2 | 13.3 |
| Secondary | 21.0 | 7.0 | 3.3 | 8.0 | 26.5 |
| Tertiary | 10.0 | 0.8 | 0.1 | 0.9 | 13.6 |

Source. Special tabulation, Encuesta de Hogares sobre Ingresos y Gastos, Dirección General de Estadística, 1980-81.

public services have thus been aggravated; at the same time, the rapid migration of an unskilled labour force has been an additional factor in labour unrest, and has added to the downward pressure on wages.

# VII. Formal and informal sectors

The PREALC approach to disaggregation of labour markets and production distinguishes four main economic sectors: the modern urban, the informal urban, the modern rural and the traditional rural. In Guatemala the modern urban sector produces a range of industrial products and public services, concentrating the activities of a highly qualified or experienced labour force in medium-to-high income categories, and frequently using advanced technology. There is a large share of profits in value added, and a high capital-output ratio. Production is mainly large or medium scale, and it dominates the other sectors.

*Table 4.9.    Distribution and level of utilisation of the urban labour force in formal and informal
sectors, 1980 (thousands of persons and percentages)*

| Level of utilisation | Total urban | | Modern sector | | Informal sector | |
|---|---|---|---|---|---|---|
| | No. | % | No. | % | No. | % |
| Total labour force | 1 012.7 | 100.0 | 498.6 | 100.0 | 514.1 | 100.0 |
| Employed | 822.9 | 81.2 | 486.6 | 97.5 | 336.3 | 65.4 |
| Unemployed [1] | 189.8 | 18.8 | 12.0 | 2.5 | 177.8 | 34.6 |

[1] The definition of unemployment used in this study is unknown, but it differs from that used in tables 4.6 and 4.7. It appears to
include a substantial adjustment for underemployment.
Source. SEGEPLAN, 1980.

   The informal sector, on the other hand, has low levels of technology
and productivity, produces little surplus and has a subsistence orientation; the
number employed in this sector depends on the number of workers not absorbed
by the modern sector, and on the opportunities that they have to produce or
sell something which generates some income. In this sector we find those with
little education, own-account workers, occasional and home workers and recent
migrants from rural areas. The majority of those concerned is of indigenous
origin. Low education levels are partly explained by the need for family
members to join the labour force at an early age to supplement family income,
for incomes are frequently less than the legal minimum wage. Labour supply
to this sector tends to grow more rapidly than the labour requirements of
production, particularly because of migration, which in turn has its origins in
the inadequate labour absorption of rural modern and traditional sectors. These
characteristics of the informal sector make for a high incidence of poverty, and
informal sector activities thus tend to be concentrated in marginal areas of the
city, and to be associated with poor housing and lack of basic services.
   The sector is also characterised by economic instability, which in turn
reinforces the tendency for incomes to be low, and promotes high levels of
unemployment and underemployment. One result is a relationship of dependency vis-à-vis the modern sector. This dependency shows up in links of various
sorts — many forms of operation, maintenance or repair are provided by the
informal sector, and domestic service is particularly widespread, in view of its
low cost. A study by SEGEPLAN (1980) gives an idea of the scale of these
phenomena in urban areas overall (data for Guatemala City alone were not
available). According to this study (table 4.9), in 1980 the majority of the
economically active population was engaged in the informal sector, slightly
more than in the modern sector. Of those who were fully employed, however,
59 per cent were in the modern sector, while among the unemployed and
underemployed 94 per cent were classified as belonging to the informal sector.[5]
Correspondingly, less than 3 per cent of the modern sector workforce was
unemployed, compared with 35 per cent of the informal sector workforce. The
sectoral distribution of informal sector workers is quite narrow, consisting
essentially of artisans, personal services and commerce.

*Table 4.10. Growth of the urban labour force by sector, 1950-80 (percentages)*

| Period | Sector | | | |
|---|---|---|---|---|
| | Total | Modern | Informal | Domestic service |
| 1950-60 | 3.4 | 4.0 | 3.6 | 1.2 |
| 1960-70 | 3.4 | 4.3 | 2.4 | 1.9 |
| 1970-80 | 3.3 | 3.2 | 4.0 | 1.7 |

Source. PREALC, 1986, p. 72.

Between 1950 and 1980 the overall urban labour force grew at about 3.4 per cent per year according to PREALC, and on average the modern sector grew faster than the informal. In the 1970s, however, this trend was reversed, as table 4.10 shows. The rate of growth of the informal sector, which was 1.9 points behind that of the modern sector in the 1960s, was 0.8 percentage points ahead of it in the 1970s despite a slight decline in the overall growth of the labour force. Since the crisis was concentrated in the late 1970s, the actual impact on informal sector growth was no doubt even larger. Thus, as in other countries of the region, the informal sector continues to play an important role in the absorption of labour supply in Guatemala, especially labour with low levels of education and qualification, but it does so in conditions of low productivity and poverty.

# VIII. Qualitative aspects of the labour market insertion of the poor

There have been no general statistical studies providing an overall picture of the behaviour and reactions of poor families, or of the socio-economic conditions found in marginal areas of the capital. It is thus necessary to use qualitative data from case studies, a risky procedure; in the past, well-intentioned policy measures based on a limited number of case studies have not had the expected results, and have sometimes even been harmful.

However, empirical material of this type permits us to identify certain characteristics of poor families living in marginal areas of the city, including the existence of free conjugal unions, illegitimate children, disintegrating households, absent parents, a constant fight for survival, alcoholism, low educational levels, insufficient medical care, poor health conditions, malnutrition, hunger, economic shortages, low life expectancy, a young population, unemployment, underemployment and low wages. Poverty implies not only shortages of material goods, but also inadequacies at the level of human dignity, of social and political participation, of work stability. Problems are frequently resolved by violence. Inadequate housing leads to a lack of privacy and to early sexual initiation of adolescents. Life at the subsistence level implies a constant struggle, the pawning of personal goods to obtain cash, the use of second-hand clothes and household effects, and uncertainty about the future.

Those who live in poverty belong to what Oscar Lewis called the "culture of poverty", based on the idea that misery is not just a state of economic deprivation, of disorganisation, or simply the absence of something, but rather that it has its own structure, raison d'être, and defence mechanisms without which continued existence would be virtually impossible. It is a persistent way of life, which is transmitted from one generation to another. The social organisation of marginal areas cannot be separated from the overall social context; the economic and social factors which were responsible for the formation of these areas also affect the ways in which their inhabitants live, the daily concerns of the households concerned and the social organisations which develop around them. Trade unions, co-operatives or "improvement committees" meet with failures and frustrations, in part because of the instability of the work of their members, who have to devote themselves to obtaining a daily subsistence by any of the few opportunities offered to them by other social groups. The organisations which develop are generally not representative of the whole, but are rather the results of efforts by small groups formed on the basis of economic needs and social class. "Improvement committees" have had relatively more success because they were formed to deal with urgent, visible problems, e.g. lack of water, of lighting, etc.

Attempts to establish co-operatives have failed because they did not eliminate intermediaries, because of the heterogeneity of their members and because of the lack of continued economic support from members, in turn the result of work instability. Trade unions, too, have faced difficulties. In the past 20 years there has been a decline in the number of new unions authorised by the Ministry of Labour and Social Security: from 1966 to 1975, 285 were authorised, compared with only 72 from 1976 to 1984; for non-agricultural workers the numbers were 85 and 32 respectively. This process was partly the result of cumbersome procedures for legalisation of new trade unions. According to Ortiz (1977), the number of trade unions declined by 11.2 per cent between 1969 and 1975. If we suppose that the number of unions is proportional to the number of firms involved,[6] then the number of firms in which workers had enough bargaining power to negotiate wage contracts was declining, which in turn led to declines in real wages and living standards. Although from 1969 to 1975 there was an annual increase of 700 in the number of trade unionists, the proportion of unionists in the working population remained both small and practically stable.

The characteristics of working families and their communities, and their ways of thinking and behaving, all affect labour supply; these have to be compared with the pattern of labour demand, to determine the points of convergence and divergence. The National Employment Service of the Ministry of Labour is the agency responsible for matching labour demand and supply. However, it mostly maintains contact with small firms, since the larger firms maintain their own registers of job applicants. Its coverage has been limited and unproductive to date. Most of the unemployed have to visit worksites personally, to follow press advertisements, and to search for vacant posts in public and private enterprises where friends and relatives work. In some cases they may have to take up own-account work, despite the risks faced by those without sufficient economic backing to enable them to survive.

## IX. Conclusion: Strategies and policies to overcome poverty

Although the economy expanded rapidly from 1960 to 1980, the surplus generated by this growth was not distributed equitably. A large proportion of the population continued to live in poverty. Given current downward trends in living standards, it is likely that the number of people living in poverty will increase unless there is a change in the style of development. Such policies as have been introduced to remedy this situation have been ineffective. Absolute poverty should not be treated as an isolated phenomenon, but as interdependent with other social processes. Thus, policies to overcome poverty should form part of the broader development strategy; and in this strategy the generation of employment should be a priority because labour is the primary source of income of the poor. The creation of new jobs and an equitable income distribution should be considered as objectives of equal priority with the growth of production.

The majority of the labour force is outside the modern sectors of the economy, and in the short and medium term it will be impossible to absorb the bulk of this labour supply in these sectors. This implies a need for the development in the medium term of other, labour intensive activities, such as agricultural production for the domestic market, the urban informal sector and small-scale formal production. Such policies are perhaps the most appropriate to attain the objective of basic-needs satisfaction, but they have to be co-ordinated with social policies aimed at improving the living conditions of workers in terms of housing, education and nutrition through subsidies or free distribution, for these in turn directly affect the capacity of poor families to obtain work and adequate incomes.

### Notes

[1] Respectively, Decano de la Facultad de Ciencias Económicas, Universidad Mariano Galvez de Guatemala, and Asesor Estadistico, Dirección General de Rentas Internas, Ministerio de Finanzas Públicas, Guatemala.

[2] These figures are derived from a poverty line calculated on the basis of nutritional recommendations from the Instituto de Nutrición para Centroamérica y Panamá (INCAP), adjusted for non-food needs. For 1980 food costs were estimated at Q.6.25 per day per family in Guatemala City (average family size 4.7), and families with incomes below this level were regarded as destitute; total minimum living costs were estimated at Q.14.95 per day, and families below this

level were regarded as poor (source: SEGEPLAN, 1983, on the basis of the Encuesta de Hogares sobre Ingresos y Gastos, Dirección General de Estadística, 1980-81). Similar calculation were made for other urban and rural areas. In 1980 Q.1.00 = US$1.00.

[3] The costs of the basket are estimated per family, so the comparison is not perfect. However in urban areas 80 per cent of households are supported by only one or two workers.

[4] The adjustments and estimations made in the ECLA study are not all clear; details were not available at the time of writing, so the figures should be regarded as order of magnitude estimates only.

[5] For the unemployed this presumably means that their last job was in the informal sector, or that they came from families whose dominant source of income was the informal sector; we do not have the precise definition.

[6] This is not necessarily true, but is a convenient simplification.

### References

ECLA, 1982: *Guatemala: la pobreza y la distribución del ingreso en los sectores urbanos* (Santiago de Chile).

———, 1983: *Satisfacción de las necesidades básicas de la población en el Istmo Centroamericano* (Santiago de Chile).

Ortiz, Rolando Eliseo, 1977: *La inflación, el costo de la vida y el sindicalismo,* Paper presented to the IV Congreso Nacional de Economistas, Contadores Públicos, Auditores y Administradores de Empresas, Guatemala City, 12-15 October 1977 (mimeographed).

PREALC, 1986: *Cambio y polarización ocupacional en Centroamérica* (San José).

SEGEPLAN, 1980: *Perspectivas y políticas de empleo en el corto plazo* (Guatemala City).

———, 1983: *La familia: Perfil de la pobreza en Guatemala* (Guatemala City).

# Chapter 5

## Labour market performance and urban poverty in Panama

DANIEL CAMAZÓN
GUILLERMO GARCÍA-HUIDOBRO
HUGO MORGADO [1]

## I. Socio-economic background

Panama's labour market in the 1980s displays one of the most modern profiles in Latin America. It has a high proportion of wage and salary earners in total employment (70 per cent); urban modern activities dominate employment (over 70 per cent); professional and technical occupations constitute a significant fraction of total employment (10 per cent); female labour force participation has grown steadily and has already reached one of the highest levels in the region (41 per cent in urban areas); and the quality of women's jobs is high by international standards, with two-thirds of female employment consisting of professional and technical occupations. The progressive nature of the labour market is a result of both a relatively modern economic structure, with a predominant urban sector, a dynamic process of capital accumulation, and a Welfare State that has pursued a number of redistributive measures, especially in housing, education and health.

Per capita income exceeded US$2,000 in 1985, the illiteracy rate registered by the Population Census of 1980 was 13 per cent, life expectancy has reached 70 years, the fertility rate has declined to 2.8 children per woman, the infant mortality rate is 20 per thousand live births, the average schooling of the non-agricultural labour force is almost nine years, there are ten medical doctors per 10,000 inhabitants, over 82 per cent of the population have good drinking water, over 89 per cent enjoy health services, and almost half the population is covered by the social security system. In 1982 the per capita daily intake of nutrients was over 3,000 calories and 69 grams of protein.

But despite all these socio-economic achievements, Panama still suffers from severe poverty. The modernisation process has as yet not reached the whole socio-economic structure. Workers with low levels of education tend to belong to and constitute the poor families. Likewise, higher proportions of underemployment and poverty are found among workers in the urban informal sector and in low-productivity activities. But as we shall see in this chapter, poverty in urban Panama presents complex relationships, since workers in the urban modern sector are by no means free from the scourge of poverty. For these reasons we believe that Panama represents a very special case among Latin

Table 5.1.   *Urban metropolitan region: Poverty incidence, 1983*

|  | Poor | Non-poor | Total |
|---|---|---|---|
| Number of families | 40 105 | 139 512 | 179 617 |
| Percentage | 22.3 | 77.7 | 100.0 |
| Number of persons | 215 204 | 560 147 | 775 351 |
| Percentage | 27.8 | 72.2 | 100.0 |
| Family income |  |  |  |
|     Total (millions of Balboas) | 117.3 | 1 400.1 | 1 517.4 |
| Percentage | 7.7 | 92.3 | 100.0 |
| Average family income | 2 924.82 | 10 035.70 | 8 447.98 |

Source. Encuesta Socio-Económica de 1983 (Ministerio de Planificación y Política Económica, 1985).

American countries, a case of poverty in the midst of wealth. This chapter aims to document this, and to examine the role of the labour market in determining the incidence of and trends in poverty.

## II. The extent and characteristics of urban poverty

Around 22 per cent of families and 28 per cent of individuals in the Urban Metropolitan Region fell below the official poverty line in 1983 (table 5.1). These families as a group received less than 8 per cent of the region's total family income, and their average family income was only a third of the national average.[2] The number of poor families was estimated using a per capita income line based on the Panamanian official basket of basic foods, which consists of 16 basic products (dairy products, eggs, meat, vegetables, fruits, cereals, etc.) whose yearly cost in 1983 was US$406.98 for the urban areas. Then the cost of this basket of basic nutrients, which is used to define the income level for critical poverty, was doubled in value − following the UN-ECLA criteria − in order to obtain an "extended basic basket" of goods and services, that in addition to nutrition covers items such as the cost of housing, clothing, transport, education, health, and so on. The per capita cost of the extended basic basket is used as the threshold to classify families as "poor" or "non-poor".

Many factors intervene in the poverty situation of families. Some are related to the demographic characteristics of the household (family size, dependency rate, etc.), others concern the personal characteristics of their members (level of education, migration status, etc.), and others refer to labour conditions, namely the insertion in the economic structure through the employment in a particular job.

The socio-demographic profile of Panama's urban poor depicts a relatively large family size, with few economically active members, and with high unemployment and dependency rates (see table 5.2). However, what is very special about Panama, compared with other Central American countries, is that

*Table 5.2.  Urban metropolitan region: Profile of poor families, 1983*

| Characteristics | Poor | | Non-poor | Total |
|---|---|---|---|---|
| | Lowest 10% [1] | All | | |
| Total population | 90 830 | 215 204 | 560 147 | 775 351 |
| Average size (number of members) | 5.03 | 5.37 | 4.02 | 4.32 |
| Population aged 15 years and above | 50 310 | 115 273 | 404 515 | 519 788 |
| Average number of members of working age | 2.79 | 2.87 | 2.90 | 2.89 |
| Economically active population (EAP) | 26 581 | 60 174 | 229 433 | 289 607 |
| Average number of EAP per family | 1.47 | 1.50 | 1.64 | 1.61 |
| Employed persons | 22 642 | 52 493 | 220 628 | 272 121 |
| Average number of employed per family | 1.25 | 1.31 | 1.59 | 1.52 |
| Unemployed persons | 3 939 | 7 681 | 8 805 | 16 486 |
| Average number of unemployed per family | 0.22 | 0.19 | 0.06 | 0.09 |
| Non-economically active population (NEAP) | 23 729 | 55 099 | 175 082 | 230 181 |
| Average number of NEAP per family | 1.31 | 1.37 | 1.25 | 1.28 |
| Labour force participation rate (%) | 52.80 | 52.2 | 56.7 | 55.7 |
| Unemployment rate (%) [2] | 14.80 | 12.8 | 3.8 | 5.7 |
| Dependency rate | 4.01 | 4.10 | 2.53 | 2.84 |

[1] As a proxy for the situation of destitutes we have taken the lowest 10 per cent of the household income distribution.  [2] The definition of the unemployment rate used by this survey is less refined, both in terms of the reference period and the number of components, than the one used in the normal Panamanian Household Surveys. Consequently, its value is not directly comparable with the 1983 Household Survey unemployment estimate.

Source. See table 5.1.

*Table 5.3.  Urban metropolitan region: Workers from poor families by segment of the labour market, 1983 [1]*

| Labour market segments | Poor workers | | All urban workers |
|---|---|---|---|
| | No. | % | |
| Total | 52 493 | 100.0 | 100.0 |
| Urban modern sector | 33 910 | 64.6 | 70.0 |
| Urban informal sector | 15 538 | 29.6 | 24.0 |
| Domestic services | 3 045 | 5.8 | 6.0 |

[1] As far as possible, we used the standard PREALC definition of "modern" and "informal" sectors. See, for instance, PREALC, 1982b.

Source. See table 5.1.

a high proportion (64.6 per cent) of the workers from urban poor families work in the modern sector (table 5.3). This is because the urban modern sector has a clear predominant role in the urban labour market, both in size and in

*Table 5.4.   Urban metropolitan region: Household income and unemployment distributions, 1983*

| Categories | Cumulated percentage of households by income class | | | | | | | | | |
|---|---|---|---|---|---|---|---|---|---|---|
|  | 10 | 20 | 30 | 40 | 50 | 60 | 70 | 80 | 90 | 100 |
| Household income | 1.9 | 6.2 | 11.7 | 18.0 | 25.3 | 33.9 | 43.1 | 55.6 | 72.8 | 100 |
| Open unemployment | 23.8 | 37.8 | 58.7 | 72.5 | 79.1 | 84.4 | 90.9 | 93.8 | 98.1 | 100 |

Source. See table 5.1.

leadership, and because within the urban modern sector, tertiary activities such as services and commerce account for more than 50 per cent of total employment. The basic explanation for this apparent paradox is that a significant number of workers in tertiary activities are paid wages very close to the legal minimum. In fact, according to the official 1983 Household Survey, almost a third of workers in trade and commerce earned salaries close to the minimum wage. But while the absolute number of the poor is larger in the modern sector (64.6 per cent of those classified as poor), the intensity of poverty is very much greater in the urban informal sector.

Personal characteristics are also very important in explaining why such a large fraction of the poor work in modern activities. Almost 50 per cent of the poor has had only primary education. On the other hand, almost 45 per cent of the poor engaged in modern activities has had either complete or at least some secondary education, which strongly suggests neither education nor access to the modern sector can guarantee freedom from want in Panama. Open unemployment comes out as one of the most important urban labour market problems that cause poverty. As seen in table 5.2, the unemployment rate is clearly higher among the poor and the destitute (lowest 10 per cent) than among the non-poor. Given that poor families are larger than average and have high dependency rates, open unemployment of the head of the household or among adult household members brings almost immediate poverty to the family.

As table 5.4 shows, the distribution of the unemployed is highly concentrated among the lowest 30 per cent of family income brackets, where almost 60 per cent of the total unemployed are to be found. Consequently any change in labour market conditions that might lead either to an increase or a decline in open unemployment would have a very large impact. A similar relationship is no doubt present for underemployment, which is one of the principal explanations why the lowest 20 per cent of the families receive as a group only 6 per cent of total family income.

## III. The role of the Welfare State

Apart from the effect on the labour market of the modernisation process of Panama's economic structure, the State has played a very important role through direct policies to alleviate poverty, involving a wide spectrum of

*Table 5.5.  Household income distribution, 1970-83*

| Decile | 1970 [1] | | 1983 | |
|---|---|---|---|---|
| | Total | Metropolitan area | Total | Urban |
| Total | 100.0 | 100.0 | 100.0 | 100.0 |
| 1st | 0.6 | 0.1 | 0.7 | 0.1 |
| 2nd | 1.2 | 0.3 | 2.1 | 0.6 |
| 3rd | 2.0 | 0.8 | 3.6 | 1.8 |
| 4th | 3.3 | 1.8 | 5.2 | 3.5 |
| 5th | 4.8 | 3.1 | 7.0 | 5.8 |
| 6th | 6.5 | 5.3 | 8.2 | 7.4 |
| 7th | 8.6 | 7.5 | 10.5 | 10.4 |
| 8th | 11.8 | 11.5 | 12.5 | 13.4 |
| 9th | 17.8 | 18.3 | 16.9 | 18.8 |
| 10th | 43.4 | 51.3 | 33.3 | 38.2 |
| Mean income [2] | 2 539 | 3 666 | 2 926 | 4 052 |

[1] In 1970 there was no distinction between urban and rural areas, but between the Metropolitan area and the rest of Panama. However, these categories are good approximations to the urban and rural areas in those years.    [2] In 1970 balboas: for 1983, current incomes adjusted by the GDP deflator (227.1).

Sources. Dirección de Estadística y Censo, 1975; Dirección de Estadística y Censo, 1986a.

policy instruments that have contributed to the improvement in income distribution and in the situation of the poor. Housing conditions, for example, improved greatly during the 1970s. The proportion of the population living in poor housing conditions dropped from 30 per cent in 1970 to 17 per cent in 1980, as a result of a substantial state investment in housing. Public expenditure on education has fluctuated between 5 and 6 per cent of GDP, and as a result, illiteracy has dropped significantly. For example, in the Urban Metropolitan Region the illiteracy rate is only 3.3 per cent. The national rate fell between 1970 and 1980 from 18 per cent to 13 per cent, and in urban areas from 6 to 4 per cent. Enrolment rates are about 94 per cent; and 46 per cent of the Metropolitan Area labour force has had at least three years of secondary education. The number of students enrolled in the educational system was almost 600,000 out of a total population of 2 million. Health policy has had a clear "pro-poor" emphasis as well. The extension of the coverage of the social security system, together with the integration of the different health services throughout most provinces, has contributed greatly to the reduction of infant mortality and extension of life expectancy mentioned earlier.

Besides these achievements, the overall national household income distribution improved from 1970 to 1983. The proportion of total national income received by the lowest 20 per cent grew from 1.8 per cent in 1970 to 2.8 per cent in 1983 (table 5.5). Consequently, the Gini coefficient fell from .57 in 1970 to .47 in 1983. The improvement was even greater in the Metropolitan Urban Area, where the bottom 20 per cent received 6.3 per cent of total incomes,

*Table 5.6.    Evolution of the share of salaries and wages in total GDP, 1970-83*

| Year | Percentage of total GDP | Real monthly average wages (US$) per month at 1970 prices |
|------|------------------------|----------------------------------------------------------|
| 1970 | 50.0 | 139.8 |
| 1971 | 51.6 | 137.3 |
| 1972 | 53.8 | 140.9 |
| 1973 | 52.7 | 139.8 |
| 1974 | 54.0 | 134.6 |
| 1975 | 51.2 | 132.0 |
| 1976 | 51.5 | 130.7 |
| 1977 | 50.8 | 125.1 |
| 1978 | 49.7 | 119.1 |
| 1979 | 49.7 | 119.1 |
| 1980 | 45.7 | ... |
| 1981 | 46.4 | ... |
| 1982 | 47.5 | 126.9 |
| 1983 [1] | 50.0 | 131.6 |

... = not available.
[1] 1983 was added by the authors, and estimated from official data.
Sources. PREALC, 1985a; Dirección de Estadística y Censo, Series of Household Surveys, 1970-83.

and the Gini coefficient was .36 in 1983. This improvement in household income distribution in the 1970s was mainly due to a general rise in income share for all the lower household income strata, mainly at the expense of the top decile, as shown in table 5.5. Among the different causes that contributed to the improvement of income distribution are: the new Labour Code of 1972 which brought about the application of legal minimum wages to all branches of economic activity (but see comments on this below); the new and enhanced economic and social role of the State, which alone generated 50 per cent of new jobs created from 1970 to 1983 and expanded the public educational system at an extraordinary rate; and the high levels of public investment that contributed heavily to the modernisation of the labour market through a dynamisation of urban areas and the development of rural areas.

The changes in labour market structure, as will be explained later, also contributed to the improvement of household income distribution, especially through the relative reduction in the number of workers with work statuses such as self-employed and unpaid family workers, groups with the lowest average productivity and earnings per worker, particularly in the rural areas.

Although the overall household income distribution improved substantially in the 1970s, the share of salary and wage earners in total national income, as measured by the national accounts, had its ups and downs (table 5.6). There was a sharp rise from 1970 to 1974, from 50 to 54 per cent of total GDP, and then a steady decline from 1974 to 1980 from 54 to 45.7 per cent. However, from 1980 to 1983 the share recovered to the 1970 level. Despite low rates of

*Table 5.7.   Wage and salary distribution, 1970-83 (in constant prices, 1970)*

| Decile | 1970 | | 1983 | |
|---|---|---|---|---|
| | Percentage of earnings | Average annual earnings | Percentage of earnings | Average annual earnings |
| Total | 100.0 | 2 040 | 100.0 | 1 626 |
| 1st | 0.9 | 174.0 | 2.6 | 418.9 |
| 2nd | 2.0 | 414.8 | 4.6 | 741.1 |
| 3rd | 3.4 | 684.5 | 5.5 | 901.0 |
| 4th | 4.9 | 1 000.2 | 6.5 | 1 053.2 |
| 5th | 6.4 | 1 301.7 | 7.4 | 1 197.5 |
| 6th | 7.5 | 1 530.9 | 8.3 | 1 358.1 |
| 7th | 9.2 | 1 871.3 | 9.6 | 1 562.8 |
| 8th | 12.0 | 2 441.7 | 11.4 | 1 852.8 |
| 9th | 20.9 | 4 259.4 | 14.8 | 2 401.4 |
| 10th | 32.8 | 6 700.7 | 29.3 | 4 768.7 |

Sources. Dirección de Estadística y Censo, 1975; Ministerio de Planificación y Política Económica, 1985.

inflation and high rates of productivity growth, median real wages fell from 1970 to 1983. This pattern can be partially explained by the high proportion of new jobs created by the State at lower average wages than in the private sector. On the other hand, the system of wage readjustments applied in the 1970s (fixed amounts for everyone) implied large improvements for the lower strata, and relative penalties for the highest income brackets. This is clearly shown in table 5.7, where real wages rose for the bottom 40 per cent of the earnings distribution, but fell quite sharply at the top.

Despite the improvement registered in the size distribution of wages and salaries, the average level of real wages deteriorated in almost all sectors, except the construction sector and the banana plantations, perhaps owing to the existence of strong labour unions and effective collective bargaining in these sectors. The level of real minimum wages also deteriorated considerably in the 1970s. Notwithstanding the new Labour Code, minimum wages have been readjusted infrequently (1972, 1974, 1979 and 1983) and insufficiently, with the sole purpose of compensating for inflation, and although price rises were moderate, the real level of the minimum wages deteriorated by 29 per cent from 1972 to 1982. The negative impact on the overall income distribution was small, however, since only 10 per cent of workers earn less than the minimum wage, and it does not show up in the 1983 Household Income Survey data because a large readjustment in minimum wages occurred in 1983 just before the survey.

*Figure 5.1.   Open unemployment, 1970-83*

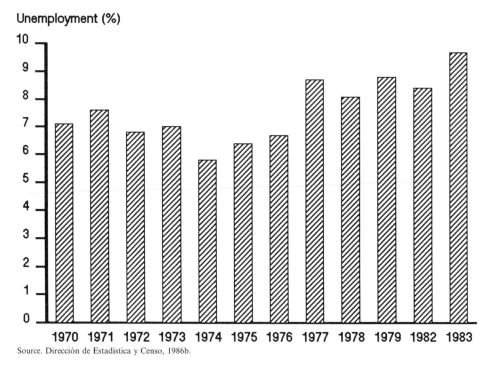

Source. Dirección de Estadística y Censo, 1986b.

# IV. The role of the labour market

### 1. Structural performance

From a long-term perspective, the labour market has played a major role in the modernisation of the economic structure and in social development. The proportion of wage earners in the total labour force grew from 44 per cent in 1950 to 70 per cent in 1980 [3] and the share of unpaid family workers declined from 17 per cent to 4 per cent over the same period. Furthermore, the relative importance of the rural traditional sector of the labour force, which accounts for the bulk of labour force underutilisation, fell by 28 per cent from 1950 to 1980, partly because of the growth of the rural modern sector and of non-agricultural rural activities.

These favourable labour market conditions were promoted to a certain extent, especially in the 1970s, by a very active economic policy and direct economic intervention by the State. For example, the rural modern sector benefited from the development and modernisation of crops such as rice and sugar, and non-agricultural rural activities profited from the state decentralisation policy of the 1970s and its vigorous public investment programme. Because of the development path of those years, the bulk of the new entrants to the labour market were incorporated in urban modern activities,

*Table 5.8.  Overall labour market characteristics, Metropolitan area, 1978-83*

| | 1978 | | 1983 | |
|---|---|---|---|---|
| | Volume | Rates | Volume | Rates |
| Population of 15 years old and above | 562 353 | | 665 089 | |
| Economically active population | 319 842 | 56.9 | 378 428 | 56.9 |
| Employed | 286 465 | 50.9 | 333 983 | 50.2 |
| Unemployed | 33 377 | 10.4 | 44 445 | 11.7 |
| Visibly underemployed (VU) [1] | 11 947 | 3.7 | 14 622 | 3.9 |
| Invisibly underemployed (IU) [1] | 26 351 | 10.3 [2] | 26 359 | 12.8 [1] |
| Equivalent unemployment for VU [1] | 4 887 | 1.6 | 6 688 | 1.8 |
| Equivalent unemployment for IU [1] | 7 613 | 3.0 [2] | 15 165 | 5.6 [1] |
| Median weekly nominal wage [3] | 44.3 | | 68.8 | |
| Median weekly real wage | 27.7 | | 30.6 | |
| Average monthly nominal wage [4] | 310.11 | | 400.38 | |
| Average monthly real wage | 193.58 | | 178.03 | |
| Percentage of informal sector employment | 25.3 | | 30.0 | |
| Percentage of salaried workers in EAP | 81.5 | | 81.3 | |
| Percentage of self-employed | 15.3 | | 15.0 | |
| Percentage of employers | 1.7 | | 1.8 | |
| Percentage of unpaid family workers | 1.3 | | 1.8 | |
| Male participation rate | 74.7 | | 75.8 | |
| Female participation rate | 40.7 | | 38.8 | |

[1] Visible equivalent unemployment is defined as the number of those working less than 40 hours, times the average deficit in hours, divided by 40; i.e. the percentage deficit in working time as compared with a 40-hour week. Invisible equivalent unemployment is based on a comparable calculation in terms of income in relation to the minimum wage.  [2] This figure refers only to salary and wage earners.  [3] Obtained through the official household surveys.  [4] Obtained through the social security system statistics. Real wages were obtained by deflating nominal wages by the Consumer Price Index.
Sources. Dirección de Estadística y Censo, 1982, 1986b; PREALC, 1982a.

while the relative importance of the urban informal sector (UIS), as a percentage of the urban labour force, remained almost unchanged.

From the occupational point of view, the proportion of agricultural workers in the labour force was halved in 30 years, while the group of professional and technical workers expanded threefold, and administrative, managerial and white-collar workers doubled. This spectacular transformation on the demand side of the labour market was possible on the supply side thanks to a huge state effort in education — university enrolment grew sevenfold in the period and secondary education tripled.

Despite all these positive developments Panama's labour market suffers from some very important problems. First, the open unemployment rate has been relatively high (figure 5.1), reflecting on the one hand the leading role of the modern sector and, on the other, the relatively higher levels of earnings per worker and more sophisticated welfare mechanisms that the labour force enjoyed as compared with other Latin American and developing countries in general. Second, the modernisation process has left some notorious islands of labour force underutilisation (mostly in rural areas). Third, the modernisation

*Table 5.9.   Urban labour market segmentation, 1978-83 (percentages)*

|  | Informal sector | | Modern sector | |
|---|---|---|---|---|
|  | 1978 | 1983 | 1978 | 1983 |
| Employment | 25.3 | 30.0 | 74.4 | 70.0 |
| Men | 23.3 | 30.6 | 76.6 | 69.4 |
| Women | 28.4 | 28.9 | 71.6 | 71.1 |
| Younger than 20 years | 54.8 | 59.2 | 45.2 | 40.8 |
| Older than 49 years | 35.9 | 47.3 | 64.1 | 52.7 |

Source. Dirección de Estadística y Censos-Ministerio de Trabajo, special tabulations of the 1983 National Household Survey.

process, particularly among certain sectors of activity, has contributed to a substantial increase in productivity, but the new technological mix has greatly lowered labour absorption per unit of capital. Fourth, the international economic crisis of the early 1980s has affected Panama, since its economy is very open and closely interlinked with the American economy.

## 2. Recent performance

Looking at the 1978-83 period to identify the recent performance [4] of the labour market and its repercussions on urban poverty, we find that there has been a deterioration in the labour market conditions, and that as a result poverty may have increased (table 5.8). The rate of open unemployment in the Metropolitan area rose from 10.4 to 11.7 per cent,[5] while modern sector real average wages fell by 8 per cent. Underemployment increased too, both in terms of insufficient working hours ("visible" underemployment) and earnings ("invisible" underemployment). The relative importance of the modern sector shrank by 4 per cent. As a whole, the Metropolitan area employment problem increased from 1978 to 1983, and the quality of the labour market structure deteriorated. In fact, the employment rate of the working-age population fell slightly because of the higher unemployment and lower female participation rates.

From the point of view of urban poverty the deterioration of the urban labour market conditions meant that a higher proportion of heads of households were forced to enter the informal sector as a survival strategy for their families, in order to avoid open unemployment, which they could not afford; meanwhile, there was pressure on other family members to enter the informal sector too, as a secondary labour force in order to generate a decent family income around the poverty line. Table 5.9 suggests that the main effect was on household heads, since the change was more pronounced for men and for those aged over 49. There are however also signs of increased entry of secondary workers into the urban informal sector, probably in an attempt to avoid extreme poverty, since the proportion of workers in the youngest (under 20) age group in this sector also rose.

*Table 5.10.  Relative importance of different work status categories by urban labour market segment, 1978-83 (percentages)*

|  | Economically active population | | Informal sector | | Modern sector | |
|---|---|---|---|---|---|---|
|  | 1978 | 1983 | 1978 | 1983 | 1978 | 1983 |
| Total | 100.0 | 100.0 | 100.0 | 100.0 | 100.0 | 100.0 |
| Wage/salary workers | 85.2 | 81.1 | 47.9 | 42.2 | 98.1 | 97.9 |
| Self-employed | 12.1 | 14.6 | 45.0 | 47.3 | 0.6 | 0.6 |
| Employers | 2.0 | 2.7 | 4.9 | 6.2 | 1.0 | 1.2 |
| Unpaid family workers | 0.7 | 1.5 | 2.2 | 4.3 | 0.2 | 0.3 |

Source. See table 5.9.

Labour conditions in the informal sector deteriorated as well. In fact, growth in this sector from 1978 to 1983 consisted mainly of self-employed workers and unpaid family workers, both engaged for the most part in very low-productivity activities such as commerce and services (table 5.10).

### 3. The economic cycle, the labour market and poverty

The economic cycle has a distinctive impact on Panama's labour market. In many Latin American countries during the downswing of the economic cycle the modern sector first reduces its employment absorption, then its volume of working hours, then starts generating open unemployment and finally reduces the average real wages; the informal sector, on the other hand, tends to act counter-cyclically: during the downswing it increases its volume of employment by absorbing both some of the modern sector unemployed and a part of the increased labour supply by secondary members of low-income families, who enter the labour market as a strategy for survival.

Panama, however, does not fit this model: during abrupt recessions both the modern and informal sectors reduce their employment absorption, and open unemployment rises rapidly. The reason is that when final demand falls too sharply, the informal sector loses final demand along with the modern activities; in Panama there are no automatic adjustment mechanisms like those in other Latin American countries, where for instance foreign exchange scarcity induces the promotion of informal sector repair services and substitution of modern sector goods by informal sector products and services with a smaller import content. In Panama the modern sector acts in those circumstances much more as a competitive sector vis-à-vis the informal activities than as a complementary sector. The complete absence of foreign exchange controls and low protection means that the informal activities are always facing fierce competition from cheap imports (clothing, for example).

However, the overall elasticity of employment in relation to GDP growth tends to increase in Panama in periods of slow (but positive) rates of growth, and it tends to decrease during the upswing of the economic cycle

*Table 5.11.    Economic cycle and employment elasticities*

| Period | GDP growth (% per annum) | Employment growth (% per annum) | Elasticity |
|---|---|---|---|
| 1970-80 | 5.5 | 2.2 | 0.40 |
| 1970-73 | 6.5 | 2.3 | 0.35 |
| 1973-76 | 2.0 | 0.5 | 0.25 |
| 1970-79 | 4.5 | 2.2 | 0.49 |
| 1973-83 | 4.6 | 2.2 | 0.49 |
| 1970-83 | 5.0 | 2.3 | 0.47 |
| 1979-82 | 8.2 | 2.7 | 0.33 |

Source. PREALC, 1985a, plus updated data.

(table 5.11). Consequently, during periods of slow growth the average labour productivity of new entrants tends to be lower, reflecting the expansion of activities with lower levels of productivity, particularly urban informal activities. The economic cycle then affects both the overall volume of employment and the composition of the labour market in terms of the distribution of workers across major segments (modern sector-informal sector), and the internal composition (work status, the age distribution of workers, etc.) of each.

In Panama the economic cycle brings widespread poverty through open unemployment in the modern and informal sectors when an abrupt reduction in the rate of growth occurs (e.g. 1973-76). When the growth rate is relatively low, over a long period (i.e. 1970-79, 1973-83), the employment elasticity tends to increase, reflecting the relative enlargement of the informal sector. In those periods poverty grows among families engaged in informal activities in the form of underemployment. When there is an energetic economic upswing (i.e. 1970-73, 1979-82), the employment elasticity tends to shrink, showing the overall increase in productivity in both modern and informal sectors. Poverty is consequently reduced among informal sector families that suffered from underemployment and becomes more concentrated among families that suffer from open unemployment.

## 4. Relationships between underemployment and poverty

While underemployment hits individual workers, poverty affects families; and while underemployment is related to productivity, poverty is connected with overall family income. We use an earnings criterion to identify underemployment — those falling below the official minimum wage (US$140.30 per month). This can be compared with the income measure of poverty used in section II. If one worker supports a family of average size (4.3 persons) then the annual per capita income provided by the minimum wage would be US$391.50, a little below the cost of the official basic food basket. It should be

*Table 5.12.    Metropolitan area employment* [1] *by main characteristics of workers with monthly earnings below US$140.30, 1983*

| Main categories | Total employment | Percentage of workers below US$140.30 | No. of workers below US$140.30 | Average monthly earnings |
|---|---|---|---|---|
| Total employment | 309 546 | 17.8 | 55 212 | 349 |
| Informal sector | 71 914 | 52.0 | 37 424 | 198 |
| Domestic services | 16 926 | 88.7 | 15 018 | 90 |
| Informal less domestic | 54 988 | 40.8 | 22 406 | 231 |
| Modern sector | 237 632 | 7.5 | 17 788 | 395 |
| Salary wage earners | 271 547 | 15.1 | 40 981 | 352 |
| Government | 95 152 | 5.7 | 5 418 | 369 |
| Private | 164 223 | 21.5 | 35 284 | 318 |
| Canal area | 12 172 | 2.3 | 279 | 674 |
| Self-employed | 31 924 | 39.6 | 12 632 | 237 |
| Industry | 39 871 | 13.0 | 5 189 | 334 |
| Construction | 21 934 | 15.1 | 3 318 | 297 |
| Transportation | 28 149 | 8.2 | 2 309 | 388 |
| Commerce | 58 623 | 16.4 | 9 594 | 305 |
| Primary schooling | 89 200 | 34.6 | 30 835 | 214 |
| 1st to 3rd degree | 13 392 | 43.6 | 5 836 | 169 |
| 4th to 6th degree | 75 808 | 33.0 | 24 999 | 222 |
| Household heads | 164 614 | 12.6 | 20 669 | 417 |

[1] These figures exclude self-employed in the agricultural sector (18,224) and unpaid family workers (6,140).
Source. 1983 Household Survey. Special tabulations made by the Planning Ministry.

remembered, though, that the latter income line, from the family's point of view, represents a critical poverty threshold that allows one to differentiate between destitute and non-destitute families.

There is indeed strong evidence that there is a close relationship between underemployment and poverty, but the individuals involved are not necessarily the same. In Panama it is interesting to see that while 16.8 per cent of the families residing in the Metropolitan area in 1983 were classified as destitute by a study on critical poverty made by the Ministry of Planning (MIPPE, 1985), 17.8 per cent of the workers of the same region earned incomes below the official urban average monthly minimum wage (US$140.30) (table 5.12). Of the total number of workers earning below US$140.30 per month in their primary jobs, the majority was concentrated in the informal sector (67 per cent), and among workers with primary schooling (56 per cent). In the informal sector domestic services accounted for 40 per cent of workers below the defined income line. Underemployment was highest in the informal sector (52 per cent), even if domestic services are excluded (40.8 per cent). Next highest was the self-employed with 39.6 per cent (this group accounts for 47 per cent of the informal sector labour force). Underemployment was particularly high among workers with primary education (34.6 per cent).

*Table 5.13.   Age profiles of the urban labour force by labour market segment, 1983*

| Age strata | | Informal sector | Modern sector | | |
|---|---|---|---|---|---|
| | | | Total | Public | Private |
| Both sexes | 15-19 | 12.6 | 5.7 | 1.3 | 5.3 |
| | 20-24 | 13.6 | 17.1 | 11.4 | 16.5 |
| | 25-29 | 11.0 | 18.5 | 19.6 | 18.0 |
| | 30-39 | 23.5 | 31.3 | 36.4 | 31.3 |
| | 40-49 | 18.1 | 17.7 | 20.3 | 18.8 |
| | 50-59 | 11.5 | 7.5 | 9.4 | 7.2 |
| | 60+ | 9.7 | 2.2 | 1.6 | 3.0 |
| | | 100 | 100 | 100 | 100 |
| Men | 15-19 | 9.6 | 6.2 | 1.5 | 5.6 |
| | 20-24 | 11.5 | 16.6 | 12.2 | 15.3 |
| | 25-29 | 10.9 | 16.9 | 17.8 | 16.5 |
| | 30-39 | 13.8 | 19.5 | 33.8 | 30.5 |
| | 40-49 | 19.4 | 18.7 | 20.5 | 20.1 |
| | 50-59 | 12.6 | 9.0 | 11.5 | 8.4 |
| | 60+ | 12.2 | 3.1 | 2.6 | 3.6 |
| | | 100 | 100 | 100 | 100 |
| Women | 15-19 | 18.1 | 4.9 | 1.1 | 4.4 |
| | 20-24 | 17.6 | 18.1 | 10.3 | 19.8 |
| | 25-29 | 11.3 | 21.2 | 21.7 | 21.9 |
| | 30-39 | 22.9 | 34.4 | 39.5 | 33.5 |
| | 40-49 | 15.7 | 15.9 | 20.1 | 15.1 |
| | 50-59 | 9.4 | 4.9 | 6.9 | 4.0 |
| | 60+ | 4.9 | 0.7 | 0.4 | 1.3 |
| | | 100 | 100 | 100 | 100 |

Source. Dirección de Estadística y Censos-Ministerio de Trabajo, special tabulations of the 1983 National Household Survey.

## 5. Main characteristics of informal sector workers

The statistical evidence shows that a significant share of the urban poor belong to families whose head or other members work in the informal sector. Since such a relationship exists, in the following sections we shall try to identify the main personal and occupational characteristics of the informal sector workers that are associated with urban poverty.

### A. The age and sex profiles

In Panama, as in many other countries, informal sector workers are disproportionately found among women, the less educated, the extremes of the age pyramid, and the recipients of low incomes and salaries. In fact, as table 5.13 shows, the proportion of young and old workers is twice as high in the informal

*Table 5.14.    Urban labour force educational level by sex and labour market segment, 1983*

| Level | Informal sector | Modern sector | |
|---|---|---|---|
| | | Public | Private |
| *Men* | | | |
| No schooling | 5.9 | 0.8 | 2.8 |
| 1-3 Primary | 14.0 | 3.3 | 5.3 |
| 4-6 Primary | 44.4 | 21.2 | 29.4 |
| 1-3 Secondary | 16.9 | 17.9 | 20.0 |
| 4-6 Secondary | 15.6 | 30.9 | 26.4 |
| University | 3.3 | 25.9 | 16.1 |
| | 100 | 100 | 100 |
| *Women* | | | |
| No schooling | 5.5 | 0.1 | 0.7 |
| 1-3 Primary | 7.7 | 0.8 | 2.4 |
| 4-6 Primary | 46.0 | 8.8 | 15.5 |
| 1-3 Secondary | 21.6 | 12.5 | 18.6 |
| 4-6 Secondary | 15.2 | 39.1 | 39.7 |
| University | 3.9 | 38.7 | 23.5 |
| | 100 | 100 | 100 |

Source. See table 5.13.

as in the modern sector. This suggests that members of poor families are forced at a young age to stop studying and to start working in order to contribute earnings to the household. Similarly, at the other end of the age range, older family members cannot retire since they are not covered by the social security system, or simply because they have to keep contributing with their full earnings to the family income. The relationship is much stronger for women than men.

### B. The educational profile

A notorious difference between workers in the informal and the modern sectors is their respective levels of education. Almost two-thirds of informal sector workers have not completed primary schooling, while in the modern sector nearly three-quarters of the labour force has attained secondary or university levels. The population groups among which this situation is particularly extreme are women, and independent and unpaid family workers (table 5.14).

### C. Underemployment

As a result of the personal characteristics of informal sector workers and their point of insertion in the economic structure, over half of them (at the

*Table 5.15.   Income situation by sex and labour market segment, 1983*

| Monthly income (US$) | Informal sector | | Modern sector | |
|---|---|---|---|---|
| | Men | Women | Men | Women |
| Less than 140.30 | 51.3 | 76.8 | 8.4 | 8.9 |
| 140.30 and more | 48.7 | 23.2 | 91.6 | 91.1 |

Source. See table 5.13.

national level) earned in 1983 incomes that fell below the line we have used to identify invisible underemployment, but this affected only 9 per cent of the total urban modern sector workers. As has already been noted regarding other personal characteristics, women were more affected than men in this regard, with 77 per cent of informal sector women falling below the fully employed income line (table 5.15). This is because most women engaged in domestic services (90 per cent) fall within this income bracket.

The distribution of earnings by labour market segment also bears witness to the close relationship between urban poverty and underemployment, particularly in the urban informal sector. As shown in table 5.16, modal earnings in the informal sector are below US$70, half the official minimum wage, compared with US$350 per month in the modern sector. Another interesting finding is that the public sector paid salaries and wages between US$200 and US$500 per month to almost 80 per cent of its employees. Since the public sector wage bill represents nearly half the total urban area wage bill, its much better earnings distribution profile is an important element that contributes to the improvement of the overall national income distribution.

In brief, Panama's urban informal sector can be characterised as a labour market segment with a high proportion of very young and very old workers, with relatively low educational levels, a high concentration of workers earning incomes below the full employment line, and among which women are over-represented. Recent experience shows, on the other hand, that the informal sector has become an important refuge for heads of household.

### 6. Family options, responses and strategies in the face of poverty

When facing a particular employment problem, different members of a family may resort to differing solutions or strategies. Some, the most fortunate, find a satisfactory wage job, while others have to embark on some self-employed activity to survive; and some stay in the educational system until reaching the level required for access to a particular occupation. In order to learn about the strategies that poor families apply to the urban labour market, a small-scale survey was conducted among the poorest areas of Panama City: San Miguelito District, El Chorrillo, Curundu, San Sebastian and Panama Viejo; 59 per cent of interviewees were wage workers in relatively large units of

*Table 5.16.  Urban monthly incomes by labour market segment, 1983*

| Monthly income (US$) | Informal sector | Modern sector | | |
| --- | --- | --- | --- | --- |
| | | Total | Public | Private |
| | 100.0 | 100.0 | 100.0 | 100.0 |
| Less than 70.15 | 36.3 | 2.2 | 0.6 | 3.4 |
| 70.15 to 105.22 | 16.5 | 1.8 | 1.0 | 2.4 |
| 105.22 to 140.29 | 7.0 | 4.6 | 3.0 | 5.9 |
| ——————————— Full employment-underemployment line ——————— | | | | |
| 140.30 to 157.37 | 8.3 | 8.6 | 5.6 | 11.0 |
| 157.38 to 210.44 | 10.6 | 14.0 | 12.3 | 15.1 |
| 210.45 to 280.59 | 6.6 | 18.5 | 19.4 | 16.9 |
| 280.60 to 420.89 | 9.2 | 27.5 | 34.4 | 22.1 |
| 420.90 to 561.19 | 2.3 | 9.8 | 11.8 | 8.2 |
| 561.20 to 701.49 | 1.2 | 4.4 | 4.7 | 4.2 |
| 701.50 to 982.09 | 0.9 | 4.5 | 4.3 | 4.7 |
| 982.10 to 1 262.69 | 0.0 | 2.0 | 1.5 | 2.4 |
| 1 262.70 to 1 283.59 | 0.2 | 1.4 | 1.0 | 1.8 |
| 1 283.60 and more | 0.3 | 1.1 | 0.4 | 1.7 |

Source. See table 5.13. The underemployment line is defined in terms of income (see section IV.4).

production by Panamanian standards (above 50 workers per establishment). When asked how they got their job, 54 per cent replied "through a friend or a relative", and only 7.5 per cent said they got it through the Labour Exchange Service. In areas such as San Miguelito, where there is a high concentration of rural-urban and urban-to-capital-city migrants, a fairly high proportion of workers (28 per cent) had changed occupations between 1978-86. However, this mobility did not imply important social or economic changes for those workers, since the moves were mostly to closely related occupations. Around 30 per cent of interviewees wanted to work more hours per week; 40 per cent of them in turn were already working over 40 hours per week. This suggests that members of poor families see secondary jobs or extra hours, and probably shift work too, as possible alternatives for their insufficient family incomes.

From the existing structure of employment, as measured by the official Household Survey, some additional answers were found regarding options that might provide labour market access for particular groups affected by poverty. Wage work in the informal sector provides some options for young female workers, but mostly as domestic servants. It also provides opportunities in micro-enterprises (fewer than five employees) for the young. Labour conditions among wage workers in micro-enterprises tend to be better than in other parts of the informal sector since they benefit from institutional mechanisms such as the Labour Code and minimum-wage legislation.

Self-employment, on the other hand, is more widespread among workers aged above 50, which can have two meanings: either self-employment demands a substantial previous experience, or employers tend to avoid hiring older workers. Conversely, the young tend to be wage earners, perhaps because they lack the experience and the savings required to start an independent job; and furthermore, employers prefer the energy and flexibility of younger workers.

Gender tends to narrow the options with respect to both sectors of activity and occupations. Male workers concentrate in activities that involve the production of goods (i.e. agriculture, industry, construction, etc.), while female workers are concentrated mainly in services and commerce.

As for labour force participation rates, there is a clear and positive correspondence between the Panamanian economic cycle and overall participation rates. But at a disaggregated level, there is an inverse relationship between the economic cycle and the specific participation rates of poor families. Economic depression hurts poor urban families badly, especially when it results in open unemployment of the head of household. In such cases other members of the family are forced to enter the labour market, engaging themselves mostly in informal activities of very low productivity (i.e. children become beggars, older family members engage in informal services or commerce). In the absence of unemployment insurance or social security benefits, the affected urban poor tend to resort to indirect social compensations, such as stopping paying rent, water or electricity bills, creating through such means a de facto subsidy financed either by the State (public utilities) or by specific groups in the community (landlords).

## V. General conclusions

Urban poverty in Panama, as we pointed out earlier, means poverty in the midst of wealth. With its present per capita income, Panama should not suffer from want. Urban poverty is a result of unequal income distribution and lack of opportunities in the labour market. The income gap of the poor is around 4 per cent of total family incomes. Such a percentage of income could easily be obtained if the present unemployment rate were reduced to the level of the 1970s. Why, then, do 22 per cent of the urban families fall below the poverty line?

As we have shown, there are numerous demographic and socio-economic factors that enter the scene. Those which we have noted include large families with few economically active members; a lack of occupational opportunities that leads to unemployment and underemployment; the relatively lower levels of education of the poor; female-headed households; the unfavourable labour market situation for the very young and old; and low salaries within the tertiary activities.

The important role of the State, as an agent of income redistribution, emerges clearly, especially with regard to its public policies in housing, education and health, employment creation, and its investment role as well. However, that role is at present threatened by the need for economic structural adjustment, and the conditions under which such adjustment is being carried out.

Last but not least, the labour market can play a central role with regard to poverty alleviation. As has been shown, there exists a close but not a perfect correlation between the rhythm of economic activity and the performance of the labour market. Employment and income policies could, in consequence, play a very important role in alleviating the direct social impacts of temporary adverse economic conditions, and could correct structural weaknesses that prevent the achievement of a better distribution of income and of basic-needs satisfaction.

### Notes

[1] Respectively, specialist on employment matters at the Ministry of Planning, Republic of Panama; representative of ILO-PREALC for Central America and Panama; specialist on employment matters at the Ministry of Labour, Republic of Panama. The authors would like to thank Gerry Rodgers for his careful reading of earlier drafts of this chapter and for his very helpful comments and suggestions. The responsibility for the views expressed and for any remaining errors lies with the authors.

[2] The urban Metropolitan Region considered in this study includes 22 per cent of the total number of poor families of the country and consequently represents a significant proportion of the urban poor. However, it should be pointed out that most poor families in Panama are located in rural areas, and thus fall outside the scope of the present chapter.

[3] Accordingly the importance of the urban modern sector labour force increased from 35 per cent in 1950 to almost 60 per cent in 1980. For additional and detailed information see PREALC (1985a).

[4] In that period the growth rate of GDP reached 5.8 per cent per year. The high growth rate was mostly explained by the inclusion of the revenues generated by the new oil pipeline and the Panama Canal Commission as part of the measurement of the national accounts. These two activities, however, generated almost no additional employment during the period.

[5] By 1987 the urban unemployment rate reached 15 per cent.

### References

Comité Técnico de Población, 1984: *Población y desarrollo* (Panama, COTEPO).

Dirección de Estadística y Censo, several years: *Panamá en cifras* (Panama, DEC).

———, 1975: *Encuesta Especial sobre Ingresos a través de los hogares, año 1970* (Panama, DEC).

———, 1982: *Situación Social, Estadísticas del Trabajo, año 1978* (Panama, DEC).

———, 1983: *Situación Económica, Cuentas Nacionales 1970-81* (Panama, DEC).

———, 1986a: *Estadística Panameña, Boletín 991* (Panama, DEC).

———, 1986b: *Situación Social, Estadísticas del Trabajo, año 1983* (Panama, DEC).

———, 1987: *Situación Económica, Cuentas Nacionales 1982-84* (Panama, DEC).

———, 1987: *Estadística Panameña, Boletín 6* (Panama, DEC).

Haan, H., 1985: *El sector informal en Centroamérica* (Santiago, PREALC).

Ministerio de Planificación y Política Económica (MIPPE), 1980: *Evolución, problemática, perspectivas y lineamientos de empleo* (Panama, DEC).

———, 1985: *Estudio de Pobreza Crítica* (Panama, MIPPE; preliminary draft).

Ministerio de Trabajo y Bienestar Social (MITRABS), 1986: *Información estadística sobre recursos humanos*, Boletin No. 3 (Panama, MITRABS).

PREALC, 1974: *Situación y perspectivas del empleo en Panama* (Geneva, ILO).

PREALC, Panama, 1982a: *Segmentación del mercado de trabajo — información estadística básica* (Santiago).

PREALC, 1982b: *Mercado de trabajo en cifras 1950-80* (Santiago).

———, 1984a: *Panama: Situación y perspectivas del empleo femenino* (Santiago).

———, 1984b: *Panama: Situación y perspectivas del empleo en el sector informal urbano* (Santiago).

———, 1985a: *Evolución y estructura de los salarios* (Santiago).

———, 1985b: *Programas especiales de empleo en Panamá, 1978-84* (Santiago).

# Chapter 6

## Poverty and the labour market: Greater Santiago, 1969-85

MOLLY POLLACK
ANDRAS UTHOFF [1]

## I. Introduction

Chile's economy underwent substantial fluctuations between 1969 and 1985. In order to re-establish basic macro-economic equilibrium at different points in this period, economic policy was so drastic that it could only have been implemented by an authoritarian regime such as the one in power since September 1973. This resulted in large changes in the Greater Santiago labour market, where unemployment, real wages, labour market structure and mobility all varied considerably. In so far as wages were the sole source of income for the majority of Chilean families, these changes affected both the extent and the characteristics of poverty. It follows that the design of policies to ensure the satisfaction of basic needs requires an understanding of the relation between the dynamics of the labour market and of poverty.

This relation is explored in this chapter through the analysis of two phenomena: first, the ways in which different categories of workers are affected by labour market adjustment — through unemployment, through reductions in real incomes, through reducing the length of the working day or through shifting to occupations where entry is easy (e.g. many services), but where productivity and incomes are low; and second, the incidence of poverty in the families to which these workers belong. In order to pursue these two issues simultaneously, we develop a criterion for the definition of poverty; quantify its magnitude between 1969 and 1985; and describe the socio-demographic and occupational profile of families falling in different poverty strata. This permits us to distinguish three types of factors characterising poverty in the economic cycle from 1969 to 1985.

First, we distinguish the structural factors which discriminate between poverty strata. We include one demographic factor: the degree of dependency — the ratio between the inactive population and the population of working age in each group of families; an economic factor: the capacity of the economy to generate productive employment for this population of working age; and a labour factor: the level of productivity (remuneration) at which individuals are employed. These factors vary across poverty strata, generating particular characteristics at different poverty levels. Second, we distinguish the micro-household level factors which discriminate between poverty strata. These include a supply factor: the manner in which work is sought by the population of working age; and a family subsistence factor: the composition of labour supply between household heads and secondary workers (spouse and children). Third, we distinguish institutional factors, including the segmentation of labour markets, and the conditions of employment and of underemployment in different segments.

We pick out the ways each of these factors operates in determining the magnitude and characteristics of poverty between 1969 and 1985 in Greater Santiago. The above classification of factors permits us to distinguish various policy actions aimed at combating poverty, within the context of family survival strategies, taking the household as unit of analysis. Within the household, overall labour supply decisions are conditioned by the employment profile of the main household workers, and these in turn determine the possibility to overcome or alleviate poverty.

The information used comes from the Employment and Un-employment Survey of the Economics Department of the University of Chile. The monthly cost of a basket of basic food items is compared with the corresponding values of family income per capita declared for the month of May in 1969, 1976, 1979, 1980, 1982, 1984 and 1985. The years selected for study correspond to the periods of boom and slump in the economic cycle between 1969 and 1985. This choice requires a discussion of the macro-economic conditions in this period (see section II). Between 1969 and 1985 the rates of open unemployment had passed the historic high of around 6 per cent and reached over 20 per cent. However, when this is adjusted to include the beneficiaries of the special assistance programmes (PEM and POJH) it is thought that the rate would be close to 30 per cent (Meller, 1984). Real wages in 1975 were 38 per cent lower than in 1970, and had scarcely reached the 1970 level again by 1981 before declining once more in the period 1983-85. A tertiarisation of the structure of employment occurred, especially through an expansion in the service sectors.

The relationship between these signs of labour market adjustment and the evolution of poverty is covered in section III through a detailed analysis of the profile of poverty. We distinguish, on the one hand, occupational conditions: the institutional sector, the sector of economic activity, the labour market segment to which access is obtained; and, on the other hand, the individual characteristics of those working: levels of education, age, sex and hours worked, for each active member of the family, broken down by relation to the household head. Evidence is also provided on the demographic characteristics of the family, such as the size and age, composition and the overall participation rates in economic activity of its adult members, and the relationship with poverty of each of these characteristics of households and of economically active family members is documented. Finally, in section IV some policy implications are suggested.

## II. Macro-economic aspects

In order to study the incidence and characteristics of poverty in the 1970s and 1980s, we need to review some events that influenced resource allocation in the economy, and hence affected different groups of the population in different ways. Three such occurrences should be mentioned: (i) the changes that took place in the openness of the economy to foreign commercial and financial dealings; (ii) the fall in investment and employment in the country; and (iii) changes in the distribution of income.

### 1. External openness

Chile's degree of openness, measured by the share of imports in the total supply of goods and services, grew from 18 per cent in 1974 to a maximum of 25 per cent in 1981 before declining to around 18 per cent in 1983-84 and 16 per cent in 1985. During this period the terms of trade continued to deteriorate, falling by approximately 50 per cent. Moreover, parallel to this, a large influx of external resources, resulting from the increase in international liquidity, was channelled towards the country under a regime of fluctuating and often distorted prices. The value of the domestic currency fluctuated greatly, without, however, a significant devaluation, which implied that in some years it was overvalued. The real cost of domestic credit rose to as much as 50 per cent. These factors contributed to discouraging the allocation of resources for investment, relative to speculation and consumption.

### 2. Investment and employment

The capability of the economy to generate employment for the population of working age, measured as the number of jobs in relation to the population above 14 years old, was seen to deteriorate seriously in the period 1963-84 (figures 6.1, 6.2). This was the result of the weakness of the accumulation process, and of the fall in real external savings in relation to the deterioration of the terms of trade and the high import coefficient of the economy. In contrast, there was no significant change during the period in overall labour force participation rates. The unemployment rate increased principally as a result of demand deficiency, responsible for a low rate of creation of jobs, far below that necessary to employ a growing workforce. This growth in the workforce was mainly the result of demographic factors, due to the previous periods of high fertility, and not necessarily due to changes in the supply behaviour of the population of working age.

At the same time there has been a bias in the technological, demographic and educational transformations that accompanied the changes in the economy. One observes a substantial increase in average labour productivity, and a beginning of the process of substituting skilled for unskilled workers, while saving labour at all skill levels. As a result, the generation of jobs has been highly biased towards the occupations which require higher levels of qualifications, reducing employment opportunities for those with lower educational levels.

*Figure 6.1.* *Employment, labour force participation and unemployment rates: Greater Santiago,*
*1963-84*

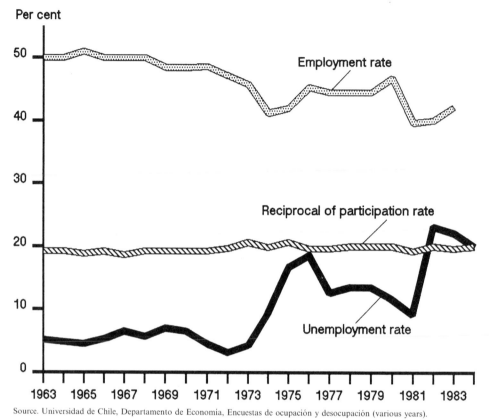

Source. Universidad de Chile, Departamento de Economía, Encuestas de ocupación y desocupación (various years).

Finally, there has been a change in the role of the State as a generator of employment between 1973 and 1985, from active to secondary, although the net effect on employment is uncertain. According to one study (Echeverría, 1985), public sector employment increased at an average rate of 7 per cent per annum between 1964 and 1973, principally as a consequence of a growth in public enterprises for economic development, as well as the growth of employment in social services. Thereafter it declined by 50.2 per cent in absolute terms between 1974 and 1983 (excluding the special employment programmes PEM and POJH). The largest reductions in employment occurred in the public enterprises, which by 1978 had already reduced their employment to approximately one-third of the 1973 level.

### 3. Distribution of income

Because the process of economic transformation favoured the market as the mechanism for resource allocation, the outcomes were in large measure

*Figure 6.2. Employment rate, gross capital formation and external trade balance: Chile 1963-84*

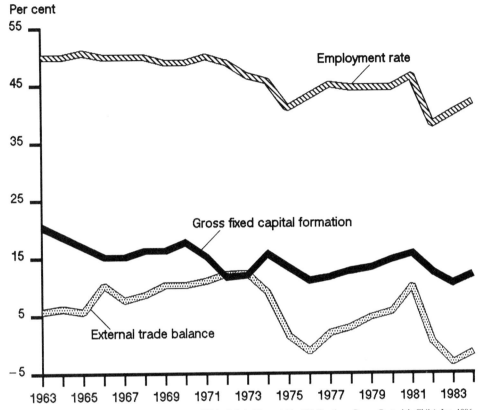

Sources. Figure 6.1; Banco Central de Chile, 1984; and ibid.: *Boletín Mensual*, No. 695 (Santiago, Banco Central de Chile), Jan. 1986.

dictated by consumers, whose influence is felt in direct relation to their purchasing power. In this way the distribution of income constitutes an important factor in the allocation of resources within the economy.

There are no relevant detailed studies on the evolution of inequality during the period under study, mainly because of the limited diffusion of the results of the 1978 Incomes and Expenditure Survey. Nevertheless, some evidence exists indicating large reductions in the real levels of consumption of the poorer families, and increases in the levels of the richer families. Between 1969 and 1978 it has been estimated that although the level of total consumption did not increase, there were changes within different poverty strata. Those in the lowest three quintiles of the income distribution suffered reductions in their real levels of consumption of 31, 20 and 12 per cent respectively. Those in the highest two quintiles, however, gained 3 and 16 per cent respectively (Cortázar and Marshall, 1980).

As a result, the economy was biased towards recovery in the levels of activity in the "non-tradeables" sector, especially in commerce, finance and

*Table 6.1.    Indicators of income levels and poverty incidence, Chile, 1969-85*

| Year | GDP per capita (US$, 1977) | Poverty line per capita, Greater Santiago (US$, 1977) | Indices, 1969 = 100 | | | Percentage of poor families, Greater Santiago | | |
|------|------|------|------|------|------|------|------|------|
| | | | GDP per capita | Real wages | Poverty line | Destitute | Other poor | Total |
| | (1) | (2) | (3) | (4) | (5) | (6) | (7) | (8) |
| 1969 | 30 155 | 3 027 | 100.0 | 100.0 | 100.0 | 8.4 | 20.1 | 28.5 |
| 1970 | 30 310 | – | 100.5 | 108.7 | – | – | – | – |
| 1971 | 32 353 | – | 107.3 | 133.4 | – | – | – | – |
| 1972 | 31 421 | – | 104.2 | 93.6 | – | – | – | – |
| 1973 | 29 182 | – | 96.8 | 87.4 | – | – | – | – |
| 1974 | 28 980 | – | 96.1 | 70.7 | – | – | – | – |
| 1975 | 24 817 | – | 82.3 | 68.4 | – | – | – | – |
| 1976 | 25 255 | 3 659 | 83.8 | 70.5 | 120.9 | 27.9 | 29.0 | 56.9 |
| 1977 | 27 274 | – | 90.5 | 77.6 | – | – | – | – |
| 1978 | 29 015 | – | 96.2 | 82.6 | – | – | – | – |
| 1979 | 30 887 | 3 548 | 102.4 | 89.5 | 117.2 | 11.7 | 24.3 | 35.9 |
| 1980 | 32 730 | 3 792 | 108.5 | 97.1 | 125.3 | 14.4 | 25.9 | 40.3 |
| 1981 | 34 021 | – | 112.8 | 107.4 | – | – | – | – |
| 1982 | 28 696 | 3 283 | 95.2 | 106.1 | 108.5 | 10.8 | 20.4 | 30.8 |
| 1983 | 28 254 | – | 93.7 | 94.4 | – | – | – | – |
| 1984 | 29 547 | 3 686 | 98.0 | 98.4 | 121.8 | 23.0 | 25.2 | 48.2 |
| 1985 | 29 773 | 3 308 | 98.7 | 94.3 | 109.3 | 19.2 | 26.2 | 45.4 |

Sources. Column (1): Banco Central de Chile, 1983, and Boletin Mensual del Banco Central, September 1986 and July 1985. Column (2): Estimated by the authors as explained in the text, deflated by the Consumer Price Index. Column (3): Estimated from column 1. Column (4): INE, deflated by the Consumer Price Index. Column (5): Estimated from column 2. Columns (6), (7) and (8): Estimated by the authors as explained in the text.

construction, but not in the "tradeables" sector, producing importables (industry) and exportables (agriculture and mining, and subject to international competition). The large differences in technical production relationships and the absorption of the labour force among these sectors of the economy have in turn influenced the levels of unemployment, underemployment and poverty. A marked concentration of growth in non-tradeable sectors led less to an increase in employment than to a recomposition of employment towards higher skills and higher pay. It can be seen in table 6.2 that the tradeables sectors, which declined in economic importance between 1970 and 1983, are those where workers have the lowest levels of schooling, and it is here that poverty is concentrated.

The calculations reported in the next section show that as a result of these large fluctuations, the incidence of poverty among families of Greater Santiago has varied from 29 per cent (1969) to a maximum of 57 per cent (1976), declining in the period of recovery to 31 per cent (1982) before increasing immediately after the recession of 1982-83 to 49 per cent (1984) and 45 per cent (1985).

*Table 6.2. Labour force composition by sector, literacy and schooling, 1970-83 (percentages)*

| | Schooling | | | | | |
| --- | --- | --- | --- | --- | --- | --- |
| | Illiterate, without schooling | 1-6 years (primary) | 7 and more years (other) | Unknown | Total | Percentage of total employment |
| Exportables | | | | | | |
| 1970 | 15.9 | 60.1 | 19.8 | 4.2 | 100.0 | 20.7 |
| 1977 | 15.0 | 59.7 | 21.2 | 4.1 | 100.0 | 21.1 |
| 1980 | 13.8 | 57.3 | 26.1 | 2.8 | 100.0 | 18.5 |
| 1983 | 12.1 | 55.5 | 31.3 | 1.3 | 100.0 | 17.7 |
| Importables | | | | | | |
| 1970 | 2.9 | 46.9 | 47.6 | 2.6 | 100.0 | 16.8 |
| 1977 | 2.7 | 43.8 | 51.5 | 2.0 | 100.0 | 16.8 |
| 1980 | 2.7 | 38.2 | 56.8 | 2.3 | 100.0 | 16.1 |
| 1983 | 2.4 | 32.9 | 63.6 | 1.0 | 100.0 | 12.6 |
| Non-tradeables [1] | | | | | | |
| 1970 | 3.5 | 37.7 | 55.4 | 3.4 | 100.0 | 62.1 |
| 1977 | 3.4 | 36.9 | 56.2 | 3.5 | 100.0 | 62.1 |
| 1980 | 3.2 | 33.0 | 60.5 | 3.3 | 100.0 | 63.4 |
| 1983 | 3.0 | 30.7 | 65.0 | 1.3 | 100.0 | 69.7 |
| All workers | | | | | | |
| 1970 | 5.9 | 43.7 | 47.0 | 3.4 | 100.0 | 100.0 |
| 1977 | 5.7 | 42.8 | 47.9 | 3.3 | 100.0 | 100.0 |
| 1980 | 5.1 | 38.3 | 53.6 | 3.0 | 100.0 | 100.0 |
| 1983 | 4.5 | 35.3 | 58.8 | 1.3 | 100.0 | 100.0 |

[1] Unknown sectors were included with non-tradeables.

Source. Ministerio de Economia, Fomento y Reconstruccion, Instituto Nacional de Estadisticas, *Encuesta Nacional del Empleo*, 1977 and 1983, October-December. Whole country.

# III. The magnitude and characteristics of poverty in Greater Santiago

## 1. The concept of poverty

Without introducing in detail all the possible definitions of poverty, it is sufficient to indicate that for this study we use "absolute poverty" in the biological sense. According to this definition, those considered as destitute or in a situation of "primary poverty" (Rowntree, 1901) are individuals whose total incomes are insufficient to satisfy their basic nutritional needs. The latter criterion refers to the minimum nutritional requirements per person as defined by ECLA (Altimir, 1979). The goods contained in the basic ECLA needs basket are valued at the prices given by the CPI in May of each year of the study, in order to obtain the value of the basic basket for each of the periods (details are given in an annex). Poverty is thus defined by comparing the cost of the basic-needs basket per person with the family income per capita obtained from

*Table 6.3.    The poverty line and real wages, 1969-85*

| (A) | Cost of the basic basket (May) (US$ per year) | Price index for basic basket (May 1969 = 100) | CPI/C-M (May 1969 = 100) | CPI INE (May 1969 = 100) | CPI INE, annual average (1969 = 100) | Food price index, INE, annual average (1969 = 100) |
|------|------|------|------|------|------|------|
| 1969 | 0.075 | 100.0 | 100.0 | 100.0 | 100.0 | 100.0 |
| 1976 | 154.40 | 2 058.7 [1] | 1 703.1 [1] | 1 007.1 [1] | 1 147.2 [1] | 1 519.6 [1] |
| 1979 | 702.02 | 9 360.3 [1] | 7 985.5 [1] | 3 897.1 [1] | 4 114.8 [1] | 4 993.3 [1] |
| 1980 | 1 041.74 | 13 889.9 [1] | 11 089.0 [1] | 5 411.7 [1] | 5 560.7 [1] | 6 794.2 [1] |
| 1982 | 1 151.47 | 15 352.9 [1] | 14 156.2 [1] | 6 908.6 [1] | 7 316.9 [1] | 8 042.1 [1] |
| 1984 | 2 025.04 | 27 000.5 [1] | 22 195.8 [1] | 10 832.2 [1] | 11 161.0 [1] | 12 243.3 [1] |
| 1985 | 2 400.86 | 32 011.5 [1] | 29 293.3 [1] | 14 296.0 [1] | 14 586.0 [1] | 15 708.2 [1] |

| (B) | Index of money wages and salaries (1969 = 100) | Index of real wages and salaries (1969 = 100) | | | | |
|------|------|------|------|------|------|------|
| | | Price indices | | | | |
| | | Basic basket | CPI/C-M | CPI INE | CPI INE, annual | Food price |
| 1969 | 100.0 | 100.0 | 100.0 | 100.0 | 100.0 | 100.0 |
| 1976 | 1 076.3 | 52.1 | 63.2 | 106.9 | 93.5 | 70.6 |
| 1979 | 7 607.8 | 81.3 | 95.3 | 195.2 | 154.5 | 127.3 |
| 1980 | 11 326.6 | 81.5 | 102.1 | 209.3 | 184.4 | 150.9 |
| 1982 | 17 111.6 | 111.5 | 120.9 | 247.7 | 219.2 | 199.5 |
| 1984 | 22 722.2 | 84.2 | 102.4 | 209.8 | 203.6 | 185.6 |
| 1985 | 28 018.9 | 87.5 | 95.6 | 196.0 | 192.5 | 178.4 |

[1] These figures are divided by 100.
Sources. PREALC on the basis of Cortázar and Marshall, 1980, and Banco Central Bulletins.

the Employment and Unemployment Survey undertaken by the Economics Department of the University of Chile.

Food-expenditure elasticities are not used for family size, which means that economies of scale in family consumption are not considered. The cost of the basket is compared directly with family income per capita, and adults and children have been given the same weights in determining the number of members belonging to the household. The total household income includes income received by all members, not only resulting directly from work (in cash or in kind) but also from other sources, such as pensions and other incomes. One criticism concerning the data in the Employment and Unemployment Survey is that there is under-reporting of non-wage and salary income; and that under-reporting is erratic (Cortázar and Marshall, 1980). Nevertheless, considering that the central interest of this investigation is poverty, this omission is not very significant, as the analysis focuses on the bottom part of the income distribution (the poor) where such under-reporting is less.

To estimate the magnitude of poverty, using the above criteria, three

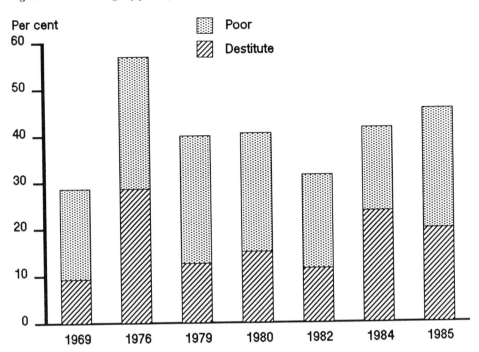

*Figure 6.3. Percentage of poverty and destitution, Greater Santiago, 1969-85*

types of families and households can be identified: those whose total income per capita is lower than the cost of the basket, those whose income is between once and twice its cost, and those whose income is greater than twice its cost. The first group of families is classified as "destitute", the second as "poor but not destitute" and the third as "not poor".[2]

## 2. Wages, prices and the cost of the basic basket

Table 6.3 shows the values of the basket compared with those of the general CPI basket and its food components (columns 2, 5 and 6).[3] Presented in the same table is the price index of Cortázar and Marshall (C-M) who reconstructed the series on the basis of price data from INE, but who also maintained the weights of the goods in the basket fixed throughout the period (Cortázar and Marshall, 1980). Real wages are examined using various estimates of the changes in the cost of living.

The results are important inasmuch as they show marked differences between the changes in the official CPI of the INE and that obtained by C-M. The index of the value of the subsistence basket in column 2 is similar to that of the CPI of C-M, and reveals that between 1969 and 1976 real wages and salaries appear to have suffered a fall of about 50 per cent, followed by a gradual increase until 1982, when they barely surpassed the 1969 level, falling again

*Table 6.4.   Indicators of poverty, unemployment and real wages: Correlation matrix*

| Variables | Percentage of poor households | | | Unemployment rate | Real wage index |
|---|---|---|---|---|---|
| | Destitute | Non-destitute poor | Total | | |
| Destitute (%) | 1.000 | 0.861 | 0.987 | 0.430 | −0.686 |
| Non-destitute poor (%) | — | 1.000 | 0.937 | 0.158 | −0.929 |
| Total poor (%) | — | — | 1.000 | 0.357 | −0.784 |
| Unemployment rate | — | — | — | 1.000 | 0.014 |
| Real wage index | — | — | — | — | 1.000 |
| Mean | 16.0 | 24.1 | 40.1 | 15.1 | 80.4 |
| Standard deviation | 7.8 | 3.4 | 10.8 | 5.8 | 19.9 |
| Maximum | 27.9 | 29.0 | 56.9 | 22.8 | 104.5 |
| Minimum | 8.4 | 20.1 | 28.5 | 6.9 | 52.1 |

Source. PREALC, on the basis of data from figure 6.1 and table 6.1.

thereafter. The results are totally different if the official CPI is used to deflate the series. In that case the index of real wages and salaries would scarcely have diminished between 1969 and 1976 (and would actually have increased if the calculations had corresponded to the May values of each year) and by 1982 would have more than doubled.

### 3. The magnitude and evolution of poverty

The percentage of households in the different strata of poverty during the years of the study were presented in table 6.1. Figure 6.3 summarises the trends. The figure shows considerable fluctuations in the magnitude of poverty during the economic cycle. The year 1976 was the worst in terms of poverty, when it affected 56.9 per cent of the households of Greater Santiago. In that year poverty was particularly affected by two factors: *(a)* the international recession caused by the rise in the price of oil; *(b)* the "shock" policy implemented by the economic authorities, in order to contain the inflationary process. After the subsequent period of expansion (1981, with effects persisting in May 1982), the levels of poverty were only slightly above the 1969 level, although they returned to high levels in 1984 and 1985. The poverty situation during this latter period reflects the effects of the recession of 1982-83. It can be seen that the largest changes occurred in destitution (affecting from 8 to 28 per cent of the families) while the "poor but not destitute" changed less (between 20 and 29 per cent of families).

Although the time series is very short for drawing definitive conclusions, table 6.4 reveals a high correlation *(a)* between the incidence of destitution and the overall rate of unemployment in Greater Santiago and *(b)* between the incidence of non-destitute poverty and the real wage and salary index. Both the wage index and the unemployment rate varied markedly in this

*Figure 6.4.    Destitution and unemployment in Greater Santiago, 1969-85*

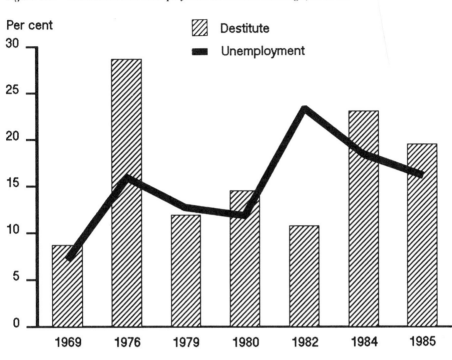

From the above we can infer that the elimination of poverty in its most extreme forms requires an attack both on unemployment and on the problem of low productivity and real incomes — which characterise the traditional sectors of the labour market and/or modern wage sectors with low bargaining power.

period (coefficient of variation of 0.25 and 0.39 respectively), but the proportion of destitutes varied more (see figures 6.4 and 6.5).

From the above we can infer that the elimination of poverty in its most extreme forms requires an attack both on unemployment and on the problem of low productivity and real incomes — which characterise the traditional sectors of the labour market and/or modern wage sectors with low bargaining power.

### 4. Poverty characteristics

Three groups of factors can be identified which characterise poverty at the family level: structural, micro-household and institutional.

### A. Structural factors

These factors reflect characteristics of the Chilean economy and society, and affect poverty in three ways. The first is through demographic factors: family size and composition. The size is simply the number of household members, whereas the composition for our purposes concerns the distribution of these members between children (under 14 years old) and adults. These variables differ greatly between poverty strata and also change significantly after 1976 (see table 6.5). In fact, the pattern in the table is a result of the sharp decline

Figure 6.5. *Poverty and real wages in Greater Santiago, 1969-85*

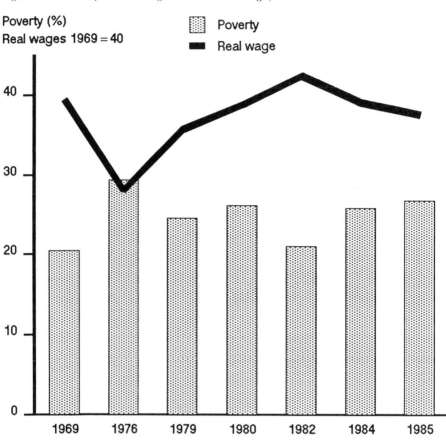

in fertility which started around 1960. After 1976 nuclear family size fell by about 10 per cent, extended family size by 8 per cent. This essentially reflects a decline in the number of children. One in three family members were children in 1969, one in four in 1984. These relationships differ across poverty strata, family size and proportion of children being larger in the poorest strata, although the differences decline between 1969 and 1985.

A second structural factor, and one which increases in importance, is the capacity of the economy to create jobs for the population of working age. Around 1969 there was one job for roughly 2.1 persons of working age; by 1984-85 the latter figure had risen to 2.3. However, the most serious aspect of the relationship between job creation and poverty is that it is destitute households which are most affected. Among this group there was one job for 2.7 persons of working age in 1969, and one for 3.0 in 1984. It is clear that destitution is closely linked to unemployment.

A third factor, relevant only for those in work, is productivity. In so far as productivity is proxied by occupational incomes in the households

*Table 6.5.  Characteristics of households by poverty strata and demographic composition, 1969-85*

| | 1969 | 1976 | 1979 | 1980 | 1982 | 1984 | 1985 |
|---|---|---|---|---|---|---|---|
| *Destitute* (%) | (8.4) | (27.9) | (11.7) | (14.4) | (10.8) | (23.0) | (19.2) |
| Extended family size | 6.4 | 5.3 | 5.6 | 5.4 | 5.5 | 4.8 | 5.1 |
| Nuclear family size | 5.7 | 4.7 | 5.0 | 4.7 | 4.6 | 4.3 | 4.4 |
| % children | 50 | 39 | 39 | 38 | 35 | 35 | 37 |
| Workers/adults (%) | 37 | 33 | 31 | 30 | 21 | 33 | 31 |
| Economically active/adults (%) | 49 | 47 | 46 | 43 | 46 | 49 | 47 |
| *Poor* (%) | (20.1) | (29.0) | (24.2) | (25.9) | (20.4) | (25.2) | (26.2) |
| Extended family size | 5.9 | 4.4 | 4.9 | 4.6 | 4.8 | 4.3 | 4.4 |
| Nuclear family size | 5.2 | 3.8 | 4.3 | 4.1 | 4.2 | 3.8 | 3.9 |
| % children | 45 | 31 | 33 | 31 | 32 | 27 | 27 |
| Workers/adults (%) | 41 | 42 | 39 | 41 | 33 | 40 | 41 |
| Economically active/adults (%) | 47 | 50 | 46 | 47 | 46 | 49 | 49 |
| *Non-poor* (%) | (71.5) | (43.1) | (64.1) | (59.7) | (69.8) | (51.8) | (54.6) |
| Extended family size | 4.3 | 3.7 | 3.8 | 3.7 | 3.8 | 3.7 | 3.7 |
| Nuclear family size | 3.7 | 3.2 | 3.4 | 3.3 | 3.3 | 3.2 | 3.3 |
| % children | 28 | 21 | 22 | 21 | 23 | 22 | 21 |
| Workers/adults (%) | 51 | 51 | 50 | 50 | 46 | 50 | 50 |
| Economically active/adults (%) | 54 | 54 | 53 | 53 | 52 | 54 | 54 |
| *Total* (%) | (100.0) | (100.0) | (100.0) | (100.0) | (100.0) | (100.0) | (100.0) |
| Extended family size | 4.8 | 4.4 | 4.3 | 4.2 | 4.2 | 4.1 | 4.1 |
| Nuclear family size | 4.2 | 3.8 | 3.8 | 3.7 | 3.6 | 3.6 | 3.6 |
| % children | 35 | 30 | 28 | 27 | 27 | 27 | 26 |
| Workers/adults (%) | 48 | 43 | 44 | 44 | 40 | 43 | 44 |
| Economically active/adults (%) | 52 | 51 | 50 | 49 | 50 | 51 | 51 |

Note. The figures in parentheses show the percentage of households falling in each poverty stratum.

Source. Prepared by the authors on the basis of data from the Encuesta de Ocupación del Gran Santiago, May of each year, Departamento de Economia de la Universidad de Chile.

concerned, it can be seen that the former did not increase from 1969 to 1985. Income per worker in destitute and poor households declined, and barely stayed constant in non-poor households. For 1969-85 as a whole, productivity levels higher than those of 1969 were reached only in 1982, and this was only temporary.

Table 6.6 summarises this analysis, and shows that demographic factors are now less important in explaining income per capita differences between poverty strata. The factor which grew most in importance was the economy's capacity to employ the population of working age. But the factor which contributed most to inequality was the level of income, and — implicitly — of productivity.

*Table 6.6.  Factors contributing to income per capita differentials between urban households in different poverty strata*

|  | Total | Total income | No. of workers | No. of adults |
|---|---|---|---|---|
|  |  | No. of workers | No. of adults | Household size |
| **1969** |  |  |  |  |
| Poor and destitute | 100.0 | 72.2 | 13.0 | 14.7 |
| Non-poor and poor | 100.0 | 63.0 | 13.6 | 23.4 |
| Non-poor and destitute | 100.0 | 66.1 | 13.4 | 20.5 |
| **1976** |  |  |  |  |
| Poor and destitute | 100.0 | 56.2 | 28.5 | 15.3 |
| Non-poor and poor | 100.0 | 72.3 | 13.8 | 13.9 |
| Non-poor and destitute | 100.0 | 66.2 | 19.3 | 14.4 |
| **1979** |  |  |  |  |
| Poor and destitute | 100.0 | 58.2 | 31.4 | 10.5 |
| Non-poor and poor | 100.0 | 70.7 | 16.0 | 13.2 |
| Non-poor and destitute | 100.0 | 66.7 | 21.0 | 12.3 |
| **1980** |  |  |  |  |
| Poor and destitute | 100.0 | 48.4 | 39.9 | 11.6 |
| Non-poor and poor | 100.0 | 72.9 | 12.8 | 14.3 |
| Non-poor and destitute | 100.0 | 64.7 | 21.9 | 13.4 |
| **1982** |  |  |  |  |
| Poor and destitute | 100.0 | 41.3 | 54.8 | 3.9 |
| Non-poor and poor | 100.0 | 68.3 | 19.3 | 12.3 |
| Non-poor and destitute | 100.0 | 59.6 | 30.8 | 9.6 |
| **1984** |  |  |  |  |
| Poor and destitute | 100.0 | 66.8 | 23.7 | 9.6 |
| Non-poor and poor | 100.0 | 72.0 | 13.3 | 14.7 |
| Non-poor and destitute | 100.0 | 70.3 | 16.7 | 13.0 |
| **1985** |  |  |  |  |
| Poor and destitute | 100.0 | 49.9 | 32.8 | 17.3 |
| Non-poor and poor | 100.0 | 80.9 | 13.7 | 5.4 |
| Non-poor and destitute | 100.0 | 69.4 | 20.8 | 9.8 |

Source. Calculated by the authors from data in table 6.5.

### B. Micro-household factors

At the level of household organisation, two factors can be distinguished which reflect family response to fluctuations in employment and incomes of the principal income earner, usually the household head; the spouse and children are considered as a secondary family labour force, on the assumption that their participation in economic activity attempts to complement the income of the household head. The factors examined here are the overall labour force participation rate of adult household members (over 14 years); and the composition of economically active household members by relation to the head.

Table 6.7. *Labour force participation rates by poverty strata and relation to the head, 1969-85*

|  | 1969 | 1976 | 1979 | 1980 | 1982 | 1984 | 1985 |
|---|---|---|---|---|---|---|---|
| *Destitute* |  |  |  |  |  |  |  |
| Head | 81.5 | 81.2 | 80.3 | 78.1 | 75.3 | 83.6 | 82.7 |
| Spouse | 17.5 | 21.0 | 21.3 | 18.6 | 21.0 | 23.6 | 19.2 |
| Children | 43.9 | 36.4 | 35.8 | 32.7 | 39.1 | 38.3 | 37.4 |
| Other relations | 34.4 | 37.7 | 37.2 | 29.9 | 46.6 | 38.8 | 19.9 |
| Other non-relations | 16.7 | 54.2 | 57.1 | 50.0 | 57.1 | 40.0 | 35.7 |
| Total | 48.6 | 46.9 | 45.7 | 42.8 | 46.2 | 48.9 | 46.7 |
| *Poor* |  |  |  |  |  |  |  |
| Head | 85.3 | 80.0 | 80.2 | 79.0 | 78.7 | 75.8 | 79.7 |
| Spouse | 13.2 | 22.2 | 19.8 | 18.2 | 17.0 | 19.9 | 18.5 |
| Children | 39.7 | 42.1 | 36.6 | 38.4 | 38.6 | 47.2 | 45.3 |
| Other relations | 42.2 | 45.1 | 42.5 | 40.9 | 36.4 | 42.3 | 42.1 |
| Other non-relations | 52.9 | 58.6 | 32.3 | 83.3 | 53.8 | 60.0 | 57.1 |
| Total | 47.5 | 49.9 | 46.3 | 46.6 | 45.6 | 49.1 | 49.2 |
| *Non-poor* |  |  |  |  |  |  |  |
| Head | 85.2 | 84.2 | 80.5 | 78.8 | 77.2 | 78.1 | 76.9 |
| Spouse | 24.1 | 32.7 | 30.1 | 43.8 | 28.6 | 33.7 | 30.3 |
| Children | 45.8 | 42.6 | 44.3 | 43.8 | 45.1 | 45.2 | 50.6 |
| Other relations | 46.8 | 38.8 | 42.0 | 42.2 | 46.1 | 44.7 | 40.5 |
| Other non-relations | 68.1 | 45.8 | 70.2 | 65.5 | 56.6 | 65.9 | 68.0 |
| Total | 54.0 | 54.1 | 53.0 | 52.6 | 52.3 | 54.0 | 53.7 |
| *Total* |  |  |  |  |  |  |  |
| Head | 80.9 | 79.9 | 77.9 | 75.7 | 75.2 | 75.9 | 78.8 |
| Spouse | 21.1 | 25.9 | 25.8 | 25.0 | 24.2 | 25.3 | 24.8 |
| Children | 43.2 | 40.2 | 40.0 | 39.5 | 42.3 | 43.5 | 46.3 |
| Other relations | 43.8 | 39.8 | 40.9 | 39.2 | 43.2 | 42.0 | 39.7 |
| Other non-relations | 61.3 | 47.8 | 53.7 | 64.4 | 56.5 | 55.4 | 60.3 |
| Total | 50.8 | 50.5 | 49.2 | 48.3 | 49.2 | 50.4 | 51.0 |

Source. See table 6.5.

During the period studied, the overall labour force participation rate is systematically lower among poor than among non-poor households. This is essentially due to a lower participation rate of secondary workers, that of heads being relatively low among the destitute up to 1982, but relatively high thereafter. The overall participation rate has not changed greatly over time, but there are some signs of an increase in the economic activity of spouses among the non-poor. A similar but smaller increase is seen for children (table 6.7), while the labour force participation of heads has declined.

It might be inferred from the above that income from secondary workers is an important factor in escaping from poverty in Chile. Nevertheless, in urban areas such work must be compatible with the roles of the women in domestic work, the latter falling mainly on the wife of the household head and

*Table 6.8.   Key labour market characteristics — Household heads, 1969-85 (percentages)*

|                                      | 1969 | 1976 | 1979 | 1980 | 1982 | 1984 | 1985 |
|--------------------------------------|------|------|------|------|------|------|------|
| *All households*                     |      |      |      |      |      |      |      |
| Not more than primary education      | 56.7 | 53.5 | 47.0 | 50.0 | 46.3 | 41.7 | 41.6 |
| Working less than 30 hours           | 9.9  | 10.7 | 8.5  | 6.8  | 11.5 | 14.4 | 11.8 |
| Working in public sector             | 20.1 | 19.8 | 17.8 | 13.3 | 12.5 | 18.9 | 19.6 |
| Working in construction              | 10.0 | 9.3  | 9.6  | 10.6 | 12.0 | 8.4  | 9.3  |
| Working in services                  | 40.1 | 40.1 | 42.5 | 41.9 | 40.3 | 48.4 | 47.0 |
| Working in informal sector           | 21.6 | 23.2 | 22.5 | 23.7 | 19.5 | 19.9 | 21.4 |
| Private sector manual wage labour    | 26.3 | 23.5 | 25.1 | 27.1 | 22.9 | 21.2 | 23.7 |
| Domestic service                     | 0.7  | 0.9  | 0.8  | 1.7  | 1.6  | 1.4  | 1.7  |
| Unemployed                           | 5.3  | 11.4 | 8.6  | 8.5  | 19.0 | 14.1 | 8.9  |
| *Destitute households*               |      |      |      |      |      |      |      |
| Not more than primary education      | 85.7 | 80.0 | 75.4 | 79.6 | 76.2 | 68.2 | 67.0 |
| Working less than 30 hours           | 20.5 | 19.4 | 19.5 | 15.9 | 38.8 | 34.2 | 26.8 |
| Working in public sector             | 9.5  | 14.3 | 15.6 | 8.6  | 6.7  | 25.5 | 24.4 |
| Working in construction              | 21.2 | 14.7 | 17.9 | 18.5 | 26.2 | 12.0 | 11.3 |
| Working in services                  | 33.9 | 35.3 | 36.2 | 32.2 | 32.4 | 47.9 | 49.8 |
| Working in informal sector           | 33.9 | 25.7 | 24.6 | 24.8 | 22.9 | 20.5 | 21.0 |
| Private sector manual wage labour    | 35.4 | 37.5 | 33.2 | 37.9 | 18.6 | 25.9 | 27.0 |
| Domestic service                     | 0.5  | 1.3  | 1.3  | 3.2  | 1.4  | 2.6  | 1.6  |
| Unemployed                           | 19.6 | 15.0 | 22.3 | 19.7 | 50.0 | 23.7 | 23.7 |
| *Poor households*                    |      |      |      |      |      |      |      |
| Not more than primary education      | 83.7 | 64.8 | 71.6 | 71.7 | 72.4 | 53.0 | 52.8 |
| Working less than 30 hours           | 12.8 | 8.4  | 10.0 | 15.9 | 14.3 | 13.9 | 12.7 |
| Working in public sector             | 13.5 | 19.8 | 14.4 | 10.9 | 8.8  | 15.9 | 16.5 |
| Working in construction              | 12.2 | 8.8  | 13.2 | 11.0 | 15.3 | 8.5  | 11.4 |
| Working in services                  | 34.0 | 37.5 | 35.8 | 35.7 | 32.4 | 45.7 | 43.5 |
| Working in informal sector           | 22.6 | 23.6 | 23.8 | 24.7 | 21.3 | 22.1 | 21.4 |
| Private sector manual wage labour    | 44.7 | 30.7 | 38.3 | 42.4 | 38.5 | 33.8 | 36.5 |
| Domestic service                     | 0.6  | 1.2  | 2.7  | 2.6  | 4.2  | 3.2  | 3.0  |
| Unemployed                           | 6.8  | 6.2  | 9.4  | 6.7  | 18.3 | 10.8 | 9.1  |
| *Non-poor households*                |      |      |      |      |      |      |      |
| Not more than primary education      | 45.9 | 29.9 | 32.7 | 33.4 | 34.0 | 23.4 | 26.8 |
| Working less than 30 hours           | 9.1  | 7.2  | 6.5  | 5.3  | 8.2  | 6.7  | 6.2  |
| Working in public sector             | 23.1 | 23.4 | 19.5 | 15.4 | 14.4 | 17.2 | 19.3 |
| Working in construction              | 8.1  | 6.2  | 6.7  | 8.6  | 9.0  | 6.6  | 7.5  |
| Working in services                  | 42.8 | 44.8 | 46.1 | 46.9 | 43.8 | 50.0 | 47.7 |
| Working in informal sector           | 20.4 | 24.5 | 22.4 | 23.8 | 20.8 | 20.2 | 21.7 |
| Private sector manual wage labour    | 20.5 | 13.1 | 19.8 | 19.3 | 21.8 | 14.7 | 16.1 |
| Domestic service                     | 0.7  | 0.5  | —    | 1.1  | 1.0  | 1.1  | 1.0  |
| Unemployed                           | 1.6  | 1.0  | 1.8  | 1.9  | 5.3  | 3.4  | 3.1  |

Source. See table 6.5.

*Table 6.9.   Key labour market characteristics — Spouses, 1969-85 (percentages)*

|  | 1969 | 1976 | 1979 | 1980 | 1982 | 1984 | 1985 |
|---|---|---|---|---|---|---|---|
| *All households* | | | | | | | |
| Not more than primary education | 57.2 | 49.3 | 47.0 | 43.6 | 35.3 | 36.2 | 35.1 |
| Working less than 30 hours | 27.0 | 26.0 | 23.8 | 20.6 | 20.4 | 22.6 | 23.2 |
| Working in public sector | 2.3 | 22.6 | 23.4 | 18.6 | 21.0 | 22.8 | 21.1 |
| Working in construction | 2.4 | 2.1 | 2.2 | 1.7 | 2.2 | 0.7 | 1.7 |
| Working in services | 45.0 | 46.9 | 50.7 | 49.6 | 56.7 | 58.3 | 59.9 |
| Working in informal sector | 40.6 | 28.3 | 29.3 | 31.2 | 22.3 | 20.2 | 26.1 |
| Private sector manual wage labour | 11.5 | 10.0 | 11.4 | 12.5 | 10.0 | 8.9 | 9.7 |
| Domestic service | 3.9 | 6.5 | 8.5 | 8.4 | 8.6 | 10.0 | 12.3 |
| Unemployed | 6.7 | 18.8 | 9.0 | 7.9 | 14.1 | 15.5 | 9.4 |
| *Destitute households* | | | | | | | |
| Not more than primary education | 93.3 | 84.5 | 82.6 | 82.7 | 82.9 | 72.1 | 65.8 |
| Working less than 30 hours | 48.0 | 27.9 | 36.9 | 51.4 | 37.1 | 45.2 | 50.9 |
| Working in public sector | 3.3 | 5.3 | 5.2 | 17.3 | 6.5 | 29.7 | 14.3 |
| Working in construction | 0.0 | 0.0 | 3.2 | 0.0 | 0.0 | 1.6 | 1.2 |
| Working in services | 66.7 | 43.4 | 40.8 | 60.3 | 66.0 | 65.6 | 56.1 |
| Working in informal sector | 60.0 | 35.6 | 40.4 | 25.9 | 40.4 | 23.0 | 36.4 |
| Private sector manual wage labour | 6.7 | 7.0 | 15.5 | 10.3 | 4.3 | 10.7 | 13.0 |
| Domestic service | 16.7 | 10.1 | 12.4 | 24.1 | 23.4 | 14.9 | 11.7 |
| Unemployed | 10.0 | 39.5 | 25.4 | 24.1 | 25.5 | 32.8 | 23.4 |
| *Poor households* | | | | | | | |
| Not more than primary education | 86.7 | 69.6 | 66.1 | 77.1 | 68.0 | 54.5 | 57.0 |
| Working less than 30 hours | 37.7 | 30.3 | 34.0 | 19.8 | 23.3 | 23.0 | 26.4 |
| Working in public sector | 3.3 | 15.5 | 9.9 | 4.9 | 2.8 | 16.8 | 17.5 |
| Working in construction | 1.7 | 2.0 | 2.4 | 1.9 | 5.6 | 0.0 | 1.9 |
| Working in services | 26.7 | 42.6 | 46.8 | 40.0 | 47.2 | 55.5 | 54.8 |
| Working in informal sector | 60.0 | 30.3 | 43.6 | 40.0 | 29.1 | 32.8 | 29.1 |
| Private sector manual wage labour | 11.7 | 20.2 | 9.7 | 24.6 | 13.9 | 10.9 | 13.6 |
| Domestic service | 3.3 | 12.2 | 19.3 | 17.2 | 22.2 | 20.9 | 22.3 |
| Unemployed | 15.0 | 16.2 | 14.5 | 7.7 | 19.4 | 16.3 | 14.6 |
| *Non-poor households* | | | | | | | |
| Not more than primary education | 49.2 | 23.7 | 28.8 | 28.4 | 23.4 | 18.4 | 21.6 |
| Working less than 30 hours | 23.7 | 39.1 | 19.9 | 17.4 | 18.2 | 16.9 | 17.1 |
| Working in public sector | 2.0 | 32.9 | 29.3 | 22.5 | 26.1 | 22.4 | 23.7 |
| Working in construction | 2.3 | 3.1 | 1.9 | 1.9 | 1.8 | 0.6 | 1.8 |
| Working in services | 46.3 | 50.7 | 51.7 | 50.6 | 57.4 | 56.6 | 62.4 |
| Working in informal sector | 35.9 | 26.4 | 24.2 | 29.9 | 20.0 | 16.2 | 22.8 |
| Private sector manual wage labour | 11.9 | 6.8 | 11.5 | 9.6 | 10.3 | 8.1 | 7.8 |
| Domestic service | 2.8 | 2.4 | 5.1 | 3.7 | 4.7 | 5.3 | 9.3 |
| Unemployed | 4.5 | 4.5 | 4.3 | 4.5 | 6.8 | 6.4 | 4.5 |

Source. See table 6.5.

on the older children in the poorest households. Moreover, the latter face poor job opportunities and low returns from work, perhaps insufficient to justify absence from home and the costs of job search. As a result, one of the mechanisms determining the incidence of poverty is directly linked to discrimination within the household in domestic roles, as well as discrimination in job access. This shows up clearly in levels of unemployment. Although the spouse and children have a lower overall labour force participation rate than household heads, their levels of unemployment are particularly high. Among the destitute, these rates average around twice as high as among the non-destitute poor, and among the latter the rates are again around double those of the non-poor (tables 6.8 to 6.10). This is consistent with what is often referred to as the "discouraged worker" hypothesis. It is clear that any strategy to combat poverty must respond to the factors which affect needs, incentives and restrictions concerning labour force participation, as well as the mechanisms determining real job opportunities.

### C. Institutional factors

Under this heading we include changes in employment opportunities and conditions in different labour market segments, including occupational structure, productivity and working hours. While personal characteristics such as education, sex and working experience are considered as important determinants of access to jobs and incomes in Chile (Corbo and Stelcner, 1980; Riveros, 1983), it is none the less clear that these factors have to be analysed within the broader labour market context; in particular, it is necessary to identify the point of insertion in a heterogeneous labour market structure, and equally to consider the hours of work which are available in different forms of employment (Uthoff, 1983 and 1983-84). A number of key variables are presented in tables 6.8 to 6.10. It can be seen that poverty is concentrated, as one would expect, among those with low education levels. There is also a distinct tendency for poverty to be associated with shorter working hours, for all categories of household members.

Between 1969 and 1985, along with the decrease in job creation compared with the population of working age, the occupational structure also changed radically. In parallel with the growth in unemployment there has been a tendency for the occupational structure to shift towards the tertiary sector (commerce and services); this included a distinct upward trend in domestic service. At the same time, public sector employment first diminished between 1969 and 1982, as a result of the policy of reduced state spending, and then rose again as a result of the emergency employment schemes initiated by the State. The average number of hours worked by those with a job did not vary systematically, showing that underemployment appeared mainly in the lower levels of productivity and income of the new occupational structure, rather than in a reduction in the working day.

The relationship with personal characteristics of workers does not show the problem of poverty as one of a restricted group of the population failing to benefit from economic growth. It is rather the absence of economic growth

*Table 6.10.  Key labour market characteristics — Children of head, 1969-85 (percentages)*

|  | 1969 | 1976 | 1979 | 1980 | 1982 | 1984 | 1985 |
|---|---|---|---|---|---|---|---|
| *All households* | | | | | | | |
| Not more than primary education | 53.1 | 37.2 | 31.3 | 25.3 | 24.8 | 23.8 | 18.6 |
| Working less than 30 hours | 13.8 | 16.6 | 14.7 | 11.1 | 14.8 | 19.8 | 14.8 |
| Working in public sector | 13.7 | 21.6 | 18.4 | 16.9 | 14.1 | 20.0 | 20.5 |
| Working in construction | 4.8 | 3.6 | 5.5 | 4.9 | 7.9 | 3.9 | 4.8 |
| Working in services | 36.2 | 38.2 | 40.1 | 42.5 | 38.1 | 45.3 | 48.2 |
| Working in informal sector | 8.5 | 13.6 | 11.7 | 10.0 | 11.1 | 11.2 | 9.5 |
| Private sector manual wage labour | 33.9 | 17.4 | 22.6 | 24.8 | 15.2 | 17.1 | 24.3 |
| Domestic service | 2.6 | 2.3 | 3.0 | 2.8 | 2.4 | 2.5 | 2.9 |
| Unemployed | 15.5 | 32.6 | 23.5 | 21.4 | 37.7 | 30.4 | 17.7 |
| *Destitute households* | | | | | | | |
| Not more than primary education | 86.2 | 63.1 | 65.3 | 54.4 | 46.9 | 46.7 | 43.1 |
| Working less than 30 hours | 31.0 | 24.3 | 22.0 | 16.1 | 32.6 | 37.8 | 33.6 |
| Working in public sector | — | 7.3 | 9.6 | 10.2 | 8.3 | 25.7 | 26.6 |
| Working in construction | 6.1 | 4.1 | 8.0 | 6.3 | 14.7 | 3.7 | 7.5 |
| Working in services | 25.2 | 25.3 | 30.7 | 33.8 | 30.8 | 42.7 | 45.0 |
| Working in informal sector | 18.3 | 14.6 | 14.7 | 6.9 | 10.5 | 13.9 | 12.4 |
| Private sector manual wage labour | 40.0 | 18.5 | 23.3 | 24.3 | 12.6 | 16.6 | 21.9 |
| Domestic service | 7.8 | 4.4 | 5.7 | 10.0 | 4.9 | 4.5 | 5.9 |
| Unemployed | 32.2 | 50.9 | 48.9 | 50.0 | 63.6 | 48.0 | 30.1 |
| *Poor households* | | | | | | | |
| Not more than primary education | 74.0 | 41.6 | 43.8 | 36.2 | 38.4 | 27.5 | 25.6 |
| Working less than 30 hours | 14.4 | 16.5 | 18.1 | 14.5 | 14.0 | 22.6 | 13.7 |
| Working in public sector | 4.0 | 17.8 | 12.8 | 12.6 | 8.5 | 18.5 | 17.5 |
| Working in construction | 4.2 | 4.8 | 4.8 | 5.8 | 9.2 | 3.9 | 5.7 |
| Working in services | 28.6 | 33.6 | 32.9 | 34.5 | 25.8 | 41.9 | 40.8 |
| Working in informal sector | 12.2 | 14.9 | 15.9 | 11.6 | 15.0 | 9.6 | 10.7 |
| Private sector manual wage labour | 48.4 | 25.4 | 30.9 | 37.2 | 22.1 | 25.8 | 38.2 |
| Domestic service | 4.5 | 2.9 | 4.2 | 5.2 | 2.9 | 3.9 | 5.2 |
| Unemployed | 21.8 | 30.8 | 28.4 | 22.5 | 45.4 | 30.3 | 16.5 |
| *Non-poor households* | | | | | | | |
| Not more than primary education | 42.5 | 14.6 | 18.9 | 14.4 | 15.8 | 10.2 | 7.6 |
| Working less than 30 hours | 11.7 | 12.2 | 13.6 | 9.9 | 12.2 | 12.8 | 11.6 |
| Working in public sector | 18.1 | 33.2 | 22.2 | 20.3 | 17.0 | 18.5 | 20.4 |
| Working in construction | 4.7 | 2.4 | 5.2 | 4.2 | 6.1 | 4.1 | 7.5 |
| Working in services | 39.8 | 51.3 | 45.0 | 48.6 | 43.6 | 48.7 | 45.0 |
| Working in informal sector | 6.1 | 13.4 | 9.8 | 10.3 | 10.9 | 11.8 | 8.1 |
| Private sector manual wage labour | 29.4 | 12.2 | 19.9 | 19.8 | 14.9 | 12.6 | 18.2 |
| Domestic service | 1.3 | 0.5 | 2.2 | — | 1.9 | 0.7 | 1.0 |
| Unemployed | 10.4 | 13.9 | 13.3 | 11.7 | 23.7 | 17.4 | 12.7 |

Source. See table 6.5.

during the period considered which has displaced workers from productive, formal sectors, towards the tertiary sectors of the economy. As a result, the employment problem is now one of unemployment, and of low levels of productivity and income in those occupations which provide an alternative to unemployment, in which family members try to obtain a sufficient income for subsistence.

The occupational situation varies, however, with the relationship in the household (tables 6.8 to 6.10). Household heads in the destitute or poor strata, if not unemployed, work mainly in construction, and in parts of the industrial and service sectors where there are concentrations of workers with low education levels, and they are subject to underemployment in terms of hours of work per day. Secondary workers in these households do not obtain better jobs; and they also have relatively lower education levels than the average for the labour force.[4] In general, an increasing proportion of spouses of heads have been working in sectors linked to services, and the same is true of children of the head. The service sector thus appears as a dualistic sector. It has been the most dynamic during the period studied, absorbing almost 50 per cent of household heads in 1985, compared with only 40 per cent in 1969, but it also provides job opportunities for the secondary labour force of poor households. In the latter, the most common employment status of the head is manual wage worker in the private sector; the same is true of the head's children, whereas the spouse tends to work in the informal sector (although this tendency declined in the period in question).

In destitute households, the most frequent employment status of the head is unemployment, or labourer in the private sector. Unemployment for this category rose up to 1982, but thereafter the decline in private sector wage jobs was substituted for by state emergency employment programmes, which are classified as public sector employment in the surveys.

Among spouses, after 1976 informal sector employment declined [5] and unemployment increased, especially among destitute households. Poor, non-destitute households differed from the destitute in that there was a higher proportion of private sector wage workers; and the non-poor did not reduce either non-wage formal sector employment or private sector wage employment. Among children of the head, the alternative to private sector wage work was unemployment, so that the incidence of poverty is directly related to their capacity to retain private sector wage jobs.

In sum, the work which most frequently provides an alternative to unemployment is wage labour in the private sector. It would be important to know better under what conditions (in terms of size of enterprise and/or ease of access) such jobs could be regarded as belonging to the informal sector of the labour market; unfortunately, our data do not permit a more detailed analysis of this issue.

Table 6.11 shows the relationship between occupational structure and the economic cycle, by relationship to the household head. The proportion of wage labour among heads, spouses and children has varied in direct proportion to the level of economic activity (as measured by GDP per capita). However,

*Table 6.11.*   *Correlation coefficients between labour market indicators*

| | F<br>%<br>Formal<br>sector | I<br>%<br>Informal<br>sector | W<br>%<br>Private<br>wage<br>labour | D<br>%<br>Domestic<br>service | U<br>%<br>Unemploy-<br>ment rate | UH<br>Unemploy-<br>ment rate,<br>head | G<br>GDP per<br>capita |
|---|---|---|---|---|---|---|---|
| *Heads* | | | | | | | |
| F | 1 000 | −0.013 | −0.669 | −0.777 | −0.529 | − | −0.294 |
| I | | 1 000 | 0.185 | −0.184 | −0.606 | − | −0.093 |
| W | | | 1 000 | 0.353 | −0.137 | − | 0.640 |
| D | | | | 1 000 | 0.629 | − | 0.307 |
| U | | | | | 1 000 | − | −0.238 |
| UH | | | | | | − | − |
| G | | | | | | − | 1 000 |
| Mean | 20 883 | 22 600 | 47 667 | 1 233 | 7 417 | − | 29 515 |
| Standard deviation | 3 944 | 1 599 | 2 883 | 0.489 | 3 121 | − | 2 509 |
| Maximum | 24 700 | 24 600 | 51 400 | 1 800 | 12 400 | − | 32 730 |
| Minimum | 15 000 | 20 700 | 43 800 | 0.700 | 4 100 | − | 25 255 |
| *Spouses* | | | | | | | |
| F | 1 000 | 0.376 | −0.709 | −0.629 | −0.118 | −0.301 | −0.320 |
| I | | 1 000 | −0.640 | −0.902 | −0.623 | −0.821 | 0.214 |
| W | | | 1 000 | 0.843 | −0.061 | 0.648 | 0.524 |
| D | | | | 1 000 | 0.321 | 0.657 | 0.184 |
| U | | | | | 1 000 | 0.541 | −0.855 |
| UH | | | | | | 1 000 | −0.238 |
| G | | | | | | | 1 000 |
| Mean | 22 217 | 28 083 | 29 450 | 7 650 | 12 000 | 7 417 | 29 515 |
| Standard deviation | 1 877 | 7 321 | 4 545 | 2 140 | 4 833 | 3 121 | 2 509 |
| Maximum | 24 600 | 40 600 | 33 300 | 10 000 | 18 800 | 12 400 | 32 730 |
| Minimum | 19 200 | 20 200 | 23 600 | 3 900 | 6 700 | 4 100 | 25 255 |
| *Children* | | | | | | | |
| F | 1 000 | −0.194 | 0.445 | 0.136 | −0.722 | −0.194 | −0.067 |
| I | | 1 000 | −0.845 | −0.334 | 0.666 | 0.445 | −0.713 |
| W | | | 1 000 | 0.659 | −0.933 | −0.652 | 0.808 |
| D | | | | 1 000 | −0.626 | −0.450 | 0.810 |
| U | | | | | 1 000 | 0.852 | −0.617 |
| UH | | | | | | 1 000 | −0.238 |
| G | | | | | | | 1 000 |
| Mean | 15 567 | 11 017 | 43 867 | 2 600 | 26 833 | 7 417 | 29 515 |
| Standard deviation | 2 818 | 1 766 | 7 765 | 0.261 | 8 190 | 3 121 | 2 509 |
| Maximum | 19 600 | 13 800 | 53 900 | 3 000 | 37 700 | 12 400 | 32 730 |
| Minimum | 11 100 | 8 500 | 34 500 | 2 300 | 15 400 | 4 100 | 25 255 |

Source. See table 6.5.

the pattern is different for unemployment, which responds countercyclically to economic activity, strongly for spouses and children, less so for heads, reflecting the differences between these categories in the available alternatives to wage employment. The informal sector plays a different role in each group. For heads, it varies little with economic activity. For spouses, informal sector employment rises and falls with economic activity, so that it does not absorb excess labour supply, and this ends up either unemployed or out of the labour force. For children, there is more sign that the informal sector plays some absorptive role in response to high unemployment, although the effect is weak, and the importance of the informal sector limited — quantitatively, unemployment is much more important. For heads, unemployment is relatively less important, partly — in 1984 and 1985 — because of access to emergency employment schemes.

## *IV. Conclusions*

The incidence of poverty at the household level is very closely related to the conditions of employment of household members. It follows that sharp or sudden fluctuations in labour market conditions have important repercussions on poverty. From the analysis reported above we can reach three groups of conclusions. The first concerns the importance of the economic cycle in the mechanisms and appearance of unemployment, underemployment and poverty. The second brings out the importance of the family as a unit of analysis for studying the link between employment and poverty. The third highlights the relationship between the particular circumstances of the labour market and poverty.

### *1. Macro-economic aspects*

Chile's experience underlines the importance of fluctuations in the level, composition and growth of economic activity for employment and poverty. Sharp or sudden economic fluctuations produce changes in the occupational situation of the economically active population as well as changes in the levels of family income, consumption and welfare. Several specific conclusions can be reached from our macro-economic analysis above.

First, it is necessary to be concerned with relative prices. The implementation of wage, inflation and foreign exchange policy should avoid sharp or sudden fluctuations in the relative prices of the economy. In the Chilean case there has been excessive short-sightedness in facing conjunctural problems, while neglecting the implications for the allocation of resources in the economy of prolonged distortions and fluctuations in relative prices. In general, the Chilean experience led to an over-expansion of the non-tradeable sector of the economy (construction, commerce and services) at the expense of the tradeable sector (agriculture, mining and industry). The indiscriminate commercial and financial openness towards the non-domestic market during a period of excessive international liquidity facilitated and accentuated this.

Second, and closely linked to the above, is the need to be concerned with maintaining and increasing the process of accumulation in the economy. Chile experienced a marked fall in the coefficient of investment in the economy between 1969 and 1985. This weakened the productive capacity as well as the capacity for labour absorption of the economy. In the case of Greater Santiago, job creation was insufficient in relation to the growth of the population of working age, and this situation was a major cause of the rise in unemployment. Not only did the process of accumulation slow down, but it was also biased towards the generation of employment requiring high levels of education, thus aggravating the occupational situation of the less educated, among whom poverty is concentrated.

Third, it should be emphasised that there is a need to be concerned with the distribution of income. In Chile the deterioration of the income distribution has been significant but, regrettably, one cannot resolve controversies on this subject because of the absence of reliable data. Since income limits consumption, changes in the distribution alter the composition of consumption and imports, thus affecting the allocation of resources in the economy. The concentration of income has tended to favour luxury over essential consumption, thereby distorting the structure of production and imports and hence the labour market.

## 2. Micro-family aspects

With regard to poverty, Chile provides three important lessons: first, the need to use the family as a unit of analysis. The family takes joint decisions on production, consumption, participation in family activities, and on the size and composition of the family. These are fundamental factors for all policies designed to combat poverty. The indicator of family per capita income is a good one for the purpose of stratifying families according to poverty status. In this study a nutritionally based concept of poverty has been used as a criterion for differentiating between families according to whether their per capita income is sufficient or not to buy a basket of goods that satisfies minimum subsistence requirements. For such purposes the elasticity of expenditure with respect to family size was assumed equal to one, which implies that there are no economies of scale in family consumption. This assumption could be revised in subsequent research.

Second, factors linked to employment are of growing importance in the differentiation of families by poverty status. The evidence indicates that demographic factors, such as size and family composition, have declined in importance relative to the job opportunities of adult family members, and their corresponding income levels, in discriminating between poverty strata.

Third, the study also shows how some aspects of the labour market acquire greater relevance when studied in the light of their relation to poverty. In this respect, rates of unemployment were positively associated with the incidence of poverty, while the rates of adult participation in the labour force were negatively associated with poverty. This invalidates the argument that unemployment increased because of the higher participation rates. On the contrary, the evidence reveals the importance which the following have for an understanding of the functioning of the labour market: (i) the compatibility of roles in the household with those of work; (ii) the concept of discouraged workers; and (iii) the cost of job search and labour force participation decisions.

From the micro-family aspects emerge some policy recommendations. Policies need to be oriented towards the poor communities most affected by unemployment and underemployment. They should therefore take into account the organisation of the family, allowing for the degree of compatibility of roles within poor households between domestic work and economic activities. Such policies might, for instance, focus on the provision of canteens and kindergartens that make such roles more compatible with each other, thus providing a way out for those who wish to escape from poverty through non-household work. There should also be a reduction in the time and cost of seeking work opportunities for the young, through training programmes and employment information. Among such policies, the highest priority should surely go to the reintegration of unemployed heads of households into the formal labour market.

### 3. Poverty and the functioning of the labour market

The characteristics of individuals which most markedly discriminate between strata of poverty are closely related to the labour market. In the poorest strata are those with the lowest levels of schooling; household heads are concentrated in construction and commerce (destitutes) and in industry (non-destitute poor); economically active spouses are concentrated in services (destitutes) and in industry and commerce (non-destitute poor); children of the head are concentrated in agriculture, mining and industry; a greater proportion of adult members are unemployed among the poor, although participation rates are lower; family size and the number of young children in the household are above average; and relatively fewer educational opportunities are available for their population of school age.

The principal change in poverty from 1969 to 1985 is that poverty now affects relatively younger households, with higher levels of education, more economically active women, a smaller family size and fewer children because families are both at an earlier stage of their life cycle and have reduced their fertility levels. Overall labour force participation rates in these households changed little, but the proportion of adults at work fell markedly (especially among the destitute), so that high rates of unemployment were observed.

The principal occupation for both household heads and children was wage employment in the private sector, while for spouses it was in informal, private, non-wage activities at the beginning of the period and in private wage employment towards the end, although informal sector activities continued to dominate for the poorest groups. However, we were unable to include in our informal sector estimates wage workers in small-scale enterprises, so the informal sector concept here is a rather restricted one.

Destitute households are characterised by household heads who are either unemployed, or employed primarily in the informal sector or working as wage workers. Labour market policies to improve the stability of employment and the productivity and/or incomes of those who are employed in these segments would constitute important elements of a policy against destitution. As noted above, the jobs concerned are found primarily in the construction and commerce sectors. The spouses of destitute household heads primarily enter the informal sector, domestic services or remain unemployed. The second generation in destitute or poor households is the most vulnerable to unemployment, and although the majority are employed as private sector wage workers, many are also found in the informal sector.

The relationships between poverty and the labour market in Chile call for non-traditional labour market policies. The problem is not only the high level of unemployment, but also the low level of productivity and incomes in segments linked to the informal sector and among private sector wage workers. As well as public assistance programmes for relieving unemployment, Chile requires an attempt to support economic reintegration, and to provide assistance to small firms, even in the informal sector.

It is important to emphasise that in their dynamic form, demographic factors are losing their importance in the pattern of poverty, and differences in school attendance between poverty strata are also declining because of assistance programmes. The fact that poverty continues to occur and grow permits one to advance an important issue for future research: what are the structural socio-economic factors which affect the transfer of poverty from one generation to the other? The particular role of the labour market, and the creation of various occupational alternatives, differentiated by the socio-economic background of the populations concerned, are important institutional factors affecting the manner in which this process occurs.

### Notes

[1] PREALC, Santiago de Chile. The authors wish to thank Alvaro García, Pablo Ortuzar, Ricardo Paredes and Carlos Samaniego for comments on earlier drafts of this chapter. However, the authors are solely responsible for its contents.

[2] We use the terms household and family interchangeably. The concept of the household includes all those who cook under the same roof except domestic employees.

[3] The values of the basket compare fairly well with that of an alternative basket defined by FAO/WHO, which is presented in the annex.

[4] Children in poor households are of course entering the labour force with higher education levels than their parents. But education alone appears to be insufficient to escape from poverty because of the strength of the underlying structural factors.

[5] The definition of the informal sector used here is the standard PREALC one, incorporating essentially non-professional self-employment, unpaid family work and domestic service. Wage workers in small-scale enterprises could not be included for lack of data.

## Annex: The basic food basket for Chile

The values of the basic basket for the determination of poverty lines in Greater Santiago are estimated on the basis of the minimum nutritional requirements suggested by ECLA (Altimir, 1979). These used the prices of the CPI for May of each year of the study: 1969, 1976, 1979, 1980, 1982, 1984 and 1985. Table 6 A.1 shows the estimated values of this basket, as well as an alternative estimate from "Eco-Salud" (FAO/WHO) based on minimum calorie and protein requirements. For details of the calculation see the Spanish original of this chapter (Pollack and Uthoff: *Pobreza y mercado de trabajo en el Gran Santiago, 1969-85* (Santiago, PREALC; mimeographed), Dec. 1986).

**Annex Table 6.A 1.**   *Value of the basic food basket, Eco-Salud and Pollack-Uthoff, 1969-85*

| Year | US$, c/year | | US$, 1977 | |
|------|-------------|------|-----------|------|
|      | Eco-Salud | P-U | Eco-Salud | P-U |
| 1969 | 0.0727 | 0.07471 | 307.0 | 315.0 |
| 1976 | 175.4 | 154.40 | 375.0 | 330.1 |
| 1979 | 858.4 | 702.02 | 429.0 | 350.8 |
| 1980 | 1 154.9 | 1 041.74 | 427.1 | 385.3 |
| 1982 | 1 225.4 | 1 151.17 | 344.4 | 323.7 |
| 1984 | 2 134.2 | 2 025.04 | 393.4 | 373.5 |
| 1985 | 2 602.4 | 2 400.86 | 367.2 | 338.8 |

## References

Altimir, O., and Piñera, S., 1977: *Análisis de descomposición de las desigualdades de los ingresos en países de América Latina* (Santiago, ECLA).

Altimir, O., 1979: "La dimensión de la pobreza en América Latina", in *Cuadernos de la CEPAL* (Santiago, ECLA).

———, 1981: "La pobreza en América Latina: Un examen de conceptos y datos", in *Revista de la CEPAL* (Santiago, ECLA), Apr.

Arellano, J. P., 1984: "Una nota sobre las causas del desempleo en Chile", in *Colección Estudios CIEPLAN* (Santiago, CIEPLAN), Sep.

Banco Central, 1983: *Indicadores económicos y sociales, 1960-82* (Santiago, Central Bank).

———, 1984: *Cuentas Nacionales de Chile, 1960-83* (Santiago, Central Bank).

Castañeda, T., 1984: *Evolucion del empleo y desempleo en el impacto de cambios demográficos sobre la tasa de desempleo en Chile: 1960-83*, Serie de investigación núm. 64 (Santiago, University of Chile, Department of Economics).

CELADE, 1981: *Boletín Demográfico* (Santiago, CELADE), July.

Corbo, V., and Stelcner, M., 1980: "La segmentación del mercado laboral reconsiderada. El caso de los asalariados. Gran Santiago 1978", in *Estudios de Economía* (Santiago, University of Chile, Department of Economics), 1st semester 1980.

Cortázar, R. and Marshall, J., 1980: "Indice de precios al consumidor en Chile, 1970-1978", in *Colección Estudios CIEPLAN* (Santiago), Dec.

Dirección de Estadísticas y Censos, 1960: *XIII Censo de población. Resumen del país*, Serie A (Santiago, Statistical and Census Bureau).

Eco-Salud, n.d.: *Desnutrición infantil: manual de prevención y tratamiento* (Santiago).

Echeverría, R., 1985: *Empleo público en América Latina*, Investigación sobre Empleo/26 (Santiago, PREALC).

FAO-WHO, 1971: *Necesidades de energía y proteínas*, Informe de un comité especial de expertos.

García, A. y otros, 1983: *El problema alimentario y nutricional en Chile: Diagnóstico y evaluación de políticas*, Monografías sobre empleo/33 (Santiago, PREALC/ISS).

Heskia, I., 1980: *Distribucion del ingreso en el Gran Santiago, 1957-79*, Serie de Investigación núm. 53 (Santiago, University of Chile, Department of Economics).

Instituto Nacional de Estadística, various years: *Encuesta nacional de empleo. Total país* (Santiago, INE).

———, 1970: *Población. Resultados definitivos del XIV Censo de población 1970. Total país* (Santiago).

Le Fort, G., 1984: "El tipo de cambio real y la experiencia de países del Cono Sur, 1974-1982", in *Cuadernos de Economía* (Santiago, Catholic University of Chile), Apr.

Meller, P., 1984: "Análisis del problema de la elevada tasa de desocupación chilena", in *Estudios de CIEPLAN* No. 14 (Santiago, CIEPLAN), Sep.

Piñera, S., 1979: *Medición, análisis y descripción de la pobreza en Costa Rica* (Santiago, ECLA).

PREALC, 1982: *Mercado de trabajo en cifras 1950-80* (Santiago).

———, 1984: *Determinantes estructurales y coyunturales de la producción en la industria manufacturera chilena: 1969-83*, Working paper/249 (Santiago).

———, 1985: *Población y fuerza de trabajo en América Latina 1950-80*, Working paper/259 (Santiago).

Riveros, L., 1983: "Verificación de diferencias estadísticas en los mecanismos de determinación de los ingresos entre sectores mediante la forma reducida de un modelo de capital humano", in *Estudios de Economía* (Santiago, University of Chile, Department of Economics), 2nd semester 1980, 1st semester 1981.

Riveros, L., and Labbé, F. J., 1985: "Situación distributiva y el impacto del desempleo: Un análisis de largo plazo", in *Estudios de Economía* (Santiago, University of Chile, Department of Economics), Apr.

Rodgers, G., 1984: *Poverty and population. Approaches and evidence* (Geneva, ILO).

Rodríguez, J., 1985: *Magnitud de la pobreza, distribución del ingreso e impacto del gasto social en Chile* (draft).

Rosende, F., and Toso, R., 1984: "Una explicación para la tasa de interés real en Chile", in *Cuadernos de Economía* (Santiago, Catholic University of Chile), Apr.

Rowntree, S., 1901: *Poverty: A study of town life* (London, Macmillan).

Roza, M., and Torche, A., 1985: *Medición de intensidad de pobreza en Chile*, Draft presented to the annual meeting of economists in Santiago, Chile.

Schkolnic, M., 1986: *Sobrevivir en la población J. M. Caro y en Lo Hermida*, Working paper/42 (Santiago, PET).

Sen, A., 1978: *Three notes on the concept of poverty* (Geneva, ILO).

———, 1981: *Poverty and famines. An essay on entitlement and deprivation* (Oxford, Clarendon Press).

Universidad de Chile, Departamento de Economía, various years: *Encuestas de ocupación y desocupación en el Gran Santiago*, various issues (Santiago, Department of Economics, University of Chile).

Uthoff, A., 1983: "Otra mirada al modelo de capital humano. Gran Santiago 1961-78", in *Estudios de Economía*, 1st semester (Santiago, University of Chile, Department of Economics).

———, 1983-84: "Subempleo, segmentación, movilidad ocupacional y distribución del ingreso del trabajo. El caso del Gran Santiago 1969 y 1978", in *Estudios de Economía*, 2nd semester 1983, 1st semester 1984 (Santiago, University of Chile, Department of Economics).

# Chapter 7

# *Urban poverty and labour supply strategies in Jakarta*

*HANS-DIETER EVERS* [1]

## *I. Introduction*

### *1. Urban poverty and the labour market*

Metropolitan Jakarta is Indonesia's largest single labour market. Despite a concentration of commercial and industrial development in and around the city and the resulting demand for labour, widespread urban poverty persists. This chapter studies the extent of urban poverty from 1960 to 1980, with some reference to earlier data; examines the labour supply strategies of poor urban households in terms of allocation of labour both for the reproduction of households and for income-generating activities; and considers the policy implications.

The extent and long-term trends of urban poverty are measured using data from household expenditure surveys. There are problems of data comparability in measuring trends, but using data from recent social surveys, and government statistics, some conclusions can be drawn. The urban poor will be differentiated in terms of household structure, migration, duration of residence in Jakarta, social mobility, education, income, and other socio-economic variables to measure changes in the composition of households below and above the poverty line.

On the basis of household survey data and a number of ethnographic case studies, it will be shown:

— how the supply of different forms of labour (wage labour in the formal and informal sectors, own-account work, and household work in an urban subsistence sector) is utilised as a flexible strategy to maximise overall levels of economic security or incomes;

— how poor urban households define their basic needs and how they distribute incomes from wage labour, own-account work in the informal sector and household work for their own consumption to meet these self-defined basic needs.

Trends in the distribution of urban poverty over about 20 years are shown, and the impact of changing access to different forms of labour in the formal, informal and subsistence sectors on consumption patterns (satisfaction of basic needs) is analysed. Particular attention is paid to the growing importance of household work (subsistence production) and informal sector employment with declining incomes, and the importance of these in maintaining satisfactory levels of income to support household members in search of formal sector employment. In these discussions the so far neglected "subsistence sector" will be defined and analysed. Our own 1979 survey data form the basis of this discussion.

## 2. The urban economy and society of Jakarta

Indonesia's capital grew rapidly from 4.5 million inhabitants in 1971 to over 7 million in 1983, while its population density increased from 7,500 to over 10,000 per square kilometre (table 7.1). Situated on the north shore of Java, its population is primarily Sundanese and Javanese, but also includes migrants from all over Indonesia and from neighbouring Asian countries. Jakarta's basic sociological structure, or rather its skeleton, can still be discerned: the old seventeenth century *kota* with its small harbour frequented by sailing vessels, warehouses, the town hall and other historical remains; the Chinese commercial area; the big central markets and shopping districts, the old Dutch upper-class quarters of Menteng and the newer upper-class area of Kebayoran Baru built after independence. The major central road, Jalan Thamrin, is lined by high-rise hotels, embassies, offices of multinational corporations, banks and ministries. However, the city is not clearly differentiated socially. Next to Jalan Thamrin is the densely settled area of Tanah Abang, not a slum, but an area where general housing conditions are far from satisfactory, including living quarters in which small traders or labourers take turns in using beds to sleep; although there are also houses of rich merchants and civil servants. Jellinek (1977, 1978) gives an excellent account of the life of various types of people in this area.

In the distinctly upper-class area of Kebayoran Baru with a high proportion of embassy personnel, development experts, customs officials and Chinese businessmen living in luxurious villas, we also find, though with some difficulty, squatters hidden between gardens along streams and flood control canals. Between the landmarks described above, there are the vast areas of *kampungs* (urban villages) of differing quality but invariably made up of an intricate network of small alleys, served by *becaks* (bicycle rickshaws) or street vendors on foot. It is estimated that 80 per cent of Jakarta's population live in these *kampungs* (Krausse, 1978). Household incomes are low, though higher than in rural areas or small towns. The average income in 1976 was around US$40 per month, according to the 1976 Government Socioeconomic Survey (SUSENAS). The average income figures, however, hide the fact that, even among the urban poor, differences between the relatively rich, poor and very poor are considerable.

Not only income differences from family to family, but also variations from year to year, or even month to month, are perhaps the most characteristic features of Jakarta *kampung* society. The changes for any family are aggravated by frequent changes in family composition because of short-term migration, and attempts to adjust to a constantly changing economic and social environment. It is perhaps, therefore, justified to use the vivid Indonesian expression *masa*

*Table 7.1.   Jakarta: Population and growth, 1960-83*

| Year | DKI Jakarta | | Year | Growth (Per cent per annum) | |
|------|-------------|--------|------|--------|-----------|
|      | Population  | Sex ratio |      | Jakarta | Indonesia |
| 1960 | 2 740 477   | 103.8  | 1961-70 | 4.5  | 2.1 |
| 1970 | 4 401 040   | 104.0  | 1971-80 | 3.9  | 2.3 |
| 1980 | 6 503 449   | 105.9  |      |      |      |
| 1983 | 7 307 000   | 106.3  |      |      |      |

Sources. BPS (A), 1980/81, 1983; KSJ, 1972. See references for details of data sources.

*apung* ("floating mass") to describe the poorest section of Jakarta's urban poor (Evers, 1980).

Jakarta's economy is dominated by the tertiary sector, particularly trade and government services. Industry is much less developed than might be expected by comparison with other Asian cities. About half of the estimated regional GDP comes from trade, and almost three-quarters of all private sector firms are small trading companies. The government sector is also of great importance. In the wake of general bureaucratisation the number of civil servants increased rapidly, particularly in the mid-1970s (Evers, 1987).

Manufacturing has been less important, its output and employment probably declining during the 1960s. A Department of Manpower survey, admittedly of dubious reliability, showed that in 1967 only 25.7 per cent of employees of registered enterprises in the survey worked in manufacturing firms, and more than half of these firms had fewer than ten employees. Between 1969 and 1975 industrialisation gathered pace in Indonesia, though from a very low level. From 1975 to 1982 the process continued; the number of firms declined throughout Indonesia, so that concentration increased, but manufacturing employment rose (McCawley, 1984, p. 159). Nevertheless, the impact on Jakarta has been less than expected. This may be partly because the most rapid industrial development took place outside the city limits, but also because after the end of an "import substitution phase" industrial development was either raw material based or was concentrated in the informal sector.

Construction, transport and tourism have also grown, although these branches of the Jakarta economy are dominated by small companies, informal sector enterprises, own-account workers, and self-help activities. Apart from occasional office blocks or housing development schemes, most construction work is done by craftsmen or by the owner-occupiers of *kampung* houses. The once frequent trishaws *(bejak)* have been banned from the city centre and main roads, depriving a large section of the migrant population of their livelihood. Instead the minibus traffic has increased and the public bus network improved. Tourists, foreign businessmen and a steady stream of government officials reporting to their ministries have boosted the hotel business, but still the vast majority of visitors find accommodation with relatives or friends of the same ethnic group. Needless to say, many of these informal or self-help activities do not find their way into the calculation of regional GDP or into other government statistics, despite the fact that many of these services are paid for in kind or in labour, even among relatives.

To sum up, Jakarta still has a large labour absorption capacity, centred on the informal and the subsistence sectors with which the majority of the urban poor are associated.

## II. Incomes and poverty

### 1. Trends in levels of living

Before addressing the question of the incidence, growth or decline of urban poverty, we have to review the development of personal income over time. As income data are very scarce, we rely mainly on household expenditure data from SUSENAS and use these as proxies for income. To be able to argue on the basis of data which are at least roughly comparable over time, we have to make use of time series on urban Java, of which Jakarta forms, of course, a major part.

The first data set is for 1964. Collected in a time of political turmoil and high inflation, the figures are very unreliable and should be treated with extreme caution. The next data set of 1968 refers only to Jakarta and excludes other urban areas of Java. It thus overstates incomes for urban Java as a whole. Broadly comparable data are thereafter available for 1970, 1976, 1978, and 1980. From 1968 on, new economic strategies were pursued, intended to integrate Indonesia into the world economy, to strengthen market forces and to stimulate economic growth. GNP has indeed grown at high rates, particularly after the increase in oil prices and the growth of oil revenues since 1972, but there has been considerable controversy about the impact on household expenditure, income distribution and poverty following the change in development strategies. We shall first present the views of various analysts and then try to reach conclusions on the basis of a comparative evaluation of existing data.[2]

If we compare the existing official income data from SUSENAS, deflated by a cost-of-living index for Jakarta that we have constructed out of various price indices, the following picture emerges (table 7.2). Average incomes, proxied by consumption expenditure, decreased somewhat in the late 1960s. This holds true even if we take into account that the Jakarta-based figure for 1968 is overestimated by approximately 20 per cent in comparison to the figure for urban Java as a whole. From 1970 to 1978 there was an annual increase in urban incomes of about 7 per cent, and then a decline at a similar rate to 1980, still leaving a substantial growth in levels of living between 1967/70 and 1976/80.

Income levels in Jakarta have no doubt been higher than the average for urban Java, but there are few reliable figures. In the 1970s the average

*Table 7.2.* **Trends in monthly per capita expenditures, urban Java, estimates, 1967-80 (in constant 1966 prices)**

| Year | Expenditure (Rp.) | Food as percentage of expenditure | Cost-of-living index [1] (Base, December 1966) |
|------|-------------------|-----------------------------------|-----------------------------------------------|
| 1967 [2] | 303.64 | 67.75 | 206 |
| 1968 [2] | 301.62 | 53.80 | 464 |
| 1970 | 280.07 | n.a. | 612 |
| 1976 | 389.54 | 60.36 | 1 788 |
| 1978 | 452.89 | 51.01 | 2 235 |
| 1980 | 383.67 | 57.85 | 3 129 |

n.a. = not available.

[1] Cost-of-living index, September each year for Jakarta. [2] Data for 1967/68 decreased by 20 per cent to adjust for differences between Jakarta and urban Java.

Sources. Sundrum (1974, 1976, 1979); BPS (A)(D)(E); World Bank (1980, 1984a).

monthly per capita expenditure in Jakarta is said to have risen from Rp.2,234 in 1970 to Rp.9,846 in 1976 (Rp.3,372 in 1970 prices), an annual growth of 8.5 per cent (Sundrum, 1979, p. 138). This figure appears to be somewhat high, particularly since the regional GDP per capita for Jakarta (non-mining, at 1973 constant prices) was estimated to have grown by only 6.6 per cent per annum between 1971 and 1979 (World Bank, 1984a, p. 175).

Data on wages are incomplete and unreliable, and it is impossible to establish overall time series. A number of studies, however, indicate that real wages of unskilled workers declined in Jakarta in the early 1970s. Thus, interviews with contractors revealed that real wages of unskilled construction labour declined from an index of 100 in 1972 to 63 in 1976 (World Bank, 1980, p. 62). This trend is confirmed by other data on construction workers in government INPRES programmes, in which real wages declined by 49.7 per cent from 1971 to 1978. But the wage trends are very diverse according to occupation or economic sectors, even though in most sectors a decline of real wages could be confirmed (World Bank, 1980, p. 64). On the other hand, salaries for government workers fluctuated wildly but showed an upward trend between 1969 and 1981 (World Bank, 1985, p. 147).

### 2. Inequality

An analysis of data for the 1970s reveals large regional differences in standards of living between urban and rural areas, and between Jakarta and other Javanese cities. "Urban incomes have increased nearly two-and-a-half times as fast as rural incomes . . . The most rapid increase of income occurred in Jakarta, more than three times as fast as in the rest of the country (16.6 per cent) . . . The general impression we get is that the rural distributions had become more equal while the urban changes are more unequal . . . On the whole, inequality increased in urban areas and declined in rural areas, and increased in Java and declined in Outer Islands, so that there was little change in the national average" (from 1970 to 1976) (Sundrum, 1979, p. 139, 141). These

*Table 7.3.  Distribution of per capita expenditure, urban Java, 1963-81*

| Year | D1 | D1-2 | D1-3 | D1-4 | D5-8 | D9,10 | D10 | Total | Gini coefficient |
|------|------|------|-------|-------|-------|-------|-------|--------|------------------|
| 1963 | — | 9.50 | — | 22.10 | 41.20 | 36.70 | — | 100.00 | — |
| 1964 | 3.50 | 8.50 | — | 21.30 | 39.20 | 39.50 | 23.02 | 100.00 | .30 |
| 1967 | — | 9.00 | — | 22.10 | 38.10 | 39.80 | — | 100.00 | .29 |
| 1969 | — | 7.80 | — | 20.00 | 38.50 | 41.50 | — | 100.00 | .33 |
| 1970 | — | — | — | — | — | — | — | — | .33 |
| 1976 | 3.30 | 7.84 | 13.05 | 19.56 | 37.47 | 42.97 | 27.29 | 100.00 | .35 |
| 1978 | 2.85 | 6.70 | 11.59 | 17.30 | 34.31 | 48.39 | 28.72 | 100.00 | .41 |
| 1980 | 3.08 | 7.31 | 12.82 | 19.34 | 36.21 | 44.45 | 27.96 | 100.00 | .36 |
| 1981 | 3.20 | 7.52 | 13.35 | 20.34 | 36.39 | 43.22 | 28.92 | 100.00 | .35 |

Note. D: deciles; D1: bottom; D10: top. Data 1963-69: urban Java, excluding Jakarta. Data 1978 and 1980: D1-4, D9,10 underestimated.
Sources. King and Weldon, 1977, p. 702; Sundrum, 1976; BPS (D) 1980; BPS (F) 1983.

views have been challenged, however, mainly on grounds of data unreliability — especially under-enumeration.

In table 7.3, if we compare the Gini coefficients for urban Java between 1964 and 1970 we find relatively little overall change. From then until 1978 urban inequality rose very sharply (at least in terms of this index of inequality). Hughes and Islam (1981, pp. 53-54) use a number of different indices besides the Gini coefficient and also conclude that there was a substantial increase in inequality from 1970 to 1976.

The Gini coefficient slightly decreased after 1978. This may result from systematic underestimation in 1980 due to a reclassification of the urban/rural population and other changes in enumeration procedures (BPS (D), 1980, p. XVII). On the other hand, there is evidence that the real income of the bottom 40 per cent declined from 1978 to 1980 (table 7.4). A closer look at the distribution of expenditure groups suggests how changes in income may have affected the urban population. Expenditure data are used here as proxy for income. If we can trust the 1968 SUSENAS figures at all, the average income of the bottom 40 per cent of the urban population showed a general tendency to fall throughout the period (table 7.4). At the same time, the average expenditure of the top 20 per cent showed a distinct tendency to rise. All this leads to the conclusion that income distribution has become less equal in the long run. Evidence given below from non-official surveys and ethnographic field work will throw further light on the question of levels of living and consumption.

Whatever the reliability of the data and the justification of various indices (in our case the 1966-based cost-of-living index), we would hesitate to endorse the euphoric statement that "between 1970 and 1980 there was a *very sharp* reduction in urban poverty" (World Bank, 1984, p. 129). This will, however, be discussed further.

*Table 7.4.    Monthly per capita expenditure in 1966 prices, top 20 per cent and bottom 40 per cent of households, 1968-80*

| Year | Total | Food | Housing | Miscel-laneous | Clothing | Durable goods | Taxes | Ceremonial |
|------|-------|------|---------|----------------|----------|---------------|-------|------------|
| *Top 20 per cent* | | | | | | | | |
| 1968 | 810.13 | 289.11 | 173.79 | 236.37 | 86.48 | included in miscellaneous | | |
| 1976 | 832.72 | 362.38 | 181.40 | 137.10 | 81.35 | 33.55 | 9.32 | 11.42 |
| 1978 | 1 141.88 | 393.10 | 319.55 | 187.32 | 91.43 | 100.24 | 22.11 | 20.71 |
| 1980 | 932.76 | 380.69 | 200.79 | 182.79 | 72.05 | 61.71 | 21.47 | 24.93 |
| *Bottom 40 per cent* | | | | | | | | |
| 1968 | 189.87 | 109.96 | 31.07 | 25.46 | 8.95 | included in miscellaneous | | |
| 1976 | 145.69 | 93.45 | 17.85 | 11.01 | 13.03 | 0.64 | 0.64 | 0.93 |
| 1978 | 158.21 | 98.24 | 24.43 | 11.27 | 10.52 | 1.16 | 1.40 | 2.32 |
| 1980 | 132.41 | 83.65 | 17.89 | 9.29 | 10.48 | 1.79 | 0.57 | 1.94 |
| *All households* | | | | | | | | |
| 1964 | 106.27 | 69.67 | 7.12 | 7.47 | 5.48 | 2.10 | 0.19 | 1.64 |
| 1967 | 404.85 | 248.90 | 25.98 | 55.71 | 47.22 | 8.57 | 2.38 | 5.71 |
| 1968 | 402.18 | 185.24 | 68.45 | 93.29 | 33.71 | included in miscellaneous | | |
| 1970 | 280.07 | – | – | – | – | – | – | – |
| 1976 | 389.54 | 204.08 | 67.69 | 50.55 | 37.64 | 9.20 | 3.32 | 4.02 |
| 1978 | 452.89 | 202.39 | 102.06 | 61.20 | 35.54 | 23.17 | 8.90 | 4.02 |
| 1980 | 383.67 | 193.78 | 103.52 | 57.06 | 30.86 | 15.76 | 5.02 | 3.35 |

Source. See table 7.3.

### 3. Urban income levels in 1979: The PLPIIS survey

A more detailed picture of living conditions in Jakarta emerges from our survey of 1,038 sample households, carried out from May to August 1979 as part of a research training programme for lecturers at the University of Indonesia (*Pusat Latehan Penelitian Ilmu Ilmu Sosial*, PLPIIS; see Sumardi and Evers, 1982, for details). The diversity of the sampled population and the difficulties in carrying out a survey in a highly volatile population make it difficult to claim that our sample represents the society, the urban masses, or the urban poor of Jakarta. However, as areas were selected that appeared to be typical in their own right for certain features of Jakarta society, while the sample is not necessarily representative in the strict statistical sense it is at least typical from a descriptive-analytical point of view for the urban *kampung* dwellers. In addition, our sample matches census figures for certain characteristics of Jakarta's population, such as average household size, age distribution, education and income distribution, which speaks for its representativeness.

Our survey shows that households spend or consume on average Rp.56.740 (about US$92), which comes close to the "minimum needs" expenditure for an average household (discussed in detail in the next section). Using this latter as a standard, in 1979 roughly half the households had an

*Table 7.5.*   *Percentage distribution of population by monthly household per capita expenditure*
*classes, Jakarta, 1979*

| Per capita expenditure (Rp.) | Percentage of households |
|---|---|
| 2 000-3 999 | 3.0 |
| 4 000-5 999 | 10.1 |
| 6 000-7 999 | 17.4 |
| 8 000-9 999 | 16.3 |
| 10 000-11 999 | 12.7 |
| 12 000-15 999 | 17.5 |
| 16 000-19 999 | 10.3 |
| 20 000-29 999 | 8.7 |
| 30 000+ | 4.0 |

Source. Evers, 1981, p. 93.

actual expenditure that was less than the self-defined minimal basic-needs requirements (see table 7.5). This result tallies with the SUSENAS data collected a few months earlier (World Bank, 1984b, Vol. II, p. 32). It also means that the other half of the households, though still by no means rich, could make a living and fulfil at least their most basic needs. The *kampungs* of Jakarta, which casual visitors might too easily classify as slums, are viable communities, with many poor people it is true, but they are not necessarily places of absolute and dismal poverty alone. Income differences are pronounced, even within the urban *kampungs*, a fact already noted by Papanek (1976) in his analysis of surveys on Jakarta's poor.

Most households satisfy their needs by buying small quantities of food and other household items on a daily basis, from a host of vendors who retail everything from kerosene for lighting to water for cooking and washing. Their income, even for those who work in the formal sector and receive a weekly or monthly salary, tends to vary from day to day as supplementary activities, such as trading or occasional work, bring in additional monetary income. Thus, urban households differ considerably from rural ones, whose income tends to be tied to the agricultural cycle, even if they are landless agricultural labourers.

The proportion of migrants is high. Two-thirds of household heads have lived less than ten years in the same district. But perhaps more significant is that 60 per cent have stayed less than half their lives in Jakarta. In one area of Jakarta (Kelurahan Pulo Gadung), a more detailed study of migrants was undertaken. Of the 120 household heads interviewed, 47 per cent had their last place of residence in central Java. Most came as occasional workers (35 per cent) or small traders *(pedagang kaki lima)* (10.8 per cent), though by the date of the survey 23 per cent were government officials, 39 per cent employees, mostly in small shops or enterprises, and only 15.8 per cent were still occasional workers, which shows considerable upward mobility through the use of employment opportunities in Jakarta.

*Table 7.6. Calculation of poverty thresholds following Sayogyo, 1968-80 (monthly per capita expenditure in rice equivalents)*

| Year | Categories/thresholds in Rp. | | | | Percentage of population below threshold | | |
|------|------|------|------|------|------|------|------|
| | Rice (price/kg) | Poor | Very poor | Destitute | Poor | Very poor | Destitute |
| 1968 | 12 | 480 | 360 | 270 | 54 | 16 | n.a. |
| 1970 | 37 | 1 500 | 1 125 | 844 | 55 | 43 | 26 |
| 1976 | 120 | 4 800 | 3 600 | 2 700 | 43 | 28 | 17 |
| 1978 | 140 | 5 600 | 4 200 | 3 150 | 37 | 24 | 12 |
| 1980 | 228 | 9 120 | 6 840 | 5 130 | 50 | 34 | 17 |

n.a. = not available.
Note. Poverty thresholds in rice equivalents: poor: 40 kg per month; very poor: 30 kg per month; destitute: 22.5 kg per month.
Sources. BPS(D): 1976, 1978, 1980; BPS(E): 1968/69; World Bank (1980): 1970, 1976.

There are hardly any old people. Only 255 of the more than 5,000 persons surveyed were 65 or older. The average dependency ratio (children and old people divided by adults aged 15 to 65) is, therefore, only 1.15. The level of education is quite high: 43 per cent of heads of households attended high school and only 8 per cent received no formal schooling at all. The figures are lower for poorer groups but nevertheless even the poorer sections of the *kampung* dwellers have surprisingly high educational levels. Only 10 per cent of our sample households could be classified as both poor and predominantly illiterate. This was confirmed by another survey on Jakarta's *kampung* population (Krausse, 1985, p. 122). However, the positive trend towards higher qualifications is apparently not matched by a sufficient increase in the demand for labour in the formal sector, where schooling is of major importance. Though our survey data still show a reasonably high correlation between level of education and household income, the difficulty in finding suitable jobs for educated youth is painfully evident. The group of young, educated poor is likely to grow.

### 4. Poverty

While expenditure estimates for the lowest 40 per cent of households in table 7.4 give one indicator of the level and trend of poverty, there are many other approaches to the definition and analysis of poverty. An early attempt to measure poverty in Indonesia was made by the Indonesian rural sociologist Sayogyo, who, on the basis of surveys on adequate food consumption, used average consumption in terms of rice equivalence to define his poverty line. The expenditure of the rupiah equivalent of 40 kg of rice per month per person was defined as the threshold below which people could be designated as "poor". The "very poor" fell below the equivalent of 30 kg of rice and the destitute below 22.5 kg. This concept is applied to expenditure data for 1968 to 1980 in table 7.6.

*Table 7.7.*    *Trends in urban poverty according to various indices, urban Java; percentage of population below different poverty lines, 1968-80*

| Year | Below average expenditure | Below Rp.5,000 in 1976 prices | Sayogyo, line 1 | Sayogyo, line 2 | World Bank line |
|------|------|------|------|------|------|
| 1968 | 72.9 | 38.1 | 54 | 16 | n.a. |
| 1970 | 78.0 | n.a. | 55 | 43 | 56.3 |
| 1976 | 65.6 | 46.0 | 43 | 28 | 46.0 |
| 1980 | 64.4 | 47.6 | 50 | 34 | 29.6 |

n.a. = not available.
Sources. Based on tables 7.4 and 7.6, and on World Bank (1984b), Vol. II, p. 28-30.

The World Bank constructed a new poverty line measure by establishing the minimum income required to satisfy a normative calorie requirement and then inflating the minimum purchasing power to cover non-food basic needs as well. The cost of 16 kg of rice per month plus an additional sum of 25 per cent of the rice price was used to estimate the minimum cost of the required food intake of 1,935 calories. For urban Java another 35 per cent is added as a required minimum of non-food items. Using a rice price of Rp.210 per kilo for urban Java in 1980, the poverty line was fixed at Rp.6,462 per capita per month (World Bank, 1984b, pp. 29-30). Using these and other ways of measuring poverty we come to a wide variety of levels and trends in poverty (table 7.7). These are perhaps more useful to shatter confidence in any single estimate than to establish firm estimates of the incidence of poverty. Nevertheless, we can be reasonably certain that urban poverty is still widespread. Only the World Bank estimate shows a sharp decline in poverty, and this is questionable because the rural/urban classification changed in 1980, and World Bank adjustments do not take into account that urban areas have expanded and that the urban poor have partly been relocated to the urban fringe, where their numbers were increased by recent migrants. This view is based on our survey of internal migration in Jakarta. In fact, the evidence suggests that real incomes in the lower-income groups were declining, and urban poverty was increasing around 1980. This was confirmed by observations and interviews in Jakarta and other Javanese cities, when we conducted large-scale surveys on the satisfaction of basic needs and on specific low-income groups between 1978 and 1980. Given the unsatisfactory nature of these poverty estimates, we present below what we believe to be a superior approach based on the expressed preferences of the poor themselves.

For Java in 1979, the PLPIIS Survey made a detailed investigation of poverty in terms of "minimum basic needs" defined by respondents in 120 households. Some 47 expenditure items were ranked, and needs adjusted for household size and age structure. We do not give the details here, but the outcome was a "minimum need" per month per adult of Rp.14,800. Because of varying household sizes, there was considerable variation in household

*Table 7.8.  Monthly household income by poverty status, Jakarta, 1979*

| Income (Rp.'000) | Poor households (%) | Other households (%) |
|---|---|---|
| 0-20 | 33 | 66 |
| 20-50 | 51 | 49 |
| 50-80 | 28 | 72 |
| 80+ | 0 | 100 |
| Total | 40 | 60 |

Cramer's V = 0.30, n = 120.
Source. PLPIIS Survey, 1979.

*Table 7.9.  Monthly household expenditure by household education index, Jakarta, 1979*

| Household income (Rp.'000) | Mainly illiterate | | Primary-school level | | Higher than primary school | |
|---|---|---|---|---|---|---|
| | No. | % | No. | % | No. | % |
| 0-20 | 16 | 9.1 | 32 | 5.5 | 4 | 1.3 |
| 20-50 | 108 | 61.7 | 272 | 46.4 | 70 | 21.7 |
| 50-80 | 40 | 22.9 | 223 | 38.1 | 127 | 39.4 |
| 80+ | 11 | 6.3 | 59 | 10.0 | 121 | 37.6 |
| Total | 175 | 100 | 586 | 100 | 322 | 100 |

Cramer's V = 0.29 significant at 0.5 level; n = 1.083 households.
Note. The education index measures the average educational attainment of household members of 14 years and above.
Source. PLPIIS Survey, 1979.

expenditure needs with a mean of Rp.48,980, a median of Rp.44,680 and a standard deviation of Rp.21,553. The median minimal household expenditure of Rp.44,680 is, in fact, close to the poverty line proposed by Sayogyo (see above); the standard deviation of our sample shows, however, the wide range of minimal expenditure. Using as a measure of poverty the satisfaction of self-defined basic needs in these terms, we are now able to look more closely at households which can satisfy their basic needs and thus rise above the poverty line, in comparison with those unable to do so (see Evers et al., 1983 for further findings). Applying our poverty line to the sample households we find that total monetary income is only a weak predictor of poverty. This is shown in table 7.8, in which monthly monetary household expenditure is used as a proxy of income and the satisfaction of basic needs as a poverty threshold.

In addition, our survey shows that poor households tend to be large, especially those with three generations, whereas small households without children and older dependants face fewer problems in combating poverty, so poverty is very much influenced by the domestic development cycle. Households come under stress with increasing age of their founding members and might then face declining social mobility, and a much larger proportion of old migrant households find it more difficult to satisfy their basic needs than recent arrivals, who tend to be younger (Evers et al., 1982, pp. 58 ff.). Our data show, like other similar surveys, that low educational attainment is highly correlated with levels of living (table 7.9).

Of primary importance for the urban poor is, however, access to employment, own-account work and subsistence production. If we take subsistence production into account, many households in the middle-income brackets are pushed across the poverty line. This can be deduced from our survey results which show that 60 per cent of the households below the poverty line met more than 20 per cent of their consumption needs from subsistence production. We can therefore argue with some justification that access to resources, both labour and facilities for subsistence production, are important for a correct evaluation of urban poverty.

## III. Labour supply strategies among the urban poor

### 1. Trends of labour supply in Jakarta, 1960-80

Keeping in mind the problems in defining jobs and employment in a city like Jakarta, we shall briefly discuss the changing structure of employment as reflected in the census and national survey data. Surprisingly, the overall changes are smaller than we would expect from the example of other Third World metropolises. The city population, at least according to census data, rose at a fairly constant rate of about 4 per cent between 1960 and 1980. The economically active population has risen but its distribution by status and industry has not changed dramatically. One is thus tempted to apply the term "urban involution" to designate a situation of increasing quantity with little change in distributional patterns.

But if we scrutinise the data carefully, we find, if not tremendous dislocations, nevertheless significant changes in trends that call for an answer. There are distinct periods distinguished by different political environments and changes in economic strategy: 1961-65 was the period of the deteriorating "old order", ending in political turmoil in 1965-66 and severe social and economic dislocations; 1966-70 can be seen as a phase of transition to the "new order" regime dominated by the Indonesian military who followed the advice of a group of "technocrats" in economic planning. Policies aimed at increasing integration into the world market and at economic growth were pursued, leading to high GNP growth rates for Indonesia and particularly Jakarta, aided by rising oil production and oil prices after about 1972. Growing social and economic inequality in the distribution of the fruits of economic growth led to increasing popular unrest from 1974 to 1978, when a rather severe devaluation changed the course of the economy.

From 1961 to 1971 employment rose only slowly, and unemployment almost doubled, from 7 to 13 per cent. Analysts noted the sharp drop in

**Table 7.10.  Labour force, Jakarta 1961-80** [1]

*A. Percentage of population by type of activity*

| Year | Labour force | | | | Not in labour force | | | | Total |
|------|----------------------------------|----------|--------------|-------|--------------|------------------|--------|-------|-------|
|      | Economically active population | Employed | Seek work | SWFFT | At school | House-keeping | Others | Total |       |
| 1961 | 34.01 | 31.49 | 2.52 | —    | 10.09 | 20.23 | 4.29 | 34.60 | 68.61 |
| 1971 | 29.59 | 25.82 | 2.30 | 1.48 | 12.83 | 18.45 | 7.58 | 38.87 | 68.46 |
| 1976 | 28.47 | 26.74 | 0.66 | 1.07 | 13.67 | 18.65 | 6.50 | 38.81 | 67.28 |
| 1978 | 31.64 | 29.63 | 0.75 | 1.27 | 15.08 | 16.57 | 4.49 | 36.14 | 67.78 |
| 1980 | 30.82 | 29.64 | 0.25 | 0.93 | 20.04 | 16.99 | 7.07 | 44.10 | 74.92 |

[1] Denominator includes children under 10 (excluded from numerator).

*B. Percentage of economically active population by type of activity*

| Year | Employed | Seek work | SWFFT | Total |
|------|----------|-----------|-------|--------|
| 1961 | 92.58 | 7.42 | —    | 100.00 |
| 1971 | 87.24 | 7.76 | 5.00 | 100.00 |
| 1976 | 93.94 | 2.32 | 3.75 | 100.00 |
| 1978 | 93.64 | 2.36 | 4.01 | 100.00 |
| 1980 | 96.17 | 0.82 | 3.02 | 100.00 |

Note. Seek work: seeking work excluding SWFFT; SWFFT: seeking work for the first time; Others: income recipients, others and not stated.
Sources. BPS(A) 1977/78, 1980/81; BPS(B) 1961, 1971; BPS(C) 1980; BPS(F) 1983.

manufacturing employment in that period and a reduction in the labour force participation rate for males from 77 to 66 per cent, especially in the 15-24 age group (Sethuraman, 1976, pp. 13, 61 and 88). Economists express bewilderment but offer no explanation for this puzzle. The political history of Indonesia, however, suggests that political unrest following the 1965 coup attempt, the killing of an undisclosed number of people, probably mostly young males, and the deportation of communist suspects and members of CPI-affiliated organisations, particularly trade unions, to concentration camps, reduced the labour force considerably. The age distribution of working-class districts shows quite visible dents in the population pyramid on the male side.

Though no detailed data are available, we can assume that many manufacturing firms had to close down following the increase of imports after 1967. It should not, therefore, come as a surprise that both the rate of employment in manufacturing and the overall labour force participation rate were lower in 1971 than in 1961 (although classification changes were also clearly important) (tables 7.10 to 7.12). In the 1970s employment picked up

*Table 7.11.*  *Percentage of employed population by employment status, Jakarta, 1961-80 (in relation to total employment)*

| Year | Own-account workers | Employer | Employee | Family unpaid workers | Total employed |
|------|------|------|------|------|------|
| 1961 | 24.60 | 2.02 | 71.72 | 1.66 | 100.00 |
| 1971 | 21.32 | 3.06 | 69.64 | 5.97 | 100.00 |
| 1976 | 21.95 | 6.38 | 66.69 | 4.98 | 100.00 |
| 1978 | 19.61 | 5.29 | 69.82 | 5.29 | 100.00 |
| 1980 | 20.32 [1] | 2.41 | 73.36 | 3.91 | 100.00 |

[1] Excludes assisting family members.
Sources. BPS(A) 1977/78, 1980/81; BPS(B) 1961, 1971; BPS(F) 1983.

*Table 7.12.*  *Percentage of employment by industry, Jakarta, 1961-80 (in relation to total employment)*

| Year | Agri-culture, fishing, hunting | Mining, quarry-ing | Manu-facturing | Elec-tricity, water, gas | Con-struc-tion | Trade, restaurants, hotels | Transport, storage, communi-cation | Insurance, real estate, business services | Community, social and personal services | Activities not ade-quately defined | Total |
|------|------|------|------|------|------|------|------|------|------|------|------|
| 1961 | 4.84 | 0.24 | 16.11 | 0.49 | 8.72 | 24.21 [1] | 11.97 | — | 32.11 | 1.32 | 100.00 |
| 1971 | 3.65 | 0.33 | 8.66 | 0.39 | 6.82 | 23.53 | 10.21 | 2.70 | 33.78 | 9.73 | 100.00 |
| 1976 | 1.26 | 0.37 | 12.02 | 0.42 | 7.89 | 30.90 | 9.94 | 1.97 | 34.97 | 0.25 | 100.00 |
| 1978 | 1.22 | 0.08 | 10.92 | 0.43 | 7.05 | 26.89 | 6.05 | 0.55 | 46.75 | 0.06 | 100.00 |
| 1980 | 1.93 | 0.74 | 14.93 | 0.57 | 6.73 | 24.63 | 8.33 | 3.36 | 38.75 | 0.03 | 100.00 |

[1] Includes insurance, real estate, banking and business services.
Sources. BPS(A) 1977/78, 1980/81; BPS(B) 1961, 1971; BPS(F) 1983.

again despite massive immigration. After 1971 employment expanded at least until 1978, and the rate of employment in manufacturing reached 15 per cent of the economically active population, almost the 1961 level. As would be expected, employment in the service sector increased continuously from 1961 to 1980. Trade, however, fell back from a maximum in the mid-1970s to the rate of 1961 (table 7.12). Changes in these sectors are very much tied to the development of the informal sector discussed below. A number of other changes appear significant. Thus, the employment of females in trade rose considerably between 1961 and 1980, at 3.3 per cent above the growth of the economically active population. As a 1975 survey showed, two-fifths of the informal sector participants were in sales occupations and at least a quarter were females (Moir, 1978, p. 133).

Another significant change which appears to pull Jakarta out of a situation of urban involution is the steep rise in the rate of professional, administrative and clerical workers since 1971 (table 7.13). These rates have risen above the 1961 level and indicate both the growth of government

*Table 7.13.*    *Percentage of employment by occupation, Jakarta, 1961-80 (in relation to total employment)*

| Year | Profes-sional, technical and related | Admini-strative and mana-gerial | Clerical and related | Sales workers | Service workers | Farmers | Production and related workers, transport equipment operators | Others | Total |
|------|------|------|------|------|------|------|------|------|------|
| 1961 | 3.48 | 1.77 | 11.78 | 19.60 | 15.14 | 4.65 | 40.22 | 3.36 | 100.00 |
| 1971 | 4.14 | 1.77 | 14.25 | 22.20 | 16.05 | 3.31 | 25.92 | 12.36 | 100.00 |
| 1978 | 4.48 | 0.92 | 13.75 | 28.54 | 22.81 | 1.33 | 26.90 | 1.26 | 100.00 |
| 1980 | 6.58 | 0.95 | 14.68 | 22.36 | 17.53 | 1.92 | 32.79 | 3.19 | 100.00 |

Sources. BPS(A) 1980/81; BPS(B) 1961, 1971 and 1981; BPS(F) 1983.

employment (Evers, 1987) and possibly a significant structural change in Jakarta's economy. A recent World Bank mission suggests, however, that the growth of large enterprises in the formal sector will not provide enough employment for the rapidly growing workforce (World Bank, 1985, p. 148), and that only employment in the informal sector can provide a safeguard against a rapidly deteriorating employment situation.

## 2. Formal sector employment

So far most studies on the labour market have relied primarily on labour force statistics, i.e. on those defined as "salaried employees and wage earners". But who is a wage earner? Labour force statistics are not only a compromise between fact and fiction, necessary because of lack of time, funds and trained census personnel, but they may be misleading because of conceptual weaknesses. The image of a male European wage earner or employee, working his eight-hour shift and supporting his wife and two children is still, despite better knowledge, the standard in international statistics. In Indonesia wage labour still carries a positive connotation. A census taker is likely to receive a positive response to the category of "employee" or "wage earner", even if the respondent draws wages only occasionally and is using his or her labour for all sorts of other activities. This bias in favour of wage labour was particularly strong in the 1980 Census, which allowed a classification in this category if the respondent had worked for wages for one hour during the previous week! Of course improvements have been advocated and implemented, especially in special social surveys. But the task is formidable and much detailed empirical work is needed to come to grips with what we have called the "stratum of the insecure" (Elwert et al., 1983) or the "floating mass" (Evers, 1980). In these low-income groups one type of work is normally not sufficient to sustain a person or household, but different types of work have to be combined to ensure survival in an urban setting. In short, the usual conceptualisation of "wage labour" does not do justice to a very complex situation, and it would be wrong to think that all those classified as wage earners in Jakarta statistics make their living primarily from wages and/or are employed in the formal sector — demand for wage labour is high and probably growing in the so-called informal sector.

### 3. The development of informal sector employment

Considering the overall increase in employment and the relatively poor showing of formal sector employment, particularly in manufacturing, it goes without saying that particular importance has to be attached to the so-called informal sector. There are no official data but estimates from survey research are available (table 7.14). There is no general agreement on the definition of the informal sector, but normally the problem is approached from the point of view of the enterprise rather than the workforce. Sethuraman (1976, pp. 1-6) thus includes in the informal sector *(a)* all unregistered commercial enterprises; and *(b)* all non-commercial enterprises that have no formal structure in terms of organisation and operation. He thus estimated informal sector employment by deducting from the total labour force those employed by registered enterprises, government servants and some others. He arrives at an estimate of 435,000 people who depended on informal sector employment in 1967. In a survey by LEKNAS (the National Institute for Economic and Social Research) in 1975, a more restrictive definition was used and enterprises were sampled accordingly. Nevertheless, this survey yielded an estimated 757,000 employed in the informal sector (Moir, 1978, p. 140). It is, therefore, reasonable to assume an increasing proportion of informal sector employment during the 1960s and 1970s. This assumption is also backed by ethnographic reports which speak of an increasing entry of circular migrants into informal sector activities in the early 1970s (Jellinek, 1978, p. 149). Another measure of informal sector employment used in recent World Bank reports must, however, be regarded as totally unreliable. In these reports the ratio of the number of employers and employees to total employment is defined as formal sector employment (World Bank, 1985, p. 142). This ratio has, in fact, changed little between 1961 and 1980 (table 7.11).

It can safely be assumed that a large proportion of the urban poor is employed in the informal sector, but we cannot assume that the wages or income derived from the informal sector are necessarily lower than formal sector wages. The informal sector is not equivalent to the urban poor, though high wages tend to be associated with the formal sector, as discussed below (table 7.18 shows that only 13 per cent of households deriving their income primarily from formal sector employment are classified as poor). The informal sector is not homogeneous but highly differentiated in terms of activities and incomes. Generally the characterisation used by the early ILO studies on Kenya's informal sector still holds, namely ease of entry, reliance on indigenous resources, family ownership of enterprises, small-scale operations, use of labour-intensive and adapted technology, use of skills acquired outside the formal school system, and the sale of products on unregulated and competitive markets.

*Table 7.14.　Employment in the informal sector, selected industries, 1967 and 1975 (estimates)*

| Year | Total | Manufacturing | Construction | Trade | Transport | Services |
|------|-------|---------------|--------------|-------|-----------|----------|
| *Percentage of all employment* | | | | | | |
| 1967 | 41.2 | 22.1 | 84.7 | 35.5 | 68.3 | 31.3 |
| 1975 | 52.2 | 49.4 | 23.3 | 28.1 | 42.1 | 26.3 |
| *Percentage distribution* | | | | | | |
| 1967 | 100.00 | 6.3 | 16.2 | 20.8 | 19.1 | 29.1 |
| 1975 | 100.00 | 11.0 | 3.5 | 59.5 | 8.1 | 17.8 |

Sources. Sethuraman, 1976, p. 128 (1967); Moir, 1978, pp. 101, 140 (1975).

Given the complexity of the informal sector, it is difficult to generalise beyond these criteria and to describe the labour supply strategies for the whole sector. However, there seem to be few individual strategies in the sense of going to a labour exchange, registering for a particular job and eventually fulfilling one's job aspirations. Labour supply strategies and survival strategies are pursued collectively in the household, kin group, neighbourhood, or loose organisation of migrants originating from the same home village. Some case studies will illustrate this.

Migrants entering Jakarta in search of jobs or income will stay with relatives for a prolonged period of time, or join a *pondok*, a rooming house, which is at the same time an enterprise in the informal sector. In our sample areas, we found *pondoks* for trishaw drivers and construction workers, but also for labourers in large formal sector firms. A good report on a *pondok* serving mobile ice cream vendors is given by Jellinek (1978) and summarised below. Other informal sector enterprises might produce iron gates to protect the houses of the rich, or manufacture cooking utensils, or repair automobiles. Others might — contrary to the semi-official definition of the informal sector — employ a large number of people, such as the vegetable marketing syndicate described by Jellinek. In most cases, profit-sharing rather than payment of regular wages appears to be widespread. On the basis of the 1981 SUSENAS data, it was estimated that of all urban Javanese households falling below the World Bank poverty line, 52 per cent were in the formal and 48 per cent in the informal sector (World Bank, 1985, p. 163). To designate households as belonging totally to either sector is, to us, completely unacceptable. However, the point that a large proportion of those deriving their income from the informal sector do not fall below the poverty line is well taken, and can be substantiated by data from our PLPIIS survey.

### 4. Work in the subsistence sector

#### A. A description of the subsistence sector

One type of work generally excluded from the economically active population or the labour force is own-account work producing goods and services to be consumed by the worker and his or her household, not to be sold in the market. Work in the subsistence sector adds considerable "income" to poor urban households, in many cases to such an extent that survival in the urban environment without subsistence production would be impossible and the household would perish or be forced to migrate. We found that much labour time was used to construct or repair housing for own use, to do backyard gardening, to teach children, to walk long distances to fetch water or search for firewood, to mend clothes, cook food and look after children. Though monetary income is very important in urban areas, it is supplemented by a host of activities which contribute to household consumption, are not mediated by any market and do not involve cash payments. We use the term "urban subsistence production" to designate this part of urban household income (Evers, 1980, 1981; Evers and Schiel, 1979). We defined all unpaid work for own use, i.e. for the immediate consumption of goods and services by the producer or his or her household as "subsistence labour". We could thus distinguish between formal sector wage labour, wage labour or work on own account in the informal sector, and subsistence labour. If subsistence labour is combined with means of production used free of charge or owned by the worker or his/her household we speak of subsistence production. A characteristic of subsistence labour and production is that it is not mediated by a market and therefore has no price. Measurement is thus a problem.

Subsistence production with household labour is production for own consumption. It does not increase the supply of goods and services on the market, but is also unlikely to reduce overall demand, since the cash income of poor urban households is low anyway. There may, however, be a change in the demand structure, i.e. less demand for food or construction and repair of housing as these are partly provided in the subsistence sector. However, there is likely to be higher demand for inputs for the subsistence sector — tools, bicycles, sewing-machines, fishing tackle and other "means of production" for the subsistence economy. Subsistence production itself is extremely complex. Vegetables grown on tiny plots between the *kampung* houses, chickens raised in makeshift huts, and fishing at the beach or in urban rivers contribute significantly to food production. Construction and maintenance of houses accounts for another big share of subsistence production. Waste materials such as old boxes, nails, broken tiles, etc., are collected and used for the construction of housing. Yearly floods and occasional heavy rainfalls make reconstruction and repair of housing a permanent activity in which *kampung* dwellers have to invest much of their labour.

Improvements in labour productivity through subsistence production are difficult to measure, but probably significant. Informal education, training, health care, improved nutrition through direct access to fresh vegetables, poultry or fish are likely examples. Most important appears to be, however, the reduction of social cost and the increased security in times of household crisis (death, birth, illness). Fluctuating access to labour in the informal or formal sector and thus to monetary income is also cushioned by receipts from subsistence production. Neighbourly help and other forms of self-help organisation are another important aspect.

*Table 7.15.  Subsistence production by household expenditure*

| Subsistence production (%) | Percentage of households in monthly monetary expenditure classes (Rp.'000) | | | |
| --- | --- | --- | --- | --- |
| | 0-19.9 | 20-39.9 | 40-59.9 | 60 and more |
| Over 20 | 71.2 | 46.3 | 20.5 | 13.6 |
| 10 to 20 | 14.4 | 29.3 | 58.6 | 35.8 |
| Less than 10 | 14.4 | 24.5 | 21.0 | 50.6 |

n = 1,083 households.
Source. PLPIIS Survey, Jakarta, 1979 (Evers, 1981, p. 96).

### B. Subsistence labour and incomes

The following income sources are covered by the questionnaire of the PLPIIS Survey of 1979:

(1) Monetary income from the formal and informal sectors:

   *(a)* employment — main occupation; regular additional occupation; seasonal occupation, overtime pay, commissions, irregular jobs;

   *(b)* self-employment — net profit from independent work/trade; net profit from selling self-produced plants/livestock; interest from moneylending, renting out land and houses;

   *(c)* monetary transfers — gifts and donations; consumed savings; annuities; selling or pawning of land; receiving debts, instalments from moneylending; prizes in a lottery.

(2) Subsistence sector income:

   *(a)* non-monetary receipts — estimated value of received goods from relatives, neighbours, etc. (food items and non-food items);

   *(b)* estimated market value of unpaid services — estimated rent for self-owned house; housework; shopping; value of free medical treatment;

   *(c)* estimated market value of self-produced goods — food crops; livestock and fishing; clothes; commodities and tools; scavenged items needed for house repairs; other scavenged items; *jamu* (traditional medicine).

All economic activities could then be classified into three basic categories: wage labour, informal sector labour and subsistence labour.

According to our 1979 PLPIIS survey, the average monthly income from subsistence production, if calculated at local market prices, amounts to Rp.9,377 (about US$15) per household,[3] or 18 per cent of monthly household expenditure on average. In general, the contribution of subsistence production to consumption tends to be higher, the lower the monetary expenditure of a household (table 7.15). In other words, if money income is low the deficit is to some extent made up by subsistence production. This also means that subsistence production becomes more and more important, the poorer the family or household. Particularly for very poor families, subsistence production is not only important but essential to their survival. For 34.5 per cent of all households, subsistence production contributes more than one-fifth of the household budget. It therefore appears justified to identify subsistence production as one of the major sectors of the urban economy. Income from wage labour, profit from work on own account in small commodity production or services and subsistence production thus constitute the three main sources of urban incomes. In addition, transfers from the rural subsistence sector, subsumed here under subsistence production, are important.

It is difficult to separate out a category of worker in the subsistence sector except for "housekeeper"; in 1980, 10,195 males and 1,094,852 females were classified as housekeepers. As they were not counted as part of the labour force, it makes sense to look at their importance in relation to total population (table 7.10). The percentage totally engaged in housekeeping fell from 20 per cent in 1961 to 17 per cent in 1980. Whether or not this indicates a decline of subsistence production in general is uncertain, as other types of subsistence labour such as backyard gardening, house repair and construction, transporting of goods for own use, and related activities, are carried out by those whose main occupation may be in either the formal or informal sector. Even if the major part of work is done in the subsistence sector in terms of working hours or income, the worker would still be classified under a different occupation under current census definitions. As working hours of the poor are likely to be extremely long, we can suppose that the very poor have little time left for subsistence production. This is supported by our 1979 survey data: very poor households add less subsistence production to their incomes than households just below the poverty line.

There are as yet no time series to indicate the growth or decline of the subsistence sector. However, subsistence labour is, according to our data, very much tied in with informal sector activities, as can be seen from table 7.16. It is therefore quite possible that the growth of the informal sector is accompanied by a growth of the urban subsistence sector. Labour supply in general is very much influenced by work in the subsistence sector. After all, one of the main functions of the subsistence sector is to reproduce and maintain the labour force!

## 5. Survival strategies of the urban poor

### A. Sharing of poverty and combination of resources

Of course, lack of income or access to other resources is the defining characteristic of the urban poor. A major problem is, however, social and economic insecurity. Low-income groups with a low but stable income may still be poor, but as long as their survival is not threatened, they would not regard their situation as desperate. Large segments of the urban poor may have above-average income, but their livelihood may be threatened by insecurity of access to income and resources. We consider this "strata of the insecure" as the core group of the urban poor in need of assistance (Elwert et al., 1983). Strategies for the allocation of their major asset, labour power, seem to be

Table 7.16.    *Subsistence production by informal and formal sector employment*

| Subsistence production as percentage of expenditure | Employment in informal sector (%) | Employment in formal sector (%) |
|---|---|---|
| 0-9 | 0 | 100 |
| 10-19 | 19.2 | 80.8 |
| 20-29 | 35.9 | 64.1 |
| 30 and more | 93.7 | 6.3 |

n = 356 persons. Cramer's V = 0.22, significant at .001 level.
Source. Subsample of PLPIIS Survey, Jakarta, 1979.

mainly directed at reducing this insecurity. Maximisation of income is only one strategy among many. In the following sections several such strategies will be analysed as far as they concern the use of labour. Pooling of resources and co-operation as in the *pondok* system, the multiple job structure leading to excessively long working hours, and the combination of different types of labour will be singled out as important labour supply strategies of Jakarta's urban poor.

### B. The **pondok** *system*

Survey research figures on the average household size reveal a high standard deviation. This figure would probably be even higher if the *pondoks* (large institutional households) were correctly enumerated. These *pondoks* (particularly for circular migrants following one or several related occupations) are operated by the landlord or landlady, quite often a squatter. In the sample areas selected during our PLPIIS household survey there were several such *pondoks*. One housed more than 30 *bejak* (trishaw) drivers who took turns in sleeping in the narrow bunks provided there. They either operated their own *bejaks* or rented them from the owner of the *pondok*. If their journeys did not take them to distant areas, the *bejak* drivers would go home for their meal, for which they paid individually. Solidarity was high, *bejaks* were exchanged and drivers who suffered one of the many calamities such as confiscation of their vehicle by the police or accidents were helped through a rotating credit system.

Many different forms of *pondok* exist in Jakarta, estimated by Jellinek to number several thousand. Some resemble large boarding-houses, such as several *pondoks* in our research which were owned by former peasants whose land had been taken over by industrial firms because of urbanisation, and who rented sleeping places to gangs of construction workers or to daily wage labourers in the industrial estates. When such workers bring their wives and children, individual households are established and the *pondok* changes to a normal boarding-house with little or no institutional identity.

Jellinek's (1978) study on a *pondok* of ice cream sellers shows how resources such as ice cream making equipment are shared and how communal living allows survival in an insecure environment. The *pondok* is owned and run by a couple who sell food and supply equipment and ingredients to the ice cream vendors. The ice cream is prepared individually by each vendor in the *pondok* yard and sold in various parts of the city. These traders are all circular migrants originating from the same village in West Java. Income from this *pondok* trade, which surpasses rural and urban wages, is usually sent back to support the family in the village. "The earnings of the ice cream traders depended on the amount of ice cream they could sell but generally they earned surprisingly well by comparison with their fellow *kampung* dwellers. Those employed by the Government in unskilled jobs, such as watchmen, tea makers, etc., had the security of a regular wage and received a supplement of rice, but the ice cream traders could earn more than twice the wage of such employees" (Jellinek, 1978, p. 144). None the less, living conditions were appalling, working hours stretched from 6 a.m. until the evening, and health standards suffered in consequence.

### C. Multiple jobs

In order to compensate for low wages and salaries many people turn to either permanent or occasional additional work. This is facilitated by working hours, especially in the public sector, that run from about 7 a.m. to 2 p.m., leaving ample time to do additional work after the heat of the afternoon has subsided. It is, therefore, surprising that census figures and survey data show relatively small figures. An urban unemployment survey by the University of Indonesia in 1972 showed that only 4 per cent of employed males and 1 per cent of employed females held more than one job. The low figures may be due to the definition given to "multiple jobs" during data collection. Jakartans tend to make a distinction between a job and additional income. A construction worker who occasionally repairs doors and windows in the evening would not regard this as an additional job. A lecturer in a university transferred to permanent duty at the National Planning Agency and teaching in a private institution in the evening, besides being a regular newspaper columnist and a long-term consultant to several international agencies, would in all probability declare himself just a "civil servant". A daily worker in the informal sector will, as we know from observations and field reports, work for different employers at different hours and for different lengths of time. Whether this is regarded as a "multiple job structure" remains a matter of definition. In the Census, such a worker will simply be enumerated as an employee in an industry he happened to have worked in during the past week for at least one hour. Instead of "multiple jobs", one should therefore speak of another form of "combinations of types of work", which finds expression in the extremely long working hours mentioned in several surveys (Atma Jaya University, 1976; Moir, 1978; Karafir, 1977; Krausse, 1985, Ch. V). In the mid-1970s nearly 60 per cent of the employed worked more than 44 hours per week (Sethuraman, 1976, p. 78); in 1980 this had increased to 65.4 per cent (Manning and Papayungan, 1984, p. 350). Women in particular combined different types of work, to such an extent that more than a third of those employed in Jakarta in 1980 worked over 60 hours per week! This does not even include housework and other types of subsistence labour.

### D. Combinations of different types of work

In the course of our PLPIIS study it became apparent that household members tried to apply their labour power to sectors which offered the best opportunity to satisfy their basic needs and ensure their reproduction. The combination of different types of labour, however, changes with total household income. Our original hypothesis that subsistence labour grows in importance with declining household income was only partly confirmed. For very poor households, subsistence labour − though still essential for survival − amounted to a lesser share than for somewhat "richer" households. Access to land and resources, and "capital equipment" for household production, such as sewing-machines, stoves, or bicycles, appears to be as important as the composition of the household labour force or the dependency ratio. For similar reasons the total value of subsistence labour increases with growing household income, while its relative value declines. In other words, wage labour provides an increasing share of household income, but the monetary input also gives access to resources used for subsistence production.

In terms of the inner logic of poor urban households it makes little sense to classify households or even individuals by their "main economic activity", occupation or source of income. The combination of incomes from the formal, informal and subsistence sectors, and changes in this combination with the domestic development cycle, characterises the urban household economy. The claim that 12.7 per cent of Jakarta's labour force is unemployed (Census, 1971 (BPS(B)) and Sethuraman, 1976, p. 72) is rather misleading in this respect. One of our subsamples of 120 households in East Jakarta, which has been subjected to intensive analysis, shows that of their total income 58.2 per cent came from formal sector employment, 25.4 per cent from the informal sector and 16.4 per cent from subsistence production (Evers et al., 1983). The three sources of income were, however, combined in widely different proportions in each household.

Comparing wage labour in the formal and informal sector will shed further light on the importance of subsistence production. According to our survey data, subsistence production is much more important for labourers working in the informal sector, such as workshops producing furniture and other household implements, than for government employees. Half the informal sector workers had to add more than 30 per cent in subsistence production to their incomes in order to survive, in contrast to only 2 per cent of government employees, who, however, had other additional sources of income. This adds fuel to the argument that subsistence production subsidises wage labour and, in fact, facilitates the payment of wages below the subsistence level. In line with our earlier arguments, however, it makes little sense to look at the three types of labour separately. Which typical combinations occur and which combinations tend to ensure the survival of households? Which combinations result in a better satisfaction of basic needs?

Of the theoretically possible 64 types of labour combination, only 21 actually occurred. These could be grouped into five types, ignoring insignificant contributions to household income (table 7.17). The households representing

Table 7.17.   *Distribution of types of labour combination*

| Labour combination | Households | Percentage |
|---|---|---|
| (1) F | 7 | 6.9 |
| (2) F + S | 46 | 39.3 |
| (3) F + I + S | 22 | 18.8 |
| (4) F + I | 4 | 3.4 |
| (5) I + S | 37 | 31.6 |
| Not classifiable | 3 | |

Note. F = Formal sector wage labour; I = Informal sector work; S = Subsistence labour. (Estimated contribution of less than 10 per cent of subsistence labour to total household labour ignored.)
Source. PLPIIS Survey, 1979.

each type show different characteristics in terms of demographic composition, such as dependency ratio and proportion of migrants, educational attainment and, last but not least, household income (see Evers et al., 1983, pp. 27-37 for a more detailed statistical analysis).

The results of our analysis can be summarised as follows: access to wage labour remains the major avenue to assuring the satisfaction of basic needs and pulling the household across the poverty threshold. As sufficient education is a precondition for getting a formal sector job, households with a larger proportion of educated persons are found in types F and F + I, which in turn have higher incomes. The F type with the highest average income (and the highest net savings) is made up primarily of small households with young, relatively highly educated migrants, whereas the F + I + S type consists mainly of large households and long-term residents. The largest households (average 7.6 persons) of this type, with low levels of education, find it difficult to satisfy basic needs and can thus be identified as a typical poverty group. They have to do different types of work in order to survive, including a high input of subsistence labour (see table 7.18).

Earlier we indicated that employment trends in Jakarta seem to lead to increasing difficulties in absorbing young educated workers in the formal sector. If workers try instead to gain access to informal sector or unwaged subsistence employment, income among these workers will probably decline. In any case, our survey data indicate that employment outside the formal sector, i.e. in the informal or subsistence sectors, is associated with a greater incidence of poverty. But urban poverty would be even greater if access to informal and subsistence activities were to be curtailed.

## IV. Conclusions

On the basis of several field studies, it has been argued that wage labour rarely occurs alone, but is typically combined with work in the informal sector and with subsistence labour. In the discussion of subsistence labour and

*Table 7.18.  Types of labour combination by characteristics of households*

| Characteristic | Labour combination | | | | |
| --- | --- | --- | --- | --- | --- |
| | F | F + S | F + I | F + I + S | I + S |
| Average household income (Rp.1,000) | 127.0 | 54.4 | 81.1 | 59.5 | 41.6 |
| Average subsistence production (Rp.1,000) | 9.1 | 9.8 | 7.3 | 10.1 | 9.2 |
| Households above poverty line (%) | 87 | 76 | 75 | 40 | 40 |

Source. PLPIIS Survey, 1979.

production, several problems have been addressed, e.g. the definition and description of these concepts, problems of measurement and the creation of typologies of labour combinations. But an essential question remains: what is the practical relevance of these findings? It seems that the following avenues for discussing this question could be fruitful:

— it can be demonstrated to policy-makers that the subsistence sector is both large and productive;

— typical social relations of subsistence labour, such as exploitation of child and female labour or other unpaid work in the household, can be drawn into the open; and

— the inter-relation between wage labour and subsistence labour can be studied with the aim of avoiding the destruction of socio-ecological systems which have a high survival value for poor populations.

Our study of the *kampung* population shows certain characteristics that seem typical of Jakarta's poverty in general. Though the study is not representative in the strict statistical sense, the results are an indicator of living conditions of Jakarta's lower classes. Most striking is the variety and differentiation of income, expenditure and life-styles in the *kampungs*. Many migrants, but also long-term residents, have to adjust constantly to changing economic conditions and changes in their domestic development cycle. Analytically we can discern three sources of income: wage labour, income from small commodity production and services, and subsistence production; we may also use another classification scheme: income from the formal, informal and subsistence sectors. The latter appears to be important, particularly for the survival of the lowest income groups. Whereas the informal sector has drawn more attention in recent years, the contribution of subsistence production to the urban economy in general and the low-income groups in particular should not be neglected.

In this chapter we have used statistical data from various government surveys, and expressed serious doubts about their reliability due to enumeration errors and conceptual problems. The data show that from 1960 to 1980 average household expenditure rose in urban Java and particularly Jakarta, suggesting that the incomes of the urban masses may have improved. How much real wages rose is extremely difficult to ascertain because of lack of data. Overall household incomes that include wages from the formal and informal sectors, transfers, profits from small-scale activities and own-account work, and also from subsistence production, own consumption and housework, may be higher than the official statistics claim. But this does not mean that incomes, especially of the lower income classes, have risen dramatically. The evaluation of the statistics depends very much on the often criticised cost-of-living indices, which have, especially in the 1960s, given great weight to government-controlled prices of food items. These items were often not available to the urban poor at government price levels, and increases in the "cost of urban living" (transport, housing, food, clothing, protection fees and illegal levies) have been particularly severe and have reduced the percentage of food in household expenditures.

Notwithstanding the partly contradictory statistical data, we have the impression, from long-term field observation in Jakarta and other urban areas, that urban poverty has not fallen dramatically in terms of personal incomes. Indeed it may have increased, although public services such as road construction, flood control, education and health improved in the 1970s. It appears that growing public sector employment has provided incomes as well as greater access to public services. Otherwise the increase of formal sector employment has been less than satisfactory. Own-account work in the informal sector, especially in trade and commerce, showed a considerable labour absorption capacity. We can only speculate whether the increase of petty trade reflects a reduction of subsistence production, i.e. work for own consumption outside the market. Our surveys have, however, shown that in the late 1970s subsistence production was still important and essential to the survival of large sections of the urban poor.

The Government has instituted some income- and employment-generating programmes, such as *kampung* improvement or the construction of market-places. The former has been acclaimed a success, but the latter has often limited market access for poor traders and so led to a more inequitable distribution of income. The same can be said of banning small human-powered vehicles such as *bejaks* from most areas of Jakarta, which certainly led to a higher "cost of urban living" and falling incomes of the urban poor.

Last but not least, an increasing absorption of the young into schools reduced the pressure on the labour market throughout the 1970s, but also added a major expenditure item for poor urban households. School uniforms, illegal school levies, expenses for books and writing materials are excluded from the older cost-of-living indices. It can be expected that the wave of graduates looking for work after completing secondary or tertiary education will produce higher unemployment rates and a higher *de facto* dependency ratio. As shown above, educational attainment in the *kampung* areas is already quite high and consequently these poorer sections of the population will also be severely hit by this new trend. Most of these conclusions are based on estimates, incomplete observation or simply guesswork. But we can legitimately conclude that on present trends the problems of urban poverty and unemployment are not going to be solved by the end of this century.

### Notes

[1] Sociology of Development Research Centre, University of Bielefeld. This chapter was prepared with the help of Friedhelm Betke and Heiko Schrader. Extensive use has been made of the PLPIIS survey, directed by Mulyanto Sumardi and the author (then Universitas Indonesia, Jakarta). The author has benefited greatly from discussions with Gerry Rodgers and S. V. Sethuraman (ILO, Geneva) and colleagues at the Sociology of Development Research Centre.

[2] Data from income and expenditure surveys such as SUSENAS have to be interpreted cautiously because of many sources of error. In addition to the usual socio-statistical problems of survey research, such as sampling errors or inaccuracies in responses, some major systematic under- and over-estimations are vaguely known but hardly ever accounted for. Income and expenditure of the highest and lowest income groups are known to be underestimated. Though the category of "own consumption" or "income in kind" is usually included in most income and expenditure surveys, the importance of these items as a major contribution to household income is hardly ever recognised (Fisk, 1975, pp. 252-279). The contribution of goods and services provided by the consumers themselves, or received free of charge outside the market economy, remains unclear. SUSENAS, the major source of expenditure data, includes some goods produced or received by the consumers for own consumption, but no services. Other surveys such as the Inter-Censal Population Survey (SUPAS) exclude even this limited enumeration (Evers, 1981, p. 90). Apart from these specific problems, most official data and the analysis based on them tend to be completely divorced from the descriptive accounts of anthropologists, sociologists and geographers. A wall of "objective", though often quite unreliable, statistical data and a "detached" scientific language tend to hide the underlying realities.

[3] Monetary estimates were obtained from in-depth interviews within a household budget approach, in which were identified all consumption, all services utilised, and all activities within and outside the household. Shadow prices were (reluctantly) used at times, especially for housework. Despite this detail, the estimates should be considered as minima.

### References

Atma Jaya University, 1976: *Hawkers in Jakarta* (Jakarta, Jaya Research Centre).

BPS (A); Biro Pusat Statistik, 1961 ff: *Statistik Indonesia, statistical pocketbook of Indonesia* (Jakarta).

——— (B); Biro Pusat Statistik, 1961, 1971, 1981: *Sensus penduduk DKI Jakarta Raya* (Jakarta).

——— (C); Biro Pusat Statistik, 1979: *Indikator kesejahteraan rakyat* (Jakarta).

——— (D); Biro Pusat Statistik, 1967, 1976, 1978, 1980: *Survey sosial economi nasional, Pengeluran untuk konsumi penduduk* (Jakarta).

——— (E); Biro Pusat Statistik, 1968/9: *Survey biaya hindup* (Jakarta).

——— (F); Biro Pusat Statistik, 1983: *Statistik Indonesia* (Jakarta).

——— (G); Biro Pusat Statistik, 1976-78: *Indikator sosial* (Jakarta).

Elwert, G., Evers, H. D. and Wilkens, W., 1983: "Die Suche nach Sicherheit: Kombinierte Produktionsformen im sogenannten 'informellen Sektor'", in *Zeitschrift für Soziologie* (Stuttgart), 12, 4, pp. 281-296.

Evers, Hans-Dieter, 1980: "Subsistence production and the Jakarta 'floating mass'", in *Prisma* (English edition, Jakarta), 17, pp. 27-35.

———, 1981: "The contribution of urban subsistence production to incomes in Jakarta", in *Bulletin of Indonesian Economic Studies* (Canberra), 17, 2, pp. 89-96.

———, 1987: "The bureaucratisation of South East Asia", in *Comparative Studies in Society and History* (Cambridge), 29, 4.

Evers, H.-D., Betke, F. and Sundoyo, S., 1983: *Die Komplexität der Grundbedürfnisse. Eine Untersuchung über städtische Haushalte der untersten Einkommensschichten in Jakarta*, Working Paper No. 43 (Bielefeld, Sociology of Development Research Centre).

Evers, H.-D. and T. Schiel, 1979: "Expropriation der unmittelbaren Produzenten oder Ausdehnung der Subsistenzwirtschaft — Thesen zur bäuerlichen u. städtischen Subsistenzproduktion", in H.-D. Evers et al.: *Subsistenzproduktion und Akkumulation* (Saarbrücken, Breitenbach).

Evers, H.-D., Sundoyo, S., Betke, F. and Buchholt, 1982: *A survey of low income households in Jakarta*, Working Paper No. 17 (Bielefeld, Sociology of Development Research Centre).

Fisk, E. K., 1975: "The subsistence component in National Income Accounts", in *The Developing Economies* (Tokyo), 13, 3, pp. 252-279.

Hammado, Tantu, 1979: "Sektor informal di Jakarta", in M. Sumardi and H.-D. Evers (eds.): *Urbanisasi, Masalah Kota Jakarta* (Jakarta, YTKI/FES), pp. 36-46.

Hughes, G. and Islam, 1981: "Inequality in Indonesia: A decomposition analysis", in *Bulletin of Indonesian Economic Studies*, 27, 2, pp. 42-71.

Hugo, G. J., 1977: *Population mobility in west Java* (Yogyakarta).

Jellinek, Lea, 1977: *The life of a Jakarta street trader — Two years later*, Working Paper No. 13 (Melbourne, Monash University, Centre of SEA Studies).

————, 1978: "The pondok system and circular migration", in Jellinek, L., Manning, C. and Jones, G.: *The life of the poor in Indonesian cities* (Melbourne, Monash University).

Karafir, Yan Pieter, 1977: *Pemupukan modal pedagang kaki-lima* (Jakarta, PLPIIS/Universitas Indonesia).

KSJ; Kantor Sensus dan Statistik, 1970-77: *Jakarta dalam angka* (Jakarta).

King, D. Y. and Weldon, P. D., 1977: "Income distribution and levels of living in Java, 1963-70", in *Economic Development and Cultural Change* (Chicago).

Krausse, Gerald H., 1978: "Intra-urban variation in Kampung settlements of Jakarta", in *Journal of Tropical Geography* (Singapore), 46, pp. 11-26.

————, 1982: "Themes in poverty. Economics, education, amenities, and social functions in Jakarta's kampungs", in *Southeast Asian Journal of Social Science* (Singapore), 10, 2, pp. 49-70.

Krausse, Gerald H. (ed.), 1985: *Urban society in Southeast Asia*, Vol. I: *Social and economic issues* (Hong Kong, Asian Research Service).

Magiera, S. L., 1981: "The role of wheat in the Indonesian food sector", in *Bulletin of Indonesian Economic Studies*, Vol. 17 (3).

Manning, Chris and Papayungan, Michael (eds.), 1984: *Analisa ketenagakerjaan di Indonesia* (Jakarta, Biro Pusat Statistik).

McCawley, Peter, 1984: "A slowdown in industrial growth?", in *Bulletin of Indonesian Economic Studies*, 20, 3, pp. 158-174.

Moir, H., 1978: *Jakarta informal sector* (Jakarta, Indonesian Institute of Science (LEKNAS-LIPI)).

Papanek, Gustav F., 1976: "Pendukuk miskin di Jakarta", in *Prisma* (Jakarta), 5, 1, pp. 59-83.

Sayogyo, 1978: "Lapisan masyarakat yang paling lemah di pedesaan Jawa", in *Prisma* 7, 3, pp. 3-14.

Sethuraman, S. V., 1976: *Jakarta, urban development and employment* (Geneva, ILO).

Sumardi, Mulyanto and Evers, Hans-Dieter (eds.), 1982: *Kebutuhan pokok dan kemiskinan* (Jakarta, CV Rajwali/Yayasan Ilmu-Ilmu Sosial).

Sundrum, R. M., 1974: "Household income patterns", in *Bulletin of Indonesian Economic Studies*, Vol. 10, 1.

————, 1976: "Consumer expenditure patterns: An analysis of socio-economic survey", in *Bulletin of Indonesian Economic Studies*, Vol. 9, 1.

————, 1977: "Changes in consumption patterns in urban Java, 1970-76", in *Bulletin of Indonesian Economic Studies*, 13, 2.

————, 1979: "Income distribution, 1970-76", in *Bulletin of Indonesian Economic Studies*, Vol. 15, No. 1.

VT, 1930; DPT van Landbouw, Nijdverheid en Handel, 1933: *Volkstelling 1930: Deel I: Inheemsche Bevolking van west Java* (Batavia).

World Bank, 1978: *Indonesia, poverty and inequality*, Draft, confidential, Report No. 2093-IND (Washington, DC).

————, 1980: *Indonesia, employment and income distribution in Indonesia* (Washington, DC).

————, 1984a: *Indonesia, policies and prospects for economic growth and transformation*, Report No. 5066-IND (Washington, DC).

————, 1984b: *Indonesia, urban services sector report* (Washington, DC).

————, 1985: *Indonesia, policies for growth and employment*, Report No. 55597-IND (Washington, DC).

# Chapter 8

## Trends in poverty and labour market outcomes in the Metro Manila area

RUPERTO P. ALONZO [1]

## I. Introduction

### 1. Background

Poverty redressal programmes have long been the concern of social workers in the Philippines, but only in the 1970s did economists and other social scientists start to show serious interest in poverty issues.[2] Among the many factors influencing this increased awareness of Philippine poverty was the general disappointment with the pace at which the economic growth of the 1950s and 1960s had "trickled down" to the poor. In fact, income distribution data which became available in the early 1970s showed an increase not only in relative inequality but also in poverty incidence between 1961 and 1971, even though GDP was growing at a respectable 5 per cent per year. Instead of prosperity trickling down to the masses, more and more people were being pushed into poverty. Even before statistics allowing the estimation of trends in income inequality and poverty incidence began to be published, outward manifestations of the growing poverty problem were becoming too frequent to be ignored. By the early 1970s the plight of the poor was finding expression in constant street demonstrations in Manila and growing insurgency in rural areas, and gave rise to many studies which explored different dimensions of the country's poverty. Economists in particular have been concerned with macro poverty issues, proposing various definitions of poverty thresholds and estimating the number of families falling below such thresholds. Research along these lines often looked at poverty in terms of income and expenditure, although the growing concern with basic needs also led to the measurement of poverty in terms of other welfare dimensions such as housing, health, nutrition and education. Sociologists and anthropologists, on the other hand, examined specific segments of the poor population in their micro-case studies such as fishermen, upland farmers and landless workers in rural areas and squatters, slum dwellers and scavengers in the cities.

Despite the extensive documentation of the deterioration in material welfare of a growing number of Filipino families, the Government in the 1970s, and well into the 1980s, continued to pursue policies that would in general be characterised as anti-poor (De Dios, 1984). The trade policy regime maintained a system of protection that imposed penalties on agriculture and the labour-intensive industries, where most of the poor found their living. Fiscal policy was characterised by regressivity in both taxation and public expenditure. Financial policy also showed a bias in favour of big capital-intensive firms. Direct intervention programmes, which were ostensibly addressed to the poor (especially in the more highly visible urban areas), were launched with much fanfare, but the beneficiaries often ended up being the not-so-poor, as the experience of the national shelter and livelihood programmes showed (Angeles, 1985).

Even information on poverty was in a way suppressed by the Government, with constant changes in statistical definitions and procedures. On employment, the reference period for those considered as employed was changed in 1976 from the "past week" to the "past quarter", effectively increasing the numerator of the employment rate (Tidalgo and Esguerra, 1984). Thus, even in 1984 and 1985, while the country was in the deepest recession in the post-war period, with GDP declining by 10 per cent, open unemployment was officially registered at only 5-7 per cent. On nominal and real wages, the series monitored by the Central Bank based on surveys of workers in various establishments was discontinued in 1981 and replaced by a new series on legislated minimum wages, though compliance with wage legislation was known to be very weak. The main reason for the change, in the view of most observers, was the bad picture of government performance painted by the sharply declining real wages in the Central Bank series. On inflation, the number of commodities and services comprising the market basket for the Consumer Price Index (CPI) was reduced from 644 to 393 items; the relative weights were also changed in 1982 to favour items under price control (De Dios, 1984). The net effect was to understate the true inflation rate, since commodities under price control were not always sold at official prices.

## 2. The study's objectives and coverage

With the advent of a new political order in the Philippines, a review of past trends in poverty is called for, especially since 1984 and 1985 witnessed an unprecedented decline in domestic output, which certainly worsened poverty. The recession has been particularly harsh on the industrial sector, with foreign exchange constraints limiting capital and raw materials imports, such that the ranks of the urban poor grew as workers lost their jobs.[3] This chapter reviews urban poverty trends, concentrating on Metro Manila, although data constraints will often oblige us to examine urban areas in general. It will also cover concurrent trends in labour market outcomes and try to evaluate the relative importance of labour market mechanisms in the evolution of poverty. It aims to contribute to an understanding of the influence of labour market policies on poverty, so that the design of poverty redressal strategies could better take advantage of labour market complementarities.

Metro Manila was chosen because of its dominant position among urban areas in the Philippines. In population density, industrial concentration and overall economic activity it outranks all the other 12 regions in the country.

Its share of total population grew from 10.8 per cent in 1970 to 12.3 per cent in 1980, and it accounted for about a third of the total urban population. Moreover, many of the other "urban" places are really rural based, with low population densities. If, in the other cities classified as urban areas, only the "urban centres" are included, Metro Manila would constitute around 50 per cent of the total urban population. Metro Manila is also dominant in the economy: in 1983 it accounted for 32.3 per cent of GDP; the Census of Establishments gives its share in manufacturing value added in 1975 as 58.1 per cent, and the Annual Survey of Establishments places its share of value added in wholesale and retail trade for 1981 at 59.6 per cent (these data sources, however, may have some bias in coverage towards bigger and formal sector enterprises).

The employment structure in Metro Manila also differs from the rest of the country. Statistics from the Integrated Survey of Households for the third quarter of 1983 show that industrial employment comprised 30 per cent of total Metro Manila employment, while other areas had only 12.5 per cent of their employed labour force in industry. The proportion of wage and salary workers in Metro Manila was 80 per cent, compared with 36 per cent in other areas.[4] But while patterns of employment and economic activity look favourable in aggregate, pockets of poverty abound, especially in blighted areas. For 1981 the National Housing Authority estimated that about 25 per cent of Metro Manila's total population was living in slums and squatter communities. Most relocation efforts have been met with violence, as people resist being moved away from their sources of livelihood.

### 3. The related literature and data sources

Among recent studies on Filipino poverty are several bibliographical listings and reviews of the literature which help in documenting trends. In particular, the bibliography by Abad and Eviota (1985) contains over 600 annotated entries of social science works written between 1979 and 1983, grouped under five major headings: general works, social institutions and poverty, disadvantaged groups and communities, social processes, and general policies. It is especially helpful in tracing micro-case studies of poverty groups undertaken by sociologists and anthropologists. The National Economic and Development Authority (NEDA) also prepared an inventory of surveys covering different aspects of poverty in the Philippines, including private as well as government studies (NEDA, 1980a). A companion volume reviews poverty issues and discusses government programmes addressed to poverty-related problems (NEDA, 1980b). Complementing these works are the surveys by Alburo and Roberto (1980) on major research efforts on Philippine poverty, and by Mangahas and Barros (1980) on the closely related issues of the distribution of income and wealth. Two World Bank studies (1980, 1985) are especially useful, as they contain previously unpublished cross-tabulations from National Census and Statistics Office (NCSO) surveys. The 1985 study was able to draw a panel of 3,300 households from the third-quarter surveys of the 1979 and 1983

Integrated Surveys of Households (ISH); data on household sizes and incomes, and on household heads' occupations and educational attainments were analysed. Most of the macro-level data on labour market outcomes used here are from the NCSO's ISH and Annual Surveys of Establishments. The ILO-sponsored survey of the informal sector in Metro Manila in 1976 (Jurado and Castro, 1979) offers a broad view of the groups which are the focus of socio-anthropological micro-level studies such as Keyes (1974) on scavengers and Guerrero (1975) on hawkers and vendors.

## II. Trends in urban poverty incidence

### 1. Defining poverty thresholds

In the post-war period official concern with measuring poverty lines dates back to 1948, when the then Bureau of the Census and Statistics, in collaboration with the then Department of Social Welfare, proposed the Rice-Wage Formula, which was meant to indicate the minimum income (in rice equivalents) that a low-wage earner needed to provide the minimum basic needs of a family of five in terms of food, clothing, shelter, education and health. This approach has been criticised on various grounds, not least the biases induced by changing relative prices between rice and other goods, but the basic idea (along with its biases) has been retained in many later computations of poverty thresholds.

In 1974 the Development Academy of the Philippines sponsored the Social Indicators Project (SIP), which attempted to make a systematic evaluation of the trends in different aspects of national welfare (Mangahas, 1976). One of the major areas of concern of the SIP was the measurement of the extent of poverty in the country (Abrera, 1976). Two poverty lines were defined and calculated: the food threshold, based on a recommended diet for a reference family (to represent the level of absolute poverty); and the total threshold, including other basic needs (to represent the level of "secondary" poverty). An allowance was made for cost-of-living differences between Metro Manila and the rest of the country. A linear programming approach to the determination of the least-cost food menu that would satisfy minimum nutritional requirements defined by the Food and Nutrition Research Institute (FNRI) was used by Tan and Holazo (1979). They also computed a total poverty threshold including separate estimates of costs of housing, medical care, clothing, schooling and utilities. This produced poverty lines that were much lower than those of the SIP. The composition of the regional food baskets has been criticised as unrealistic in terms of the standard Filipino food tastes, even among poor families (Mangahas, 1979). For example, rice — the staple cereal in the Philippines — was replaced by noodles in the least-cost solution for most areas. The World Bank studies (1980, 1985) also drew their own poverty lines. The 1980 study started from the national survey of some 1,000 households by the National Food and Agriculture Council (NFAC) in late 1970, estimating

*Table 8.1. Comparative poverty lines, 1971 and 1975 (pesos per family per year, in current prices)*

| Study [1] | 1971 | | 1975 | |
|---|---|---|---|---|
| | Urban | Rural | Urban | Rural |
| Tan and Holazo | 2 025-<br>2 634 | 1 865-<br>2 349 | 3 688-<br>4 984 | 3 680-<br>4 287 |
| World Bank, 1985 | 2 989 | 2 341 | 5 514 | 4 570 |
| World Bank, 1980 | 3 751 | 2 633 | 6 618 | 4 879 |
| Social Indicators Project (SIP) | 5 762-<br>7 203 | 5 000 | 9 905-<br>11 872 | 8 668 |

[1] For Tan and Holazo and the SIP, the upper limit for urban is the value for Metro Manila. These two studies used a reference family of six, while the World Bank studies used observed family sizes for the urban and rural areas.
Sources. World Bank (1980, 1985); Abrera (1976); Mangahas (1977); and Tan and Holazo (1979), as reported in Mangahas (1979).

the actual income level at which calorie intake recommendations were achieved, taking into account both the elements of a least-cost food budget and actual preferences, and adjusting for urban-rural price differences. The 1985 study defined thresholds for urban and rural areas: a food threshold based on rice (60 per cent) and other food items, and a total threshold including 40 per cent of non-food expenditures in urban and 30 per cent in rural areas.

Poverty lines obtained from these various techniques are reported in table 8.1. The World Bank studies give poverty thresholds much lower than those of the SIP and only slightly higher than Tan and Holazo. For 1971, for example, the 1985 World Bank threshold was only P2,989 per family per year for urban areas, compared with the SIP's P7,203 for Metro Manila and P5,762 for other urban areas. Tan and Holazo's estimates for the same year, on the other hand, were even lower at P2,634 for Metro Manila and P2,204 for other urban areas.[5] The main reason for the low poverty thresholds in the 1985 World Bank study is the removal of fish, meat and poultry from the poor family's menu. This food category has been observed from nutrition surveys to constitute as much as 30 per cent of the average Filipino family's food budget, so removing this from the diet even for poor families is perhaps unrealistic.

Perhaps the only institution in the Philippines that has made periodic estimates of poverty lines for Metro Manila (and lately also for Metro Cebu) is the Center for Research and Communication (CRC). The latest CRC methodology (Antonio, 1984) defines three poverty lines. The first computes basic food needs for families of differing age-sex compositions, using FNRI nutritional guide-lines. A second line is then drawn for total family needs by applying a food expenditure factor of 0.60. For the third line above which a family would be able to maintain a "decent" standard of living, the food expenditure factor falls to 0.43, as allowance is made for entertainment and a small amount of family savings. This third "threshold family income" thus goes beyond mere survival and provides "at least the barest requirements consistent with the dignity of the family members as human beings" (Reyes, 1985).

Estimates of the three CRC thresholds, including the food poverty line, have
been higher than those made by other researchers.

Poverty lines drawn on the basis of minimum requirements have been
criticised as being imposed by the value judgements of the researchers. The first
documented effort to measure directly the people's perceptions of the meaning
of being poor was a socio-economic survey of urban areas conducted in 1971
by the Asia Research Organisation (ARO) for Gallup International (Abrera,
1976). The survey asked respondents how much income per week they thought
a family of four would need for health and comfort. Sixty-two per cent of the
urban respondents (from Metro Manila, Cebu, Davao and Bacolod) answered
in the range of P51 to P150 per week. Converting these figures to an average
annual figure comparable with table 8.1 gives a perceived threshold of P7,013
in Metro Manila, very close to the SIP estimate of P7,203. A similar approach
used by the Development Academy of the Philippines in Metro Manila in 1981
produced a median poverty threshold as perceived by the respondents of about
P16,800 per family per year (using the mid-point of the median range), double
the World Bank (1985) estimate of P9,965 for that year. There has been much
discussion among economists since the early 1970s on the proper poverty lines
to follow and on the types of income and expenditure data to use, such that the
poor themselves tend to be forgotten in the debate. This review, instead of
remaining confined to any particular approach to poverty measurement, tries
to be eclectic and reports on primary poverty studies as they come, but at the
same time points out whatever peculiarities and limitations they may have.

## 2. Data problems and limitations

The primary data requirement for measuring poverty incidence is the
distribution of families according to income and expenditure classes. In the
Philippines the main source of such data is the Family Income and Expenditures
Survey (FIES), which has been conducted by the NCSO for 1957, 1961, 1965,
1971, 1975 and 1985. These data sources have been subject to much controversy
and debate. The recall period is long (mostly one year), and there is evidence
of undercoverage, especially in 1975 (Mangahas et al., 1977) and in the earliest
surveys. Apart from the FIES, the NCSO began collecting household income
data in 1976 through its annual Integrated Survey of Households (ISH), which
provides information on labour force participation, employment and earnings
patterns for all household members, together with detailed accounts of
household income; however, it does not gather any data on household
expenditures. The reference period for the survey is the quarter immediately
preceding the field interview; the income data are thus only for one quarter. The
ISH results also show a high degree of undercoverage of income when compared
with the National Income Accounts.[6] Mangahas (1982) estimates the coverage
for 1978 to 1980 as ranging from 42 to 54 per cent. Comparisons for 1981 to
1983, however, do show an increase in coverage, reaching 66 per cent in 1983
(World Bank, 1985).

Dissatisfaction with the quality, frequency and publication delays of

*Table 8.2.  Comparative estimates of poverty incidence, 1965-75 [1] (percentage of families below threshold)*

|  | 1965 | 1971 | 1975 |
|---|---|---|---|
| **Metro Manila** | | | |
| *Food threshold* | | | |
| SIP-income | 24 | 34 | 58 |
| SIP-expenditures | 17 | 25 | – |
| *Total threshold* | | | |
| SIP-income | 49 | 59 | 75 |
| SIP-expenditures | 47 | 52 | – |
| Tan and Holazo-income | 11 | 16 | 41 |
| Tan and Holazo-expenditures | 6 | 9 | – |
| World Bank, 1980 [2] | – | 15 | 31 |
| World Bank, 1985 | – | 35 | 53 |
| **Range outside Metro Manila [3]** | | | |
| *Food threshold* | | | |
| SIP-income | 41-49 | 39-64 | 58-62 |
| SIP-expenditures | 27-39 | 25-48 | – |
| *Total threshold* | | | |
| SIP-income | 69-81 | 64-83 | 80-90 |
| SIP-expenditures | 61-76 | 52-76 | – |
| Tan and Holazo-income | 32-68 | 31-66 | 38-66 |
| Tan and Holazo-expenditures | 15-71 | 12-51 | – |
| World Bank, 1980 | – | 16-61 | 29-73 |
| World Bank, 1985 | – | 57 | 64 |

[1] See table 8.1 for the respective poverty thresholds.  [2] Both World Bank studies use the expenditure distribution. The 1980 study applies the per capita threshold to the distribution of families by per capita expenditure class. The Metro Manila figures for the 1985 study are really for urban areas, and those for outside Metro Manila are for rural areas.  [3] The SIP range is for rural and other urban areas; the Tan and Holazo and the World Bank (1980) ranges are for other regions.
Sources. World Bank (1980, 1985); Abrera (1976); Mangahas (1977); and Tan and Holazo (1979); as reported in Mangahas (1979).

the NCSO surveys has led some researchers to conduct their own household surveys in monitoring poverty conditions. The CRC, in collaboration with Consumer Pulse (a marketing research organisation), has been conducting its own "poverty audit" for Metro Manila since the early 1980s, through a periodic survey of income and expenditure patterns of 800 households. The Social Weather Station (SWS) Project of the Development Academy of the Philippines also conducted its own primary surveys of 500 Metro Manila households in 1981, including many questions on respondent attitudes and perceptions.

While there are problems with using FIES and ISH data on income distribution, this does not mean that such data are entirely useless for analysing poverty trends. It is generally agreed that the FIES figures up to 1971 are on the whole acceptable. The possible undercoverage of income in the 1975 FIES is felt to fall in the upper-income classes, so that while the reported income distribution may not give an accurate notion of relative inequalities, it may serve

*Table 8.3.  Poverty incidence by occupation of family head, 1971* [1]

| Occupation | Metro Manila | | Philippines |
| --- | --- | --- | --- |
| | All families ('000) | Poor (%) | Poor (%) |
| Professional, technical and related workers | 61 | 0.5 | 3.2 |
| Administrative, executive and managerial workers | 30 | 0.0 | 5.3 |
| Clerical and related workers | 61 | 2.5 | 8.4 |
| Sales workers | 91 | 5.8 | 20.0 |
| Transport and communications workers | 82 | 12.8 | 28.7 |
| Craftsmen, production workers and labourers not elsewhere classified | 187 | 13.8 | 31.7 |
| Services, sport and recreation workers | 67 | 14.5 | 27.7 |
| Farm, fishing, logging, mining and related workers | 15 | 7.3 | 53.0 |
| Occupation not reported or inadequately described | 76 | 9.3 | 28.7 |
| All occupations | 670 | 9.1 | 38.7 |

[1] The poverty line is defined here at P500 per capita per year.
Source. 1971 FIES, as reported in World Bank (1980).

reasonably well in studies of poverty incidence. The ISH series for 1980 to 1983 looks consistent and may indicate actual poverty trends in the period. Nevertheless, the data limitations cited should be kept in mind in the discussions that follow.

### 3. Trends in urban poverty in the 1960s and 1970s

Even before the economic crisis of the mid-1980s, statistics on the distribution of income and expenditure over the past 20 years already indicated a general increase in both urban and rural poverty, no matter how the poverty line is defined and on what distribution it is applied (whether on income or expenditure, and on per capita or per family measures). Table 8.2 shows trends in poverty gleaned from various studies using the 1965 to 1975 FIES,[7] and shows increasing poverty with all types of measure, especially for Metro Manila. For areas outside Metro Manila there was a relative decline from 1965 to 1971, but an increase again in 1975. It can also be seen that in 1965 the incidence of poverty in Metro Manila was much lower than in other areas (following the SIP or Tan and Holazo accounts); however, this difference was eroded by 1971, as poverty spread faster in Metro Manila. Earlier trends from the 1957 and 1961 FIES showed a decline in poverty up to 1965 (Abrera, 1976; World Bank, 1980).

Who were the urban poor in the 1970s? Tables 8.3 to 8.5 give rates of poverty incidence, as computed from the 1971 FIES by the 1980 World Bank study. The poverty line used is a national cut-off of P500 annual expenditure per capita; the Metro Manila (and urban) rates would be higher if urban-rural cost-of-living differences were accounted for. Nevertheless, for any given

*Table 8.4.  Poverty incidence by industry of family head, 1971* [1]

| Industry | Metro Manila | | Philippines |
|---|---|---|---|
| | All families ('000) | Poor (%) | Poor (%) |
| Manufacturing | 162 | 7.5 | 26.5 |
| Electricity, gas, water and sanitary services | 13 | 7.7 | 19.6 |
| Construction | 55 | 20.5 | 33.2 |
| General commerce | 97 | 5.8 | 19.8 |
| *Sari-sari* stores | 14 | 0.7 | 16.4 |
| Hawking and peddling | 5 | 52.0 [2] | 43.0 |
| Transport, storage and communication | 80 | 13.5 | 27.7 |
| Government and community services | 109 | 3.4 | 10.6 |
| Domestic services | 15 | 16.7 | 48.3 |
| Personal services other than domestic | 28 | 13.2 | 26.7 |
| Agriculture, fishing, forestry and mining | 16 | 3.8 | 53.0 |
| Industry not reported or inadequately described | 76 | 9.5 | 28.9 |
| All industries | 670 | 9.1 | 38.7 |

[1] The poverty line is defined here at P500 per capita per year.   [2] The sample size is deemed too small for statistically valid inference. Source. 1971 FIES, as reported in World Bank (1980).

geographical area, the tables indicate which particular groupings are more poverty-prone.

Table 8.3 shows that in Metro Manila in 1971 blue-collar workers and manual labourers had the highest poverty incidence in terms of absolute numbers (25,800 families) and the second highest in the proportion of families involved (13.8 per cent). The services category had the highest relative incidence at 14.5 per cent (9,700 families), but in absolute numbers this was exceeded by workers in transport and communication — mainly tricycle, jeepney, and bus drivers and conductors — among whose families 10,500, or 12.5 per cent, were below the poverty line. These three occupational categories accounted for 75 per cent of poor families, although they comprised only 50 per cent of all families in Metro Manila. By unemployment sector, poverty incidence in Metro Manila was highest among those in construction (20.5 per cent), where most manual labourers worked (table 8.4),[8] followed by those in domestic services with 16.7 per cent. Transport and services other than domestic also had high rates of poverty, at just over 13 per cent. Workers in manufacturing, while having a low poverty incidence at 7.6 per cent, had the largest absolute number of families (12,200) below the threshold. As in the occupational groupings, the proportion of poor families was lower in Metro Manila than the country as a whole in every sector. Education data in table 8.5 are available only for urban and rural areas in general, without separate tabulation for Metro Manila. However, there is no reason to expect Metro Manila's pattern to differ from the overall urban pattern, which is very clear: the incidence of urban poverty declined with the educational

Table 8.5.   *Poverty incidence by education of family head, urban and rural, 1971* [1]

| Highest grade completed | Urban | | Rural | |
|---|---|---|---|---|
| | All families ('000) | Poor (%) | All families ('000) | Poor (%) |
| Elementary, 1 to 3 | 155 | 35.7 | 928 | 55.5 |
| 4 to 5 | 218 | 31.8 | 1 098 | 55.2 |
| 6 to 7 | 342 | 25.9 | 889 | 48.3 |
| High School, 1 to 3 | 254 | 19.3 | 367 | 38.1 |
| 4 | 320 | 9.3 | 238 | 27.0 |
| College, 1 to 3 | 201 | 5.9 | 96 | 20.0 |
| 4 | 259 | 1.9 | 109 | 4.3 |
| 5 or higher | 79 | 0.9 | 27 | 4.0 |
| No grade completed or reported | 86 | 33.0 | 681 | 49.8 |
| All levels | 1 914 | 17.6 | 4 433 | 47.8 |

[1]  The poverty line is defined here at P500 per capita per year.
Source. 1971 FIES, as reported in World Bank (1980).

Table 8.6.   *Selected social indicators in the 1970s*

| | Metro Manila | Urban | Rural | Philippines |
|---|---|---|---|---|
| *1973* | | | | |
| Infant mortality rate (per thousand) | 51.2 | 57.5 | 70.8 | 67.6 |
| Life expectancy at birth (in years) | 64.3 | 62.8 | 59.9 | 60.6 |
| *1978* | | | | |
| Percentage of children below cut-off in: | | | | |
| Weight-for-age | | 34.2 | 41.1 | 39.1 |
| Height-for-age | | 31.8 | 36.0 | 34.7 |
| Weight-for-height | | 4.6 | 4.8 | 4.7 |
| *1978-79* | | | | |
| School enrolment ratio (%): | | | | |
| Elementary | 94.8 | – | – | 89.7 |
| Secondary | 73.2 | – | – | 40.2 |

Sources. Mangahas (1976); NEDA (1982); World Bank (1980).

attainment of the household head. Finishing college had a particularly marked effect, as fewer than 2 per cent of those in urban areas with four or more years of college could be considered poor. Basic-needs indicators in general showed that in the 1970s Metro Manila residents fared better than those living in other urban and rural areas (see table 8.6).

Unfortunately, despite efforts by researchers to press for the regular monitoring of social indicators, it remains very difficult to find out what has happened over time and across areas of the country. There was some initial

*Table 8.7.   Poverty lines and poverty incidence, 1980-83 (third quarter)*

| Year | Poverty line (Pesos per family per year) | | Poverty incidence (percentage of families) | | Survey to national average income ratio |
|------|---------|---------|---------|---------|------|
|      | Rural   | Urban   | Rural   | Urban   |      |
| 1980 | 5 537   | 7 758   | 46.7    | 28.5    | 0.55 |
| 1981 | 6 384   | 8 965   | 47.8    | 28.4    | 0.58 |
| 1982 | 6 892   | 9 790   | 42.2    | 24.6    | 0.67 |
| 1983 | 7 363   | 10 584  | 45.4    | 26.0    | 0.60 |

Source. World Bank (1985) computations from ISH 1980-83.

government enthusiasm after the SIP published its report (Mangahas, 1976), as inter-agency committees were organised to formulate additional indicators. This culminated in the 1982 NEDA social development report; however, the report did not contain much by way of new data that would allow the monitoring of welfare trends in the 1970s.

### 4. The years immediately before the crisis

After the 1975 FIES the NCSO did not conduct a nation-wide family income and expenditure survey until 1985. Instead, it expanded its labour force survey series into the ISH, conducted in selected quarters each year since 1976. However, as of 1985, the income data for 1976-79 had not yet been cleaned. A 1984 World Bank mission, though, did get tabulations on aggregate income distributions for 1980 to 1983, and built a data file on 3,300 families for 1979 and 1983 (World Bank, 1985). The ISH results presented in the 1985 World Bank study thus constitute the only major body of information on macro poverty trends since 1975.[9]

Measures of poverty incidence for 1980 to 1983, based on the distribution of family income, show a decline in 1982 and an increase in 1983, with the absolute number of poor families rising steadily in urban and rural areas (table 8.7). The movements in poverty incidence, however, seem to correspond to the degree of undercoverage (compared with the National Income Accounts), suggesting a lack of reliability of the observed trend. The more interesting aspect of the 1985 World Bank tabulations from the ISH is the breakdown of urban poverty by source of income, drawn against the distribution of families by income class (see table 8.8). Apart from the high incidence of poverty among those engaged in farming and fishing, who of course constituted only a small proportion of urban families, the table shows a rather flat poverty incidence across different income source categories. The bulk of the urban poor fell in the category of "non-agricultural labour", including all families whose main source of income is wages and salaries from outside agriculture. This was followed by those receiving dividends, rents and pensions

*Table 8.8.*   *Urban poverty incidence by main source of income, 1982-83 (third quarter)*

| Main source of income | 1982 | | 1983 | |
|---|---|---|---|---|
| | All families ('000) | Poor (%) | All families ('000) | Poor (%) |
| Farming | 192 | 43.1 | 178 | 45.7 |
| Fishing/livestock | 63 | 43.8 | 65 | 48.9 |
| Manufacturing | 90 | 15.5 | 83 | 23.8 |
| Wholesale/retail trade | 300 | 20.7 | 344 | 20.1 |
| Other services | 156 | 21.3 | 138 | 17.4 |
| Dividends/rent/pensions | 584 | 18.6 | 616 | 18.5 |
| Non-agricultural labour | 1 610 | 15.4 | 1 650 | 16.3 |
| All urban | 2 995 | 19.2 | 3 074 | 19.7 |

Source. World Bank (1985) computations from ISH 1982-83.

*Table 8.9.*   *Perceived change in level of living, 1978-81 and 1979-81, by self-rated socio-economic status, Metro Manila (percentages of respondents)*

| Self-rated status | Period | Better | Same | Worse |
|---|---|---|---|---|
| Not poor | 1978-81 | 51.7 | 21.8 | 26.4 |
| | 1979-81 | 44.7 | 30.7 | 21.8 |
| Border line | 1978-81 | 41.2 | 29.4 | 29.4 |
| | 1979-81 | 43.5 | 33.5 | 17.0 |
| Poor | 1978-81 | 34.0 | 30.5 | 36.6 |
| | 1979-81 | 29.1 | 29.7 | 30.2 |
| Total | 1978-81 | 42.1 | 27.1 | 30.8 |
| | 1979-81 | 38.5 | 30.8 | 23.9 |

Source. Mangahas, Miranda and Paqueo (1982).

and those in wholesale and retail trade (including *sari-sari* or small variety store owners and hawkers and vendors). It should be noted that the classification in this table is not directly comparable to occupation or industry groupings. The 1985 World Bank study also analysed income data for the 3,300 families in the 1979 and 1983 third-quarter ISH. Among the urban poor in 1979, 57 per cent were still poor in 1983, while among the non-poor, 20 per cent became poor, following the World Bank (1985) thresholds.

The monitoring of trends in social indicators did not appear to have generated as much interest in the early 1980s as in the mid-1970s. The second oil price shock, low export price, and the concomitant balance-of-payments problems were the major concerns of policy-makers. The 1982 NEDA Social Development Report was actually part of a project begun in 1978 and, as stated

*Table 8.10. Poverty incidence in Metro Manila, 1983-84*

|  | 1983, second quarter | 1984, first quarter | 1984, fourth quarter |
|---|---|---|---|
| Percentage of households earning below: |  |  |  |
| Basic food needs | 18.7 | 25.0 | 44.9 |
| Basic poverty threshold | 39.1 | 49.6 | 61.7 |
| Decent income threshold | 50.1 | 62.8 | 70.9 |

Source. Reyes (1985).

earlier, contained hardly any new information. One of the few regular monitoring efforts was that of the nutritional status of children by FNRI; but the reports showing an increasing incidence of malnutrition were suppressed by the Government itself.

Meanwhile, periodic surveys of perceptions of poverty in Metro Manila were conducted in 1981 by the Development Academy of the Philippines. The findings roughly conform with the ISH-World Bank panel data. The Social Weather Station Surveys asked the respondents to rate themselves as "poor, border line, or not poor", and about one-third fell under each category (Mangahas, 1982). Table 8.9 summarises the distribution of responses regarding the question on perceived changes in levels of living.

## 5. Current urban poverty profiles

A post-1983 macro profile of Metro Manila's poor is presented in the CRC's periodic "poverty audit report" (Reyes, 1985).[10] As discussed earlier, the CRC identifies three thresholds, shown for Metro Manila in table 8.10. In terms of satisfying basic food needs, the CRC surveys show a marked increase in poverty from the second quarter of 1983 to the fourth quarter of 1984. The CRC food basket, however, is rather expensive — P250 per person per month in October 1983 (Buencamino and Guerrero, 1984).[11] Nevertheless, the figures are a clear indication of the worsening trend in this critical period. Direct evidence of the effects of the crisis on nutrition comes from the results of an FNRI survey in Metro Manila in February-March 1984. From a sample of 400 households, FNRI found that "the quantity and quality of diets in Metro Manila households tended to become inferior, as manifested in the shift of the energy and protein intake from upper to lower levels of adequacy when compared with a similar data base for 1982" (FNRI, 1984, quoted in Herrin, 1986).

The most recent body of data on poverty in the Philippines comes from the 1985 FIES (see table 8.11).[12] With the poverty line at P2,500 per capita per year, only 8.3 per cent of families in Metro Manila would be considered poor; if the line were raised to P5,000 per capita per year, the proportion below this threshold would rise to 22.4 per cent.[13] For either threshold, the incidence of

*Table 8.11.   Poverty incidence by family size and threshold basis, Metro Manila, 1985*

| Family size | All families ('000) | Basis for poverty threshold | | | |
|---|---|---|---|---|---|
| | | Per capita income | | Family income | |
| | | P2,500 per year | P5,000 per year | P15,000 per year | P30,000 per year |
| | | Poor (%) | Poor (%) | Poor (%) | Poor (%) |
| 1 | 18.4 | 0.0 | 3.3 | 22.6 | 58.3 |
| 2 | 55.6 | 0.0 | 3.3 | 11.2 | 45.4 |
| 3 | 123.9 | 0.5 | 8.2 | 8.2 | 42.5 |
| 4 | 214.0 | 2.5 | 18.3 | 7.4 | 40.1 |
| 5 | 263.5 | 7.5 | 19.7 | 7.5 | 41.4 |
| 6 | 213.7 | 9.7 | 28.5 | 2.4 | 28.5 |
| 7 | 147.4 | 7.9 | 25.2 | 2.5 | 25.2 |
| 8 | 114.0 | 24.5 | 43.9 | 3.5 | 24.5 |
| 9 | 64.5 | 18.9 | 30.5 | 1.0 | 18.9 |
| 10+ | 95.5 | 11.1 | 23.2 | 1.2 | 11.1 |
| Total | 1 310.5 | 8.3 | 22.4 | 5.4 | 33.0 |

Source. 1985 FIES, Vol. II.

poverty was highest for families with eight members. In absolute numbers, however, the bulk of the poor in 1985 was comprised of six-member households, based on the higher threshold.[14] When the poverty line is defined in terms of family income, setting the income cut-off at P15,000 per family per year (or P2,500 per head per year for a family of six) would show a poverty incidence of only 5.4 per cent for Metro Manila. If the threshold is doubled to P30,000, poverty incidence would increase more than sixfold, to 33 per cent. In both cases, single-member families had the highest incidence of poverty while five-member families constituted the modal group among the poor.

The 1985 FIES shows that families relying primarily on wages and salaries fared worse than those whose main source was either entrepreneurial activities or non-work income, no matter where the poverty line is defined (table 8.12). This suggests that one should avoid the convenient practice of considering all wage and salary workers as belonging to the "formal sector", and that further breakdowns of this category are necessary for a clearer understanding of the nature and characteristics of poverty groups. It should also be noted from the table that families depending mainly on remittances and gifts from abroad constituted almost 12 per cent of all families in Metro Manila and had a relatively low incidence of poverty, attesting to the significant amount of material relief provided by job opportunities abroad. Even for the rest of the country, 9 per cent of families depended on cash and gifts from abroad for their main source of income.

*Table 8.12.  Poverty incidence by main source of income, Metro Manila, 1985*

| Main source of income | All families ('000) | Threshold level | | |
|---|---|---|---|---|
| | | P15,000 per year | P30,000 per year | P40,000 per year |
| | | Poor (%) | Poor (%) | Poor (%) |
| *Wages and salaries* | 766.2 | 5.8 | 36.8 | 56.4 |
| Agricultural | 6.6 | 18.6 | 65.0 | 74.4 |
| Non-agricultural | 759.6 | 5.7 | 36.5 | 56.2 |
| *Entrepreneurial activities* | 218.7 | 4.7 | 33.2 | 49.1 |
| Agricultural | 1.2 | 0.0 | 52.9 | 52.9 |
| Non-agricultural | 217.5 | 3.6 | 32.0 | 49.1 |
|   Wholesale/retail | 141.9 | 6.2 | 35.7 | 51.1 |
|   Manufacturing | 19.3 | 3.1 | 28.9 | 54.4 |
|   Community/personal services | 27.8 | 3.8 | 43.2 | 63.4 |
|   Transport/communication services | 21.5 | 0.0 | 15.6 | 23.4 |
|   Mining and quarrying | 0.6 | 0.0 | 0.0 | 0.0 |
|   Construction | 2.2 | 0.0 | 23.6 | 23.6 |
|   Entrepreneurial activities not elsewhere classified | 4.2 | 0.0 | 0.0 | 0.0 |
| *Other sources* | 325.6 | 4.8 | 23.9 | 37.2 |
| Net share of crops, etc. | 3.3 | 0.0 | 15.7 | 15.7 |
| Cash, gifts from abroad | 153.0 | 0.7 | 12.0 | 22.2 |
| Cash, domestic gifts | 46.1 | 14.6 | 58.4 | 75.6 |
| Rental, non-agricultural | 25.1 | 2.1 | 24.8 | 49.0 |
| Interest income | 0.6 | 100.0 | 100.0 | 100.0 |
| Pensions, social security | 12.2 | 8.0 | 21.8 | 21.8 |
| Imputed housing rental | 74.4 | 5.5 | 25.9 | 39.9 |
| Family sustenance activities | 0.6 | 0.0 | 100.0 | 100.0 |
| Dividends from investments | 0.2 | 0.0 | 0.0 | 0.0 |
| Goods/services received as gifts | 9.0 | 19.4 | 32.9 | 55.4 |
| Other sources not elsewhere classified | 1.1 | 0.0 | 0.0 | 91.6 |
| Total | 1 310.5 | 5.4 | 33.0 | 50.4 |

Source. 1985 FIES, Vol. II.

## 6. Summary

The foregoing suggests that poverty incidence has generally been lower in Metro Manila than other parts of the country, even if allowance is made for the higher cost of urban living. However, in sheer numbers, Metro Manila constitutes the country's largest geographical concentration of poor families, many of them in slums and squatter areas. The main variable correlating with poverty, among those for which data were available, is the educational level of the family head. Poverty is ubiquitous among families whose heads have had little or no schooling. The links between education and earnings are of course not simple, but as learning is a basic need it is unfortunate that government spending on education declined in real terms from the late 1960s onward. Only in 1986 was the trend reversed, as the new Government asserted a strong commitment to the provision of basic education for all.

## III. Concurrent trends in labour market outcomes

### 1. Statistics on employment and earnings

The main source of data on the labour force over the past ten years is the ISH of the NCSO, which began as the Philippine Statistical Survey of Households (PSSH) in 1956.[15] The ISH, first conducted in the third quarter of 1976, changed the reference period for employment data from the PSSH's "past week" to the "past quarter" (see section I). The change was meant to capture workers in irregular, short-term or seasonal jobs who would otherwise be classified as out of the labour force. While the intention of the change may have been well-meaning, the result was a break in the consistency of the labour force series. Table 8.13 shows that the "past quarter" definition comes up with consistently higher participation rates and lower open unemployment rates than the "past week" definition, and the difference in measured unemployment rates can be substantial. In 1987 there was an official shift back to the "past week" reference period.

Another significant break of the ISH from the old series concerns the age span covered by the labour force definition. The old series included 10 to 14 year-olds, who were excluded by the ISH "to conform with the Labor Code of the Philippines". Based on the 1960 and 1970 Population Censuses, they constituted about 6 per cent of the labour force, with a participation rate of 15 per cent. Published tabulations from the old series usually present statistics for the 10 to 24 year-olds aggregatively, so that it is difficult to make the necessary adjustments for consistency. The other main data sources on employment and earnings — establishment surveys — have limited sectoral coverage and tend to omit small firms. These limitations make it problematic to analyse long-term employment trends.

The NEDA has also recently been monitoring wage trends in manufacturing through its monthly Survey of Key Establishments. The Central Bank used to run a series on nominal and real wages for Metro Manila, but it was discontinued in 1981 when the function was transferred to the NEDA. What replaced the Central Bank series initially was a NEDA report of legislated minimum wages (see section I). The National Wages Council is the agency assigned to monitor non-agricultural wages; it started a quarterly occupational wage survey in June 1984, but the results have only recently come out, and only for areas outside Metro Manila. Another agency, the Office of Compensation and Position Classification (OCPC), collects information on wages and salaries for different occupations every two or three years from private enterprises, but

*Table 8.13.    Comparative statistics on employment status, using "past week"[1] and "past quarter" definitions, Philippines, third quarter, 1976-86 (percentages)*

| Year | Labour force participation rate | | Unemployment rate | |
|------|-------------|--------------|-------------|--------------|
|      | Past week | Past quarter | Past week | Past quarter |
| 1976 | 59.5 | 60.5 | 6.3  | 5.2 |
| 1977 | 56.6 | 58.2 | 9.1  | 4.5 |
| 1978 | 61.1 | 62.5 | 7.1  | 4.1 |
| 1981 | 61.3 | 61.7 | 9.8  | 5.3 |
| 1982 | 63.5 | 63.6 | 9.5  | 6.0 |
| 1983 | 63.6 | 63.8 | 7.9  | 4.9 |
| 1984 | 63.5 | 63.3 | 10.6 | 7.0 |
| 1985 | 63.4 | 63.9 | 11.1 | 6.1 |
| 1986 | 63.8 | 64.2 | 11.1 | 6.4 |

[1] Past week falls in July or August for the third-quarter ISH.

Source. NCSO, Integrated Survey of Households, third quarters, 1976-78, 1981-86.

its sample is dominated by large firms. Up to now, the Government is the only institution in a position to conduct regular data collection activities on employment and earnings. However, private researchers have often undertaken surveys, dealing especially with those activities which are not transparent from official statistics. Specific occupational and area studies of low-income groups are often the domain of sociologists and anthropologists, although economists occasionally conduct their own primary surveys, as in the research on the informal sector in Metro Manila undertaken in 1976 (Jurado and Castro, 1979) and in the series of studies on the poor in Metro Manila sponsored by the Institute of Philippine Culture (e.g. Keyes, 1974).

## 2. Trends in urban labour market outcomes

Metro Manila has consistently shown lower labour force participation rates than other areas, as one would expect of a highly urbanised area.[16] The trends for Metro Manila and the Philippines, however, appear to have moved in opposite directions (table 8.14). Between 1967 and 1974 the participation rate in Metro Manila increased by 9 per cent, while the national rate declined by 8 per cent; between 1976 and 1980 the trends were reversed, as Metro Manila's labour force participation rate fell by 8 per cent while the national rate rose by 6 per cent.[17] Beginning in 1981 the participation rates for both areas increased, as more people were probably pushed into the labour force because of declining real wages. Table 8.14 also shows that open unemployment rates have been about twice as high in Metro Manila as in the Philippines, because of the high share of wage and salary work in total employment. From 1967 to 1980 the unemployment rate for Metro Manila fluctuated without any sign of a long-term trend; but thereafter signs of the impending crisis began to appear,

*Table 8.14.  Labour force participation and unemployment rates, Metro Manila and the Philippines, 1967-86 (percentages)*

| Year [1] | Metro Manila | | Philippines | |
|---|---|---|---|---|
| | Participation rate | Unemployment rate | Participation rate | Unemployment rate |
| 1967 | 43.8 | 10.8 | 54.7 | 7.7 |
| 1971 | 47.5 | 10.8 | 50.0 | 5.2 |
| 1972 | 48.8 | 12.5 | 50.8 | 6.3 |
| 1974 | 47.8 | 9.8 | 50.2 | 4.0 |
| 1976 | 58.5 | 12.1 | 60.5 | 5.2 |
| 1980 | 53.3 | 10.4 | 59.8 | 5.0 |
| 1981 | 54.6 | 11.6 | 61.7 | 5.3 |
| 1982 | 55.7 | 13.2 | 60.1 | 6.0 |
| 1983 | 55.0 | 12.2 | 64.1 | 5.4 |
| 1984 | 60.0 | 17.9 | 64.8 | 7.3 |
| 1985 | 59.5 | 22.1 | 63.4 | 7.1 |
| 1986 | 53.6 | 19.3 | 63.8 | 6.7 |

[1] Figures for 1967 to 1974 are averages for the year; the reference period is the "past week" and the labour force definition begins with 10 year-olds. Figures for 1976 onwards are for the third quarter; the reference period is the "past quarter" and the labour force starts with 15 year-olds.

Sources. For 1980-86, ISH, as reported in the Ministry of Labour and Employment *1984 and 1987 Yearbooks of Labour Statistics*; for 1967-76, PSSH and ISH, as reported in Domingo and Feranil (1984).

as the open unemployment rate crept up in the early 1980s. It jumped to 17.9 per cent by 1984, and 22.1 per cent by 1985. As the participation rate increased, the ranks of the unemployed in Metro Manila swelled by 68.4 per cent from 1983 to 1984. The severe contraction in job opportunities affected the sexes almost evenly, as 22.6 per cent of males and 21.4 per cent of females were openly unemployed.[18]

Patterns of unemployment by educational attainment show the incidence of joblessness increasing with years of schooling completed, except for those who finished college (table 8.15). The more educated members of the labour force must have borne the brunt of the crisis. However, many of the educated unemployed were likely to be new entrants to the labour force and not main breadwinners. For Metro Manila in 1985, 57.3 per cent of the unemployed were inexperienced, and only 10.3 per cent were heads of households (compared with an average of 1.9 workers per household). Nevertheless, a high incidence of unemployment among household members would mean lower household income.

Changes in the sectoral distribution of the employed labour force in Metro Manila from 1980 to 1985 are indicative of the deterioration in the economy in the 1980s (table 8.16). The share of manufacturing declined from 26.6 per cent in 1980 to only 19.8 per cent in 1985. The share of the more "formal" sector of finance and business services also declined to only 5.9 per cent of total employment, from 7.9 per cent in 1980 and even 18.4 per cent in

*Table 8.15.    Unemployment rates and distribution of the unemployed by educational attainment, Metro Manila, third quarter, 1980-85 (percentages)*

| Schooling completed | 1980 | | 1983 | | 1985 | |
|---|---|---|---|---|---|---|
| | Unemployment rate | Percentage distribution | Unemployment rate | Percentage distribution | Unemployment rate | Percentage distribution |
| No schooling/ not reported | 4.2 | 0.3 | 0.0 | 0.0 | 7.4 | 0.2 |
| Elementary 1-5 | 13.5 | 8.8 | 5.4 | 2.7 | 15.5 | 4.4 |
| Elementary graduate | 8.3 | 12.2 | 10.4 | 12.9 | 14.1 | 9.0 |
| High school 1-3 | 13.8 | 16.5 | 17.6 | 17.9 | 26.3 | 14.2 |
| High school graduate | 10.6 | 27.5 | 15.4 | 30.6 | 26.3 | 36.1 |
| College 1-3 | 14.2 | 22.5 | 14.9 | 21.7 | 28.0 | 23.2 |
| College graduate | 6.1 | 12.2 | 7.3 | 14.2 | 15.5 | 12.9 |
| All levels | 10.4 | 100.0 | 12.2 | 100.0 | 22.1 | 100.0 |

Source. ISH, 1980, 1983 and 1985.

*Table 8.16.    Distribution of employment in Metro Manila, by industry, occupation and class of worker, third quarter, 1980-85 (percentages)*

| | 1980 | 1981 | 1982 | 1983 | 1984 | 1985 |
|---|---|---|---|---|---|---|
| *Industry* | | | | | | |
| Agriculture | 1.5 | 1.6 | 1.3 | 1.4 | 1.2 | 1.3 |
| Mining | 0.1 | 0.2 | 0.3 | 0.1 | 0.1 | 0.1 |
| Manufacturing | 26.7 | 25.9 | 24.4 | 22.7 | 19.7 | 19.8 |
| Electricity, gas, water | 0.8 | 1.1 | 0.8 | 1.0 | 0.8 | 0.6 |
| Construction | 6.8 | 5.1 | 6.4 | 6.6 | 6.2 | 6.0 |
| Wholesale, retail trade | 14.6 | 15.2 | 15.5 | 16.9 | 20.6 | 22.7 |
| Transportation | 10.0 | 7.7 | 8.4 | 8.2 | 8.1 | 9.6 |
| Finance, business services | 7.9 | 7.1 | 8.9 | 7.8 | 8.5 | 5.9 |
| Community, personal services | 31.6 | 36.1 | 34.0 | 35.3 | 34.8 | 34.0 |
| *Occupation* | | | | | | |
| Professional, technical | 11.8 | 12.5 | 13.0 | 12.3 | 11.3 | 9.5 |
| Administrative, managerial | 2.9 | 3.1 | 3.1 | 3.2 | 3.5 | 3.5 |
| Clerical workers | 14.4 | 13.9 | 14.0 | 13.5 | 11.7 | 11.8 |
| Sales workers | 15.0 | 15.6 | 16.1 | 16.9 | 20.0 | 21.1 |
| Service workers | 17.9 | 18.1 | 17.9 | 18.7 | 20.2 | 19.4 |
| Agricultural workers | 1.3 | 1.6 | 1.1 | 1.4 | 1.1 | 1.2 |
| Production, transport, etc. | 36.7 | 35.2 | 34.8 | 34.0 | 32.2 | 33.5 |
| *Class of worker* | | | | | | |
| Wage and salary | 86.7 | 83.3 | 83.0 | 80.8 | 77.5 | 75.1 |
| Own-account | 10.6 | 13.8 | 13.7 | 15.5 | 18.4 | 21.5 |
| Unpaid family workers | 2.7 | 2.9 | 3.3 | 3.7 | 4.1 | 3.4 |

Source. ISH, 1980 to 1985.

*Table 8.17.*    *Real average quarterly earnings in cash and in kind of wage and salary workers and own-account workers in urban areas by industry, third quarter, 1980-85 (in pesos at constant 1978 prices [1])*

| Industry | 1980 | 1981 | 1982 | 1983 | 1984 | 1985 |
|---|---|---|---|---|---|---|
| *Wage and salary workers* | | | | | | |
| Agriculture | 893 | 838 | 960 | 899 | 603 | 603 |
| Mining | 2 342 | 2 035 | 2 572 | 3 143 | 966 | 1 227 |
| Manufacturing | 1 748 | 1 596 | 1 753 | 1 783 | 1 027 | 1 263 |
| Electricity, gas, water | 2 720 | 2 709 | 2 527 | 2 653 | 1 827 | 1 718 |
| Construction | 1 629 | 1 418 | 2 225 | 1 593 | 935 | 962 |
| Wholesale, retail trade | 1 146 | 1 329 | 1 508 | 1 425 | 906 | 804 |
| Transport, communication | 2 024 | 1 608 | 2 069 | 1 685 | 1 149 | 1 067 |
| Finance, business services | 3 147 | 2 868 | 2 856 | 2 548 | 1 725 | 1 469 |
| Community, personal services | 1 550 | 1 430 | 1 698 | 1 442 | 1 018 | 946 |
| All wage and salary workers | 1 725 | 1 553 | 1 841 | 1 614 | 1 040 | 1 015 |
| *Own-account workers* [2] | | | | | | |
| Agriculture | 1 344 | 1 053 | 1 391 | 1 136 | 887 | 727 |
| Mining | 17 009 | 11 133 | 10 508 | 3 109 | n.a. | 1 131 |
| Manufacturing | 3 263 | 4 977 | 4 932 | 3 226 | 1 498 | 1 231 |
| Electricity, gas, water | n.a. | 5 619 | 6 079 | 5 637 | n.a. | n.a. |
| Construction | 4 524 | 3 195 | 5 298 | 7 875 | 2 130 | 2 027 |
| Wholesale, retail trade | 2 228 | 2 405 | 2 732 | 2 789 | 1 686 | 1 301 |
| Transport, communication | 2 774 | 2 680 | 2 832 | 2 659 | 1 997 | 1 915 |
| Finance, business services | 8 374 | 14 802 | 6 096 | 6 349 | 5 621 | 3 886 |
| Community, personal services | 2 769 | 2 322 | 2 964 | 5 681 | 1 206 | 1 044 |
| All own-account workers | 2 305 | 2 541 | 2 759 | 2 747 | 1 449 | 1 186 |

n.a. = not available.

[1] Quarterly earnings in current prices are deflated by the third quarter Consumer Price Index (base year 1978).    [2] Own-account workers include both employers and the self-employed.

Sources. Quarterly earnings in current prices from computer print-outs of the ISH; price deflators from the NEDA, *Philippine Statistical Yearbook.*

1976. Labour was absorbed by the relatively more "informal" sectors such as the wholesale and retail trade (where the neighbourhood *sari-sari* stores belong), and community and personal services (including domestic service).

Significant reductions in the share of what are generally considered as high-paying jobs can be seen in the 1980s, as employment moved towards sales and service occupations. Production workers, in particular, who comprised the largest group, suffered a net loss in their share in total employment. Similarly, as more and more firms retrenched or shut down with the worsening economic conditions, a bigger proportion of the labour force was pushed into self-employment.[19] Wage employment in Metro Manila did not grow at all, even though total employment increased at an average of 2.8 per cent per year.

Earnings patterns across industries are presented in table 8.17, for urban areas in general, as no breakdowns are yet available by region. The trends in earnings, however, are probably also indicative of the situation in Metro

Table 8.18.    Real annual wages and salaries of paid employees in small and large establishments, by industry, Metro Manila, 1972-83 (in pesos at constant 1978 prices)

| Industry | Size of establishment [1] | | Small/ large (%) |
| --- | --- | --- | --- |
| | Small | Large | |
| *1972* | | | |
| Manufacturing | 7 690 | 9 998 | 76.9 |
| Construction | 9 020 | 9 154 | 98.5 |
| Trade | 5 380 | 9 584 | 56.1 |
| Transport | 5 161 | 8 982 | 57.5 |
| Services | 4 845 | 9 587 | 50.5 |
| *1975* | | | |
| Manufacturing | 3 079 | 7 103 | 43.3 |
| Construction | 3 227 | 5 753 | 56.1 |
| Trade | 3 875 | 7 216 | 53.7 |
| Transport | 5 073 | 14 252 | 35.6 |
| Services | 3 219 | 5 581 | 57.7 |
| *1978* | | | |
| Manufacturing | 3 694 | 8 234 | 44.9 |
| Construction | 6 516 | 11 451 | 56.9 |
| Trade | 2 288 | 9 492 | 24.1 |
| Transport | 10 065 | 11 380 | 88.4 |
| Services | 3 395 | 8 744 | 38.8 |
| *1983* [2] | | | |
| Manufacturing | 2 749 | 8 834 | 31.1 |
| Construction | 5 065 | 10 153 | 49.9 |

[1] Small establishments are those with fewer than ten workers.   [2] Published results for Metro Manila are available only for manufacturing and construction.
Sources. Annual wages and salaries in current prices from NCSO, Census of Establishments; price deflators from NEDA, *Philippine Statistical Yearbook*.

Manila. They show that real earnings, after rising from 1980 to 1982, declined sharply for all classes of workers in all sectors thereafter, mainly because increases in nominal earnings did not keep up with inflation. The price index for Metro Manila more than doubled over this period. Own-account workers were hit even harder than wage and salary workers, with a 57 per cent fall in income from 1982 to 1985 against 45 per cent for wage workers, perhaps indicating growth of underemployment among the self-employed. The wage and salary workers hit hardest by inflation were those in construction, where real earnings declined by well over 50 per cent. Public utilities and manufacturing were less affected. Among own-account workers, excluding mining (where the numbers are small), the steepest decline was in manufacturing. On the whole, the earnings gap between the two types of worker narrowed. The sectors with big shifts in employment were not necessarily those where earnings changed the most, nor is there a close relationship between the initial level of earnings in 1982 and the change up to 1985 — both high- and low-income sectors have suffered considerable earnings declines. More disaggregated data are needed to pursue this question.

Lumping all wage and salary workers together also often hides the diverse characteristics of paid employment. As table 8.18 shows, workers receiving wages and salaries in small establishments employing fewer than ten people earn much less than their counterparts in big establishments. In the 1970s the gap widened across all sectors except transport. The trend continued into the 1980s for manufacturing and construction. From 1982 to 1985, without any adjustments for cost-of-living differentials, the gap in the ratio of rural to urban real earnings for wage and salary workers narrowed from 0.54 in the third quarter of 1982 to 0.70 by the third quarter of 1985 (Tidalgo-Miranda and Herrin, 1986).

### 3. The informal sector in Metro Manila

The standard industrial and occupational classifications of the labour force often fail to highlight the significant volume of activities in what is often called the "informal" sector, where it is generally considered that most of the poor eke out their living, either as petty entrepreneurs or as paid workers. Definitions of the informal sector abound, sometimes dictated by the availability of data. The common notion, however, is that this sector is one where free entry exists, enterprises are small and use indigenous resources, workers have limited formal training, and markets are highly competitive and unregulated (Sethuraman, 1981). Because of its low profile and inherent difficulties in extracting information from its participants, very little is usually known about the economic characteristics of the sector from official statistical sources, and researchers often conduct their own primary surveys.

For Metro Manila a study was undertaken in 1976 of the structure of informal sector enterprises, operationally defined as those employing ten people or fewer covering manufacturing, transport, retail trade, construction and service sectors (Jurado and Castro, 1979). The focus was on productivity, employment and equity; each subsectoral study began with an analytical description of the participants (the enterprises, heads of enterprises and workers) as gleaned from the survey, and then examined the determinants of value added per enterprise, earnings of enterprise head and output per worker. The findings brought out various characteristics. In informal manufacturing, for example, formal schooling did not seem to be a major factor in explaining productivity and earnings (Canlas, 1979). In service activities most enterprises displayed hardly any growth in output, were slow in adopting new techniques, financed investment and working capital needs with home-generated savings, and had hardly any links with the formal sector (Tidalgo and Jurado, 1978). In transport the owners of the enterprise (the jeepney and tricycle operators) were not themselves poor, as setting up such a firm required substantial capital. However, the drivers, especially the so-called "extras" who did not have any regular driving days, did verge on poverty. What characterised these operators as belonging to the informal sector was the illegality of their franchises. There appeared to be diseconomies of scale in operations (one or two jeepneys would not need a garage, and supervision of drivers would be relatively easy), but economies of scale in dealing with the government agencies which granted the franchises. It was thus typical for somebody having many franchises to operate only a few units and illegally lease out the rest (Alonzo, 1980).

The poverty research series of the Institute of Philippine Culture, meanwhile, focused on case studies of particular poverty groups (defined *a priori*) and examined economic and psycho-social aspects of the groups being studied. A study on scavengers living in a Manila locality traced the chain of transactions that identified linkages to the formal sector (Keyes, 1974). Scavengers would unload their daily haul, mainly of used paper, at the *bodega* (warehouse) which often provided the carts. The *bodega* owner would then sort out the materials and sell to a dealer who would then sell to the paper mill or a bigger dealer. The *bodega* owner, although not rich, might sometimes give loans to the scavengers. It was estimated that scavenging supplied a fourth of the raw materials requirements of the Manila paper mills at that time.

A recent survey of the "underground economy" (mainly referring to activities without proper business permits) in Manila adds some insights on the socio-economic and labour force characteristics of this segment of the urban poor (Gatchalian et al., 1986). Vendors and other "underground" workers plying the busy sections of the four major cities in Metro Manila were interviewed in 1986, and several findings are noteworthy. Over 80 per cent of enterprises were engaged in vending food and other items. Only 20 per cent of workers earned fixed wages; 57 per cent were unpaid family workers, with the rest sharing in food and profits. Two-thirds of heads of enterprises had not finished high school, compared with only a third of the employed labour force in Metro Manila in 1985. Job mobility appeared restricted, as almost half the enterprise owners had been trading in the same places for at least four years, despite low incomes (49 per cent earned less than P50 per day). Fifty-six per cent were primary breadwinners.

Most other case studies lean on the descriptive side, discussing the socio-economic characteristics of the low-income groups. Many, however, describe the link with the formal sector, particularly the way certain laws and regulations affect the livelihood of these groups; one example is the study on hawkers and vendors in Metro Manila which surveyed government officials as well and proposed a more positive attitude towards peddling activities (Guerrero, 1975).

## *IV. Concluding remarks*

We began with a description of Philippine development over the past 15 years and the macro policies that influenced this, and pointed out that government policies appeared to have been biased against the poor, as reflected in their adverse effects on employment and labour earnings. The bias further operated against the rural poor, as import-substituting industrial activities located mostly in urban areas (dominated by Metro Manila) received favoured treatment. The urban poor were not particularly advantaged, however, since the policies also favoured big, capital-intensive firms, thus dampening urban employment expansion. The financial and economic crisis in late 1983, brought about by external shocks and internal economic and political factors, pushed more families further below the poverty line (however defined), bearing down more heavily on urban-based, import-dependent industries and their workforces. The rural-urban wage gap narrowed in the 1980s. The contractionary structural adjustment policies imposed by the multilateral lending agencies, while enabling the country to pay part of its foreign debt, were seen by many as having aggravated the economic crisis, with the heavier burden placed on the poor.

We then surveyed studies that have tried to define poverty thresholds, and looked at how these thresholds relate to trends in employment and earnings for Metro Manila and urban areas in general, adding a broader perspective to the macro poverty studies that, often constrained by the nature of their data bases, tended to focus on characteristics of the family head. Macro and micro studies of the labour market were surveyed, including socio-anthropological and economic research. The trade and services sectors appeared to be the major pockets of poverty, but a more detailed look, from informal sector studies, showed that other sectors such as manufacturing and transport did have vulnerable segments within them. But while these studies give insights on the nature and characteristics of urban poverty, they rarely offer much guidance in the design of effective labour market interventions, for indeed the causes of poverty extend beyond labour market outcomes.

### Notes

[1] School of Economics, University of the Philippines.

[2] Alburo and Roberto (1980) enumerated Philippine poverty research at little more than 70 books and articles from the 1960s. Abad et al. (1978) includes 234 studies from 1970 to 1978. An update by Abad and Eviota (1985) contains over 650 entries from 1979 to 1983. The extent of poverty in Metro Manila has been particularly visible. Slums and squatter communities have kept on sprouting and expanding, in spite of the previous Government's efforts to relocate them and hide them from public view. From these communities come most of the beggars, scavengers, hawkers and vendors.

[3] Agriculture has not been insulated from the current crisis. World prices of major export crops such as sugar and coconut products have been very low in recent years. Many sugarcane planters stopped production in 1985, causing considerable unemployment, especially in Negros Occidental province.

[4] By the third quarter of 1986, industrial employment in Metro Manila had dropped to 24.7 per cent, while the proportion of wage and salary workers was down sharply (see table 8.16). These figures, however, remained much higher than those for the rest of the country.

[5] Tan and Holazo did not really have strict urban-rural breakdowns; "other urban areas" refers to Central and Southern Luzon, both highly urbanised regions.

[6] There is also of course the possibility that the national income estimates are themselves overstated.

[7] The FIES data show a high level of dissaving for lower-income groups, so that a poverty line applied across the expenditure distribution gives a lower poverty incidence than when applied to the income distribution. It has been noted that family expenditure increases, but per capita expenditure declines with family size (World Bank, 1985); cutting across the expenditure distribution will catch not the poor with large families but those with low per capita expenditures.

[8] Those in hawking and peddling were reported in the World Bank (1980) study as having 1,600 out of 5,000 families below the poverty threshold, but the sample was considered too small for valid statistical inference.

[9] The various limitations on the ISH data, noted earlier, should be kept in mind in the discussion of the World Bank (1985) findings that follow. One should perhaps also avoid comparing ISH results with those from the FIES; ISH income covers only one quarter, while FIES income covers a full year.

[10] August 1983 marks a significant milestone in Philippine history, when the assassination of a major opposition figure triggered economic and political turmoil that led to the eventual downfall of the old regime.

[11] The World Bank (1985) threshold for the same period was only P140 per person per month, although the National Wages Council in 1981 defined a "necessities line" of P287 per person per month (P57.42 per family per day) as a guide-line for its minimum wage recommendations.

[12] Published results from the 1985 FIES came out in late 1987. An earlier set of unpublished tables was prepared by the NCSO for the NEDA's Low Income Study Group Project, but these tables covered only the first semester. The ratio of total family income from the 1985 FIES to personal income from the National Accounts is 0.63, which is better than the ISH coverage for most of the 1980s (see table 8.7).

[13] Earlier studies also demonstrate that the relative incidence of poverty is highly sensitive to the value chosen for the poverty threshold. For Metro Manila, from the 1975 FIES, a 20 per cent increase in the poverty line will raise the proportion of families below the line by 39 per cent, while a 20 per cent decrease will reduce it by 21 per cent (World Bank, 1980).

[14] The low threshold of P2,500 per capita per year is the level below which 30 per cent of all Filipino families would fall in 1985. This cut-off was used by NEDA for a low-income study project in 1985. The higher threshold of P5,000 per capita per year is close to the World Bank (1985) poverty line, after allowing for inflation.

[15] This is the same ISH used for information on household incomes (see section II). The PSSH was called the BCS Survey from 1965 to 1973 and became the National Sample Survey of Households in 1974 and 1975.

[16] Most high schools and colleges are in urban areas. Therefore, there is a bigger proportion of 15- to 24-year-olds in the urban population (38 per cent for urban versus 34 per cent for rural in 1980), but the labour force participation rate is also much lower (39 per cent for urban, 49 per cent for rural in 1980).

[17] Before 1975 the labour force measure included 10- to 14-year-olds and the reference period was the "past week" instead of the "past quarter".

[18] In the third quarter of 1983 the unemployment rate was 10.4 per cent for males and 14.9 per cent for females (from unpublished NCSO computer print-outs of the ISH).

[19] Tidalgo-Miranda and Herrin (1986) say that 60,000 workers per year were sacked in Metro Manila due to retrenchments and shutdowns from 1982 to 1984.

### References

Abad, Ricardo G., Villanueva, Nora S. and Picazo, Oscar F., 1978: *Philippine poverty studies in the seventies: A preliminary annotated bibliography* (Quezon City, Institute of Philippine Culture).

———; Eviota, Elizabeth U., 1985: *Philippine poverty: An annotated bibliography, 1970-83* (Quezon City, Institute of Philippine Culture and PIDS).

Abrera, Ma. Aclestis, 1976: "Philippine poverty thresholds", in Mahar Mangahas (ed.), *Measuring Philippine development: Report of the Social Indicators Project* (Manila, Development Academy of the Philippines).

Alburo, Florian A. and Roberto, Eduardo L., 1980: "An analysis and synthesis of poverty research in Philippines", in PIDS, *Survey of Philippine development research I* (Makati, PIDS).

Alonzo, Ruperto P., 1979: "Employment and earnings among college graduates", in *Philippine Economic Journal*, 18, 3.

————, 1980: "The informal transport sector in the Greater Manila Area", in *Philippine Review of Business and Economics* (Quezon City) 17, 1 and 2.

Angeles, Edna S., 1985: *Public policy and the Philippine housing market* (Makati, PIDS).

Antonio, Emilio, Jr., 1984: "Looking beyond those magic targets and totals", in *CRC Staff Memos* (Manila), Dec.

Barreto, Felisa R., 1973: *An analytical study of the rice wage formula*, Technical Paper No. 4 (Manila, Bureau of Census and Statistics).

Buencamino, J. A. S. and Guerrero, R. A., 1984: "The threshold family income in Metro Manila and Metro Cebu", in CRC, *Economics and society* (Manila).

Bureau of the Census and Statistics (BCS), 1973: *Indicators of social development* (Manila).

Canlas, Dante B., 1979: "Output, productivity and earnings: The informal manufacturing sector in the Greater Manila Area, 1976", in *Philippine Review of Business and Economics* (Quezon City), 16, 3 and 4.

David, Cristina C., 1983: *Economic policies and Philippine agriculture*, (Makati, PIDS).

De Dios, Emanuel (ed.), 1984: *An analysis of the Philippine economic crisis* (Quezon City, University of the Philippines Press).

Domingo, Lita J. and Feranil, Imelda Z., 1984: *Changing labor force in the Philippines*, CAMS Discussion Paper Series 84-14.

Food and Nutrition Research Institute (FNRI), 1984: *Annual Report* (Manila).

Gatchalian, Jose C. et al., 1986: *The nature, consequences and prospects of underground employment in the four major cities of Metro Manila* (Quezon City, Institute of Industrial Relations, University of the Philippines).

Guerrero, Sylvia H., 1975: *Hawkers and vendors in Manila and Baguio* (Quezon City, Institute of Social Work and Community Development, University of the Philippines).

Herrin, Alejandro N., 1986: *The impact of external shocks and adjustment policies on the welfare of low-income groups in the Philippines*, Report prepared for UNICEF.

Jurado, Gonzalo M. and Castro, Judy, 1979: "The informal sector in the Greater Manila area, 1976: An overview", in *Philippine Review of Economics and Business*, 16, 1 and 2.

Keyes, William J., 1974: *Manila scavengers: The struggle for urban survival*, IPC Poverty Research Series, No. 1 (Quezon City, Institute of Philippine Culture, Ateneo de Manila University).

Mangahas, Mahar K. (ed.), 1976: *Measuring Philippine development: Report of the Social Indicators Project* (Makati, Development Academy of the Philippines).

————, 1977: "Measuring poverty and equity through perception variables", in *Philippine Economic Journal* (Manila), 16, 4.

————, 1979: "Poverty in the Philippines: Some measurement problems", in *Philippine Economic Journal*, 18, 4.

————, 1982: "What happened to the poor on the way to the next development plan?", in *Philippine Economic Journal*, 21, 3 and 4.

———— and Barros, Bruno, 1980: "The distribution of income and wealth: A survey of Philippine research", in PIDS, *Survey of Philippine development research I* (Makati, PIDS).

————; Miranda, Felipe B. and Paqueo, Vicente, 1982: *Measuring the quality of life: A 1982 social weather report*, Unpublished monograph.

————; Quizon, Jaime and Lim, Antonio, 1977: *A critique of the NCSO 1975 family income and expenditure survey*, PREPF Equity Project Technical Paper.

National Census and Statistics Office (NCSO): *Family income and expenditures surveys*, 1957, 1961, 1965, 1971, 1975 and 1985 (Manila).

————: *Integrated survey of households*, 1976 to 1986 (Manila) (unpublished computer print-outs for recent years).

National Economic and Development Authority (NEDA), 1980a: *An inventory of poverty-related surveys in the Philippines* (Manila).

————, 1980b: *Poverty issues and problems in the Philippines* (Manila, limited circulation).

————, 1982: *Social development in the Philippines, 1970-80* (Manila).

————, 1984: *Philippine Statistical Yearbook* (Manila).

Nguiagain, Titus, 1986: *Trends and patterns of internal migration in the Philippines: 1970-80*, Discussion Paper No. 8606 (University of the Philippines, School of Economics).

Oshima, Harry T., 1983: "Sectoral sources of Philippine growth", in *Journal of Philippine Development* (First semester).

Reyes, Florangela R. E., 1985: "The rising tide of poverty in Metro Manila", in CRC, *Economics and Society* (Manila, CRC).

Sethuraman, S. V. (ed.), 1981: *The urban informal sector in developing countries* (Geneva, ILO).

Tan, Edita A. and Holazo, Virginia, 1979: "Measuring poverty incidence in a segmented market", in *Philippine Economic Journal*, 18, 4.

Tidalgo, Rosa Linda P. and Esguerra, Emmanuel F., 1984: *Philippine employment in the 1970s* (Makati, PIDS).

———— and Jurado, Gonzalo M., 1978: "The informal services sector in the Greater Manila area", *Philippine Review of Business and Economics*, 15, 1.

———— and Herrin, Alejandro N., 1986: "An overview of the impact of adjustment policies on welfare", Unpublished paper.

World Bank, 1980: *Aspects of poverty in the Philippines: A review and assessment*, Vol. II, East Asia and Pacific Regional Office.

————, 1985: *The Philippines: Recent trends in poverty*, East Asia and Pacific Regional Office.

# Chapter 9

## Poverty and employment characteristics of urban households in West Bengal, India: An analysis of the results of the National Sample Survey, 1977-78

*PRANAB BARDHAN* [1]

## I. Introduction

A large part of the analysis of poverty in the existing literature is based on data that are much too aggregative. The main purpose of this chapter is to utilise a fairly rich data set, which is large enough to generate statistically valid generalisations and yet disaggregative enough to capture variations in the meaningful relationships between demographic, employment and other economic characteristics of the poor. In 1977-78 the National Sample Survey Organisation (NSSO) undertook what was to date the largest sample survey ever conducted in India focusing on employment and unemployment characteristics of rural and urban households. But beyond some useful aggregative tables on selected items of employment and unemployment, no detailed statistical analysis of the mass of information collected at the local, household and individual levels was carried out. After considerable effort, we gained access [2] to the raw data set for one Indian state, West Bengal. The cross-tabulations and statistical analysis on this data set [3] try to relate urban poverty to individual age, sex, education and skill characteristics, the nature of the household and the urban labour market and some features of the surrounding agricultural economy in which the urban area is located.

West Bengal is a densely populated (second highest density among major Indian states) and poor region, with paddy and jute-based agriculture dependent on heavy rainfall, and with pockets of relatively advanced (though very sluggishly growing) industry and commerce in the urban agglomeration around Calcutta, drawing raw materials and migrant labour from a large and backward hinterland of eastern India. Our sample contains 5,168 urban households with 23,142 individuals (6,806 individual workers) in them. The survey took a stratified two-stage sample, with urban blocks as the first-stage units and households at the second stage. The survey period of one year was divided into four subrounds of three months each. A quarter of the sample blocks was surveyed in each subround, and each sample block was visited only once in the year. The data collected for each household may be classified in three groups: *(a)* data relating to characteristics of the household as a whole (location, size, caste, monthly per capita expenditure, principal occupation,

**Table 9.1.**   *Distribution of households and persons by expenditure size classes in urban West Bengal, 1977-78*

| Per capita monthly household expenditure size class (Rs.) | Percentage of total households | Percentage of all persons |
|---|---|---|
| 0-25 | 0.9 | 1.1 |
| 25-55 | 17.1 | 23.2 |
| 55-75 | 16.7 | 21.4 |
| 75-100 | 19.4 | 20.0 |
| 100-250 | 40.4 | 31.1 |
| Above 250 | 5.4 | 3.1 |

primarily self-employed or wage-employed, number of economically active members, etc.); *(b)* characteristics of each individual member of the household — age, sex, education, skill, day-to-day time disposition particulars over the reference week along with wage and salary earnings reported for the week for those who are currently in the labour force, principal and subsidiary activity of members by *usual* activity status (i.e. status of activity prevailing over the major part of the preceding year); *(c)* response to various probing (and sometimes hypothetical) questions about work pattern, job search, acceptable work types and earnings, nature of domestic work commitments, etc.

# II. Labour force characteristics

Table 9.1 gives the percentage distribution of households and persons by per capita monthly household expenditure size class. Since the average size of household declines in general with a larger per capita expenditure class of household, the percentage of poor people is larger than that of poor households. If one takes a per capita monthly expenditure of Rs.20 at 1960 prices as a very rough and ready "poverty line", then in 1977-78 this poverty line is estimated to be at Rs.60.5 at current prices (using the average of index numbers of consumer prices in Calcutta, Asansol, Kharagpur and Jalpaiguri for consumers with monthly expenditure level of up to Rs.100), and about 30 per cent of the urban population was below it.

We do not have any information on the wealth distribution among households which underlies this expenditure distribution. But we have, in table 9.2, the percentage distribution of individuals by age-sex groups in terms of general education categories (which can be a very rough proxy for at least one kind of "human capital" distribution). The majority of adult males and a much larger majority of adult females are either illiterate or have only primary education or below. Less than 10 per cent of adult males and less than 5 per cent of adult females have an above-secondary education level.

Of all individuals with some "gainful" occupation, only 2.3 per cent could be described by the principal occupational category of working

**Table 9.2.** *Distribution of persons aged 15-59 by general education categories for each age-sex group in urban West Bengal, 1977-78*

| General education categories | Percentage distribution of males in each age group (in years) | | | Percentage distribution of females in each age group (in years) | | |
|---|---|---|---|---|---|---|
| | 15-29 | 30-44 | 45-59 | 15-29 | 30-44 | 45-59 |
| 1. Illiterate | 13.4 | 16.5 | 17.2 | 24.0 | 34.7 | 47.5 |
| 2. Primary and below | 29.0 | 32.2 | 34.4 | 26.7 | 35.6 | 35.9 |
| 3. Middle and secondary | 49.4 | 38.6 | 40.1 | 43.5 | 24.7 | 15.0 |
| 4. Above secondary | 8.2 | 12.8 | 8.4 | 5.7 | 5.1 | 1.6 |
| All education categories | 100.0 | 100.0 | 100.0 | 100.0 | 100.0 | 100.0 |

**Table 9.3.** *Different employment characteristics of households (for each expenditure size class) in urban West Bengal, 1977-78*

| Per capita monthly expenditure size class (Rs.) | Percentages of | | | | | |
|---|---|---|---|---|---|---|
| | Households which are primarily self-employed | Active workers in the household who are unemployed by usual status | Active workers in the household who are casual labourers by usual status | Active males in the household who are in the labour force in the current week | Active females in the household who are in the labour force in the current week | All females in the household who are in the labour force by usual status |
| 0-25 | 18.4 | 9.6 | 10.6 | 76.8 | 92.3 | 64.0 |
| 25-55 | 35.1 | 9.5 | 13.4 | 95.3 | 77.3 | 28.7 |
| 55-75 | 32.8 | 11.4 | 11.5 | 95.2 | 70.2 | 18.1 |
| 75-100 | 30.6 | 7.8 | 9.0 | 95.9 | 73.8 | 13.9 |
| 100-250 | 23.6 | 6.3 | 5.3 | 97.3 | 69.5 | 17.7 |
| Above 250 | 19.8 | 4.1 | 1.7 | 98.1 | 60.0 | 26.6 |
| All | 28.2 | 7.9 | 8.4 | 96.2 | 72.6 | 20.3 |

Note. "Usual status" refers to the activity status over the major part of the preceding year. "Active" refers to being in the labour force by usual status. Primarily self-employed households are those where more than half of income over the preceding year was from self-employment of members. "Males" and "females" in this and subsequent tables refer to the age group 15-60.

proprietors, directors and managers; 36 per cent by the category of "other" professional, administrative, clerical and sales workers (excluding street vendors); the remaining more than 60 per cent of individuals are mostly different kinds of service and production workers (including 6.4 per cent in domestic service, 2.1 per cent as cart drivers and rickshaw pullers, and 2 per cent as street vendors). Of all the professional, administrative, clerical and sales workers (including working proprietors, directors and managers and excluding street vendors) 41.5 per cent worked in their household enterprise over the major part of the preceding year (i.e. by their usual activity status) and the rest

*Table 9.4.   Percentage of households in different expenditure classes and principal occupation categories in urban West Bengal, 1977-78*

| Per capita monthly expenditure size class (Rs.) | Household principal occupation categories | | | | |
|---|---|---|---|---|---|
| | Working proprietors, directors managers | Other professional, administrative, clerical and sales work (except street vendors) | Service and production work (including street vendors) | Farm, fishing and forestry work | Others |
| *Primarily self-employed households* | | | | | |
| 0-25 | 0.0 | 0.2 | 0.4 | 0.0 | 0.0 |
| 25-55 | 0.1 | 6.7 | 12.3 | 2.0 | 0.1 |
| 55-75 | 0.4 | 7.3 | 8.9 | 2.8 | 0.0 |
| 75-100 | 1.8 | 10.1 | 6.9 | 2.3 | 0.0 |
| 100-250 | 3.1 | 15.8 | 12.7 | 2.1 | 0.1 |
| Above 250 | 0.8 | 1.7 | 1.2 | 0.1 | 0.0 |
| All | 6.2 | 41.8 | 42.5 | 9.3 | 0.2 |
| *Primarily wage-employed households* | | | | | |
| 0-25 | 0.0 | 0.2 | 0.6 | 0.2 | 0.1 |
| 25-55 | 0.0 | 2.7 | 10.2 | 1.8 | 0.8 |
| 55-75 | 0.0 | 4.0 | 10.1 | 0.7 | 0.9 |
| 75-100 | 0.0 | 6.4 | 10.5 | 0.4 | 1.5 |
| 100-250 | 0.3 | 16.7 | 22.3 | 0.4 | 3.3 |
| Above 250 | 0.3 | 3.3 | 1.9 | 0.1 | 0.4 |
| All | 0.6 | 33.2 | 55.6 | 3.5 | 7.0 |

Note. Primarily self-employed households are those where more than half of income over the preceding year was from self-employment of members. The principal occupation of the household is the occupation which is the single largest source of earnings for the household. Primarily wage-employed households are those where more than half of income over the preceding year was from wages earned by members.

were mostly working as regular employees on a wage or salary. Of the other workers, 26.7 per cent worked in their household enterprise, 54 per cent worked as regular employees on a wage or salary and about 19 per cent worked as casual wage employees.

As table 9.3 indicates, only 28 per cent of households are primarily self-employed (i.e. more than half of their income over the preceding year was from self-employment of members). The percentage of primarily self-employed households is far below average in rich as well as very poor households: the very poor do not have either the physical or human capital to be mainly self-employed, and the overwhelming majority of the relatively rich are primarily salary earners. As table 9.4 shows, households in the richest expenditure class are more likely to be in professional, administrative, clerical and sales work than in any other principal occupation category. The poor, on the other hand, are mostly in service and production work.

The steadiness of the job is, of course, a major component of income security. Table 9.5 shows that about 40 per cent of households did not have a single member with a regular wage job over most of the preceding year; the

*Table 9.5.    Percentage of all households in different expenditure classes having a household member with a regular wage-paid job in urban West Bengal, 1977-78*

| Per capita monthly expenditure class (Rs.) | Household member with a regular wage-paid job? | |
|---|---|---|
| | Yes | No |
| 0-25 | 0.5 | 0.5 |
| 25-55 | 8.0 | 9.1 |
| 55-75 | 8.8 | 7.9 |
| 75-100 | 11.4 | 8.0 |
| 100-250 | 27.5 | 12.9 |
| Above 250 | 4.1 | 1.3 |
| All | 60.3 | 39.7 |

Note. Regular work here is defined as that by usual status, i.e. over the major part of the preceding year.

majority of the poor households do not have a single regular wage earner. Withdrawals from the current labour force (probably in the form of discouraged drop-outs) on the part of *usual* members of the labour force are also higher in the case of the poor (as table 9.3, column 5, indicates, such withdrawals are unusually large for adult males in the poorest expenditure size class of households).

Regular wage jobs are not merely steadier, they are also in general higher paying. Table 9.6 shows that the male daily wage rate in regular work is one-and-a-half times or more than in casual work for non-farm service and production workers (even for illiterates). The regular wage jobs are more likely to be characterised by seniority systems, job ladders and rationing, and workers' collective bargaining power. The occupational breakdown in table 9.6 seems to suggest that in at least one occupation where these factors are unimportant (e.g. domestic servants) the male regular daily wage rate is not higher [4] than the casual rate (the *hourly* wage rate may even be lower for regular servants, since for them the "day" is usually much longer).

Table 9.7 shows that 15 per cent of households had at least one adult member unemployed by usual activity status. The percentage is, of course, lower for richer households: for example, 22 per cent of households in the monthly per capita household expenditure size classes of Rs.0-25 or Rs.55-75 had at least one adult member unemployed by usual activity status, whereas the corresponding percentage for the richest size class of above Rs.250 was only 7 per cent. This is in spite of the fact that the rich could better afford to remain unemployed over the major part of the preceding year. Table 9.3, column 3, indicates that while only 4 per cent of economically active workers in the household were unemployed by usual activity status in the richest expenditure size class, the percentage was two to three times as large in the poor households. Table 9.8 suggests that the majority of those who report availability for additional work (not all of whom are unemployed) have been seeking such work

*Table 9.6.* **Wage and unemployment rates of non-farm service and production workers in the current labour force by expenditure class and educational and occupational category in urban West Bengal, 1977-78**

| | Daily wage rate in casual work (Rs.) | | Daily wage rate in regular work (Rs.) | | Unemployment rate (percentage) | |
|---|---|---|---|---|---|---|
| | Male | Female | Male | Female | Male | Female |
| *Per capita monthly expenditure class (Rs.)* | | | | | | |
| 0-25 | 3.97 | 3.20 | 5.49 | 2.35 | 8.7 | 4.7 |
| 25-55 | 6.91 | 2.55 | 8.99 | 2.72 | 5.9 | 3.3 |
| 55-75 | 6.82 | 3.17 | 10.93 | 3.75 | 4.6 | 3.5 |
| 75-100 | 8.12 | 4.61 | 11.84 | 4.47 | 2.8 | 3.9 |
| 100-250 | 7.95 | 5.13 | 13.07 | 5.64 | 2.1 | 1.5 |
| Above 250 | 10.43 | 3.86 | 17.39 | 5.56 | 5.3 | 0.0 |
| *Educational category* | | | | | | |
| 1. Illiterate | 6.32 | 3.45 | 9.46 | 4.06 | 4.7 | 2.2 |
| 2. Up to primary | 8.10 | 3.65 | 10.76 | 4.40 | 3.8 | 3.4 |
| 3. Middle/secondary | 7.74 | 3.80 | 14.21 | 6.39 | 2.2 | 11.2 |
| 4. Above secondary | — | — | 24.88 | — | 0.8 | — |
| *Occupational category* | | | | | | |
| 1. Paid housekeeping workers | 6.47 | 3.26 | 5.94 | 3.78 | 0.8 | 0.6 |
| 2. Street vendors | 4.06 | — | 10.11 | — | 3.2 | — |
| 3. *Bidi*-makers | 5.15 | 2.05 | 6.86 | — | 6.6 | 5.6 |
| 4. Cobblers | — | — | 13.02 | — | 0.0 | — |
| 5. Cart-drivers and rickshaw-pullers | 10.67 | — | 12.55 | — | 1.8 | — |
| 6. Other non-farm service and production workers | 7.43 | 3.97 | 12.40 | 6.08 | 3.7 | 6.6 |
| *All classes* | 7.36 | 3.50 | 12.01 | 4.17 | 3.5 | 2.9 |

— = no observations.

Note. A person is defined to be in the current labour force if he/she was in the labour force for at least one hour on at least one day during the reference week. The unemployment rate is defined as the number of person-days seeking or being available for work to the number of person-days spent in the current labour force in the reference week. The daily wage rate is the total wage earnings over the reference week divided by the number of days spent in wage work over the same period. On account of the very small sample size for casual and, to a lesser extent, regular workers for the expenditure size classes Rs.0-25 and above Rs.250, the corresponding estimates have large margins of error; likewise for wage-paid *bidi* (cigarette) workers and street vendors.

for more than a year; as expected, such longer-duration search is proportionately more important for richer (table 9.8) and more educated people (table 9.9).

The unemployment referred to in the preceding paragraph is by usual activity status (i.e. over the major part of the preceding year). The person-day unemployment rate for the reference week (defined as the ratio of the number of person-days when seeking or being available for work to the total number of person-days spent in the current labour force in the reference week) for non-farm production and service workers is given in table 9.6. This unemployment rate for males averages 3.5 per cent, and is higher for the poorer and less-educated workers.

*Table 9.7.*    *Percentage of all households in different expenditure classes having any adult in the household unemployed by usual activity status in urban West Bengal, 1977-78*

| Per capita monthly expenditure class (Rs.) | Any adult in the household unemployed by usual activity status? | |
|---|---|---|
| | Yes | No |
| 0-25 | 0.2 | 0.8 |
| 25-55 | 3.3 | 13.8 |
| 55-75 | 3.6 | 13.1 |
| 75-100 | 2.9 | 16.6 |
| 100-250 | 4.8 | 35.7 |
| Above 250 | 0.4 | 4.9 |
| All | 15.2 | 84.8 |

Note. "Unemployed" here refers to someone who has been seeking or was available for work over the major part of the preceding year. An adult in this table refers to the age group 15-60.

*Table 9.8.*    *Availability for additional work of individuals in the usual labour force plus students and domestic workers and duration of job search/availability in urban West Bengal, 1977-78*

| Per capita monthly household expenditure size class (Rs.) | Percentage of such individuals seeking/available for additional work | | | | |
|---|---|---|---|---|---|
| | Seeking for up to 3 months | Seeking for 3 to 6 months | Seeking for 6 to 12 months | Seeking for more than 12 months | Seeking for any length |
| 0-25 | 0.0 | 0.0 | 0.0 | 0.2 | 0.3 |
| 25-55 | 0.2 | 0.2 | 0.5 | 3.0 | 4.0 |
| 55-75 | 0.1 | 0.2 | 0.5 | 2.8 | 3.6 |
| 75-100 | 0.1 | 0.2 | 0.3 | 2.4 | 2.9 |
| 100-250 | 0.1 | 0.2 | 0.4 | 3.3 | 4.0 |
| Above 250 | 0.0 | 0.0 | 0.0 | 0.3 | 0.3 |
| All | 0.6 | 0.9 | 1.7 | 11.9 | 15.1 |

*Table 9.9.*    *Availability for additional work of males in the usual labour force plus students and domestic workers and duration of job search/availability in urban West Bengal, 1977-78*

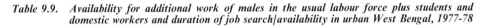

| General education category | Percentage of such individuals seeking/available for additional work | | | | |
|---|---|---|---|---|---|
| | Seeking for up to 3 months | Seeking for 3 to 6 months | Seeking for 6 to 12 months | Seeking for more than 12 months | Seeking for any length |
| 1. Illiterate | 4.7 | 6.4 | 8.7 | 80.3 | 100.0 |
| 2. Up to primary | 4.3 | 6.9 | 12.7 | 76.1 | 100.0 |
| 3. Middle and secondary | 3.4 | 5.4 | 11.3 | 79.8 | 100.0 |
| 4. Above secondary | 1.8 | 4.3 | 8.6 | 85.3 | 100.0 |
| All categories | 3.8 | 6.0 | 11.2 | 79.1 | 100.0 |

## III. Levels of living and wages

In this section we report the results of multiple regression analysis carried out on the data to capture the net effects of a whole range of variables on cross-sectional variations in levels of living and in regular wage rates. In table 9.10 the dependent variable is PCEXPR, defined as the monthly per capita expenditure of the household deflated by a cost-of-living index (with 1960 as the base year) computed for the nearest price-collection centre. The mean value of PCEXPR for urban West Bengal in 1977-78 is Rs.37.18 at 1960 prices, with a standard deviation of Rs.26.25. Some of the explanatory variables used are specific to each individual household — number of dependants in the household (DEPNO), number of members with above-secondary education (HEDU), with middle and secondary education (MEDU), and with technical education (TECHED), number of members who are unskilled (UNSKILL), proportion of unemployed among active adult workers in the household (UNEMPROP), proportion of casual workers among active adult workers in the household (CASPROP), occupation category for the principal occupation of the household (ROCCUP, taking larger values for lower-paid occupations), dummy variable for no adult male worker in the household (DLABFORM), dummy for primarily wage-employed as opposed to self-employed household (HSTYPE2), dummy for households not belonging to scheduled castes or tribes (HHG3), and the NSS subround in which the household was visited (SBRND). Some other explanatory variables are specific to the district where the household happens to be located — dummy variable for the district belonging to the main urban agglomeration in West Bengal (DSIZE), number of urban persons engaged in manufacturing and repair services in the district as percentage of total for urban West Bengal (MANFROP), and average foodgrains yield per hectare in the district (YHA).

All the explanatory variables have statistically significant coefficients and are of expected signs. Across households, levels of living are positively related to the education variables (HEDU, MEDU and TECHED), the dummy for primarily wage-employed households (HSTYPE2) — reflecting, as we have noted in the preceding section, the fact that the overwhelming majority of the relatively rich are primarily salary earners — and the dummy for higher caste (HHG3). It is negatively related to number of dependants (DEPNO), number of unskilled members (UNSKILL), lower-paid principal occupation category (ROCCUP), proportion of unemployed (UNEMPROP) and casual workers (CASPROP), and the dummy for no adult male worker in the household (DLABFORM). The household level of living is higher in districts belonging to the main urban agglomeration and where the importance of manufacturing and repair services is larger, possibly indicating a larger availability of higher-paid jobs. There is some indication that the level of living of an urban household is significantly linked to the productivity and seasonality of agriculture in the surrounding area. The level of living is higher if the household is located in a district where YHA, the average foodgrains yield, is larger, possibly indicating higher opportunity cost and hence the wages of workers. It

*Table 9.10.* *Linear regression analysis of determinants of per capita level of living in the household in urban West Bengal, 1977-78*

Dependent variable: PCEXPR (monthly per capita expenditure of the household deflated by cost-of-living index with 1960 as the base year). Mean: Rs.37.18. Standard deviation: Rs.26.25

| Explanatory variables | Regression coefficient (elasticity) | Standard error | Significant at the percentage level |
|---|---|---|---|
| 1. DEPNO (number of dependants in the household) | −3.9845 (−0.3000) | 0.1654 | 0.0 |
| 2. HEDU (number of members with above-secondary education | 10.8270 (0.0639) | 0.5908 | 0.0 |
| 3. MEDU (number of members with middle and secondary education) | 3.0140 (0.0893) | 0.2870 | 0.0 |
| 4. TECHED (number of members with technical education) | 7.2193 (0.0134) | 1.1041 | 0.0 |
| 5. UNSKILL (number of members who are unskilled) | −1.8653 (−0.1195) | 0.2675 | 0.0 |
| 6. ROCCUP (lower-paid occupation category for the principal occupation of the household) | −5.9281 (−0.4198) | 0.5614 | 0.0 |
| 7. UNEMPROP (proportion of unemployed among active adult workers in the household) | −18.0095 (−0.0340) | 1.8756 | 0.0 |
| 8. CASPROP (proportion of casual workers among active adult workers in the household) | −8.7317 (−0.0198) | 1.2727 | 0.0 |
| 9. DLABFORM (dummy for no adult male worker in the household) | −10.8702 (−0.0125) | 1.5585 | 0.0 |
| 10. HSTYPE2 (dummy for primarily wage-employed as opposed to self-employed household) | 1.8182 (0.0344) | 0.7168 | 1.1 |
| 11. HHG3 (dummy for households not belonging to scheduled castes or tribes) | 3.2151 (0.0747) | 0.9399 | 0.1 |
| 12. SUBRND3 (Jan.-Mar. quarter) | −1.5857 (−0.0107) | 0.7652 | 3.9 |
| 13. SUBRND2 (Oct.-Dec. quarter) | 1.4041 (0.0095) | 0.7651 | 6.7 |
| 14. DSIZE (dummy for the district belonging to the main urban agglomeration in West Bengal) | 4.3215 (0.0959) | 1.3694 | 0.2 |
| 15. MANFPROP (number of urban persons engaged in manufacturing and repair services in the district as percentage of total for urban West Bengal) | 0.0950 (0.0470) | 0.0379 | 1.2 |
| 16. YHA (average foodgrains yield per hectare in the district) | 2.9112 (0.1129) | 1.3629 | 1.2 |
| Constant term | 51.1347 | 2.4701 | 0.0 |

$R^2 = 0.3113$; $F = 138.1$; No. of observations = 4,906.

Note. The data for explanatory variables 1-13 are from NSS 32nd Round. The data for MANFPROP is from the 1971 Census, and those for YHA are from the State Statistical Bureau. The main urban agglomeration in DSIZE refers to Calcutta, 24 Parganas, Howrah, Hooghly, Durgapur, Kharagpur, Bardhaman and Asanol. The variable ROCCUP takes the value of 1 if the principal occupation category of the household is that of working proprietors, 2 for other professional, administrative and sales workers, 3 for service and production workers (including street vendors) and 4 for farm work (including fishing and forestry). The unemployed and the casual workers in UNEMPROP and CASPROP refer to their usual activity status (i.e. over the major part of the year). In the dependent variable, PCEXPR, the figure for per capita monthly expenditure (obtained from NSS 32nd Round data) is deflated by the cost-of-living index in 1977-78 for the monthly expenditure level of Rs.1.100 obtained by the State Statistical Bureau averaged over 25 different centres in West Bengal with 1960 as the base year.

*Table 9.11.   Linear regression analysis of determinants of daily wage rates of regular non-farm
service and production workers in the current labour force in urban West Bengal, 1977-78*

Dependent variable: REGWAGE (daily wage rate on regular work). Mean: Rs.10.98. Standard
deviation: Rs.7.44.

| Explanatory variables | Regression coefficient (elasticity) | Standard error | Significant at the percentage level |
|---|---|---|---|
| 1. FEM (dummy variable for women) | −2.6428 (−0.0316) | 0.5160 | 0.0 |
| 2. AGE (in years) | 0.4029 (1.2616) | 0.0499 | 0.0 |
| 3. AGE squared | −0.0033 (−0.4029) | 0.0007 | 0.0 |
| 4. DEP (number of dependants as proportion of the household size) | 1.8676 (0.0737) | 0.3963 | 0.0 |
| 5. REDGEN4 (above-secondary education) | 13.9741 (0.0316) | 0.8047 | 0.0 |
| 6. REDGEN3 (middle and secondary education) | 3.2655 (0.0864) | 0.3602 | 0.0 |
| 7. RSKILL2 (machinist, fitter, welder, electrician, driver, miner skill category) | 1.9972 (0.0348) | 0.3185 | 0.0 |
| 8. RSKILL3 (typist, etc., skill category) | 0.8964 (0.0044) | 0.5395 | 9.7 |
| 9. RPROCC3 (maids, nurses and other housekeeping occupation category) | −2.2992 (−0.0333) | 0.4965 | 0.0 |
| 10. RPROCC4 (street-vendor occupation category) | −3.5456 (−0.0008) | 2.3974 | 13.9 |
| 11. HHG1 (scheduled caste household) | −1.1510 (−0.0122) | 0.3764 | 0.2 |
| 12. DSIZE (dummy for district belonging to the main urban agglomeration in West Bengal) | 1.3175 (0.1083) | 0.4675 | 0.5 |
| 13. SUBRND2 (Oct.-Dec. quarter) | 0.7672 (0.0184) | 0.3337 | 2.2 |
| 14. YHA (average foodgrains yield per hectare in the district) | 1.2256 (0.1640) | 0.5500 | 2.6 |
| Constant term | −4.0202 | 1.1386 | 0.0 |

$R^2 = 0.3871$; F = 90.6; No. of observations = 2,457.

is also interesting that the level of living in the urban household is higher in the
agriculturally busy season (October-December quarter) and lower in a relatively
slack season (January-March quarter). It is possible that at times of peak
operations in agriculture the opportunity cost of labour in the urban sector goes
up, whereas in the slack season labourers from the rural sector crowd the urban
labour market and bring wages down. It is also possible that as the
October-December quarter includes some of the major festivals in the area
household expenditure (as well as bonus payments at work) reaches a seasonal
peak at this time. Another way seasonality may affect the urban standard of
living is that in the agriculturally busy (slack) season the urban household needs
to send fewer (more) remittances to relatives in the rural area.

Table 9.11 presents a regression analysis of the determinants of REGWAGE, the daily wage rate on regular non-farm service and production work for workers currently (i.e. in the reference week) in the labour force. The mean value of REGWAGE at current prices is Rs.10.98, with a standard deviation of Rs.7.44. Some of the explanatory variables are specific to each individual worker — AGE (in years), sex dummy for women (FEM), education level (above secondary, REDGEN4; middle and secondary, REDGEN3), skill category for machinist, fitter, welder, electrician, driver and miner (RSKILL2), typist and similar skill category (RSKILL3), maids, nurses and other housekeeping occupation category (RPROCC3) and street vendor occupation category (RPROCC4). Some of the other variables are specific to the household of the worker — number of dependants as proportion of the household size (DEP), dummy for households belonging to scheduled caste (HHG1) and the NSS subround in which the household was visited (SBRND). The variables DSIZE and YHA are, as in the earlier regression, specific to the district where the household happens to be located.

All these variables are statistically highly significant (except RSKILL3, RPROCC4 and all subrounds other than SUBRND2) and are of expected signs. REGWAGE is lower for women, higher with age indicating seniority and learning (although at a diminishing rate, as AGE squared has a significant negative coefficient), higher with education level, higher with skill category RSKILL2 and RSKILL3, lower for domestic service and street vendor occupation categories, lower for scheduled castes (possibly due to caste segregation of some menial jobs), higher for workers with more dependants in the household (possibly indicating more overtime, more strenuous efforts, working on more jobs for such workers with a heavier family burden [5]), and higher in areas of urban agglomeration, again possibly indicating a larger availability of higher-paid jobs in those areas. For reasons partly similar to those explained in the case of the earlier regression, the daily wage rate on regular work in the reference week is higher in districts where the average foodgrain yield is larger and in the agriculturally busy and festival season included in the October-December quarter.

# IV. Poverty and employment of women

Here we report on some of the specific poverty and employment characteristics of women in the sample. We have already noted in section III (and table 9.10) that other things remaining the same households with no adult male workers are strongly associated with lower levels of living. Table 9.12 shows that among non-farm service and production workers, while 20.5 per cent of male workers belong to the lowest two expenditure classes (with per capita household monthly expenditure of Rs.0-25 and Rs.25-55), for female workers the proportion is about double, 40.7 per cent. This is, of course, partly indicative of the fact that poorer households send out more women to service and production work than richer households. Taking all individuals, while about

*Table 9.12.*   *Distribution of non-farm service and production workers in the current labour force by expenditure size classes and sex in urban West Bengal, 1977-78*

| Per capita monthly household expenditure size class (Rs.) | Percentage of all non-farm service and production workers | |
| --- | --- | --- |
| | Male | Female |
| 0-25 | 0.8 | 3.8 |
| 25-55 | 19.7 | 36.9 |
| 55-75 | 20.8 | 19.3 |
| 75-100 | 19.6 | 11.8 |
| 100-250 | 36.1 | 23.9 |
| Above 250 | 3.0 | 4.3 |

27 per cent of all males in urban West Bengal were below our poverty line (Rs.60.5 per capita expenditure per month), the figure was about 33 per cent for all females.

We have noted in the preceding section (and table 9.11) that holding other factors (such as age, education, skill, occupation category, caste, etc.) constant, the daily wage of regular non-farm service and production workers in the current labour force is significantly lower for women than for men. Table 9.6 presents the differences in male and female daily wage rates in casual and regular non-farm service and production work by expenditure size classes of households, education levels and some occupational categories. Even for illiterate workers, the average daily wage rate of men seems to be more than double that of women in regular work, and almost double in casual work. The occupational breakdown shows that such male-female wage differences are very large, even for occupations where male greater physical strength need not be a factor (as for example in *bidi*-making) or where male advantage in skill is likely to be low (as for example in the occupation category of maids, nurses and other paid housekeeping workers).

The unemployment rate seems to be in general lower among women than men, possibly because where job prospects are poor, women drop out of the current labour force more readily. Table 9.3 shows that about 27 per cent of economically active (i.e. in the labour force by usual activity status) adult females withdrew from the current labour force in the reference week. In response to a probing question in the survey we find that even among women who are engaged in household work by usual activity status (and are thus outside the labour force), about 5 per cent report that they are so engaged because of non-availability of gainful work and about 19 per cent report their willingness to accept additional work (such as animal husbandry, spinning and weaving, tailoring, small-scale manufacturing and repairing, etc.) if it is made available to the woman's household.

On average, about a fifth of adult females in a household participate in the labour force and, as table 9.3 indicates, such participation is very high

*Table 9.13.* Linear regression analysis of determinants of female participation in the labour force in urban West Bengal, 1977-78

Dependent variable: FEMPAR (the number of adult females usually active in the labour force as proportion of total number of adult females in the household). Mean: 21 per cent. Standard deviation: 39 per cent.

| Explanatory variables | Regression coefficient (elasticity) | Standard error | Significant at the percentage level |
|---|---|---|---|
| 1. DEPNO (number of dependants in the household) | −7.0970 (−1.2527) | 0.3689 | 0.0 |
| 2. CHDOM (number of children engaged in domestic work of the household) | 14.0358 (0.0338) | 2.4157 | 0.0 |
| 3. ADTMALE (number of adult male workers in the household) | −2.6448 (−0.2001) | 0.6268 | 0.0 |
| 4. HEDF (number of adult females with above-secondary education) | 19.0083 (0.0703) | 2.1383 | 0.0 |
| 5. MEDF (number of adult females with middle and secondary education) | 3.6505 (0.0902) | 0.9179 | 0.0 |
| 6. TECHEDF (number of adult females with some technical education) | 17.2117 (0.0108) | 5.1590 | 0.1 |
| 7. PECEXPEND (monthly per capita expenditure of the household) | −0.0489 (−0.2314) | 0.0096 | 0.0 |
| 8. ROCCUP (lower-paid occupation category for the principal occupation of the household) | 3.3329 (0.4109) | 1.0256 | 0.1 |
| 9. HHG3 (dummy for households not belonging to scheduled castes or tribes) | −10.8233 (−0.4470) | 1.7985 | 0.0 |
| 10. HSTYPE2 (dummy for primarily wage-employed as opposed to self-employed households) | −2.0720 (−0.0687) | 1.3250 | 11.8 |
| 11. AWAYM (number of adult male members of the household who were away for a period of one month or more in the preceding year) | 6.0709 (0.0047) | 3.4495 | 7.9 |
| 12. REASM (number of adult male members of the household away in the reference week at work or in search of work) | 4.0570 (0.0103) | 2.1832 | 6.3 |
| 13. DSIZE (dummy for the district belonging to the main urban agglomeration in West Bengal) | −9.7797 (−0.3752) | 2.0637 | 6.3 |
| 14. MANFPROP (number of urban persons engaged in manufacturing and repair services in the district as percentage of total for urban West Bengal) | −0.1700 (−0.1438) | 0.0686 | 1.3 |
| Constant term | 60.2277 | 4.0665 | 0.0 |

$R^2 = 0.1859$; $F = 52.0$; No. of observations = 3,658.
Note. The data for explanatory variables 1-12 are from NSS 32nd Round. The data for MANFPROP are from the 1971 Census. For the denotation of urban agglomeration in DSIZE and of ROCCUP, see notes to table 9.10.

in the very poor households, declines for the middle range of income or expenditure groups and rises again for the richest households. Table 9.13 presents the results of a regression analysis of variations in female participation rates across urban households. The dependent variable is FEMPAR, the number of adult females in the labour force by usual activity status as a proportion of the total number of adult females in the household. FEMPAR has a mean value of 21 per cent in the sample with a standard deviation of 39 per cent. As in table 9.10, most of the explanatory variables are specific to the household, whereas some variables such as DSIZE and MANFPROP relate to the average for the district where the household happens to be located.

Most of the variables are statistically significant and are of expected signs. The female participation rate seems to be positively related to the number of children in the household doing domestic work (suggesting how children, particularly girls, performing these tasks ease the constraint on adult women for work outside), to the female education level (middle and secondary, above secondary and technical), indicating that the taboo against women's working outside is weaker for largely non-manual jobs taken by relatively educated women, to households belonging to scheduled castes or tribes (where the taboo is weak), to cases where the principal occupation of the household is in a low-paid category (again, the taboo is weak and need for extra income high) and to households with more adult male members away (for a period of one month or more in the preceding year or away in the reference week at work or in search of work). The female participation rate is lower for households with larger number of dependants (possibly the usual constraint of taking care of children and old people on women's participation in the labour force), for better-off households (the usual income effect coupled with a positive effect on social status achieved by the upwardly mobile, through restricting female economic activity), for households with a larger number of adult male workers (income effect again) and for primarily wage-employed households (as opposed to primarily self-employed households where women may have more opportunities to work alongside other family members). It is noteworthy that the female participation rate is lower in districts belonging to the main urban agglomeration and where manufacturing jobs may be more important: it is possible that in these areas male job opportunities are better (reducing the need for women to join the labour force) and the importance of large-scale factory-type jobs or skills (as contrasted with small-scale informal sector jobs where the mostly unskilled women are more often employed) is larger.

## V. Summary

We have tried to relate urban poverty to demographic characteristics of households, to age, sex, education, skill, occupation and employment (wage, steadiness of jobs, unemployment, withdrawal from the labour force, etc.), to characteristics of individuals and to the nature of urban agglomeration, and even to the productivity and seasonality of agriculture in the surrounding rural area. We have also indicated some of the special handicaps that women workers face. We should note, however, that while the data set used is one of the largest and most detailed in any part of urban India that has been subject to a statistical analysis, the very nature of the particular NSS survey design and schedules seriously constrains our exploration of the nature of urban poverty. One would like, for example, more information on the operation of urban labour market mechanisms, the labour recruitment and job rationing process, the nature of labour market segmentation, the network of "connections" and migration linkages, the working of intermediaries and contract systems, the formation and structure of trade unions, access to credit and marketing systems for the self-employed, the pattern of remittances and links with relatives in villages, and the qualitative and quantitative aspects of levels of living not captured in the per capita monthly consumer expenditure figures.

### Notes

[1] University of California, Berkeley.

[2] I am grateful to V. M. Dandekar, the then chairman of the Governing Council of the NSSO, for helping me gain access to the data tapes.

[3] A similarly detailed statistical analysis of the poverty and labour market characteristics of the *rural* households in West Bengal on the basis of these data has been reported in parts of Pranab Bardhan, *Land, labour and rural poverty: Essays in development economics* (Columbia University Press, New York, 1984).

[4] This, of course, is subject to larger probable margins of error in computing the cost of food consumed by the regular servant in the household as part of his or her total wage.

[5] The positive coefficient of DEP is also consistent with the nutrition-based efficiency theory of wages, but such fine worker-specific variations in wage rates as implied in this theory may not be the usual practice except possibly in very small firms.

# Chapter 10

## Vulnerable workers in the Indian urban labour market

*JOHN HARRISS* [1]

## I. Introduction — Concepts and theory

This chapter reviews evidence showing the existence of considerable heterogeneity and stratification in India's urban labour markets, such that labour markets appear to be divided into distinct submarkets. A major premise is that the livelihoods of some groups of workers are "vulnerable" on several dimensions, and that because of the forces which compartmentalise the labour market, some groups may be condemned to being vulnerable. There are conceptual difficulties and acute empirical problems in studying the structure of the urban labour markets of South Asia in this way. But there is empirical evidence of a tendency for an increasing proportion of the labour force to be piled up in vulnerable types of employment; and some evidence, though it must be treated with caution, that the wages of "vulnerable" groups have declined in comparison with those in the most protected and least vulnerable forms of employment.

### 1. Against dualistic models

There is now much evidence to show the limitations of the dualistic model of urban labour markets, which derive essentially from the way in which it obscures the heterogeneity existing in them (including in the structure of wages and earnings), and in types of economic units, and from its neglect of the particularism that characterises search procedures and access to urban employment. As Kannappan says: "The model is poorly equipped to handle the diverse economic characteristics, wage structures and labour market practices encompassed by metropolitan markets" (1985, p. 719). Evidence for India in this chapter amply supports this argument.

It has been in response to these limitations that several authors, mainly elaborating on field-work in Third World cities, have proposed other frameworks for the analysis of urban labour markets (Bromley and Gerry, 1979; Harriss, 1982). They distinguish between, first, a group of wage workers whose employment is relatively secure, and whose earnings and conditions of work are subject to certain legally defined guarantees (they are "protected"; though the extent to which the legal guarantees are implemented in practice varies in different situations); and second, workers who lack such formal guarantees (and who are thereby, in varying degrees, "vulnerable"). They are then concerned with making meaningful distinctions among "vulnerable" workers. Bromley and Gerry's categories reflect a particular concern with the vulnerability of direct producers to control and exploitation by capital: short-term wage workers are more vulnerable than permanent wage workers because they are not protected by legal guarantees (so the length of their working day may be extended, or the intensity of work increased, perhaps by avoiding safety measures); disguised wage workers and dependent workers are vulnerable because they have little or no control over raw materials (or merchandise, premises or equipment) and their output. The "truly self-employed", by contrast, enjoy considerable autonomy. There is a presumption that this autonomy also means that their livelihoods are relatively assured so that though they are not protected like permanent wage workers they may have a similar level of security.

Rodgers (1985, p. 25) suggests a framework to make this analytically more precise, based on distinctions between subordination/autonomy; (institutionally) unprotected/protected; irregular/regular (unstable/stable) employment; and their implications for the security of livelihoods. The distinctions on which the framework depends may be understood as different dimensions of "vulnerability". An implicit premise is that the way in which labour is distributed between the different categories in any specific economy is the outcome of struggle between workers and owners/controllers of means of production, and of the conditions (including those affecting demand for and supply of labour) under which this struggle takes place.

The analytical framework we advocate, and the problems to which this framework responds, recall the segmented labour market approach which developed in studies of advanced capitalist economies, and which has been elaborated because of dissatisfaction with the traditional neo-classical approach to labour market analysis. There are strong indications in the Bombay, Ahmedabad and Coimbatore studies discussed here of the existence of compartments within the labour market which are more or less self-contained and composed of non-competing groups of workers, whose options are severely constrained by social and institutional factors. The observations on which the segmented labour market approach in the study of advanced capitalist economies is based are closely comparable with those that gave rise to the framework adopted here; and the whole problematic is shared.

One attempt to develop a theory of labour market segmentation in LDCs, of particular interest to us, is the model proposed by Mazumdar (1983):

[There is a] process by which the urban market for workers of low skill tends to develop a sector of high wage, often accompanied by job security and fringe benefits unavailable to the large number of workers outside this sector. Furthermore, since the number of jobs in the high-wage sector is limited, many urban jobseekers with skills or human capital endowments similar to those employed in the sector have only limited opportunities of getting into it (Mazumdar, 1983, p. 254).

As he explains, the high-wage or "formal" sector is easily identified by the operation of labour laws and/or unionisation. But he argues that it is doubtful whether the existence of the sector should be explained in terms of these institutional factors, in view of historical evidence showing that a distinct high-wage sector had become established before unions or labour legislation. His explanation of the existence of the high-wage sector is in terms of the following framework:

*(a)* It is possible to distinguish between the supply prices of permanent and temporary migrants to the city, the latter being lower than the former. Some employers, historically, being interested in the higher efficiency of a stable, committed labour force, set wage levels high enough to attract permanent, family migrants: "Thus we find the emergence of a modern sector with wage levels that were perceptibly higher than the earnings of labour in those activities in which individual migrants dominated" (p. 255).

*(b)* The establishment of a high-wage, permanent labour force then created its own momentum, as firms had an incentive further to increase the wages of their own labour force so long as there were more than proportionate increases in efficiency. "A certain body of workers is selected (more or less at random) to provide a stabilised workforce. The subsequent increase in wage is not due to the prior scarcity of workers of a certain quality. It is due to the pursuit of a high-wage policy within a firm dealing with an exclusive body of workers — which produces net profits to be shared between management and workers" (p. 255).

*(c)* At this stage the labour force may become unionised ("as a natural consequence of the labour market segmentation produced by the previous stages, rather than being a cause of segmentation"). Unionisation may indeed be encouraged by governments, interested in political stability.

Mazumdar then reports findings (based mainly on the Bombay Labour Market Study discussed below) that, in explaining the wage differentials between "formal" and "informal" sectors, the "sector of employment" variable turned out to be the most important factor; that there is strong evidence of very limited mobility between sectors; and that the market for recruitment to formal sector jobs is located more in rural areas than in the urban "informal" sector. In other words, there is strong evidence of the existence of segmentation. On the basis of these observations and of his conceptual framework, Mazumdar postulates that in the context of LDCs (including a growth rate of employment in the formal sector well below the growth rate of the working population . . ., etc; p. 258), there must be a tendency in the urban economy towards widening wage differentials between the formal and residual sectors with a declining proportion of the labour force employed in the former. The evidence reviewed here permits some testing of Mazumdar's framework and of this prognosis.

## 2. Data problems and the dearth of relevant research

Further refinement of categories for analysing labour markets in the Third World is of limited usefulness here, for the existing secondary, statistical data from population censuses and labour force surveys in South Asia, and the existing research studies for the region, do not permit systematic analysis on the lines of Rodgers's framework. The secondary statistical sources may give us information on the distribution of the labour force among different employment statuses: conventionally those of "employer", "employee", "self-employed" and "unpaid family helper". The discussion above draws attention to the significance of distinctions among the categories both of "employee" and "self-employed", and the available employment status data do not allow these distinctions to be explored. Information on the distribution of the labour force between occupations and between activities, similarly, provides only a very blunt instrument. Indeed, about the best that can be done with the available data is to use information on numbers employed in establishments registered under some industrial or employment legislation, and which is available in returns on "establishments" or "factories", in comparison with census or labour force survey data on the total labour force in the relevant categories, so as to derive a measure of the number employed in units which are in some (specifiable) ways "protected". This is of course what has been done in studies which have attempted to measure the "informal" or "unorganised" sector in relation to the "formal" or "organised" sector of the urban economy (an outstanding study on these lines, on Bombay, is Joshi and Joshi, 1976). So in spite of the limitations of the dualistic approach, we are often in the position of having to work with it.

Few studies use anything other than the conventional categories of labour force statistics, or the formal/informal distinction. Several studies of urban labour markets in India, described in some detail in this chapter, do however make use of an approach which approximates a little more closely to Rodgers's framework. In Deshpande's study of the Bombay labour market (Deshpande, 1979), in work by Papola, Subrahmanian and others on Ahmedabad (Papola and Subrahmanian, 1975; Subrahmanian et al., 1982; Papola, 1983), and in work on Coimbatore (Harriss, 1982, 1986), workers in factories registered under the Indian Factories Act (which provides quite strong protection concerning the security and conditions of employment) are distinguished from those employed in establishments which are not covered by such legislation, and these workers in turn are distinguished from those who are considered to be daily paid "casual" workers, employed outside establishments. The distinctions made are not very precisely formulated, but they are concerned with problems of vulnerability.

Given the diverse and imprecise, unstandardised categories employed in the evidence and the research reviewed here, we should ask whether any reliance at all can be placed on comparisons that may be suggested across place and time. There are difficulties, but at least the data on numbers employed in "registered" establishments, and who are thereby "protected" in specifiable ways, seems to allow conceptually sensible comparison. The very existence of legal provisions which make registration necessary at all means that the workers so distinguished are comparable with each other and clearly distinct from other groups of workers. In fact the available data seem to allow principally for comparisons between "permanent/protected wage work" and casual, daily paid wage labour. This seems to us to be sensible in itself, though it is clearly important not to treat "casual work" as a proxy for all those types of employment other than protected wage work.

# II. Trends in population, labour force, wages and poverty

There are considerable difficulties in the interpretation of the Indian labour force data, and the arguments discussed below must be treated with caution. At the same time, none of the sources suggest that there has been any very marked structural change (see table 10.1; Krishnamurthy, 1984 and Deshpande and Deshpande, 1985).

## 1. Changes in the structure of the urban labour force

Of particular significance here is the Deshpandes' finding that non-household industry, non-registered factory employment in manufacturing increased by 84.5 per cent between 1971 and 1981, whereas according to data available under the Employment Market Information Programme of the Directorate General of Employment and Training, factory employment increased by only 42.2 per cent over the same period. (The data for employment in factories collected under the EMI programme include females, and are not strictly comparable with the Census data for male main workers relied on in the Deshpandes' paper, but as they point out the exclusion of female workers would strengthen their conclusion of the relatively faster growth of the unorganised sector):

|  | 1971 | 1981 |
|---|---|---|
|  |  | *( Thousands )* |
| Nos. employed in manufacturing in other than household industry | 9 747 | 15 834 |
| Registered factory employment according to EMI returns | 5 083 | 7 228 |
| *Therefore:* unorganised sector | 4 664 | 8 606 |
| *Therefore:* growth of |  | *( Percentages )* |
| organised manufacturing |  | 42.2 |
| unorganised manufacturing |  | 84.5 |
| Relative shares of: |  |  |
| organised manufacturing | 52 | 45.6 |
| unorganised manufacturing | 48 | 54.4 |

Source. Deshpande and Deshpande, 1985, p. 970

Table 10.1.    Percentage distribution of the workforce by main activity, 1971-81, all India (excluding
                    Assam), males

|  | Activity | All India | | | | | |
|---|---|---|---|---|---|---|---|
|  |  | Total | | Total, rural | | Total, urban | |
|  |  | 1971 | 1981 | 1971 | 1981 | 1971 | 1981 |
| I | Cultivators | 45.90 | 43.70 | 55.73 | 55.16 | 5.22 | 5.19 |
| II | Agricultural labourers | 21.54 | 19.56 | 25.61 | 24.00 | 4.70 | 4.66 |
| III | Plantations, forestry, etc. | 2.24 | 2.34 | 2.39 | 2.50 | 1.64 | 1.81 |
| IV | Mining and quarrying | 0.54 | 0.62 | 0.43 | 0.49 | 1.00 | 1.04 |
| Va | Household manufacturing | 3.42 | 3.18 | 3.19 | 2.87 | 4.40 | 4.21 |
| Vb | Non-household manufacturing | 6.70 | 8.92 | 2.49 | 3.82 | 24.15 | 26.05 |
| VI | Construction | 1.36 | 1.81 | 0.83 | 1.12 | 3.57 | 4.12 |
| VII | Trade and commerce | 6.37 | 7.33 | 2.75 | 3.27 | 21.33 | 20.96 |
| VIII | Transport, storage and communications | 2.86 | 3.32 | 0.97 | 1.37 | 10.64 | 9.88 |
| IX | Other services | 9.07 | 9.21 | 5.62 | 5.39 | 23.31 | 22.06 |
|  | Total workers | 100 | 100 | 100 | 100 | 100 | 100 |
|  | I + II + III | 69.68 | 65.60 | 83.73 | 81.66 | 11.56 | 11.66 |
|  | Va + Vb | 10.12 | 12.10 | 5.68 | 6.69 | 28.55 | 30.26 |

Note. The 1981 figures are based on the 5 per cent sample of the Census of India (excluding Assam).

At the same time employment in household industry grew by only
13.44 per cent, so that the whole "unorganised" segment of manufacturing
(household industry + non-household non-factory) grew only a little faster
than the "organised" segment and "... consequently its share within
manufacturing increased (only) marginally from 65.48 per cent in 1971 to
66.35 per cent in 1981" (ibid., p. 970).

In urban areas, according to the Deshpandes, employment in public
utilities increased by 74.8 per cent between 1971 and 1981, in construction by
66.4 per cent and in unregistered manufacturing by 65.4 per cent — all
considerably higher rates than that of urban employment as a whole, which
increased by only 44.43 per cent (compared with the intercensal increase in the
whole urban population of 44.5 per cent). Employment in trade increased by
42.24 per cent, in transport by 32.99 per cent, in services (other than finance)
by 34.35 per cent and in registered manufacturing by 42.83 per cent (all these
figures are taken from Deshpande and Deshpande, 1985, p. 970, table 3). But
because of the large shares of these sectors in total urban employment (in 1981
trade 19.82 per cent; services 23.02 per cent; registered manufacturing 17.98 per
cent; transport 10.96 per cent) they continued to account for large shares of the
total change in absolute male employment, as shown in table 10.2.

According to the Deshpandes' analysis, therefore, it seems that from
1971 to 1981 there was a marked relative and absolute expansion in employment
in unregistered manufacturing in urban areas and a notable, though in absolute
terms less significant, expansion in construction. These are sectors in which a
majority of employees, characteristically, are not much protected by labour

*Table 10.2.  Share in total change in absolute male employment 1971-81, by industry divisions: Urban areas*

| Division | Percentages |
|---|---|
| Agriculture | 2.45 |
| Mining | 1.26 |
| Manufacturing (registered) | 17.65 |
| Manufacturing (unregistered) | 20.17 |
| Utilities | 2.04 |
| Construction | 5.98 |
| Trade | 19.17 |
| Transport | 8.90 |
| Finance | 3.10 |
| Services | 19.18 |
| Total | 100.00 |

Source. Deshpande and Deshpande, 1985, table 4.

legislation, and it is fair to conclude (if the Deshpandes' methodology is accepted) that the expansion of these sectors implies relative expansion of vulnerable sectors of the labour market. The large absolute increases in trade and in non-financial services may also imply expansion of vulnerable sectors. These proportions are confirmed by the observation that among the ten occupational groups which absorbed over 50 per cent of the total increase in male employment in urban areas, several are groups which typically include a large proportion of vulnerable workers: "salesmen, shop assistants and related workers", "unclassified labourers", and "tailors, dress-makers, etc.", though "transport equipment operators" and "machinery fitters" may also include high proportions of unprotected wage workers (ibid., table 8, p. 972).

## 2. Implications of changes in the structure of the labour force; and trends in earnings and in poverty

Krishnamurthy comments that the extent to which the shift away from agriculture "... has been related to a rising share of manufacturing reflecting positive growth forces in the economy is difficult to determine" (1984, p. 2128), especially when the Census suggests a move into manufacturing and the National Sample Survey (NSS) rather into services. He goes on:

Again, if the Indian rural workforce is becoming progressively casualised [as his analysis suggests while the NSS results suggest a similar process is taking place in urban India], the declining share of agriculture could reflect ... the growing inability of agriculture to take on increased numbers added to the workforce. This in turn could be due to not only demographic pressures but adverse trends in the agrarian sector. As the land base of agriculturalists becomes progressively smaller, especially for those for whom it is already small, more and more workers would have to look for casual, intermittent employment in rural and urban areas (1984, p. 2128).

*Table 10.3.   Per capita annual earnings of employees in manufacturing industries, 1970-80*

| Year | Earnings in current prices (Rs.) | Earnings in constant 1960 prices (Rs.) | Index of real earnings |
|------|------|------|------|
| 1970 | 2 726 | 1 486 | 101 |
| 1971 | 2 821 | 1 485 | 101 |
| 1972 | 3 000 | 1 485 | 101 |
| 1973 | 3 136 | 1 329 | 90 |
| 1974 | 3 119 | 1 026 | 70 |
| 1975 | 3 147 | 980 | 67 |
| 1976 | 5 125 | 1 731 | 118 |
| 1977 | 5 614 | 1 749 | 119 |
| 1978 | No data | No data | No data |
| 1979 | 6 144 | 1 755 | 119 |
| 1980 | 6 387 | 1 637 | 111 |

Source. *Indian Labour Year Books*, various years.

These suggestions are borne out in Kalpana Bardhan's review on rural labour markets in India (1983), in which she argues that "The demographic factor, the rise in farm-size concentration, and the sluggishness of rural non-agriculture have made the number of farm labourers rise more than the demand for farm labour" (1983, p. 2). She notes indications of increased labour mobility, and comments on a twist in the story of declining labour absorption in agriculture of particular relevance in the present context:

A striking aspect of rural-to-urban migration in India, as well as of the intra-rural mobility into "modern" manufacturing and service jobs, is the proportionally low (under-represented) access of landless labour families in general, and those from tribal and outcaste groups in particular. Even as non-farm jobs multiply in urban-industrial centres and often within rural areas, the stratification of access to job opportunities and related wherewithals generate an increasing concentration of land-poor *harijans* and *adivasis* in the lowest-paid ranks of farm labour and coolie labour (Bardhan, 1983, p. 4).

Against these "pessimistic" interpretations of the structural shifts the Deshpandes set the results of an analysis of the real domestic product per main worker in 1971 and 1981. They find that "... an overwhelming majority – 88 per cent of main workers of both sexes and 96 per cent of males – are likely to be better off by the change in the structure of employment" (1985, p. 972). But according to their analysis, "income per main worker (male and female)" declined between 1971 and 1981 in agriculture, construction and (though by very little) in unorganised manufacturing. If it is true that the changes that took place have, on balance, had a favourable effect, it has been in a context showing evidence of prevailing stagnation in levels of livelihood.

According to Bardhan, the evidence indicates that employment and real earnings per agricultural labourer have not generally increased, despite

*Table 10.4.   People below poverty line/modest poverty line (urban) (percentages)*

| Period | Poverty line | Modest poverty line |
|---|---|---|
| 1972-73 | 40.1 | 19.9 |
| 1977-78 | 38.2 | 18.8 |
| 1979-80 (estimated) | 40.3 | 23.7 |
| 1984-85 (projected) | 33.7 | 18.7 |

Note. The poverty line is the mid-point of the monthly per capita expenditure class having a daily calorie intake of 2,100 per person in urban areas: Rs.88 in 1979-80.
(1972-73 and 1977-78 data are derived from NSS consumption expenditure distribution provided in the 27th and 32nd Rounds: source, Government of India, Planning Commission: *A technical note on the 6th Plan of India*, July 1981.)

agricultural growth in some regions (1983, p. 2). Wage series for activities outside the agricultural sector other than "organised" manufacturing do not exist, unfortunately, but these organised sector wages have increased only erratically and sluggishly (see table 10.3).

The studies of labour markets in Bombay, Coimbatore and Ahmedabad discussed in section III offer strong evidence of the existence of much heterogeneity, but also of differentiation and of a segmented wage structure. They indicate marked disparities between male and female wages, even for similar work (such as *bidi* rolling). In general, and for India as a whole, the finding on organised sector wages in the Boothalingam Committee's *Report of the Study Group on Wages, Incomes and Prices* (Ministry of Finance, May 1978) is noteworthy: "The determination of a homogeneous national wage structure is very difficult . . . Disparities, anomalies and irrationalities exist and have come to be regarded as 'rights'".

When there is evidence that increases in the rural labour force are not entirely absorbed productively in agriculture; when real earnings per agricultural worker have stagnated; when there is little evidence of strong growth in rural non-agricultural employment; when the total change in urban male employment has been mainly accounted for by unregistered manufacturing, trade, services and construction (sectors in which workers are commonly vulnerable); when NSS evidence shows increasing casualisation of urban labour; and when organised manufacturing wages demonstrate "disparities, anomalies and irrationalities" and have increased in aggregate only erratically and sluggishly – in such circumstances, it is not surprising to find evidence of persistent poverty.

For all the attention focused on the measurement of poverty in India, there has been very little analysis of trends in urban poverty. Dandekar and Rath reported that urban poverty had deepened in the 1960s. Planning Commission estimates for the 1970s, however, suggest at least that there has not been further deterioration in relative terms, though clearly the absolute number of urban people living in poverty has increased (table 10.4). One of the few analyses of urban poverty is by Bardhan for West Bengal (see Chapter 9), which confirms the presumptive case made here concerning the high incidence of poverty among workers in "vulnerable" sectors of the urban labour market.

# III. Evidence on the segmentation of labour markets and its implications

Two studies of Indian urban labour markets distinguish different types of employment on lines similar to those set out in our Introduction. These are on Bombay (Deshpande, 1979; Mazumdar, 1979) using survey data relating to 1974-76, and on the South Indian city of Coimbatore (Harriss, 1982, 1986) using survey data from 1980. There are some other data for Bombay for 1979 (from a study of slum dwellers: Indian Council on Social Welfare, 1983) but no other materials are available for Bombay or for Coimbatore which would permit the study of trends in wages and incomes in different segments of the labour market. Rather fragmentary data are available for Calcutta, however, which give some indications on trends, but there does not appear to be a published study of the Calcutta labour market to compare with those for Bombay and Coimbatore. Further, less comprehensive information is available also for Ahmedabad, Madras and Delhi, from studies undertaken primarily of the "informal sector" or of rural-urban migration.

## 1. The Bombay Labour Market Study (BLMS)

### A. Concepts and method

The BLMS distinguished *(a priori)* *(a)* casual workers, employed on a daily contract basis; *(b)* workers in the small-scale sector (those employed in establishments registered under the Bombay Shops and Commercial Establishments Act of 1948); and *(c)* workers in factories registered under the Indian Factories Act of 1948 (as establishments employing ten or more workers if using power and 20 or more if not). The study is based on a sample of 1,100 casual workers randomly selected from those who gathered for work in well-known market-places for casual workers distributed across the city; a sample of 2,000 workers in small-scale units drawn by using the registers of such establishments maintained by the municipal ward offices; and a sample of about 2,700 employees in factories, sampled by using the List of Factories kept by the Chief Inspector of Factories. The categories on which the research is based clearly only approximate loosely to those discussed above, though it is likely that workers on the List of Factories enjoy more protection than those in small establishments, who are distinguished in turn by the regularity of their employment from daily paid casual workers.

### B. Trends in the organised/unorganised sectors of the Bombay labour market

Casual workers and those employed in small establishments may be described as working in the "unorganised sector", as opposed to the "organised sector" of the registered factories and comparable business and service establishments. In the Indian context, attempts have been made to derive a measure of the relative sizes of these sectors, by taking data available under the Employment Market Information Programme of the Directorate of Employment and Training (covering all establishments in the public sector and private sector units employing 25 or more workers) as an estimate of the numbers employed in "organised" establishments, and comparing them with the total workforce figure from the Census. (We reported above an exercise of this kind for India as a whole in 1981, by the Deshpandes.) The very doubtful reliability of this procedure is pointed out by the different estimates of the relative sizes of the two sectors in Bombay arrived at by Joshi and Joshi (1976) and by Deshpande (1979). The Joshis concluded that the numbers of workers outside the organised sector increased absolutely and as a percentage of the labour force between 1961 and 1971. But this conclusion depends of course on the figures for "organised" employment taken for the base and terminal years, and the Directorate of Employment has in fact supplied *two* figures for each year. The higher figures attempt to take delayed response into account. The existence of two sets of figures at all reflects the practical difficulties involved in collecting the EMI data. The Directorate of Employment itself points out in the publications in which the EMI figures are recorded that the data should be treated with caution because *(a)* the frame of establishments being maintained at the local employment exchanges is not always comprehensive and *(b)* there is always an element of estimation because of defaulting establishments. Deshpande shows that Joshi and Joshi reached their pessimistic conclusion concerning the relative growth of organised and unorganised sectors because they happened to use the high figure of organised employment for 1961 and the low figure for 1971. His concludes that "The basic point is that the Directorate's data are too poor in quality to yield firm conclusions regarding the growth of the organised sector" (1979, p. 65). He goes on to show that, using the more reliable Census data on establishments *in manufacturing*, it appears that the organised sector grew faster than the labour force as a whole in 1961-71 (table II.16, p. 69, shows that employment in organised manufacturing increased from 371,914 in 1961 to 508,382 in 1971, a 36.69 per cent increase compared with the 35.03 per cent increase in the labour force over the same period).

### C. Characteristics of workers in different types of employment

The workers in Deshpande's sample were overwhelmingly male (91.7 per cent: closely comparable with the proportion for five relevant industry divisions recorded by the 1971 Census); and adult (children — those under 15 years of age — made up only 1.18 per cent of casual workers and 1.14 per cent of small establishment employees). Casual workers and those in small establishments were distinctly younger than those in factories (male casuals average age 27.3, small sector 29.6 and factory workers 37.0); and a much higher proportion of them were single men (casual workers 50 per cent, small sector 48 per cent and factory workers 15 per cent), reflecting the fact that there was a higher percentage of recent migrants amongst the casual and small establishment workers. Since most migrate young, a sector which employs a higher proportion of recent migrants shows a lower average age. Workers in the small establishments were more heterogeneous with respect to their mother tongue than those in the other two sectors where the majority were Marathi speakers. Workers in the small establishments were also the most highly educated, and they and the factory workers were distinctly better educated than the casual workers:

|                              | Literacy (%) | Average No. of years of formal education |
| ---------------------------- | ------------ | ---------------------------------------- |
| Casual workers               | 68           | 4.03                                     |
| Small establishment workers  | 86           | 6.72                                     |
| Factory workers              | 79           | 6.01                                     |

Table 10.5 gives the characteristics of migrants in Bombay according to the BLMS.

Holmström, in a discussion of these data, argues plausibly that:

> Factory workers are less educated than small establishment workers, more often Maharashtrian, and older. It is clear that earlier Maharashtrian migrants got into the factory sector and stayed there, not necessarily in the same factories. More recent migrants followed at a time when more people were being educated for longer but factory employment was stagnant, and when the few factory vacancies tended to be filled by relatives and friends of those already employed (Holmström, 1984, p. 186).

An important finding is that "... in a sense, the segmentation of an urban labour market begins in the villages" (Deshpande, 1979, p. 144). Bombay's population and to a great extent its workforce consists of migrants (57 per cent of its population and 80 per cent of its workers in 1971: 76 per cent in the BLMS sample); and the survey shows that migrant casual workers are generally older, less educated and more likely to be married at the time of migration than others. They more commonly come from backgrounds as landless rural wage labourers. They are more likely to migrate alone and to have few friends or relatives to help them find a job. Given the lack of job mobility which the study reveals (see section D) it appears strongly that "... The casual worker continues to be employed at the lowest rung of the socio-economic ladder in Bombay, just as he was in the village" (p. 144), even though the vast majority of those engaged in casual work have gained substantially by migration. It appears that factory workers probably come from rather more prestigious family backgrounds, with larger holdings, and that casual workers come generally from poorer families of lower status.

### D. Job mobility and earnings in different sectors

Amongst the workers in factories and small establishments, 57 per cent (in each sector) reported having changed at least one job, but only 13.5 per cent of them had started as casual workers. Seventy per cent of the casual workers had not changed jobs at all (and in the Indian Council of Social Welfare (ICoSW) slum surveys 94 per cent of employees in the sample were still in the first job, indicative of very restricted mobility). Deshpande was not able to find out how many factory workers had worked in small establishments, but the evidence on the way in which placements are made leads him to doubt the

*Table 10.5.  Characteristics of migrants, Bombay, 1974-76*

| | Casual | Small | Factory |
|---|---|---|---|
| 1.  *Characteristics of migrants* | | | |
| Percentage married | 29.8 | 16.4 | 22.1 |
| Average education (years) | 3.9 | 5.5 | 4.7 |
| Average age | 19.9 | 17.8 | 17.6 |
| Percentage from landless families | 49.1 | 38.0 | 28.3 |
| 2.  *Mode of migration* (%) | | | |
| Alone | 48.3 | 45.7 | 42.6 |
| With family member employed in Bombay | 32.7 | 29.0 | 31.8 |
| With relative employed in Bombay | Almost none | 11.5 | 13.9 |
| 3.  *Activity at time of migration* (%) | | | |
| Work on family farm | 38 | 32 | 49 |
| Household industry | 7 | 4 | 3 |
| Casual agricultural labour | 12 | 3 | 6 |
| Non-farm wage labour | 15 | 11 | 7 |
| Student | 16 | 36 | 22 |
| Unemployed | 19 | 12 | 13 |
| Total | 107 [1] | 98 [1] | 100 |

[1] Does not total 100 in original source.
Source. BLMS.

"graduation hypothesis" (p. 208). Overall the evidence strongly indicates that ". . . the process of recruitment by which regular jobs go to friends and relatives of those already employed helps to continue the stratification of the urban job market that began in the villages" (p. 153). This feature of the labour market in India is well known, but its significance in the present context deserves emphasis. In an extended discussion of the Indian evidence on modes of labour recruitment, which shows the vital important of "contacts" and hence primordial attachments (family, caste, neighbourhood), Holmström concludes that "Regular work looks like an enclosure, to which a limited number hold the keys . . ." (1984, p. 203: but see his whole discussion, pp. 198-227). Jobs in factories may be treated like property, as workers in some cases have rights to pass on their jobs to relations whom they name (this practice has been negotiated between unions and management in the Coimbatore cotton textile industry, for example). Survey evidence shows, without exception in the studies reviewed, that a large majority of workers both in factories and small establishments report that they obtained their jobs through "recommendations". This is a practice which serves useful purposes from the point of view of the employers, offering, for example, some guarantees of the good behaviour of those whom they employ. At the same time the importance of "recommendation" helps to account for the fact that workers in particular factories, or a particular department of big factories, commonly have the same origins — they all come from the same village or region, or they have a common

*Table 10.6.   Real wages in current occupation and changes therein, Bombay, 1974-76 (Rs.)*

|  | Casual | Small | Factory |
|---|---|---|---|
| 1. *Average monthly earnings* | | | |
| Male | 183.7 | 270.3 | 470.6 |
| Female | 80.9 | 246.6 | 344.3 |
| All persons | 164.7 | 268.9 | 463.0 |
| 2. *Percentage of workers with gain in real wage in current occupation* | | | |
| Male | 31 | 54 | 73 |
| Female | 23 | 63 | 76 |
| All persons | 29 | 55 | 73 |
| 3. *Average percentage gain in earnings in current occupation* | | | |
| Male | −2 | 17 | 78 |
| Female | −11 | 7 | 77 |
| All persons | −5 | 16.5 | 78 |
| 4. *Percentage gain in real wage: current wage over earnings in first job* | | | |
| Male | 5 | 46 | 158 |
| Female | −11 | 14 | 91 |
| All persons | 2 | 45 | 155 |

Source. BLMS.

caste background. The "principle of particularism" extends to casual work as well (as we document below, for Coimbatore).[2]

Further, BLMS data on earnings in common occupations in all three sectors indicated the existence of very marked differentials and suggest that the sectors constitute non-competing groups (out of 17 common occupations listed by Deshpande — table V.22 — 15 received a premium in the factory sector of over 100 per cent, by comparison with wages in casual employment). Mazumdar reports findings from these data (see table 10.6) that:

Differences between earnings are substantial between sectors of the labour market, and are only reduced — not eliminated — when we control for factors (such as education) typically allowed for in earnings function analysis. Workers in the largest factories earn just above twice as much as casual workers (Mazumdar, 1979, p. 43).

In addition to the existence of these marked differentials between wages in different sectors of the labour market, Deshpande's study shows that many more factory workers than small sector or casual workers have gained increases in real wages in their current occupations; and that those who received such gains among the factory workers will have had much greater increases in their real wages than small sector workers who have obtained some increase (table 10.6). Casual workers are likely to have experienced a slight *decline* in their real wages in their current occupations, by contrast; and very few of them have experienced much increase in their real current wages over their earnings in their first jobs. On the basis of these data (and of his earlier argument concerning the growth

*Table 10.7.  Women's participation in the labour force, Bombay, 1974-76 (percentages)*

| Participation rates | Casual | Small | Factory |
|---|---|---|---|
| Crude | 23.0 | 6.3 | 5.18 |
| Net | 35.3 | 10.3 | 8.5 |

Source. BLMS.

of organised sector employment compared with that of the labour force), Deshpande argues (tendentiously) that "... the demand for labour in the organised sector is likely to have increased faster than the supply of labour ... the rise in the real wage of the factory sector need not be attributed to institutional factors alone" (1979, p. 181). Casual workers, on the other hand:

> ... are exposed as no other workers are, to the fierce competition from fresh migrants. According to an estimate by S. Deshpande, 47 per cent of the male migrants with duration of residence of half a year outmigrate before they complete their third year in the city. The "target workers" and the floating population prevent any improvement in the earnings of casual labour, and may even cause a decline in the real wage, notwithstanding the state of demand for labour (Deshpande, p. 181).

Given the data we have referred to on the lack of mobility between sectors, it seems that when the organised sector expands it does not recruit all its workers from the unorganised sector.

In sum, the BLMS data provide quite strong evidence of the existence of distinct compartments in the labour market, those employed in different sectors having distinct personal characteristics, with little mobility certainly between casual work and regular employment, and marked differentials in wages and lifetime earnings prospects. Casual workers clearly stay at the bottom with few exceptions, though they may not get any poorer over time. Factory workers' real incomes appear to have risen substantially because of the increased demand for labour, and there has been a general rise in wages as well as individual gains from job changes and promotion. Real wages in small establishments have risen, but less fast; casual workers' real wages have stagnated or even declined.

### E. Family characteristics, incomes and poverty in different sectors

The family size of workers in the BLMS sample is on average much smaller than those of all Bombay residents (3.43 per family as compared with 4.5). Migrants' families are usually smaller than those of non-migrants and there are more migrants among workers than among the general population of Bombay. As many as 58 per cent of the families have no children living with them.

The crude labour force participation rate among family members of the respondents in the sample was 22.7 per cent, or 38 per cent among family members aged 15-59 (as compared with a rate for the city as a whole of 40 per cent in 1971). Participation rates are low because women, who form the majority

*Table 10.8.    Dependency by sector, Bombay, 1974-76*

| Sector | Non-earners per 100 earners | Non-earners per 100 principal earners |
|--------|-----------------------------|----------------------------------------|
| Casual | 79 | 127 |
| Small | 100 | 147 |
| Factory | 185 | 256 |

Source. BLMS.

of the family members, are economically far less active than men. Both the crude and the specific participation rates are highest among male members of casual workers' families and lowest in factory workers' families — the higher incomes of the principal earners in the factory sector evidently enabling teenagers and older people to withdraw from the labour force. Women in casual workers' families are far more active (table 10.7). Marriage reduces the participation of women, especially in factory workers' families, and the presence of children is generally associated with lower rates of female participation — though the activity rate of casual workers' wives actually *increases* with the number of children.

Corresponding with these observations there is clear evidence of higher levels of dependency in the factory workers' families (table 10.8). A striking fact is that the principal earners in casual workers' families are on average worse off than the secondary earners in small and factory sector workers' families (a further indicator of the existence of segmentation). The average family incomes of small sector workers (Rs.428.6 per month) are 61 per cent higher than those of casual workers (Rs.266.8 per month); and the factory workers' family incomes are 149 per cent higher. In terms of per capita incomes the differentials are not so great (Rs.92.7; 147.27; 168.0: i.e. small sector workers 59 per cent higher than casual workers; and factory sector family members 81 per cent higher). Income per adult equivalent is negatively associated with the size of family (in adult equivalent units). In terms of per capita expenditure, average levels are actually higher in small sector workers' families than in those of factory workers (table 10.9). Poverty (as measured according to the Dandekar and Rath criterion) is, unsurprisingly, very much more extensive among casual workers than those in regular employment. Perhaps surprising is the fact that the incidence of poverty is slightly higher among factory workers than small sector workers.

## 2. The Coimbatore Labour Study (CLS)

### A. Concepts and method

The Coimbatore data come from a study of workers in a random sample of units in engineering (in both "organised sector", officially designated "factories" — 123 workers in six units; and "unorganised sector" small

*Table 10.9.   Expenditure (Rs. per month) and poverty amongst workers in different sectors, Bombay, 1974-76*

|  | Casual | Small | Factory |
|---|---|---|---|
| Family expenditure | 207.2 | 347.7 | 422.8 |
| Index | 100 | 167.8 | 204.0 |
| Per capita expenditure | 72.3 | 117.4 | 103.3 |
| Index | 100 | 162.5 | 142.9 |
| Percentage of families below poverty line | 40.0 | 10.1 | 12.5 |
| Percentage of persons below poverty line | 63.8 | 15.8 | 19.5 |

Source. BLMS. Poverty line uses Dandekar and Rath estimate of Rs.22.5 per month at 1960-61 prices (= Rs.65.5 in 1975).

workshops — 85 workers in 15 units), and a survey of 827 households in five "slum" areas selected to represent the range of working-class residential areas in the city (the procedure is explained in detail in Harriss, 1986). The data clearly do not have the statistical validity of those of the BLMS, and data on workers collected from a sample of industrial establishments and those collected from a household survey are not strictly comparable with each other. The data are also less detailed in important respects, notably on wages and incomes. But they do provide a representative cross-section of the workers of Coimbatore in 1980, while the detailed information collected — on the social characteristics of workers in different types of employment, on their mode of entry into the labour market and on mobility between different types of employment — strongly bears out the evidence of the Bombay study on the segmentation of the labour market and the degree of determination of chances in the market exercised by ascriptive social characteristics. The "principle of particularism" is clearly very strong in this case.

### B. Characteristics of workers in different types of employment

Distinctions between different groups are quite clear, though not of the same kind as in the BLMS. We start by comparing engineering workers in sectors 1 ("organised" or "permanent") and 2 ("unorganised" or "short-term"). About one-third of the workers in sector 1 in the engineering industry are migrants, though they are mainly from elsewhere in Coimbatore district; while only about a quarter of workers in sector 2 are migrants, a majority of them being from Kerala. Also, more workers in sector 2 than in sector 1 are natives of or long-term residents of Coimbatore city (see Harriss, 1982, table 10). These differences are related to the more strongly agricultural background of workers in sector 1 (see table 10.10). Permanent wage workers come equally from agricultural families (23 per cent from families of agriculturalists and 7 per cent from agricultural labourer families) and families which already included permanent workers (23 per cent were organised sector workers and 7 per cent in government service). Otherwise the sons of hereditary artisans (mostly Acharis — blacksmiths, carpenters and goldsmiths) are

*Table 10.10.    Coimbatore: Fathers' occupations, education and castes of different groups of workers, 1980 (percentage distribution)*

| | Worker sample | | Household sample | | | |
|---|---|---|---|---|---|---|
| | 1 | 2 | 1 | 2 | 3 | 4 |
| *1. Fathers' occupations* | | | | | | |
| Agriculture | 23 | 7 | 11 | 6.5 | 3 | 11 |
| Agricultural labour | 7 | 3.5 | 22 | 16.7 | 28 | 18 |
| Trading/business | 5.7 | 4.7 | 0.7 | 12.3 | 8.8 | 19 |
| Artisans | 20 | 18 | 18 | 22 | 4 | 26 |
| Weavers | – | – | – | 2.2 | 6.2 | 2.1 |
| Coolies/*kalasi* | 3.3 | 4.7 | 7.2 | 15.2 | 31 | 6.7 |
| Organised sector | 23 | 24 | 28 | 8 | 6.6 | 3.8 |
| Government service | 7.3 | 2.4 | 6.5 | 1.5 | 0.4 | 1.3 |
| Others | 10 | 35 | 6.6 | 16 | 12 | 12 |
| *2. Education* | | | | | | |
| Technical training | 22 | 1 | 2.2 | – | – | – |
| 8th Standard and above | 60 | 24 | 40 | 20 | 8 | 13 |
| Beyond primary | 78 | 53 | 51 | 35 | 16 | 26 |
| No formal education | 3 | 13 | 23 | 26 | 51 | 36 |
| *3. Castes* | | | | | | |
| Dominant castes [1] | 16 | 8 | 3 | 2 | 2 | 2 |
| Agricultural castes | 25 | 20 | 6 | 9 | 3 | 5 |
| Trading castes | 6 | 6 | 4 | 3 | 2 | 3 |
| Acharis [2] | 15 | 15 | – | 7 | – | 7 |
| Other artisans | 10 | 6 | – | – | 1 | 1 |
| Muslims | – | – | 6 | 33 | 42 | 38 |
| Christians | 10 | 8 | 7 | 7 | 1 | 3 |
| Pallan [3] | 2 | 5 | 14 | 4 | 4 | 2 |
| Chakkiliyan [4] | 4 | 7 | 39 | 24 | 38 | 24 |

[1] Dominant castes in the Coimbatore region are Kamma Naidus and Kongu Vellala Gounders.    [2] Acharis are hereditary carpenters, blacksmiths and goldsmiths.    [3] Pallans are a scheduled caste, historically agricultural labourers.    [4] Chakkiliyans are also a scheduled caste, historically leatherworkers and scavengers.

Note. In this table the first two columns (reading from the left) refer to the samples of workers in the engineering industry, 1 = permanent wage workers and 2 = short-term wage workers. The remaining four columns refer to principal earners in the household survey, 1 = permanent wage workers, 2 = short-term wage workers, 3 = casual workers, 4 = self-employed.

Source. CLS.

prominent, and the sons of petty producers or traders are represented rather little. Altogether 45 per cent of these workers had an agricultural background of some kind (i.e. they or their families own land, or have owned land until recently; or their fathers were tenant farmers or agricultural labourers). By contrast only 28 per cent of short-term wage workers have an agricultural background (defined in the same way) and fewer of them own land (17 per cent as opposed to 23 per cent), and the average size of their holding is smaller (4 acres as opposed to the average of 7 acres). About as many of them as of permanent wage workers come from artisanal or organised sector backgrounds, but a majority (one-third of the total) have fathers engaged in other occupations — including carters and watchmen, a variety of small tradesmen such as house painters and plumbers, workers in small workshops, barbers and *dhobis*. In other words, quite commonly their fathers are also short-term wage workers or petty producers. This finding corresponds with the observations that more short-term workers come from Coimbatore itself. Permanent wage workers in engineering are relatively highly educated (see table 10.10) and a substantial minority have had specialised technical training. Short-term wage workers in unregulated production units are rather unlikely to have had any technical training, but they are generally fairly literate.

The dominant castes (politically and economically) in the region of Coimbatore are the Kammavar Naidus and the Kongu Vellala Gounders; and they are more strongly represented among permanent wage workers than short-term wage workers. Agricultural castes in general are also more prominent among permanent wage workers; and among the agricultural castes the more highly ranked among them (such as Thevars and Pillais) are also more strongly represented in sector 1 than in sector 2. Trading castes, hereditary artisans, the Acharis, and Christians are about equally represented among the two groups, while members of the scheduled castes (such as Chakkiliyans and Pallans), although they are more strongly represented among short-term wage workers, are still not well represented. (It was found that even companies which in some respects could be described as exemplary employers had policies, unofficially, of not employing scheduled caste people.) Among workers in regulated workshops, scheduled caste people are most likely to be found working in the moulding shops where work is particularly unpleasant and low skilled, or in casting gangs, where the work is physically hard and somewhat dangerous.

In sum, therefore, permanent wage workers in the engineering industry commonly have agricultural backgrounds and come from small landowning families; and many more of them than of other groups of workers are from locally dominant castes or other leading agricultural castes. Otherwise almost a third of them come from families in which there is already someone working in the organised sector. They are almost all relatively highly educated and many have had technical training. Corresponding with these observations are the facts that these workers come almost equally from *(a)* Coimbatore, *(b)* "commuter" villages nearby and *(c)* other places in Coimbatore district or elsewhere in Tamil Nadu. These characteristics are related to the industry's demand for well-educated men, who in turn are likely to come from the families of the prosperous agriculturalists around Coimbatore, and families having a base in the organised sector. Alternatively they may be drawn from the communities of hereditary artisans. The demand for well-qualified people means that recruits to the industry may be drawn from a considerable distance. A further factor influencing recruitment is that the industrialists who own the organised-sector companies are themselves predominantly from the two dominant castes of the region, and have strong connections with agriculture and with the villages from which some of the hereditary artisans have come. Workers themselves say that

Kammavar Naidu industrialists give preference to other Naidus (though this is not quite so much the case in practice as is commonly believed). While there may be no open discrimination against members of the scheduled castes (on grounds of their caste), members of these castes are much less likely than others to find employment as permanent wage workers because they are less likely to be sufficiently well educated or well connected. But there is also some evidence of discrimination by employers, as we reported; and one of the very few Chakkiliyans in the sample said that he had concealed his true caste identity from his workmates.

Short-term wage workers are younger (average age in the sample was 25 compared with 31 among permanent wage workers); they have a less strongly agricultural background; come less commonly from the dominant castes of the region or from leading agricultural castes; and are less well educated. Many more of them than of permanent wage workers come from short-term wage work backgrounds in Coimbatore city; and there is an important minority of workers who are migrants from Kerala. These characteristics seem to be related to the demand of the unregulated units for cheap labour rather than for well-educated or technically trained people; and another factor is that the owners of these units may also come from a similar background. The better-educated (and often higher-caste) people working in these units are more likely to be "passing through" to other jobs in the organised sector, or as employers themselves, than are others.

Turning now to the *sample of principal earners from the household survey*, we find that some of the same features distinguish *permanent wage workers* in sector 1 from those in sector 2, though the differences between these two groups of workers in the household sample are not quite the same as in the engineering industry sample. This is not surprising given the range of activities included within each group in the household sample (see Harriss, 1986, table 2, which shows that sector 1 workers include municipal sweepers in permanent employment as well as mill workers and engineering workers, and that sector 2 includes salesmen and workers in tea shops as well as "helpers" and temporary workers in manufacturing). But even in this sample, permanent wage workers are now clearly more highly educated than short-term workers (see table 10.10), while short-term wage workers are in turn better educated than those in self-employment, with casual workers distinctly the least well educated (only 8 per cent having gone beyond primary education, and 51 per cent having had no formal education at all). In terms of social background (as judged from the distribution of their fathers' occupations), permanent wage workers in the household sample are rather similar to those in the engineering worker sample, though agriculturalists from dominant and leading agricultural castes are much less strongly represented. Permanent wage workers in the household sample are distinguished from others particularly by the prominence of work in the organised sector in their backgrounds. *Short-term wage workers* come more from petty trading or service caste or casual workers' families (generally, as in the engineering worker sample, they have more diverse backgrounds than others). *Casual workers* are predominantly Muslims and Chakkiliyans, and more of them than of other workers come from Coimbatore city (see Harriss, 1982, table 10). A third of them come from families in which the principal occupation was casual work (daily paid wage labour); a significant minority are sons of weavers; and another minority are sons of organised sector workers (most are sons of mill workers who have not been able to follow their fathers into mill employment, given the stagnation of demand for labour in the cotton textile industry). Otherwise casual workers come from agricultural labour families (28 per cent). Those who are engaged in various forms of *self-employment* in the sample come rather from hereditary artisanal or service caste families, and from families of small traders and businessmen, or from families of small agriculturalists. A large number of them, too, come from agricultural labour backgrounds. Migrants from Kerala and from places in Tamil Nadu outside Coimbatore district are prominent in this group.

In sum, therefore, *casual wage workers* are most likely to come from historically low-ranking urban communities which have always been largely engaged in unskilled and even degrading work, such as the Chakkiliyans, or which have supplied petty services in the towns, such as poor Muslims. Others come from agricultural labouring families and may have recently migrated from rural areas nearby, in Coimbatore district or adjacent parts of Kerala. Such migration sometimes follows marriage and it seems that there have long been connections between urban and rural members of these low-ranking communities. The level of education among these workers is low — and it might be thought that this is a group to which the term "lumpenproletariat" could be applied. It should be noted, however, that these workers are relatively strongly organised in unions; and that entry to casual employment, as a market porter, for example, is by no means open to all. It is necessary to belong to a gang operating a particular street or market area; and the basis for membership may well be ethnic or neighbourhood background.

The petty producers and traders of Coimbatore, in various forms of *self-employment*, also come mainly from urban backgrounds — from Coimbatore, from other towns in Coimbatore district or elsewhere in Tamil Nadu or Kerala. Only about a quarter of them are from urban or rural labour families (and most are in fact kerosene sellers, who are highly dependent on commission). A majority are from petty trading or artisanal backgrounds; and certain activities are still the almost exclusive preserve of particular caste communities.

There are very strong indications in these observations of the way in which particular combinations of ethnic (caste, religious community) and social background factors (including migration status and the geographical origin of a family) influence the supply of labour into particular activities and sectors of the labour market. The level of education is also important, but often in association with the other factors referred to. When we examine the significance of different background factors, and of education, in different residential areas of Coimbatore, the relationships involved are made clearer (see Harriss, 1986, for detailed discussion).

The area known as Ammankulam, for example, is part of an extensive area of workers' housing, partly squatted and partly an old-established residential area where people hold titles to their house sites. The former area is inhabited almost entirely by a very low-ranking group of hereditary leather workers and scavengers (Madharis), the great majority of whom are migrants from villages in Coimbatore district and come from agricultural labouring households. They are mainly employed as commission sellers of kerosene; a few are short-term wage workers, mainly moulders in small foundries; and of the five in permanent wage work, three are employed as sweepers in government offices. It has evidently been extremely difficult for Madharis to obtain permanent wage work or anything other than highly dependent commission selling.

The old part of Ammankulam, by contrast, is occupied especially by Pallans, also an untouchable caste, but who have relatively higher status than Madharis, and are old residents of this area. Some were owners of small pieces of farmland earlier in this century when the area was still rural and not yet incorporated into the urban area. In marked contrast with the Madharis, the Pallans are most frequently employed in permanent wage work, as mill workers, in engineering factories or as peons. Few are employed as casual workers and very few are self-employed petty producers or traders. As the established residents of Ammankulam, the Pallans were prominent among those recruited into mill employment in the 1920s and 1930s, a base upon which they have been able to build. Now, of the men in permanent wage work in Ammankulam, 29 out of 37 are Pallans (or Pallan converts to Christianity), but 21 out of 33 (64 per cent) household heads in permanent wage work have had no education at all or have been educated only up to grade 5. Here caste community, with its concomitants in terms of broader social background, appears to have been a more significant determinant of entry into permanent wage work than education (see Harriss, 1986, tables 10 (i)-(iii)).

Comparable patterns, reflecting the "principle of particularism" which operates in determining entry to different activities in the urban economy, appear in the other areas studied. To give only one example, in another part of the city yet another scheduled caste community, historically engaged in boot and shoe making and the manufacture of riding accessories for the rulers, now includes a large proportion of public sector employees. The strongest relationship we observed between education and entry into the labour élite was among these people, but that relationship really only holds because education is the means whereby people from this caste community have been able to make use of reservations in public sector employment for members of scheduled castes. It was concluded:

We see ... the determining effects of caste, occupational and residential backgrounds in the case of the Pallans of Ammankulam as well as of the Chakkiliyans of Kamarajpuram. A rather high proportion of the members of both these communities is in the "labour élite". In both cases it is because of a particular history, including the fact that members of these castes were recruited into factory employment in the early days of factory industry in Coimbatore. They have been able to build on this partly through education and the possibility of making use of education in order to enter public sector employment. The importance of personal contacts and of recommendation in

*Table 10.11.  Household characteristics by labour market sector of head, Coimbatore Household
Survey, 1980*

|  | Permanent wage | Short-term wage | Casual | Self-employed |
|---|---|---|---|---|
| Average age of principal earner | 41.35 | 37.6 | 38.95 | 41.68 |
| Average size of household | 5.5 | 5.19 | 5.42 | 5.73 |
| Percentage of migrant households | 29.5 | 35.3 | 32 | 47 |
| Average age at time of migration | 22.9 | 23.9 | 21.4 | n.a. |
| Average No. of years in Coimbatore | 23.9 | 15.9 | 20.8 | 21.7 |

n.a. = not available.
Source. CLS.

entry to permanent wage work has tended to create self-reinforcing networks which may
be restricted to people from particular caste and residential backgrounds. But it is not
only to permanent wage work that this applies. In all the five "slum" areas we studied,
where special circumstances such as those we have just described do not apply, the
lowest-ranking Madharis and Chakkiliyans are most likely to be casual workers or highly
dependent sellers of kerosene (if they are not pursuing their hereditary occupations as
leatherworkers). Muslims, on the other hand, are more likely to be petty traders in
plastics, cloth, vegetables and fruit, or scrap, than are the other historically low-ranking
urban group . . . (Harriss, 1986, p. 49).

It is noteworthy, finally, that in the household sample the principal
earners in different types of employment are not very clearly distinguished in
terms of age; that there are more migrants among those in self-employment
(especially) or in short-term wage work than among casual workers; and that
among migrants it is not the case in this sample that casual workers are the most
recent arrivals or that their households are the smallest (see table 10.11).

So, in this sample, casual wage workers are not generally younger, nor
can the lower wages of more recent migrants be explained in terms of their lower
supply price (related in turn to the temporariness of their migration and smaller
family size). Neither, as we shall see, is it necessarily true that their wages are
lower than those of other workers. Little can be made of the differences between
these observations and those of the BLMS, because a sample of workers (as in
the BLMS) is not strictly comparable with a sample of principal earners in a
household survey. But still there are indications in these data of differences in
the processes operating in the labour market in Coimbatore, compared with
those apparently at work in Bombay, though in both cities the principle of
particularism is apparent.

### C. Job mobility and earnings in different sectors

There are strong indications in the Coimbatore data that mobility
between sectors is very restricted indeed, though there are greater possibilities
of movement from short-term into permanent wage work, than from casual
work or self-employment to permanent wage work. In the sample of
123 permanent wage workers in engineering only 32 (26 per cent) had entered

from other sectors of the labour market: 12 from hereditary artisanal work and 20 (16 per cent of the whole sample) from unregulated workshops or foundries in sector 2. Amongst the 827 households surveyed it was possible to find only 39 cases of movement from other sectors into permanent wage work, or vice versa (and these were equally divided between instances of movement into and out of permanent wage work: see Harriss, 1982, table 14).

It is also quite unusual to find households with members both in permanent wage work and in other sectors of the labour market. Among the 827 households only 33 (or 4 per cent) had members in permanent wage work and in other sectors too. Half of them were mill workers' households with wives carrying on a supplementary occupation or with sons working as porters or shop assistants and who might (or more likely not) succeed their fathers in their jobs. Among the 123 engineering workers in permanent wage work only ten (8 per cent) had workers in other sectors of the labour market residing in their households, though 25 per cent of the short-term engineering workers came from households in which there were also organised sector workers, and 50 per cent had relations working in the organised sector (see Harriss, 1982, table 15). Only 21 per cent of the casual workers and self-employed workers could name someone employed in permanent wage work among a wide circle of kin. Here is yet further strong evidence of the extent to which participation in different types of work is socially restricted, and (given the evidence we have referred to, the vital importance of recommendation and "contacts" in gaining entry to work) mobility is likewise very limited.

In Bombay, according to Deshpande's analysis, there is very little movement at all from casual work into regular employment either in small establishments or in factories. In Bombay it is especially poor, landless, low-status, poorly educated migrants from villages who enter casual work in the city, and remain there. In Coimbatore it is sometimes people with the same set of characteristics who enter casual work; but more frequently casual workers from historically low-ranking, poor urban groups, Muslims and Chakkiliyans. Only in particular circumstances, such as those of the Chakkiliyan leather workers, have members of those communities been able to move into regular employment. In Bombay Deshpande argues that "... in a sense the segmentation of an urban labour market begins in the villages". The same might be argued for Coimbatore also, when, as we have seen, members of the prestigious, landowning rural caste communities enter mainly into permanent wage work, while those from the bottom of the rural ladder, such as the Madharis of Ammankulam, remain in casual work and poorly remunerated dependent commission selling. But in Coimbatore there is also an old urban hierarchy, which was shaken up a little in the early phase of industrialisation, when those such as the Pallans entered employment in the cotton mills. But the evidence indicates that since that time the social and economic ladder has "set" again and that very little movement is possible for those in low-status social groups.

Comparing wage levels in different forms of employment, such evidence as there is (see Harriss, 1986, table 3) suggests that in Coimbatore there is a marked differential between wages in permanent wage work and those in other types of work. In Coimbatore in 1980 the lowest-paid permanent workers in the cotton textile industry received a payment of about Rs.20 per day, and engineering workers in the household sample received on average Rs.17.20 — compared with an average of Rs.7.50 for workers in unregistered engineering workshops, Rs.6.80 for shop workers, and only Rs.3.60 for *bidi* rollers. These wage rates for short-term wage workers are *not* clearly differentiated from those for casual workers (Rs.8.10 for one group of porters and Rs.6.10 for another; Rs.5.40 for construction coolies; and Rs.6.40 for stitchers of gunny bags). Here, as far as the evidence goes, it does not appear that casual workers' wages are, necessarily, lower than those of short-term wage workers. What is most striking in these data is the suggestion (and it is no more than that) that there can be significant differences in the wages paid for the same kinds of work, such as the difference between the Rs.8.10 received by one group of *kalasi* workers (porters, load carriers) and Rs.6.10 received by another. It is striking that permanent wage workers in engineering, who may have had specialised technical training, commonly earn less than semi-skilled workers in cotton mills. The variations in wage levels that have been recorded seem to bear out the strong indications that there are distinct compartments in the labour market. This hypothesis has not been subjected to rigorous testing, though the evidence we have referred to on the differences in wages in the textile and engineering industries is strongly indicative of the salience of institutional conditions, and it is most unlikely that it can be explained in terms of factors such as level of education. Textile workers' unions are much stronger than those of the engineering workers; and the higher-paid casual workers (such as the *kalasi* workers) are quite strongly unionised whereas the employees of small engineering workshops, or shop and sales workers, are not (see Harriss, 1986, for discussion).

### D. Family characteristics, incomes and poverty

Unfortunately, systematic data on incomes and consumption expenditure were not collected in the Coimbatore study. Data on household characteristics (from the household survey) do not suggest, however, that the same kind of levelling down as a result of larger family sizes and higher dependency ratios that was observed in the BLMS can possibly obtain in Coimbatore (table 10.12). Given the data on wages that have been referred to (from Harriss, 1986, table 3) there can be little doubt that per capita incomes are also higher in the families of permanent wage workers than in those of workers in other sectors. The earnings of those in self-employment (the average for a sample of petty producers was Rs.13.70 per day, and among petty traders ranged from Rs.8.90 to Rs.16.60 for some vegetable and fruit sellers — all of these figures include returns to capital) probably show wide variation between individuals, activities and seasons. Given their low wages and higher dependency loads there can be little doubt that per capita incomes are lowest among short-term wage workers and casual workers. How close many of them must be to the poverty line is indicated by this working: the average casual worker household has 5.4 members, say 4 adult equivalent units; assume that

*Table 10.12.  Family characteristics, Coimbatore Household Survey, 1980*

|  | Permanent wage | Short-term wage | Casual | Self-employed |
|---|---|---|---|---|
| Average size of household | 5.5 | 5.19 | 5.42 | 5.73 |
| Average No. of earners per household | 1.82 | 1.66 | 1.62 | 1.85 |
| Percentage of single-earner households | 50 | 58 | 59 | 51 |
| Dependency ratio | 1 : 3.02 | 1 : 3.12 | 1 : 3.34 | 1 : 3.1 |

Source. CLS.

each adult equivalent unit requires 2,400 Kcal per day,[3] and that rice is the principal source of calories: then the average household requires 2.66 kg of rice per day. The average price of rice in Coimbatore in 1980 was Rs.2.70 per kg. *Therefore*, the average casual worker household required at least Rs.7.18 per day for its basic livelihood requirements. Assuming 1.62 casual construction workers in the average family, daily income would have been not more than Rs.8.75.

### 3. Some evidence from other Indian cities

#### A. Calcutta

There are no studies of the Calcutta labour market at all comparable with those on Bombay or Coimbatore, but evidence of a broadly similar pattern of particularism was reported as follows by Holmström (1984, p. 61):

For a long time Calcutta people have had few chances to move between jobs. Those who had work clung to it. Sons took their fathers' jobs if they were lucky . . . There was no labour market, but a number of self-contained compartments in the workforce, and little movement within some of these compartments. This is perhaps an exaggeration, but is broadly true.

Bhattacharya and Chatterjee found that 75 per cent of a sample of jute workers were Hindi- or Urdu-speakers, 78 per cent had their own house in a rural area and 86 per cent were born there, few had ever done anything but mill or agricultural work, half were illiterate, and half the workers' households in Calcutta had no female members.

The workforce in the big engineering factories, by contrast, is mainly Bengali, Hindu and educated . . .

Small engineering workshops and foundries are concentrated in Howrah . . . in these workshops, the owners and most skilled workers are Bengali . . . but factory employment is shrinking, and the few factory jobs that become available are quickly filled by the present workers' relatives. Although many workers in the small engineering workshops are both skilled and experienced, it seems they have little chance of ever finding well-paid steady factory work.

In addition to these three self-contained groups of industrial workers . . . there are of course a large number of groups, often equally self-contained and each showing a strong concentration of one ethnic group, filling niches in Calcutta's industrial and commercial economy . . . [ethnic clustering in Calcutta has been mapped and explained as the direct result of limited opportunities] "more than any ethnic bias, occupational considerations direct a person to choose a residence".

*Table 10.13.   Calcutta: Wages (Rs. per week) for "informal sector" work (in constant 1974 prices)*

| Category of worker | 1971 | 1974 | 1982 |
|---|---|---|---|
| Employees in small industrial units | 39.9 [1] | 30.0 [2] | 34.9 [3] |
| Informal sector employees | | | |
| *(a)*    manufacturing | | 48.5 [4] | |
| *(b)*    services | | 34.5 [4] | 35.5 [5] |
| *(c)*    "informal sector workers" | | 45.85 [4] | 65.0 [6] |
| Unskilled workers in organised sector | | | 60.13 [7] |
| Service workers in "formal sector" | | | 82.15 [8] |
| "Formal sector workers" | | | 73.00 [9] |
| Day labourers | | | 50.45 [10] |
| Rickshaw pullers | | | 68.70 [10] |
| Tailors (employees) | | | |
| *(a)*    cutters | | 62.5-75 [11] | 62-103 [12] |
| *(b)*    machine stitchers | | 25-35 | 62 |
| *(c)*    button stitchers | | 10-18 | 37 |
| Carpenters (employees) | | 48-72 [13] | |
| "Skilled workers" | | | 68 [10] |
| Income per informal sector worker's household [4] | | 58.70 | |
| *(a)*    manufacturing | | 62.55 | |
| *(b)*    services | | 41.04 | |
|          (each of these *per capita*) | | 13.4 | |
| | | 13.9 | |
| | | 13.7 | |
| Poverty line, 1974 (per capita weekly) | | 14.3 | |
| Workers employed in manufacturing industry (employees earning Rs.400+ per month), all India | | 60.73 (1975) | 97.73 (1981) |

[1] Survey of Non-Registered Manufacturing in Urban West Bengal 1970-71, Bureau of Applied Economics and Statistics, West Bengal (Bose, p. 69). This figure, for Calcutta, from a survey said to have ". . . covered all the industrial units employing 1-4 persons . . .".   [2] Refers to "workers in a small unit making rubber rings and washers" (Bose, p. 103).   [3] Survey of 53 "informal" manufacturing units, 1981-82 (Romatet, p. 2124).   [4] Labour Department, Government of West Bengal. Pilot Study of Income and Expenditure of 123 informal sector workers' families in ten industry and trade groups (Bose, p. 79 and table 46).   [5] Survey of 36 informal sector households, 1982 (Shaw, p. 50).   [6] Survey of 56 slum households in 1982 (Shaw, p. 44).   [7] Romatet, p. 2124, but basis of estimate is not given.   [8] Survey of 36 formal sector households in 1982 (Shaw, pp. 50-51).   [9] Survey of 79 formal sector households in 1982 (Shaw, p. 44).   [10] Shaw, table 3; survey of 36 informal sector households, 1982.   [11] Bose, pp. 106-107.   [12] Romatet, p. 2120, for tailoring industry in Garden Reach.   [13] Bose, p. 114.

Note. Values adjusted to 1974 in line with the Consumer Price Index for industrial workers in Calcutta.

Sources. Bose, 1978; Romatet, 1983; Shaw, 1985.

He suggests, indeed, that the long-term decline in Calcutta's economy has led to particularly strong ethnic compartmentalisation of the labour market.

Although there appear to have been no systematic analyses of the labour market in Calcutta, there is some evidence in three studies concerned with delimiting and analysing characteristics of "informal sector" enterprises, which permits the drawing up of the following rough time series on wages and incomes among those in vulnerable segments of the labour market (table 10.13). Obviously it would be foolish to attempt to make too much of these figures, given that they are based on very different types of survey, or simply on one-off observations. Still, the facts that Romatet's data on wages paid in 53 small

*Table 10.14. Madras: Earnings of slum dwellers, 1979*

| Employment status | Percentage of total | Average monthly income (Rs.) | Percentage with monthly income of Rs.0-150 |
|---|---|---|---|
| Employers and owners of family enterprises | 4.0 | 340 | — |
| Employee, unorganised sector | 21.7 | 144 | 68 |
| Employee, organised sector | 21.7 | 287 | 21 |
| Family workers | 2.6 | 181 | 49 |
| Self-employment (non-establishment) | 50.0 | 140 | 72 |

Source. ORG, 1980, tables 3.1 and 3.2.

manufacturing units in Calcutta in 1981-82, when compared with survey data from 1970-71, indicate a fall in the real wage, and that Shaw's observations on informal service sector wages in 1982 show no change from those recorded in the Department of Labour Survey of 1974, do at least suggest that the earnings of many short-term wage workers may at best have stagnated over the late 1970s. The suggestion is borne out by the observations on some tailoring wages, and wages paid to carpenters/skilled workers, though contradicted by Shaw's data on all "informal sector workers" (some of whom must be quite highly paid to compensate for the low wages paid to service workers), when these are compared with the 1974 survey data.

Romatet's data for early 1982, with Shaw's for about the same time (see her table 3 especially), like the Coimbatore data show a considerable range of payments received by people doing comparable types of work, as well as a comparable differential between presumptively permanent wage workers' wages and those of people in short-term wage work (Coimbatore engineering workers' wages were more than double those of workers in small engineering workshops; Romatet's 242 manufacturing employees, also in small workshops, were paid less than half the average received by Shaw's "formal sector workers", and not very much more than half of what Romatet records as the general level of payments made to "unskilled workers in the organised sector").

It may be suggested, though very tentatively, on the basis of these figures, that the real wages of *many* short-term wage workers in Calcutta have stagnated over a period when, in India as a whole, there may have been some increase in real wages paid to permanent wage workers in large-scale manufacturing. The 1974 survey data show that per capita incomes in all informal sector workers' families were just below the Dandekar and Rath poverty line. As in Bombay, the larger family sizes and higher dependency ratios of the better-paid workers (though here all the "informal sector") mean that the differences in terms of per capita incomes are effectively eliminated.

### B. Madras

A study of slum dwellers in Madras in 1979 for the Madras Metropolitan Development Authority (ORG, 1980) gives some evidence which

*Table 10.15.* **Madras: Distribution of average income in various occupations by age group (Rs.), 1979**

| Age | Tailor | Carpenter (self-employed) | Semi-skilled construction worker (mason, painter, etc.) | Driver (self-employed) | Craftsman | Turner/ fitter | Self-employed (all) |
|---|---|---|---|---|---|---|---|
| 15-24 | 106 | 165 | 144 | 164 | 132 | 145 | 125 |
| 25-34 | 183 | 193 | 161 | 199 | 223 | 327 | 144 |
| 35-44 | 158 | 194 | 174 | 193 | 194 | 349 | 146 |
| 45-59 | 153 | 197 | 156 | 233 | 199 | 441 | 144 |
| All age groups | 141 | 187 | 161 | 199 | 193 | 319 | 140 |

Source: See table 10.14.

*Table 10.16.* **Madras: Annual growth rate in earners' income for various occupations between 1971 and 1978**

| Age | Construction labourer | Barber | Tiffin/ tea maker | Rick-shaw puller | Vege-table/ fruit vendor | Helper/ cleaner | Tailor | Fitter | Machine operator |
|---|---|---|---|---|---|---|---|---|---|
| 15-34 | 4.7 | 7.9 | Nil | 4.9 | 6.8 | 6.5 | 19.0 | 45.4 | 10.8 |
| 35+ | 6.5 | 1.4 | 0.7 | 2.5 | 2.1 | 6.0 | 7.9 | 10.9 | 16.9 |
| All age groups | 6.0 | 2.6 | 0.7 | 3.7 | 2.8 | 6.2 | 12.2 | 24.1 | 13.3 |

Source. See table 10.14.

suggests that the real earnings of employees in the "unorganised sector" and of people in self-employment probably declined during the 1970s (see table 10.14).

The extreme marginality of the great majority of slum workers' incomes is indicated by the facts that 71 per cent of these workers were in the unorganised sector or in self-employment; that almost three-quarters of workers in these categories earned less than Rs.150 per month, and that their average monthly incomes were only Rs.144 and Rs.140 respectively. A monthly income of Rs.140 means about Rs.4.60 per day, which given rice prices in Madras in 1979, was equivalent to about 2 kg of rice. Note that the differential between organised sector and unorganised sector workers' monthly incomes was about 100 per cent.

The ORG study constructed age-income occupational profiles, and compared the annual growth rates of income in different occupations, in the 1970s, with annual cost-of-living increases. The results are shown in tables 10.15 and 10.16. It appears that most of the slum workers are in occupations where income does not increase with age (see table 10.15). The growth rate of incomes in the 1970s for unskilled occupations such as rickshaw puller, construction worker, barber and vegetable/fruit vendor was low (1-6 per cent) as compared with an average increase in the CPI of more than 10 per cent per year (ORG, 1980, p. 59). Growth rates were higher in skilled occupations such as that of tailor, fitter and machine operator; and in these cases the growth in money incomes is said to have outpaced the increase in consumer prices. But it is pointed out that less than 20 per cent of slum workers are in such occupations.

### C. Ahmedabad

There have been several studies of labour and labour markets in Ahmedabad (population 1971: 1.7 million), in Gujarat, which has been dominated historically by the cotton textile industry (for a general description see Holmström, 1984, pp. 64-66). The studies referred to are Papola and Subrahmanian, 1975, on factory workers; Papola, 1983, on the informal sector; and Subrahmanian et al., 1982, on construction workers. The latter, based on a survey of 1,000 workers spread across the city in 1977, is of particular interest here. Construction workers make up only 3.2 per cent of the city's workforce but in the 1960s the growth rate in labour absorption in construction was almost three times faster than that of the workforce as a whole. Building construction is organised through a complex contracting system in which general builder-contractors are the key figures; and the vast majority of workers in the sample (97 per cent) had been recruited by specialist labour contractors. The socio-economic profile of the construction worker is described as that:

> ... of a poor, illiterate, unskilled migrant to the city. On migrating to the city he sticks to the first job he gets, and tries for another only when he loses it, in view of the relatively poor chances of his getting an alternative job in a labour surplus situation. Although the building construction worker is largely a migrant to the city, he is not highly mobile (Subrahmanian et al., 1982, p. 100).

Seventy-five per cent of the workers in the sample were males. That as much as 25 per cent were made up by women is indicative of the relatively important role of women in construction labour (compare figures on female participation in the BLMS, or the fact that women made up only 15 per cent of the workforce in the Coimbatore study). Seventy-one per cent of men and 62 per cent of women were migrants from rural areas. It is said that "It is the 'push' factor, as reflected in the low level of family income, heavy indebtedness and other economic compulsions, more than the 'pull' of city life, that explains the rural urban migration" (Subrahmanian et al., 1982, p. 165). The picture painted of construction workers recalls that of the casual workers in Bombay according to the BLMS. The construction workers are most commonly from scheduled castes and scheduled tribes, but it is argued that this "... is on account of the fact that they, being illiterate and uneducated, are disproportionately represented among the unskilled workers" (p. 165). Mobility from construction work into other occupations is very low:

> He (sic) moves from one work-site to another under same/different employers but within the building industry and within the city. There is very little inter-industry, inter-occupational and inter-regional mobility among the building workers (p. 166).

Wage rates were around or slightly lower than the legislated minimum wage for the occupations involved. Of particular interest is the following

*Table 10.17.* *Ahmedabad: Monthly wage rates in organised and building construction labour markets, by occupation, 1970s*

| Occupation | Organised labour market, 1971-72 | | Building construction labour market, 1977-78 | |
|---|---|---|---|---|
| | Average wage rate (Rs.) | Variation (%) | Average wage rate (Rs.) | Variation (%) |
| Machineman/machine operator | 158.1 | 14.6 | 185.0 | 14.6 |
| Watchman | 155.5 | 17.7 | 170.0 | 4.9 |
| Coolies/dust lifter | 115.6 | 21.9 | 105.0 | 3.7 |
| Carpenter | 222.7 | 7.7 | 240.0 | 13.0 |
| Cutter/steel bender | 258.3 | 22.9 | 235.0 | 12.0 |
| Fitter/pipe fitter (cement) | 246.9 | 35.0 | 240.0 | 13.1 |
| Moulder/smithy | 214.8 | 20.8 | 260.0 | 16.5 |

Sources. 1971-72 — Papola and Subrahamanian, 1975, Appendix table II-A1; 1977-78 — Subrahamanian, 1982.

comparison of average wage rates and their variations in the organised labour market and the building construction labour market (table 10.17). It is revealing that the average wage rates of some occupations, especially the unskilled, prevailing in the construction industry in 1977-78 were lower than those in the organised industries in 1971-72; and also —

The comparison of the values of variations is . . . instructive to the extent that the occupational wage differentials are narrower in building construction as compared to organised industries . . . One would have expected that the relative scarcity of skilled workers would have pulled up the highest wages faster than the unskilled workers' wage rates and thus widened the wage differentials. That this has not taken place in Ahmedabad's construction labour market suggests that building workers have not been consolidating their individual bargaining strength into a trade union power (p. 129).

The construction workers are indeed only very weakly organised into trade unions, and in the absence of the kind of pressure that might have been supplied by a union even legislation such as the Minimum Wages Act does not count for much.

That the workers are in stiff competition among themselves in the construction labour market is evident from the very low variations in wage rates among units and even among easily substitutable occupations in the unskilled group. But at the same time *the building workers' market seems somewhat insulated from the organised labour market of the city in so far as, in similar occupations, wages in building construction are much lower than in other, organised activities and wages have also been rising faster in the latter* (our emphasis) — and it is argued that . . . The difference in wage and earning situation is made primarily by the organised character and institutionalised practices in the manufacturing industry, and the lack of it in building construction (p. 145).

The sample shows a lack of linkage with permanent wage work, comparable with the findings for Coimbatore. The average construction worker's family consists of two earners and 2.9 non-earners. The majority of earners (79 per cent) are described as casual workers; altogether 96 per cent of the earners are employed in the "informal" sector and 4 per cent in organised manufacturing.

It was found that the average monthly earnings of the building workers were Rs.195 (Rs.247 for men and Rs.142 for women); and that a majority (63 per cent) of their households had an average monthly income of less than the average among a sample of informal sector workers' households studied in the same year (where the average was Rs.467). It was estimated, finally, that 78 per cent of the sample households and 73 per cent of persons were living below a poverty line defined in terms of expenditure corresponding to the nutritional norm of 2,250 calories per capita per day. The study also reports that the evidently abject circumstances of the construction workers are exacerbated by their high dependency burdens:

> The situation is accentuated by the typical family structure characterised by a bigger family with larger proportion of non-earning members, and higher dependency burden as compared to the workers of the organised manufacturing as well as informal sectors of the city (p. 170).

The data on which this is based are not given in the report, but it is an important observation, to be set alongside the findings of the Coimbatore study which showed a slightly higher dependency ratio among casual workers than others. In other words, there is certainly no basis for generalising the finding of the BLMS about the levelling down of disparities between factory workers and others in Bombay, as a result of their higher dependency loads, though Holmström (1984, p. 316) has tended to do just this.

In general, this study bears out those on Bombay and Coimbatore on the existence of distinct compartments in the labour market; and confirms the indications (in the Bombay study, the Madras slum study, and the "time series" constructed for Calcutta) that among the implications of the segmentation in the urban labour market is the strong possibility that real earnings in the vulnerable segments have tended to stagnate even when they have been rising in organised manufacturing. Finally, the study documents the intensity of poverty among this group of casual workers (73 per cent of persons compared with 64 per cent among casual workers in the BLMS).

## 4. The "informalisation" of labour

There is evidence of the deliberate casualisation or "informalisation" of labour in South Asia in the 1970s, as employers in the public sector and private companies found it advantageous to employ labour in such a way as to avoid the laws which protect workers. There is evidence from India of the breaking up of formerly integrated production processes in relatively large factories, covered by the Factories Act, and of the "putting out" of work to small workshops in which workers are unprotected; of how some owners choose to expand their businesses by forming a string of small firms, rather than setting up a large plant, partly to avoid the provisions of labour legislation; and of the increased use of contract labour (or "labour only subcontracting", whereby ". . . a recruiting agent or an intermediary supplies an undertaking with labour, generally for the performance of a specific job"; ILO, 1980). These practices all increase the number of workers in vulnerable sectors of the labour market. At the same time there is evidence of increased employment, especially of young, usually unmarried women in export industries, not only in the free trade zones of South-East Asia, but also in the garments industry in Delhi and in other Indian cities. The employment of women both in old industries like this, and in new ones like electronics, is frequently justified by reference to the supposed dexterity of young women for the tasks involved. But it is clear that employers have at least as much interest in the malleability of a young female workforce, which can be employed at relatively low wages. The tendency to "feminisation" in certain activities seems to us to represent another form of the informalisation of labour, and to have created a large group of vulnerable workers subject to subordination in the sexual division of labour as well as through capital-labour relations (see Kalpagam, 1981).

### A. The "informalisation" of labour in engineering in Coimbatore

The metalworking and engineering industries of the South Indian city of Coimbatore (among which the manufacturing of electric motors and irrigation pumps, textile machinery and small machine tools are prominent) are predominantly organised in officially designated "small-scale" units; and the "small-scale industries" for which the city is well known are also mostly metal based. Some of the principal reasons for this form of organisation are illustrated in the story of "Durairajan":

Durairajan owns a large workshop (officially a "medium-sized factory") producing a range of small machine tools. The workshop has a partially automated foundry section, sheet-metal and machine shops and it employs altogether about 200 people, most of whom receive provident fund and other benefits, and who are union members. Not long ago more were employed in the workshop, but it is now Durairajan's policy not to replace men who leave, whilst he is also encouraging some of the experienced workers from the machine shop to leave and to set up their own small workshops. He has helped those who have agreed to do this by selling them second-hand machinery at its book value, and by giving them orders for work. It is this that he refers to, jokingly, as "Our Socialism!" or the "sharing out" of the prosperity of his firm. Whether or not this pattern of paternalistic subcontracting does mean prosperity for the men who set up small workshops and undertake "job-work" for Durairajan is at least questionable. Durairajan himself certainly benefits, for — according to his own account — by splitting up his machine shop he has been able to reduce the costs of production of the small drilling machines for which his company first established its reputation, through lowering labour costs and by cutting down on overheads. Those who undertake job-work for Durairajan receive materials and the specifications for the parts they undertake to make; and the parts are quality controlled on their return. The job-workers are paid only for the work which is found satisfactory, and the costs of materials wasted on parts which are found not to pass the quality control are deducted from their total payments. Durairajan finds that he can get certain types of work done more quickly and more carefully in this way. He has benefited at the same time by having got rid of some workers who, whilst having valuable experience and skills, were also leading union members and at least potential "trouble-makers". . . .

By splitting up a formerly more integrated process of production Durairajan has achieved a number of objectives, relating to labour and costs and control over the labour process, whilst retaining some of the advantages of economies of scale, as in the purchase of raw materials.

In addition to assisting the establishment of job-work units Durairajan has also set up two new small workshops of his own, though they are both nominally owned by other family members, and he says that it is now his policy to set up such "ancillary" units. Because they will not be unionised, labour problems may be averted, and wage costs may be brought down. The level of taxation, via central excise, may also be reduced . . .

Durairajan's concern about the control of labour (and limitation of labour costs) is also reflected in his use of contract labour for the operation of his foundry and for the cleaning of castings (fettling). In his view ". . . the efficiency of labourers is in inverse proportion to their strength" — and those who are employed through a labour contractor who agrees to undertake a particular operation can easily be dismissed. Foundry work is generally almost unskilled, and fettling is unskilled, but Durairajan fears that if foundry workers became permanent employees they would come to demand the same levels of payment, increments and bonuses as the more skilled machine-shop, sheet-metal workers and fitters . . . (Harriss, 1985, p. 137).

This story is a paradigmatic example of tendencies in engineering in Coimbatore (and probably India in general; see Nagaraj, 1984). Many other owners of engineering firms were pursuing similar policies to "Durairajan", and there were indications (though not quantitative evidence) of a secular tendency of casualisation through such means. Certainly it illustrates factors and processes which help to account for the greater expansion of "unorganised" manufacturing in India in the 1970s, referred to in section II.

### B. *"Disorganisation of the organised sector": Contract labour in the Rourkela steel plant and elsewhere in India*

The Report of the National Commission of Labour in India, published in 1969, clearly recognises that the contract labour system gives several advantages to employers, permitting them to escape most of the provisions of labour legislation, and allowing them to "sweat" labour and pay low wages. The system was sought to be controlled by the Contract Labour (Regulation and Abolition) Act of 1970, but there are strong indications that the incidence of labour contracting — hence of an important group of vulnerable workers — may actually have increased during the 1970s:

The employment figures of Rourkela Steel Plant show that in 15 years, between 1968 and 1983, the number of directly employed labour has increased by a meagre 12.6 per cent, from 34,800 to 39,200. The number of contract labour however has increased by 100 per cent during the same period, from 4,200 to about 8,400 in 1983. The modern steel plant, which had only a nominal proportion of contract labour (and decreasing till 1968) has, by now, become a substantial employer of contract labour. The picture does not change much if the steel industry as a whole is considered, including the mines which were employing a substantial number of contract labour even in 1968. (According to a CITU estimate about 23 per cent of the total labour force in the steel industry is made up by contract labour.) Rourkela is not an exception . . . It was reported for example in IISCO (Burnpur) that the public sector management has surreptitiously introduced contract labour system in its captive coal mines (. . ., etc.) (Sengupta, 1985, p. 13).

Sengupta describes how at Rourkela, after contract labour had been almost eliminated in line with an agreement between the Steel Authority of India and national trade unions, the system came to be progressively reintroduced after contractors were called in to undertake a particularly unpleasant and dangerous task. Now it seems that loading and unloading and a range of cleaning and maintenance tasks are contracted out. These tasks all involve difficult and dangerous, or extremely unhealthy working conditions. As

Sengupta says "The management, instead of improving the conditions of work, has resorted to engagement of insecure labour compelling them to work in the same harsh conditions" (p. 29). It appears that wherever possible the management seeks to casualise labour: ". . . the restricted extension of the practice is more because of history — it is not possible to replace the permanent workers . . . the system can predominate only in the newly created jobs" (p. 29). Contract labourers are low paid (quite commonly receiving less than the stipulated minimum wage); they have virtually no possibility of mobility; they are cheated by contractors who make deductions from payments for provident fund or Employees' State Insurance but who then fail to deposit them; they suffer from violations of safety rules and they rarely have access to medical care in the event of accidents. They are recruited disproportionately from among the scheduled tribes of the region, and they include a disproportionately large number of women: "Evidently, the great majority of contract labour comes from the most depressed sections of the people in rural areas" (p. 51). There is strong evidence here of the systematic recruitment of labour on terms designed to make workers vulnerable in the range of ways that we have considered, and clear indications of a shift in the composition of the workforce in this industry at least, to increase the relative size of the vulnerable sector.

Recent reports highlight similar tendencies in textiles. In May 1984 there were massive demonstrations in Kanpur against subcontracting:

> The situation of the textile industry in Kanpur represents in a nutshell the crisis of the textile industry in the country . . . Kanpur is one of the oldest textile centres in the country with ten mills, one of them closed for several years. Out of the remaining nine mills only one is in the private sector . . . the Kanpur mills like many others had to be declared sick and were taken over by the government. All of them are in bad condition: obsolete machinery, dilapidated buildings, recurring shortage of raw materials like cotton, coal and spare-parts and electricity. The management is callous, indifferent and thoroughly corrupt . . . Most of the Kanpur mills produce coarse cloth used by ordinary people. They find it difficult to compete with the powerlooms where overhead costs are much less . . . Resorting to contract labour is one of the devices to save on production costs at the cost of the workers. The contract labourers work in the same factory, do the same job, and are involved in work of a continuous nature. Subcontracting occurs for example in the reeling section and the rule of equal wages for equal work is blatantly violated. The contract labourer gets as little as Rs.3 and at best Rs.10 while the permanent worker gets Rs.25-30. The contract labourers also do not get annual leave, bonus, gratuity or provident fund and on top of it all have longer working hours. They are not even entitled to a normal gate pass and do not get medical facilities. Most of them are young people, men and women (Dietrich, 1984).

A similar situation is reported from another old textile centre, Ahmedabad, in 1985 (Patel, 1985). There the trend is of ". . . pushing workers in the organised industry into non-organised industries" (p. 2155).

The use of ancillaries and subcontracting (as in the Coimbatore case), resort to labour contracting (as in the Indian steel and textile industries), and the employment where possible of young women, all seem to have increased in South Asia (though precise quantification of this cannot be established). These tactics deliberately push labour into vulnerable forms of employment, and impart another downward pressure on the incomes and livelihoods of urban workers.

## IV. Conclusions

The evidence reviewed here is of course limited in various ways: it is not abundant; it is fragmentary; it has been collected in a variety of ways, according to different conceptual frameworks; and some of it is, frankly, not very reliable. Nevertheless, some conclusions can be drawn which gain credibility because the sources all seem to point to them.

*First*, there is much evidence, in every study bearing on the point, of the influence of ascriptive social characteristics, commonly linked to rural class structure, on the process of recruitment of labour into different types of employment. The BLMS showed that those in rural society who are least well endowed with resources, least educated, and (probably) of lower social status, are those who are most likely to become casual wage workers. The Ahmedabad studies tell a similar story; while the Coimbatore study shows that rural migrants with these characteristics and the historically lowest-ranking urban communities are most likely to become casual workers, and also that protected wage workers come especially from the highest-ranking rural social groups. It is difficult to sort out the significance of different factors in explaining these observations: clearly, in the case of engineering in Coimbatore, for example, it might be argued that what is most important is the level of education of the labour force, and that men from the highest-ranking castes predominate among protected wage workers because they are generally better educated than others. It is difficult to escape the conclusion, however, that the overriding consideration is what we have called "the principle of particularism". It seems clear that at all levels, whether that of the collector of cigarette butts in the streets, or that of a permanent, skilled employee in a large factory, entry is influenced by personal connections, and that these are often based on neighbourhood, family and ethnic ties. The rationality of this in terms of trust and security is clear. It may well be that in the first place the pattern that became established was the result of more or less random factors, as Mazumdar suggests in his model. But thereafter the way in which recruitment is structured by "connections" is strongly apparent.

In correspondence with these observations we have found, *second*, good evidence for the existence of distinct "compartments" in urban labour markets. It is not only that entry into different types of employment is clearly channelled by the principle of particularism, but also that mobility between different sectors of the market is so clearly constrained. The evidence on this is clear and strong in the Bombay and Coimbatore studies; definite in the Ahmedabad studies. Further, Mazumdar's test using the Bombay data showed a difference of more than 100 per cent between the wages of protected factory workers and casual workers, after allowing for the factors accommodated in conventional earnings function analysis; the Ahmedabad studies showed distinct and probably increasing differentials between wages for comparable unskilled work in construction and in manufacturing; the Coimbatore studies suggest a difference of about 100 per cent between the wages paid to comparable workers in registered factories and unregistered workshops in engineering, and that relatively skilled, quite highly educated engineering workers earn less than "permanent" employees in cotton textiles who are only semi-skilled. Though the data are limited in quantity they give clear indications of compartmentalisation in the labour market (and even of segmentation in a strict sense).

*Third*, the macro-level labour force data examined show that in the 1970s there was a small shift of the labour force out of agriculture (though the evidence is less clear for India than for some other Asian countries). In India there appears to have been a rather greater expansion in all manufacturing employment than in other countries, but here too the greatest expansion relatively and absolutely has been in unregistered manufacturing and the tertiary sector. The evidence indicates that with the shift of labour out of agriculture, the kind of structural shift occurring is one in which labour is concentrated in unprotected forms of employment, and in the tertiary sector and "unregistered" manufacturing rather than in large-scale manufacturing with a protected labour force.

The *fourth* set of conclusions, on which the sources are fairly consistent, concerns wages and incomes associated with different types of work. Table 10.18 shows, for a variety of unprotected work, in different places and years, a clustering of wages between the equivalent of 2 and 5 kg of rice per day. Workings such as those presented for Coimbatore show that wage levels in this range must push many families near to, if not below, a nutritionally defined poverty line; and the few studies which attempt to measure the incidence of urban poverty this way (the findings of which are summarised in the table) confirm that a large proportion of casual workers, certainly, live in poverty. The divide between what is described as "casual work" and protected wage work — a divide which, we have seen, is commonly almost unbridgeable for the worker — is very clearly defined in all the studies offering evidence. The wages of employees in small establishments (who fit fairly well into Rodgers's category of "competitive, regular wage work") may extend over a wide range, however; and the earnings of those in self-employment very clearly cover a wide distribution, extending from the bottom end of the range for casual workers to levels above those of the great majority of protected wage workers (as seen in the Bombay slum study: ICoSW 1983; the Madras slum study; and the various studies on Calcutta). These findings probably account for the lack of clear evidence of consistent wage differentials between "formal" and "informal" sector employment in the studies reviewed by Kannapan (1985). Differentials seem much more clear-cut when the "informal sector" is disaggregated, even if only in the rather limited and quite crude way in which it has been possible to do so here. The extent to which the higher earnings of protected wage workers and some other employees, and some of those in self-employment, are levelled down by higher dependency loads in their families seems to be variable (and there seem to be no grounds for generalising, as we think Holmström tends to, the findings of the BLMS).

Finally, there is evidence, though less secure than that summarised hitherto, which shows that wages paid to casual workers and to some employees in establishments not covered by protective legislation have stagnated or

*Table 10.18.    Wages per day, in rice equivalents: Calcutta, Bombay, Ahmedabad, Madras and Coimbatore, 1971-82*

| Year | Calcutta | Bombay | Ahmedabad/Madras/ Coimbatore |
|------|----------|--------|------------------------------|
| 1971 | 5 kg (workers in small industry) | | |
| 1975 | | 3.1 kg (male casual workers) 4.6 kg (male small establishment workers) | |
| 1977 | | | 4.5 kg [Ahmedabad] (male construction workers) |
| 1979 | | | 2.6 kg [Madras] ("informal sector employee") 2.5 kg ("self-employed") |
| 1980 | | | 2 kg [Coimbatore] (male construction workers) 2.5-3 kg (male porters) 2.7 kg (male workers in small engineering workshop) |
| 1982 | 2 kg (workers in small manufacturing establishments) | | |

*Estimates of incidence of poverty (nutritionally defined)*

| | |
|---|---|
| Bombay, 1975 (casual workers) | 40% of families |
| | 64% of persons |
| Ahmedabad, 1977 (construction workers) | 78% of families |
| | 73% of persons |
| Madras, 1979 (informal sector employees) | 70% of families |

Sources. BLMS; CLS; Subrahmanian, 1982; Bose, 1978; Romatet, 1983; ORG, 1980.

declined in a period in which real wages received by protected wage workers have increased. For India there is: the cross-sectional data in the BLMS showing stagnation in the wages received by casual workers, compared with quite large increases experienced by the great majority of factory workers in their present occupations; the similar evidence for several important groups of casual and short-term wage workers in the Madras slum study; the evidence in the Ahmedabad studies of an increasing disparity between the wages of workers in construction and in organised manufacturing; and finally the indications of the time series that we were able to construct for Calcutta. None of this evidence is strong in itself, but at least there is no indication at all that disparities have been reduced in the 1970s.

This raises the question of explaining these observations. The factors involved appear to be these. First, there is some evidence in the Indian literature (such as Breman, 1985, on labour circulation in south Gujarat; as well as the BLMS) of the role of circular migration in maintaining a supply of temporary migrants offering a low supply price, and keeping down wage rates paid in a range of "casual" work. Secondly, increases in the labour force have evidently not been absorbed as much in agriculture as in some rural, non-agricultural activities, in the urban tertiary sector, and in manufacturing in unregistered establishments. The extent of organised manufacturing employment, where wage work is protected, has expanded in India but has absorbed only a small proportion of the increase in the labour force. At the same time the operation of the principle of particularism in recruitment to protected wage work means that the number of potential recruits has been restricted, and a large proportion of the expanded labour force has been pushed into other types of employment. Some combination of institutional factors, and of the development of firm-specific labour markets postulated by Mazumdar in his model, has kept up real wages in organised manufacturing, meanwhile. That tendency has enhanced the interests of many employers in the informalisation of labour, of which there is evidence from the Coimbatore labour studies and recent reports relating to the Indian textile and steel industries.

In sum, the evidence bears out Mazumdar's model of the segmented labour market in LDCs. Given the existence of a high wage sector, recruitment to which is subject to the principle of particularism (and which often means, as Mazumdar suggests, that ". . . the market for recruitment to formal sector jobs is located much more in rural areas than in the urban informal sector"), in circumstances in which the rate of growth of employment in the formal sector is well below the growth rate of the working population, with employment lagging behind the growth rate of value added in the formal sector, and a variety of institutional pressures acting to keep up wage rates in the formal sector, there is a tendency for differentials between the formal and the residual sectors to widen. The conclusion, that real wages have stagnated or declined in the recent past for many groups of unprotected wage workers in South Asia, certainly seems much more strongly substantiable than the contrary hypothesis. But as Mazumdar also argues (1983, p. 258): "What happens to income distribution in the lower reaches of the urban labour force depends crucially on the dynamism of the self-employed sector of petty producers and traders — which often shows high returns to small doses of capital and entrepreneurship . . .". There is very little evidence on trends in the earnings of the self-employed. The evidence on their earnings, however, does indicate that their returns extend over a wide range, and it is certainly not impossible that some of them have improved their real incomes over the recent past. This would help to explain the hints (and they are no more than that) of some improvements in urban areas, in the aggregate, in terms of a reduced incidence of poverty. These hints certainly do not invalidate our main conclusions, which are that there is strong evidence of the existence of distinct compartments in urban labour markets in South Asia; that there is evidence of a widening disparity between the earnings of protected wage workers and unprotected "casual" workers; and that there are indications of stagnation in the earnings of such "vulnerable" workers, among whom the incidence of poverty (defined in relation to standard nutritionally based norms) remains very high.

### Notes

[1] School of Development Studies/Overseas Development Group, University of East Anglia. The author would like to thank the following for their help with different aspects of the paper on which this chapter is based: Joep Bijlmer, Chris Edwards, Hans-Dieter Evers, Ruth Pearson and Hein Streefkerk. He is grateful, too, to the library staff at the University of East Anglia, the School of Oriental and African Studies, London School of Economics, Centre of South Asian Studies, Cambridge, and the Institute of Development Studies, Sussex — and to an especially understanding librarian at IDS who allowed him to jump the Inter-Library Loan system. Gerry Rodgers encouraged the preparation of this paper, and helped a lot, though he is not in any way responsible for infelicities and errors that remain.

[2] The principle of particularism means that entry into many occupations and types of employment is effectively restricted to those with certain ascriptive social characteristics; and, consequently, that mobility within the labour market may be severely restricted. The implications of the sort of "parcelisation" of the labour market that results are explored, as far as possible, in this chapter.

[3] Of course this may greatly over-estimate minimum nutritional requirements, but it corresponds with the estimate that has conventionally been used in poverty studies in India. The working shown is concerned with a broader conception of poverty than simply minimum nutritional requirement.

### References (not including official serial statistical publications which are fully referenced in the text)

Bardhan, K., 1983: *Economic growth, poverty and rural labour markets in India: A survey of research* (Geneva, ILO; mimeographed World Employment Programme research working paper; restricted).

Bose, A. N., 1978: *Calcutta and rural Bengal: Small sector symbiosis* (Calcutta, Minerva Associates Publishers Ltd.).

Breman, J., 1985: *Of peasants, migrants and paupers. Rural labour circulation and capitalist production in West India* (Delhi, Oxford University Press).

Bromley, R. and Gerry, C. (eds.)., 1979: *Casual work and poverty in Third World cities* (Chichester, John Wiley).

Deshpande, L. K., 1979: *The Bombay labour market* (Bombay, University of Bombay, Department of Economics; mimeographed).

Deshpande, S. and Deshpande, L. K., 1985: "Census of 1981 and the structure of employment", in *Economic and Political Weekly* (Bombay), 1 June.

Dietrich, G., 1984: "Kanpur textile workers' struggle against subcontracting", in *Economic and Political Weekly* (Bombay), XIX, No. 29.

Harriss, J., 1982: "Character of an urban economy: 'Small-scale' production and urban labour markets in Coimbatore", in *Economic and Political Weekly* (Bombay), XVII, Nos. 23 and 24.

———, 1985: "'Our socialism' and the subsistence engineer: The role of small enterprises in the engineering industry in Coimbatore, South India", in Bromley, R. (ed.): *Planning for small enterprises in Third World cities* (Oxford, Pergamon Press).

———, 1986: "The working poor and the labour aristocracy in a South Indian city: A descriptive and analytical account", in *Modern Asian Studies* (Cambridge), Apr.

Holmström, M., 1984: *Industry and inequality: The social anthropology of Indian labour* (Cambridge, Cambridge University Press).

Indian Council on Social Welfare, 1983: *The urban dead end? Pattern of employment among slum dwellers* (Bombay, Somaiya Publications).

ILO, 1980: *Contract labour in the clothing industry*. Second Tripartite Technical Meeting for the Clothing Industry, May-June 1977 (Geneva).

Joll, C. et al., 1983: *Developments in labour market analysis* (London, Allen & Unwin).

Joshi, H. and V. J., 1976: *Surplus labour and the city: A study of Bombay* (Delhi, Oxford University Press).

Kalpagam, U., 1981: "Labour in small-scale industry: Case of export garments industry in Madras", in *Economic and Political Weekly*, 28 Nov.

Kannapan, S., 1985: "Urban employment and the labour market in developing nations", in *Economic Development and Cultural Change* (Chicago), 33, 4.

Krishnamurthy, J., 1984: "Changes in the Indian workforce", in *Economic and Political Weekly*, XIX, 50.

Mazumdar, D., 1979: *Paradigms in the study of urban labour markets*, World Bank Staff Working Paper No. 366 (Washington, DC, World Bank).

———— 1983: "Segmented labour markets in LDCs", in *American Economic Review*, Papers and Proceedings, Vol. 73, No. 2.

Nagaraj, R., 1984: "Subcontracting in Indian manufacturing industries", in *Economic and Political Weekly*, Annual Number.

ORG (Operations Research Group), 1980: *An economic profile of the urban poor slum dwellers of Madras* (Baroda, mimeographed).

Papola, T., 1983: *Urban informal sector in a developing economy* (Delhi, Vikas).

———— and Subrahmanian, K., 1975: *Wage structure and labour mobility in a local labour market: A study in Ahmedabad* (Ahmedabad, Sardar Patel Institute of Social and Economic Research; distributed by Popular Prakashan, Bombay).

Patel, S., 1985: "Nationalisation, TLA and textile workers", in *Economic and Political Weekly*, XX, 49.

Rodgers, G., 1985: *Labour markets, labour processes and economic development: Some research issues* (Geneva, ILO; mimeographed World Employment Programme research working paper; restricted).

Romatet, E., 1983: "Calcutta's informal sector: Theory and reality", in *Economic and Political Weekly*, XVIII, 50.

Sengupta, N., 1985: *Contract labour in Rourkela steel plant*, Madras Institute of Development Studies Working Paper No. 57 (Madras).

Shaw, A., 1985: "The informal sector in a Third World urban economy: A case study of Calcutta", in *Bulletin of Concerned Asian Scholars*, 17 (1).

Subrahmanian, K. et al., 1982: *Construction labour market* (New Delhi, Concept).